Few composers have been subjected to a greater degree of sentimentalizing extravagance and romantic misrepresentation than Franz Schubert. His short life was singularly bare of romantic encounters.

A schoolmaster's son, he was born in a suburb of Vienna in 1797, showed his musical precocity when he was four, and at the age of eleven he entered the seminary which trained choristers for the imperial court chapel. In 1813, the year of his first symphony, he became an assistant teacher in his father's school, but the young man was no schoolmaster: he quit the post in 1816 and thereafter led a bohemian existence. He never managed to get a salaried appointment of any permanence, and his main income in a hand-to-mouth life was derived from the sale of short-order compositions. Schubert was an easy-going person and he had numerous friends – none of them, unfortunately, with any influence – and with one or other of these he went on walking tours through the Austrian countryside – which tours probably explain the awareness of folk music that constantly shows itself in his compositions. During one such tour in late 1828 he contracted enteric fever and died a few weeks later. He was thirty-one.

Of the two influences that steadily show through in his work the first – his acquaintance with folk song – has been mentioned. The other is that – and this is about the only significant element in the Schubert 'legend' – unlike those other great Austrians – Mozart, Haydn and Beethoven – Schubert was Viennese to his fingertips. He was born, brought up, and lived most of his impoverished life in the city.

Schubert's orchestral music is remarkable by any standard but his enduring glory is that he created the German *lied*. His song cycles are amongst the most lyrical that the world has known, and they lead straight to Schumann, Wolf and Mahler. Dr. Alfred Einstein's masterly study, quickly disposing of the 'lilac time' nonsense, restores the essential greatness to this great composer.

KU-425-241

Alfred Einstein

Schubert

translated by David Ascoli

Panther

Granada Publishing Limited
Published in 1971 by Panther Books Limited
3 Upper James Street, London W1R 4BP

First published by Cassell & Co. Limited 1951
Made and printed in Great Britain by
Cox & Wyman Ltd.,
London, Reading and Fakenham
Set in Intertype Times

Contents

Foreword

During a discussion of one of my books, a friend of mine once asked whether it had been written as a result of 'a moral force or a being outside myself'. I do not, in fact, know of any third way in which books come to be written; in the case of this *Schubert*, both forces were jointly at work; the suggestion of the Oxford University Press that I should write it, and an inner urge to carry out this suggestion.

In spite of this, I hesitated a long time before agreeing to do so. There is a vast mass of literature about Schubert, and the Jubilee years of 1928 and 1947 in particular produced a flood of books and articles which seemed to meet every need, from the popular to the technically more ambitious. This book comes *post festum*.

Yet the two publications – both by friends of mine – which seemed most calculated to deter me were those which, in fact, confirmed me in my decision to undertake this task. One is Otto Erich Deutsch's *Schubert – A Documentary Biography* (London, 1946, J. M. Dent), translated by Eric Blom, also published in American under the title of *The Schubert Reader*, which provides incomparably full and accurate information on all matters biographical. Professor Deutsch, I should add, obliged me by reading my book in manuscript, correcting or adding some biographical details and suggesting the chapter 'Schubert and his attitude to Death'. The other publication is the fourth volume of the Paul Hirsch Music Library Catalogue (Cambridge University Press, 1947) which proved no less reliable and relieved me of all trouble in the matter of the bibliography of Schubert's works. What I lacked as a third 'foundation stone' was a thematic and chronological list of Schubert's works. This is now being prepared by Otto Erich Deutsch and the present volume may perhaps make a modest contribution to it.*

Another difficulty with which I was faced was the marshalling of my material. I could have treated Schubert's life and works separately, as I did in my *Mozart*. In the case of Schubert, however, there would have emerged an even greater disparity between the two parts than in the *Mozart*, for how much more simple, uneventful and 'undramatic' Schubert's life was than Mozart's! As in my Mozart book, I could have further divided the section entitled 'Works' into categories, and have dealt with the various sub-divisions of his music in separate chapters. Then, however, there would have been a much greater danger of constant repetition, and *one* chapter, the one on Schubert's songs, would have completely dominated the others or would have had to be shortened. Too much that was closely interwoven was condensed into the short span of his creative life for it to be separated with a single clean stroke. In this book, therefore, the lines of demarcation partly follow biographical divisions, and partly those which are determined by his musical output. The biographical chapters extend only up to the time when Schubert shook off his 'middle-class' shackles and began to follow simply the impulse of his spiritual development.

I originally started the book on the basis of a different division of my material – that of 'Preparation' and 'Fulfilment' or 'Perfection', of the 'Pupil' and the 'Master'. For me, at least, that proved impracticable. This kind of classification would have broken every rule of chronology and many of the early songs and instrumental movements would have had to be included in the 'Perfection' section, while many of the later works would have had to appear under the heading of 'Preparation' or 'Imperfection'. Schubert was a pupil and a master from beginning to end. Sir George Grove, to whom Schubert research owes so much, drew the dividing line at which Schubert's 'master' phase began in the instrumental field at the year 1822. A moment's thought is enough to make one realize the arbitrary nature of this and, in fact, *any* 'qualitative' division on the basis of a specific date.

Therefore I decided on the following approach: not to be

---

*Of the immense bulk of Schubert literature which I have read, I might mark out only a single one of another friend: Richard Capell's admirable book *Schubert's Songs* (London 1928).

deterred by the volume of existing literature on Schubert, not to divide the book into 'life' and 'works', nor to sub-divide the works into categories, but to follow his creative development from year to year within the compass of his uneventful life. The journey is admittedly broken at various points by sections of a more general nature which will perhaps contribute to the filling-in of many details and to a deeper understanding.

This book does not attempt to be complete in its listing and assessment of Schubert's works. I know that Schubert wrote many Waltzes, Ländler and 'Teutsche': I am aware that there is a movement for piano-trio dating from the year 1812; I am aware that there are a number of short vocal Terzets dating from the year 1816, which are not in the Collected Edition; and I am familiar with all these works, too. Furthermore compilers of programme-notes and radio talks will in many cases be disappointed. This book is not a collection of analyses. It is in the very nature of an analysis, that it is of no assistance to someone who does not know the work in question, and that anyone who knows the work does not need the analysis. Unfortunately one cannot arrive at the essence of music through the medium of words, either by technical analysis or by flights of poetic fancy. Mendelssohn once observed very pertinently that genuine music is more unequivocal, more positive and more incapable of mis-construction than any written attempt to explain it. But since, in writing a book about a composer, one cannot avoid words, a single suggestive phrase will often say more than a bar-by-bar description. This book is written for readers who know and love their Schubert, and who wish to under-stand him better and to know more about him. It is written for readers who are musical, but at the same time something *more* than musical. For in order to understand genuine music, one must be not only musical, but *instinct* with music. There is a world of difference between the two.

Finally, I am deeply indebted to Mr. David Ascoli, the translator, for his incessant interest in the book and for sev-eral suggestions.

ALFRED EINSTEIN

Northampton, Mass.

Chapter One

Childhood and Youth

1797–1808

Franz Schubert – or Franz Peter Schubert, to give him his full name – was born at half past one on the afternoon of 31st January, 1797, in Vienna at the House of the Red Crab, then No. 72 Himmelpfortgrund, now No. 54 Nuss- dorferstrasse. The following day he was baptized in the Leichtental parish church of the Fourteen Friends in Need by the Co-operator, Johann Wanzka, in the presence of his uncle and godfather, Karl Schubert. He was the twelfth child of Franz Schubert, who had held an official ap- pointment as a schoolmaster in the Himmelpfortgrund since 13th June, 1786, and of Elizabeth, *née* Vitz or Vietz, his wife.

Of all the great 'Viennese masters', from Johann Joseph Fux to Johannes Brahms, Schubert is the only real native of Vienna. He therefore ranked, and still ranks, as a genuine example of a 'Viennese musician' in the conventional sense, a Viennese *par excellence*. Yet that is only partially true, in both a musical and biographical sense. The epithet 'Viennese', in its musical context, the significance of which has been so variously emphasized, watered down or garbled since his day, owes much more to him than he to it. Admittedly, he grew up in this 'Viennese' musical atmosphere, but to a great extent he himself was responsible for creating and defining it. The 'Viennese' tradition already existed in the eigh- teenth century in the shape of Ländler or 'German Dances'. These, in their turn, had developed out of the inter- nationally-popular Minuet; then, towards the turn of the century, they were transformed into the Waltz and had already regained some of their former dignity at the hands of Haydn and, particularly, Mozart. Schubert inherited this tradition. But he restored these Minuets, Ländler, Waltzes,

Ecossaises and Gallops to the Viennese with, so to speak, double interest – that is to say, in a form and spirit which were themselves capable once more of acquiring a 'traditional' flavour. This was especially true when he tried his hand at writing 'Valses sentimentales' or 'Valses nobles'. He not only inherited this legacy, but added to it and established a new one.

But what else is 'Viennese' in his music? What is there 'Viennese' in that field in which he is at his greatest – in his songs? There he is much too independent to be contained by purely regional boundaries; and if we must at this stage mention the word 'independence' then we should add that his songs did not have their roots in Vienna but – as we shall see – from a musical point of view, in Swabia or North Germany, and, from a spiritual or poetical standpoint, in the general German literary renaissance. And what is there 'Viennese' in his instrumental works? Is there anything Viennese' in the last three quartets, the String Quintet, the two Piano Trios or the Piano Sonatas? Some works admittedly, such as the operas, could have originated only in Vienna for reasons of purely local circumstance, while the second subject of the first movement of the B minor Symphony could have been written by Schubert in Vienna alone. But to my mind, Robert Schumann, to whom we owe so much that is sensitive and intelligent on the subject of Schubert, put many lesser people on the wrong track when he described the great C major Symphony as being so Viennese:

... this Vienna, with its St. Stephen's spire, its lovely women, its public pageantry, encircled by the countless loops of the Danube and stretching across the verdant plain which climbs gradually towards higher and still higher mountains – this Vienna, with all its memories of the greatest German masters, must be fruitful ground for the musician's fancy. Often as I gazed at it from the mountain heights I used to imagine how Beethoven's eyes must constantly have wandered restlessly towards that distant range of Alps: how Mozart, lost in thought, must often have followed the course of the Danube which seems everywhere to merge with field and forest, and how Papa Haydn must many a time have contemplated the spire of St. Stephen's, shaking his head at the prospect of so dizzy a height. Combine these pictures of the Danube, St. Stephen's spire and the distant mountain range, suffuse them with the gentle, catholic fragrance of incense – and you have a single picture of Vienna. And as we ourselves look upon this charming landscape, the sight stirs within us chords which would otherwise never have sounded. Schubert's symphony, with the clear romantic spirit that quickens it, brings the city more vividly before my eyes today than ever before, and makes me understand once again how it is that such works come to be born in surroundings like these. . . .

But Schubert probably saw and knew a very different Vienna from that which the sensitive and poetically-inclined visitor from Zwickau in Saxony thus describes.

From the biographical point of view, Schubert would have to be classified as a Moravian or Silesian composer, if we interpret the racial laws literally. Neither of his parents was a native of Vienna. His father, Franz Theodor Schubert, was born on 11th July, 1763, at Neudorf, near Altstadt, in Moravia, while his mother came from Zuckmantel in Austrian Silesia. His father, a man of peasant origin, seems to have become a schoolmaster from choice and had already served as an assistant teacher for three years in his own home town. In 1784, however, he moved to Vienna to join his brother Karl, who had been working as a teacher for some time in the Leopoldstadt. Two years later he became 'a full-blown master in the Trivial School at No. 12 Himmelpfortgrund', having married some eighteen months previously, on 17th January, 1785.* Elizabeth Vietz, the daughter of a locksmith, was seven years older than her husband and had been employed as a cook in Vienna before her marriage. In spite of the difference in their ages, her relations with her husband seem to have been much the same as those between Mozart's mother and his father Leopold. She was 'a quiet woman, much loved by her children and greatly respected by everyone', and a self-effacing wife; for, in contrast to the aristocracy and the *nouveaux riches*, it was still customary among the humble middle-class society of Vienna to look up to the father as the head of the household. 'Humble middle-class circumstances' is an accurate description of life in the Schubert family in the early days, for the poverty of the inhabitants of the Liechtental district gave the schoolmaster little chance of a quick rise in the world.

Small wonder that the elder Schubert more than once

* The fact that his first son Ignaz was born only seven weeks after the wedding suggests that this step was to some extent forced on him. Cf. O. E. Deutsch, 'Schubert's Vater' in *Altwiener Kalender für das Jahr, 1924* (Wiener Drucke, 1924), pp. 134–48.

tried to better his lot, and applied several times for another appointment, chiefly without success. Eventually, four years after Schubert's birth, and before the disastrous depreciation of the Austrian currency which resulted from the Napoleonic Wars, he managed to acquire the school-house in the Säulengasse, and moved there with his four surviving children, not without the fervent hope that he would soon leave it again. For in 1805 he applied, once more unsuccessfully, for a post with the Carmelites in the Leopoldstadt, left vacant by the death of his brother Karl. In this house in the Säulengasse the Schubert family lived until 1818, and it can claim to be the real home of young Franz; it was here that he slept and worked during such time as he was not taking refuge with his friends. It was not until 1826 that the elder Schubert sold it at no inconsiderable profit.

On 28th May, 1812, Schubert's mother died at the age of fifty-six, and on 25th April, 1813, his father remarried, after a year as a widower, which by contemporary standards was a long rather than a short interval. This second wife was named Anna Kleyenböck. She was the daughter of a middle-class silk manufacturer, twenty years younger than her husband and only fourteen years older than her stepson, Franz. She, too, was a good mother to him and to his brothers and sisters, and he both loved and respected her. To his four brothers and sisters – another sister, Therese, had been born in 1801 – she added in due course a further five. Since she belonged to a somewhat higher level of middle-class society, she contributed towards a raising of the social status of the whole Schubert household; or to put it more accurately, the fact that she accepted the elderly widower's offer of marriage indicated the improved financial circumstances of this household. A Viennese schoolmaster in the years following the death of the Emperor Joseph was no longer the ignorant, despised Baculus of the eighteenth century. He already moved in higher cultural circles and entered into the intellectual activities of the middle class. We know little about the degree of culture which existed in the Schubert household; but it must have been more genuine, more enthusiastic and more intellectual than in many homes of the aristocracy or the *nouveaux riches*, and bore fruit not only in Schubert himself, but also in his brothers. Patriotism, too, was more genuine in this class of society which knew little or nothing of the well-concealed shabbiness of the Government. The Napoleonic Wars had intensified this patriotism, and indissolubly bound up with it was a strong sense of loyalty towards the Imperial House – a loyalty which had, if anything, been strengthened by the well-deserved blows which the monarchy had suffered between the Peace of Campoformio and the Treaty of Pressburg. Nor could it be shaken even by the vague knowledge of the personality of the Imperial sovereign who had been ruling since 1792 and within whose reign Schubert's entire life was to fall.

Closely associated with this loyalty was a profound reverence for the Church, which had been relegated to the background in the days of the Emperor Joseph but had triumphantly resumed its former status after his death. In old Schubert's household this reverence seems to have been exaggerated to the point of bigotry. As we shall see in due course, this evoked a more or less silent protest on the part of the older sons and must often have made life in the family circle scarcely bearable for them.

At any rate, loyalty and reverence for the Church played their part in the elder Franz Schubert's steady progress up the middle-class ladder. In December 1817 he was at last rescued from the hardships of Liechtental 'by a decree of the Imperial Government'. He was appointed to the teaching profession in the Rossau, and moved to the new school-building there in the New Year of 1818. His assistants Ignaz and Franz – here we are anticipating events – moved with him, though admittedly not for long in the case of Franz. On 9th February, 1826, Schubert *père* received the freedom of the city from the municipal council of Vienna, in recognition of 'his useful services to education during forty-five years and also his work for charity over a period of seventeen years'. And at the end of 1828, he was 'recommended by his superior officers for the award of the Gold Medal of Honour for Civilians, although he never in fact lived to receive it, since in the Sedlnitzky era promotions, certificates of merit and similar formalities took nearly two years'.* He died on 9th July, 1830, eighteen months after his distinguished son, his second wife surviving him by thirty years.

* O. E. Deutsch, op. cit., p. 148.

It was Schubert's good fortune to be born into this modest and loyal household, since it echoed with music. A school-master in Vienna – and not only in Vienna, but in all the hereditary lands of the Imperial Crown – had to be, among other things, a musician as well. A Cantor in Bach's day – and, indeed, Bach himself – had to be able to teach Latin; conversely, an Austrian schoolmaster had to be completely competent in matters musical. Consequently Franz Schubert received elementary music lessons in his father's school, chiefly from his eldest brother Ignaz, who had acted first as his father's somewhat unwilling assistant, but from 1805 to 1830, officially, in the same capacity. Ignaz gave Franz his first piano-lessons, while his father taught him the violin.

The musical precocity of the youngster must, however, have demonstrated itself so plainly that his brother and father soon recognized their inadequacy as teachers. So at the age of seven, apparently – that is to say, in 1804 – he was apprenticed to the choirmaster of the Liechtental parish church, one Michael Holzer (born in 1772 in the Him-melpfortgrund, died 1826), who taught him singing, organ-playing, and counterpoint. Schubert showed his gratitude and sense of obligation by dedicating his C major Mass to him in July 1816, originally in the manuscript, and then pub-licly in 1825, when the work was published by Diabelli as op. 48. His brother Ferdinand, who makes no mention of in-struction in the organ and counterpoint but only in piano-playing, violin and singing, has told us in Schumann's *Neuer Zeitschrift für Musik* (1839) that Holzer frequently assured him with tears in his eyes that he had never had such a pupil. 'For,' he used to say, 'whenever I wanted to teach him any-thing new, he already knew it. I often simply stared at him in silent astonishment.' And Schubert's father has added a final word to this comment of Holzer's: 'The result is that I [Holzer] never really gave him lessons, but simply whiled away the time with him.'

In the autumn of 1808 there occurred a decisive change in the boy's life; he left home and entered the Imperial Chapel Royal as a chorister. In May of that year there had ap-peared in the official Viennese newspaper one of the usual announcements to the effect that there were two new posts to be filled in this institution and that this number would be increased to three in the following August. 'The competitors must have completed their tenth year and must be capable of taking their places in the first Latin class.' The examination took place on 30th September. In it, the three candidates had further to show 'that they have good singing voices and are well grounded in the theory of singing'. They were also required to show evidence of physical fitness and to be past the danger of smallpox.

We do not know whether Schubert fulfilled this last condition; but as for the remainder, he passed with flying colours. We can still picture a few details of the scene. Schubert wore a light-grey suit and was duly nicknamed 'miller' or 'the miller's son' by his young friends. In the judges' chairs there sat, among others, Dr. Franz Innocenz Lang, headmaster of the Convict and a great lover of music, and Antonio Salieri, Court Music Director, a former pupil and protégé of Gluck and a resident of Vienna since 1766. He was a much maligned man on account of his opposition or rivalry to Mozart, and we shall come across him again several times, since he became Schubert's teacher in composition. 'Fra li Soprani li migliori sono: Francesco Schubert e Müllner.' – 'The two trebles Schubert and Müllner are also placed first in elementary knowledge.' Such were the verdicts of these two important personages. The third of the successful candidates was named Maximilian Weisse, and Schubert seems to have taken a great liking to him, for during his time at the Convict he wrote for the youngster an Overture for piano, of which nothing, however, is known.

The Royal Imperial Municipal Convict, founded in 1803, was housed in the old University building next to the Jesuit church, and was run by monks of the Order of Piarists. It served as a preparatory establishment for University students and also as a training-ground for choristers of the Chapel Royal. 'If the successful candidates distinguish themselves in their general behaviour and their studies, they are permitted, by order of the Emperor, to remain on in the Convict after their voices have broken; if not, they must leave as soon as their voices break.'

Franz Schubert distinguished himself not only in 'his general behaviour and his studies', but especially in all musical subjects, in singing, in the violin ('. . . plays difficult pieces at first sight') and in the piano; with the result that on one

occasion the following order was sent to the Court Music
Director by the Imperial Secretariat: 'You will convey to
Franz Schubert particular satisfaction at his excellent progress in all subjects; at the same time you will give due credit
to those music-teachers mentioned by the Headmaster and
especially to the piano-teacher Ruziczka. . . .' (28th September, 1811). Wenzel Ruzicska, viola-player at the Burg
Theatre and court organist, taught the piano and organ at
the Seminary; he also taught the boys the viola, the 'cello,
and even thorough-bass (Schubert, for example, in 1811), as
required. . . . He visited the Convict twice a day, and organized and conducted the school orchestra. Later on, Schubert
sometimes took over from him and Ruziczka used to say of
him: 'He has learnt it from God.' The violin was taught at
the Seminary by Ferdinand Hofmann, and singing by Philipp Korner. In the orchestra, which played a symphony
and one or two Overtures each evening – usually without
trumpets and trombones – Schubert soon played first violin,
and Joseph v. Spaun played second. . . .* These orchestral
practices were only interrupted during the siege and occupation of Vienna by Napoleon's troops from May until the
end of October 1809†.

It was the best possible training and experience that Schubert could have had. During these years of apprenticeship in
the Convict it was not only his innate, natural musical gift
that was developed, but also his talent for making friends.
This talent remained with him throughout his life, and in
spite of a few disappointments, it brought him much happiness. His relations with his elder brothers, too, were most
affectionate and friendly. Nothing is more characteristic of
this than the first of his letters which has come down to us. It
was written to one of his brothers, Ferdinand or Ignaz,
about a year before he left the Convict (24th November,
1812); nothing is more characteristic of his life at the Convict itself.

Let me get what I want to say off my chest at once, and come
straight to the point. I won't bore you by beating about the bush
in my usual way. I've been giving a lot of thought to life here and
have come to the conclusion that it's pretty good, though in some

*O. E. Deutsch, *Schubert – A Documentary Biography*, London, 1946,
J. M. Dent & Sons.
  † ibid., p. 12.

ways it could be better. You will know from your own experience that there are times when one could certainly do with a roll and a few apples, particularly when one has to wait 8½ hours between a moderate-sized midday meal and a wretched sort of supper. This constant longing has become more and more insistent, and the time has come when willy-nilly I must do something about it. The few Groschen that father gave me vanished into thin air in the first few days, so what am I going to do for the rest of the time? They who hope upon Thee shall not be put to shame. St. Matthew, Chap. 3, v. 4. Too true! How would it be, then, if you were to let me have a few Kreuzer each month? You wouldn't notice them, and they would make me happy and contented in my cell. As I've already said, I rely on the words of the Apostle Matthew, especially where he says: Let him who hath two coats, give one to the poor. In the meantime I pray that you will give heed to the voice which ceaselessly begs you to remember.

Your affectionate, poor, hopeful
and once again *poor* brother
FRANZ.

What a lovable letter for a boy of sixteen, who throughout the rest of his life wrote only lovable letters, with the exception of one to a publisher. One needs to have some conception of a public institution of the All-Highest Imperial State to appreciate the modesty of the writer who can euphemistically refer to his icy prison as a cell, who finds life 'by and large' good and only complains of the scantiness of the meals. How comic the biblical quotation is with its wrong reference! For you will not find it anywhere in St. Matthew's Gospel. This lovable boy will soon be capable of writing utterly lovable music, too.

It was at the Seminary that Schubert found his oldest and, at the same time, one of his most loyal friends, Joseph v. Spaun, who was ten years his senior and left the Convict in the autumn of 1809. It was Spaun who has told us in his reminiscences (*Oesterreichisches Bürgerblatt für Verstand, Herz und gute Laune*, Linz 1829) about the orchestral practices in which Schubert took an increasingly important part. According to Spaun, the resources of the school orchestra were sufficient to allow successful performances of the earlier masterpieces of Haydn, Mozart and Beethoven. Further evidence is provided by Georg Thaa, who was a pupil at the Convict at the same time as Schubert ,and in later life gave Eduard Hanslick details about the composition of the orchestra and about its repertoire for the latter's *History of Concert Life in Vienna* (1869). There were six first and second violins (three violas?), two 'cellos, two double-basses and a pair each of flutes, oboes, clarinets, bassoons, horns, trumpets and drums. (That means, therefore, that the performance of Beethoven's Fifth and Sixth Symphonies would not have been possible at this time.)

The daily practice-pieces consisted of an overture (usually by Cherubini, Weigl or Mozart), a symphony (by Haydn, Mozart and others) and then finally another overture. On special occasions such as the birthday or name-day of the Emperor (February 12th and October 4th) or the headmaster, gala performances took place to which guests were invited, either to take an active part, or merely to listen. In winter, concerts were given exclusively in private, but in summer these performances by the pupils had a considerable audience when the windows were opened. Our informant tells us that on fine evenings, the sound attracted people returning home from a stroll on the city walls and they gathered in such crowds that traffic was completely disrupted in the street and the mechanic Hanacek who lived opposite used to bring out every available chair in his house for the ladies to sit on.... Schubert had already made a bold start at composing, and without question these cheerful and well-organized amateur activities gave him a considerable stimulus and contributed largely to his practical versatility.

We have Spaun's further assurance that above all Schubert was passionately fond of Mozart's G minor Symphony and Beethoven's Second in D, and that shortly before his death he spoke of the deep and powerful impression which these two works had made on him in his youth. Spaun goes on to say that church services were a pleasure and not a penance for the boy. Of all the church music performed in the Chapel Royal, it was those works which were distinguished by their inner content and religious uplift rather than by their outward effect that made the greatest impression on his childish and naturally straightforward mind.

Hanslick was right when he said that the cheerful amateur activities in the Convict and, let us add, the somewhat mechanical, though by no means amateur, exercises in church provided Schubert with a considerable stimulus. Doubly right in the case of a talent like young Schubert's which surrendered itself unreservedly to a single impression, and yet had its 'backbone' in that 'naturally straightforward' mind, which rejected what was shallow and accepted what was significant.

This, then, is the proper place, while we are on the subject of his youthful development, to discuss the musical constellation under whose sign he stood at the moment when his musical imagination began to stir.

CONSTELLATION

If we try to imagine which were the liturgical works in which Franz Schubert took part as a chorister, either in company with his fellow-trebles or sometimes as a soloist, we can say with some certainty that they could not have included music in the 'abstract Church style', that is to say, the so-called *a cappella* works of the Palestrina period. This style was only discovered and re-assessed during the last years of Schubert's life, and then least of all in Vienna. It is much more likely that the works in question were Masses, Offertories, Vespers and hymns by the greater and lesser masters of Upper and Lower Austria, Bohemia and Salzburg. The lesser figures were men like Anton Wranitzky, Adalbert Gyrowetz, Joseph Eybler, Anton Diabelli, Abbot Maximilian Stadler, Peter Winter, and Franz Xavier Süssmayr, Mozart's pupil; the greater and really great included such names as Luigi Cherubini, Mozart himself, and the two Haydns, Joseph and Michael. Michael seems to have played a particularly large part, with his prolific output of church music which included three dozen pleasant and unexceptionable Masses alone. It can only have been the memory of those happy mornings in church that prompted Schubert, on the occasion of his trip to Salzburg in the summer of 1825, to visit, not Mozart's birthplace or home, but Michael's grave in St. Peter's churchyard. 'It seemed to me as if your gentle, serene spirit breathed upon me, dear Haydn, and even though I cannot aspire to your gentleness and serenity, there is certainly no one on earth who admires you more deeply than I do.' Thus he wrote on that occasion to his brother Ferdinand, who must have understood what he felt better than we can today. We shall, however, try to understand it when we come to consider Schubert's own Masses. For the church music with which Schubert was familiar is precisely that 'profane, worldly, operatic' (and in the particular case of Michael Haydn, pedantic) church music which sent such a shudder through the romantic purists of the nineteenth century –

Viennese, neo-classical church music, born of an instrumental spirit, which Schubert followed quite ingenuously, for the good reason that he knew no other, and which he completely imbued with his own musical sincerity and splendour. In the year 1809 there had admittedly been written a church composition which laid an unusual stress on the purely vocal side – Beethoven's Mass in C major, op. 86, which was a complete failure at its first performance in Eisenstadt during the autumn of that year, and was not published until five years later. But even if Schubert had known this work as a choir-boy – and even before 1812 this would not have been impossible in Vienna in the case of individual sections – he would have been too young to appreciate its peculiar significance, its originality and its thematic unity. He remained, even after he had become familiar with Beethoven's second great Mass, a 'neo-classical' church composer, a composer of instrumental Masses, and he carried on a tradition which achieved its ultimate splendour in the church music of Anton Bruckner. In the case of the latter, strangely enough, this characteristic of style is not a source of criticism.

In the field of instrumental music, the constellation was more favourable – though only for a learner with his innate gifts (or we should otherwise have had several Schuberts). At the time when his creative impulse was beginning to stir – that is to say, about the year 1810 – the legacy of Haydn and Mozart was complete. Mozart had already been dead twenty years, and Haydn, whom Schubert could still have met personally, had said his last word – long since, so far as his instrumental music was concerned, and, in the field of vocal music, with the appearance of *The Seasons*, in 1801. Schubert admittedly knew much less of the symphonies and chamber music of Haydn and Mozart than we do today in this age of collected editions. But of Haydn's works, he was certainly familiar with the 'London' symphonies besides a whole series of earlier ones, while he probably knew more of the quartets and piano trios than the selection to which chamber music players choose to restrict themselves today. And of Mozart's works he undoubtedly knew a certain amount of chamber music as well as the last four great symphonies, of which his two particular favourites were the E flat and the G minor. Haydn and Mozart, however, were no longer modern masters in his eyes. For, since 1792, there had lived in Vienna itself a composer, of an older generation admittedly, yet none the less a contemporary, an over-powering model and object of criticism – Ludwig van Beethoven. Schubert's relationship to Mozart and Haydn underwent hardly any change and scarcely cooled off, even when he no longer needed their stimulating influence, and even when, in his eyes, they eventually belonged to the past as creative artists. Beethoven, on the other hand, remained a disturbing influence on him throughout his life, and caused him to shift his ground. On 16th June, 1816, on the occasion of the celebrations marking the fiftieth anniversary of Salieri's arrival in Vienna, he made the following entry in his diary.

It must be a lovely and refreshing experience for an artist to see his pupils all gathered round him, while each of them strives to give of his best in honour of the occasion; to hear in all their compositions pure natural expression, free from all that eccentricity which seems to prevail among the majority of present day composers and for which one of our greatest German artists is alone responsible; to know that there is no place for this eccentricity among his pupils – an eccentricity which unites in indistinguishable confusion, the heroic with the hideous, the hallowed with Harlequin; which induces transports of frenzy among men instead of transports of delight, which provokes them to laughter instead of exalting them to God. . . .

It is disconcerting to hear a judgment such as this from the mouth of a young man, even though we may excuse it on account of the writer's youth and the fact that he was deeply influenced by his revered teacher. And it is not without an element of tragi-comedy that on the occasion of the performance of his *Rosamunde* music, at the end of 1823, a critic (in *Der Sammler*), while conceding his 'originality', at the same time accused him, too, of 'eccentricity'. Elsewhere, Spaun has told us what a discouraging effect Beethoven sometimes had on him – 'After Beethoven, who can achieve anything more?' – and this presupposes that he recognized the greatness of his predecessor. Later, his personal relationship was one of profound reverence from a respectful distance. But from a musical standpoint he persisted in his reservations about Beethoven's 'eccentricities'. There were many characteristics in Beethoven which his contemporaries found 'original' but which he himself never accepted; in his own case the association or blending of contrasts is, so to speak, involuntary, even in those instances where he was undoubtedly influenced by Beethoven. If Schubert was fascinated by Beethoven's Second Symphony during his years at the Convict, then it is reasonable to suppose that the same was true of the First and Fourth. But what did he think of the 'Eroica', the Seventh or Eighth, or even the 'Pastoral' – he, who, almost from the very beginning, found in his songs a vehicle for every kind of 'illustrative' treatment, 'aesthetic expression' and emotional 'painting'?

We have no evidence of his reaction, but in his heart of hearts he must have rejected such works. The impression made by a bright, straightforward and companionable work such as Beethoven's Septet persisted until the year 1824; at any rate Schubert raised no objections when he was commissioned to write a companion piece. Much of the older man's chamber music must equally have appealed to the younger – the early violin sonatas, for instance, or the A major Quartet from op. 18. But how about the revolutionary Quartets of op. 59, the C minor Violin Sonata from op. 30 and the 'Kreutzer' Sonata? This constant alternating between attraction and repulsion prevented Schubert from becoming Beethoven's direct successor, let alone from deliberate imitation. And on the one occasion on which he sets out to imitate, for example, the Finale of Beethoven's op. 130 during the last weeks of his life, the result is something quite different, in spite of being written in the same key.

Nevertheless, we shall have to discuss in detail his affinity to the great figures in music on many occasions during the course of this book, and indeed his sure sense of perception and his selective taste attracted him above all to the great figures. But his circle also included many lesser composers and in his eyes they were by no means to be found only on the circumference. As to the influences which were at work on him during the decisive years around 1810, we have the uncritical but at least materially reliable evidence of Johann Friedrich Reichardt's *Confidential Letters, written on a visit to Vienna ... 1808–1809*. In the field of chamber music and symphonies there were the works of Gyrowetz, Pichl, Wranitzky, Romberg, Rust, Umlauff, and those of Kozeluch and Krommer – names which have faded into oblivion today, but which were still bright stars in the musical firmament at that time. It was equally true of Schubert, as of all great composers, that he profited from the 'lesser' lights too, both in a positive and negative sense. It was musical 'food' to him in every sense of the word. We are told that while he was at the Seminary he championed the merits of a symphony by the Bohemian Leopold A. Kozeluch against those of the music of the Bohemian Franz Krommer, in the face of his colleagues, who evidently preferred the latter. Both occupied respected positions in Vienna and one of them, Krommer, succeeded the other as Director of Chamber Music at the Imperial Court and survived Schubert by several years. It would be instructive to know what it was that Schubert liked in Kozeluch and objected to in Krommer.

Reichardt also gives us some dates relating to operatic activities in Vienna round about 1810. These included not only Gluck's two *Iphigenias*, Cherubini's *Faniska*, Mozart's *Entführung* and *Don Giovanni*, but also Paër's *Sargino*, *Camilla* and *Leonore* and Weigl's *Waisenhaus*. In fact, either Weigl's *Waisenhaus* or his *Schweizerfamilie*, first performed with great success in 1809, was one of the first operas which Schubert heard. It was not without significance for him that he heard the leading roles in these two operas, as in most of the others, sung by Anna Milder, with whom he was later to have personal dealings. These operas were in different degrees large-scale, serious or, at worst, sentimental works. But in addition to them there was the whole repertoire of less pretentious ballad-operas, 'musical farces' and scenic pieces whose music the boy could not possibly, and in fact did not, escape.

In later chapters we shall have to concern ourselves at some length with Schubert's efforts in the operatic field – that field which, of all his creative work, seems on the surface to have been the most extensive, and yet was the least successful and the one which has sunk furthest into oblivion. The reasons for this lay partly in himself, without realizing it. But they also lay partly in the conditions which governed German opera in general and the Viennese stage in particular when, from 1813 onwards, he was engaged in the practical business of writing opera. We can begin to understand this when we select a few names from the list of operas which were performed in Vienna during 1811 and 1812: Isouard's *Cendrillon*, Boildieu's *Jean de Paris*, Spontini's *Vestale*,

Cherubini's *Medea* and Mozart's *Zauberflöte* – operas which belong to three distinct schools of development.

It was an intricate problem, particularly for a novice at German opera like the young Schubert; for unlike the international masters of the eighteenth century, such as Gluck or Mozart, he could not take refuge in the safe retreat of those national conventions with which French or Italian opera were hedged about. He cannot be blamed for not surmounting this problem, quite apart from his lack of years. He would have had to be a dramatist of superhuman stature to have mastered the situation. The problem would have been not merely one of setting German libretti to music, but of creating the standard pattern for a *German* opera, just as the Italians had created a native *genre* in the *opera seria* and, more especially, in the *opera buffa*, or the French in their 'tragédie, mise en musique'. For no such thing as a German operatic tradition then existed. It has often been said, and rightly so, that between Heinrich Schütz's *Daphne* and Richard Wagner's *Parsifal* there appeared a succession of magnificent German operas, but no German operatic *genre*.

It is therefore no exaggeration to say that Schubert had a wealth, indeed a superabundance, of models to draw on; but one in particular he did not have, and that was a model of style. Beethoven's *Fidelio*, which had had its first performances in 1805 and 1806 when Schubert was still a boy but which had been revived in 1814, by which time he had completed his own first experiment in opera, owed its 'revolutionary' significance solely to the powerful musical and moral personality of its creator. But considered historically it is simply a 'rescue-operation' of French origin, dozens of which had been written since the time of Le Sueur and Méhul and Cherubini. This type of opera made an impression on Schubert too, as we shall see from his *Fernando*, but from *Fidelio* he acquired nothing beyond a few superficialities; for, with his natural aversion to pathos, he could not reconcile himself to the two culminating points in this work, the explosive outburst of the prison scene and the high moral character of the Finale. (In contrast to this, imagine what feelings Wilhelmine Schröder-Devrient's singing of Leonore's 'Kill first his wife!' must have aroused in the young dramatic composer Richard Wagner!)

At this point let us look ahead a little, in order to get a

more complete picture. What of Weber's *Freischütz*, the next work of major significance in the history of German opera, which was produced in Vienna in November, 1821, a few months after its first performance in Berlin? This German opera made use of the most variegated collection of international conventions and formulae: the French 'Romance', the Italian 'Preghiera' and 'Scena ed Aria', the vocal Polonaise, the 'Lied' and the popular chorus after the model of the ballad-opera. Schubert undoubtedly liked *Freischütz*. He did not object to this medley of forms and in the light of his operatic experience he would have had no justification for doing so. But when, in Vienna of all places, Weber subsequently made a deliberate attempt at creating a German *opera seria* with his *Euryanthe* it was, significantly, not the dramatist but the composer in Schubert that firmly rejected it. Schubert completely failed to understand Weber. Weber's real achievement in *Freischütz* had been the fusion of the whole colourful motley of forms into a single musical entity by means of a particular sound-pattern to which we apply the epithet romantic; and he achieved the same result in *Euryanthe,* which is an *opera seria* in a quite different sense from Spontini's 'grand opera'. For while *Euryanthe* derives from the latter, Weber nevertheless enriches Spontini's impassioned dramatic technique with the quality of romanticism – that is to say, with something of the 'infinite'.

Schubert, as we shall see, was unwilling to overstep the limits of the contemporary operatic stage in Vienna. Unfortunately these limits were not sharply defined, and furthermore within them there was a regular glut of opera. Since Vienna was a musical capital (at the same time it contrived in many respects to be like a small provincial town), it had something of everything to offer; there was Italian opera both in the original *and* in translations, which were for the most part mechanical and slovenly; sometimes the performance of the latter version preceded the original. The waning *opera seria* in the style of works like Cimarosa's *Gli Orazi ed i Curiazi* was still being kept alive, but the new Italian Grand opera in the manner of Gaspare Spontini had also made its appearance; there was genuine *opera buffa* in the original Italian but also in the vulgarized form of the translations mentioned above. The performance of Mozart's

Nozze di Figaro or *Don Giovanni* belonged to the latter category. Then there was the French *opéra-comique* with its mixture of dramatic suspense and comedy, of the historical and the fantastic. But above all there was the German 'Singspiel' or ballad-opera in all its various forms ranging from the farcical, the idyllic, the vulgar and the sentimental to the symbolical fairy tale which had found, if not its first, at any rate its first *profound* expression in Mozart's *Zauberflöte*.

Strange as it may sound, *Zauberflöte* had an unfortunate influence on the Viennese 'German operetta'. For in its dozens of imitations and derivatives, the original was divested of all its spontaneous artlessness and significance, and all that remained was an extreme triteness allied with the most vulgar banality and philistinism. Seven years after *Die Zauberflöte* there appeared at the Leopoldstadt Theatre Ferdinand Kauer's *Donauweibchen*, 'a romantic and humorous fairy-tale, with incidental songs, and based on an old legend', with its elaborations and variants; and one year later this was followed by Wenzel Müller's *Die Teufelsmühle am Wienerberg*. Both come under the heading of musical farces, and it was only towards the end of Schubert's life that this *genre* underwent a transformation or a poetical refinement in a dramatic, though not a musical sense at the hands of Ferdinand Raimund. But Schubert would have been much too good a composer to have written the right sort of music even for Raimund's *Diamant des Geisterkönigs* or *Der Alpenkönig und der Menschenfeind*.

If the reader wishes to conjure up a picture of Vienna's metropolitan and suburban stage in Schubert's day, he need only consult the early reminiscences of Schubert's friend, Eduard von Bauernfeld, with particular reference to the chapter on the Viennese popular comedy. The favourite subjects were plays about knights and ghosts, 'in which the romantic and the comic element joined hands, although in a somewhat crude and primitive fashion'. We should not forget that the most famous of all plays about knights by the most Prussian of all dramatists, Heinrich v. Kleist's *Kätchen von Heilbronn*, had it first performance at the Theater an der Wien when Schubert was thirteen or fourteen. But whatever the category in which the plays of this dramatic repertoire belonged, music was indispensable to them all; and in the fairy play the music even fulfilled an integrating function. The dividing line between this type of fairy play and the 'German operetta' is so indeterminate that it is almost impossible for an historian of opera to define it with any accuracy.

Now Schubert's operas are nearly all centred around the 'German operetta'. As a German composer the *opera buffa* was a closed door to him, quite apart from the fact that he had no grasp of the serio-comic type of humour or the rather ruthless insight into human nature which are the stock in trade of a true *buffo* composer, and which Mozart or Rossini possessed in a high degree. And as for the *opera seria*, in which direction he once or twice had ambitions, he would have had to reform it radically, in order to have achieved even a purely artistic success in the genre. A dramatist must be a philosopher, a 'speculator'. In his operas, however, Schubert never 'speculated'. Even his literary taste, usually so sure in his choice of texts for his songs, forsook him completely in his operas. The real god of Schubert's lyrics, for all the existence of rival gods, is Goethe. The god of his opera libretti is August von Kotzebue. It is an ironical twist of chance that this unscrupulous and accomplished corrupter of German taste, this adversary of every lofty ideal which Herder and Goethe and Schiller had striven after, should have been born in Weimar, the hallowed shrine of German poetry; and it is no less a coincidence that he happened to be living in Vienna when Schubert was born. He was eleven years younger than Goethe and one year younger than Schiller, yet in his lifetime he far outstripped them both in popularity and success. 'No one assessed so accurately the common instincts of the people, no one could pander to them so cleverly, and no one provided dramatic effects so conveniently for the actor as Kotzebue. He cultivated not only the middle-class drama, but also the chivalrous drama, the comedy and the farce.* In Kotzebue the moral tendency gives place to an apotheosis of licentiousness, masquerading under the guise of virtue. Sentimental indulgence and cheap emotion are allowed to undermine the traditional ideas of morality, and generally-accepted rules of conduct are ridiculed as mere European prejudice. His caricature of the idea

---

* W. Scherer, from whose *History of German Literature*, p. 557, this quotation is taken, might well have added: '. . . and the opera libretto.'

of Humanism weakens every tragic conflict; and he is at
pains to parade vice and misery before us in all their nakedness.'

This is a harsh judgment and perhaps unjustly harsh when
we remember that Kotzebue provided the German public in
general, and Viennese audiences in particular, with exactly
what they wanted. In any event, of course, it does not strictly
apply to his opera libretti. These are not purely frivolous
like, for example, his comedy *Die beiden Klingsberg*, the
scene of which happens, by something more than a coincidence, to be laid in Vienna. His libretti are simply sentimental and trite. He is sentimental in *Dorf im Gebürge*,
set to music by Josef Weigl (Vienna, 1798), in *Fanchon das
Leiermädchen*, with music by Friedrich Heinrich Himmel
(Berlin, 1804; Vienna, 1808 and 1817) or in *Die Al-
penhütte*, with music by Conradin Kreutzer (Stuttgart,
1815; Vienna, 1822). He is trite in such works as *Der Spiegelritter* or *Des Teufels Lustschloss;* and *Des Teufels Lustschloss* is the very libretto which the young Schubert chose
for his first operatic venture, while *Der Spiegelritter* provided the subject for one of his later efforts.

In the realm of song a very different constellation existed
for Schubert compared with that in the operatic field.
Here he was born under the luckiest of stars, although we
should at once add that it is only upon an exceptional child of
Fortune that the stars cannot help but look benignly.

The aspects were favourable from both a literary and a
musical point of view. We need only recall the sort of tests
which Haydn and Mozart picked on in their Italianized fast-
nesses of Eisenstadt or Vienna, whenever it occurred to them
to set a poem to music. They were scarcely aware of the
violent change that was taking place in the German poetry
of their day, and it was almost an accident when Mozart hit
upon Goethe's 'Veilchen' or Haydn upon a text from Shakespeare. It was admittedly no accident that Mozart did not
pursue any further inquiries about the author of this poem,
since this would have been no easy matter even in Vienna. It
was, however, anything but accidental that Schubert kept
abreast of the poetry of his day and that he should have been
one of the first composers to have discovered the two Schlegels, Rückert, Platen, Uhland or Heinrich Heine.

In the realm of poetry Schubert is half beneficiary, half benefactor. But as a beneficiary, he rejected everything, or nearly everything, which did not appeal to his sensitive taste and which lacked form. He rejected every Gallicism, the elegant *perruque* which was still the height of fashion in the German poetry of 1750 or thereabouts. He rejected the 'reasonable', the moral, and the pastoral. He even rejected the religious style, dictated by reason and morality, which had made such a powerful impression on Beethoven in the shape of Gellert's *Geistliche Oden und Lieder*. He rejected the false ingenuousness which gave itself such airs in Christian Felix Weisse's *Lieder im Volkston* and Joh. Adam Hiller's *Teutsche Operetten*. Only the Anacreontic style finds an echo in him, but even then in a new feeling for the spirit of classical antiquity, and not in the vulgar or witty epigrams of the Anacreontics such as Hagedorn, who sang the praises of friendship, love, Bacchus, Terpsichore and similar cheerful philosophies around the middle of the eighteenth century.

Schubert's heritage traces itself back to the lyrical poetry of Klopstock, because Klopstock was the first German poet to come down on the side of feeling against reason and Rationalism. Klopstock's musical possibilities were discovered by Gluck, who, in 1785, published half a dozen settings of patriotic, rather than genuinely lyrical, poems by the great bard. Schubert's choice was to prove very different. When he wished to illustrate in music the bardic spirit, the blend of ancient heroic tradition and stirring sentimentality, he turned not to Klopstock's variants of the old Germanic style, but to translations from Ossian, since they were more universal, more powerful and more heart-stirring. For purely lyrical expression, he contented himself at the outset with two poets of the Göttinger Hain circle of 1772 – Stolberg and the gentle Hölty; but he is also familiar with the Swabian Schubart, who was himself a composer of songs. He ignored Bürger, except in his setting for male-voice quartet of 'Das Dörfchen', although, as we shall see later, Bürger was brought close enough to him through his musical model Zumsteeg. Possibly Bürger was too blunt for his taste – and too 'traditional'. For Schubert did not imitate the traditional manner. He created it himself without knowing he was doing so. His favourite poet in the lofty, sentimental style is Friedrich v. Matthisson, who was also one of Beethoven's favourite poets. Schubert, as it were, dug down into Matthisson's slight poetry in search of singable material, in search of an innocent, sensitive approach to Nature, in search of 'the spirit of love', not only for his songs but for his choral music as well. This choice is surprising, since he also has a spiritual affinity with Matthisson's more attractive brother, Matthias Claudius, the simple 'Wandsbecker Bote' in whom sentimentality and classical reminiscences vanish, leaving behind them only truth, simplicity and sincerity. But perhaps 'Death and the Maiden' (and the variations in the D minor Quartet) make up for the lack of quantity.

In 1773 there appeared a volume of three essays under the title of *Von deutscher Art und Kunst*; the names of two of the authors were Herder and Goethe. Herder's own poetry, with its didactic and figurative strain, did not attract Schubert; and we have already explained why there was only one instance – a year before his death, in the ballad 'Edward' – where Schubert remembered the existence of a collection of folk songs at every age and every land which Herder had published in 1778 and 1779; he similarly ignored a later anthology of epoch-making literary importance – *Des Knaben Wunderhorn*, by the two Romantics, Arnim and Brentano. Schubert had no need of the folk song; he was constantly searching for something simple, something deeply felt, but at the same time stamped with artistic individuality. And that is precisely what he found in Goethe. In Goethe he found – particularly in the poems published before 1815 – Nature instead of scenery, passion instead of rhetoric, feeling instead of sentimentality, life itself in place of mere classical imitation, in place of artlessness and sheer size. We shall have occasion to return to this subject many times; and as with Matthisson, so in the case of Goethe we shall have to study the relationship between Schubert and Beethoven; for Goethe was also a favourite poet of Beethoven's. In the case of Schiller, Goethe's antagonist from an aesthetic point of view, the comparison is more limited; for with the one celebrated exception of 'An die Freude' for which Schubert also wrote a setting, Beethoven fought shy of Schiller's poetry with its deep vein of philosophy and its reminiscences of classical antiquity. Schubert, on the other hand, advanced eagerly upon this poetry and fashioned from it some of his sublimest masterpieces.

This is roughly the extent of Schubert's literary heritage. But not only did he inherit the old; he also discovered the new. He discovered a talent for poetry not only within the close circle of his friends, but on the remotest fringes; he discovered the early Romantics and immortalized them for all time; he followed Goethe along new paths – those of the *Westöstlicher Divan*; and it can be only a matter of chance that he did not come across two Swabian poets who, each in his own way, could have filled Schiller's place for him in later life; Friedrich Hölderlin and Eduard Mörike. He had to leave the establishment of their fame to a later generation.

From the musical point of view, too, the time was ripe for Schubert, the song-writer, with his talent for using to the full the discoveries he made. True, there was no reason to expect the appearance of a great song-writer, least of all in Vienna. Or was it not most to be expected in Vienna, the city of Haydn, of Mozart, and of Beethoven? Had they not built a mighty edifice of mighty music? And was not Beethoven still composing? But the achievements of these three masters lay for the most part not in the realm of song but in other fields. As a broad generalization, it is fair to say that Mozart was not strictly a song-writer; he was even less a song-writer than his direct predecessors in Vienna, such as Johann Holzer, who was presumably a relative of one of young Schubert's teachers. Mozart wrote songs with German words, but they assume an Italian character and are transformed for the most part into canzonettas or miniature *scene*; they are Anacreontic and pastoral, even in the case of the single 'autobiographical' exception, the setting of Goethe's 'Veilchen'. Yet in spite of everything, Mozart was a true composer of vocal music, even though he treated it in the Italian manner; Haydn, on the other hand, was not even that – if we may be permitted another broad generalization. For all his occasional pride in them, his songs are like the superfluous chips from instrumental designs for sonatina movements – miniature Andantes or Adagios. There is admittedly one great and genuine strophic song among them which Schubert had probably had to sing or listen to so often that he never gave it another thought: the Emperor Hymn. But on the occasions when Schubert had this Hymn in mind, as, for example, in the variations in the 'Trout' Quintet or in the D minor Quartet, he is thinking of it in its instrumental

context in Haydn's 'Emperor' Quartet, and not in its original
form. And we shall have frequent cause to show that even
Beethoven is time and again a 'Viennese' composer in his
songs. Schubert never follows his example, either in those
cases where Beethoven confines himself within the limits of
Viennese conventions, or in the single instance where he
oversteps them.

Haydn and Mozart were severely criticized as song-writers
by their North-German contemporaries, for the North
Germans, from Berlin and Hamburg, were firmly convinced
that they themselves had created or re-created the *genre* of
the real German song. They believed, from a negative
point of view, that they had almost entirely eradicated the
influence of the Italian arioso; their positive achievement
was, in their opinion, the writing of 'songs in the traditional
manner' – simple in form, proceeding naturally from the
text and designed to fit the spirit of the poetry; all expression
was concentrated in the melody, while for the most part the
accompaniment was only lightly sketched in. This simplicity
is most clearly pronounced in the songs of Johann Abraham
Peter Schulz, who lived and worked in Berlin and Copen-
hagen. He anticipates a group of poets who belong to
Schubert's North-German heritage: Hölty, Jacobi, Stolberg, Voss, Overbeck, even Bürger (for whom Schubert
could never summon up great interest), and above all Matthias Claudius. Schulz is as full and simple as Claudius,
and when fullness and simplicity meet as in the vesper
song 'Der Mond ist aufgegangen', the result is something
which, in the purity of its conception and the intensity of
its feeling, survives far beyond the decade in which it was
written.

We are not concerned here with writing a history of song
before Schubert. Nevertheless, from the wealth of output
and the host of minor composers who preceded him, there
are two North Germans and one South German who deserve
our attention, for the two North Germans must quite
certainly have been familiar to Schubert, while the South
German exercised the profoundest influence on him.

The North Germans are Joh. Fried. Reichardt and Carl
Friedrich Zelter. The South German is Johann Rudolf Zumsteeg; and all three had a direct connection with the two
great Weimar poets with whom Schubert, too, was so deeply

preoccupied. Reichardt was associated with both of them, although they for their part were highly (and justifiably) critical of him; Zelter's closest connection was with Goethe, and Zumsteeg's with Schiller. Zelter, whose association with Goethe began in 1795, was very much an individual after the poet's own heart, both as a man and as a composer of music for his poetry. When, in 1796, there appeared Zelter's '12 Lieder am Clavier zu singen', which included several 'melodies' to songs and poems by Goethe, the latter admitted 'that he would scarcely have thought it possible that there could be anything so heartfelt in music', and on a later occasion he praised some of his friend's subsequent compositions as 'faithful reproductions of my poetic intentions'. Today, we think otherwise, thanks to Schubert, whom Goethe at best silently ignored. Generally speaking, we find Zelter too artless in a manner typical of Berliners, and, for all that, too often overlaid with a sickly Italian veneer. It is true, however, that he achieves from time to time in his artlessness an unusual economy of expression and a rare sensitivity, and since his choice of Goethe's poems frequently coincides with Schubert's, there is every opportunity for comparison. Schubert, moreover, must have been familiar with much of Zelter's work. There are certain points of affinity when he is competing with Zelter, as for example in his 'König von Thule' and 'Indische Legende'; and these points of affinity even seem to be present when he is deliberately avoiding any idea of competition, as in 'Di Braut von Korinth' or 'Das Zauberlehrling'. One must be careful not to compare songs which Schubert could not possibly have known, for Zelter survived Schubert by several years and even during Schubert's lifetime his output continued to be prolific and he revised many of his original settings.

On chronological grounds we should have mentioned Reichardt first, for he was older than Zelter and his association with Goethe started in the 1780s. In a collection of Reichardt's songs published in 1780, we find that Goethe already has pride of place along with Bürger, Voss and other lesser poets. And in 1789 Reichardt was still a welcome visitor at Goethe's house. The following principles which he had already laid down in 1770 must have had the effect of emphasizing his superiority over Zelter in the poet's eyes.

I have noticed that, however prettily people sang my songs, they hardly ever struck the right *approach*. And when I studied this fact more closely, I found that all those who missed the right approach had first played the notes as if they constituted an independent melodic composition, and had then added the words to them. This is the precise opposite of the method I adopted when I wrote the songs. My melodies always spring naturally from repeated readings of the poem, without any conscious search for them on my part. All I do afterwards is this: I run over them in my mind again and again with slight alterations and do not write them down until I am fully convinced that the various stresses—grammatical, logical, emotional and musical— are so perfectly blended one with another that the melody rings true and lies easily on the voice; and I do this not only with one verse, but with all of them. But if this process is to be conveyed with equal clearness in performance, then the singer must read and re-read the words beforehand until he feels that he is reading them with the correct expression. Then and only then can he sing them.

Two years later he simplified these principles still further:

The melodies of songs in which anyone who has ears and a throat can join, must be able to stand on their own, independent of all accompaniment, and must, by the simplest sequence of notes, the most precise rhythmic movement, and the most exact interrelationship of the sections and divisions, etc., of the melodic line, so catch the *mood* of the song, that, after a single hearing one can no longer imagine the melody without the words or the words without the melody; that the melody becomes indispensable to the words, and is nothing by itself. Such a melody will always have the true character of unison (unisono) (to choose a *single* word for the artist's benefit) and will therefore neither require nor indeed permit any accompanying harmony.

Only a North German could talk like this, never a Viennese and least of all Schubert with his teeming musical imagination. Fortunately Reichardt himself did not always adhere rigidly to such principles. His songs are much richer in style and richer in contrasts, too. As early as 1788 he wrote a setting of Goethe's free-verse, hymn-like song 'An Lida' in a declamatory, quasi-recitative style which alternates smoothly between 'recitative' and 'aria'. This is a particularly important model for the young Schubert, who resorts to a similar method of treating free poetic form, the blend of narrative and emotion which is so essential a part of Ossian's poetry. In some of his later work, such as a fragment from Goethe's 'Euphrosine', 1809, Reichardt achieves a freedom of form and a richness of expression in the accompaniment, in the later development of which Schubert is his immediate successor.*

There is no shadow of doubt that the third of these composers, J. R. Zumsteeg, was a direct forerunner of Schubert and exercised an important influence on him. Zumsteeg (1760–1802) was a South German and had started to publish, in 1791, his large-scale Ballads and less ambitious songs, including 'Colma, ein Gesang Ossian's von Goethe' (that is to say, the version of Ossian's poem as it appears in Goethe's *Werther*), and more especially Büger's crude and quasi-traditional ballads 'Des Pfarrers Tochter von Taubenhayn', 'Die Entführung' and 'Lenore'. The reactions to his setting of 'Lenore' varied between delight and horror, thanks to its profoundly dramatic effect and its flexible accompaniment. Even today it has not entirely lost its violent impact. From 1797 onwards, Zumsteeg also published collections of his songs. The first contained seven under the title of *Gesänge der Wehmut, von J. G. v. Salis und F. Matthisson*, the second, twelve, and the third, three; and after 1800 there appeared four volumes of *Short Ballads and Songs*, each larger than its predecessor. The first begins with Schiller's 'Ritter Toggenburg' which Schubert, in 1816, imitated so naïvely that his setting is really little more than a somewhat richer version of Zumsteeg's. But we scarcely require this striking proof of Schubert's intimate knowledge of Zumsteeg's songs, for there are many of his texts which could only have been taken from Zumsteeg's various collections (in addition to those mentioned above, a further three were published after his death). Zumsteeg, moreover, was a livelier, less affected composer than his two North-German contemporaries, with their sickly veneer of aestheticism. His melodic vein is richer; he tries to convey the changing moods and changing scenery of a ballad, or the association of ideas in a song; in some degree he heralds the spirit of Schubert, almost as if he were his John the Baptist. The story goes that, as a child, Schubert not only wrote pieces for strings and for the piano, but also little songs. If this is true, then it is more than likely that they were imitations of Zumsteeg.

* It is significant that Schubert copied Reichardt's *Monolog aus Goethes Iphigenia als Probe musicalischer Behandlung jenes Meisterwerks*, preserving the title of the first edition.

Chapter Two

First Steps at the Convict

1808–1813

With the significant exception of his songs, everything which Schubert wrote during his time at school is designed for a particular purpose in music, that is to say, to be played in the family circle at home; or for the enjoyment of his fellow-pupils, either on the piano or in the orchestra; or for performance in church. In April 1810, when he was in his fourteenth year, he started work on a Piano Fantasia for four hands (IX, 30). Now Mozart, in his fourteenth year, after numerous experiments, began to write his first *opera seria,* and consequently Schubert's precocity is in no way comparable with Mozart's. But musically Schubert was already much more advanced than this long dialogue for two players reveals. If we are to take it seriously, then we must admit that it is altogether too emotional. It begins thoughtfully in G and ends majestically in C. In between there is a succession of gaily-coloured musical threads, broken only by a passage near the middle where the opening subject develops into a march, the first of many, and by the recurrence of a trumpet theme, expressly marked as such. It is all very childish, but with this difference. Unlike other boys of the same age, Schubert does not spend his time painting picture books, but instead, amuses himself at the piano with one of his friends. The martial subject is mere boyish fancy and is un-Schubertian; but the excessive length of the piece and a certain voluptuousness of sound produced by chords repeated in the same rhythm are both typically Schubertian. And is it not arch-Schubertian to start with music for four hands? Schubert is later to become not only the most prolific but also the greatest composer of music for four hands, because the playing of duets on one instrument – as opposed to the 'concerto' principle on two pianos which always presupposes an idea of rivalry – is symbolic of friendship. Almost all his compositions for four hands bear dedications, and it was not a quartet or a volume of songs that he inscribed to his revered Beethoven, but a set of variations for piano duet. The last of his long list of such works bears the motto: 'Notre amitié est invariable'.

When we consider the two later Fantasias for four hands (IX, 31 and 32), the first written in September 1811 and the second between April and 10th June, 1813, we can dismiss the earlier work of 1810 as a boyish joke. If, however, it is meant to be treated seriously, then we can say that between 1810 and September 1811 Schubert, so to speak, 'woke up' and became a composer. For the two later Fantasias are admittedly imitations, but conscious, even self-conscious imitations. The model in each case was one or both of Mozart's pieces for the mechanical organ (K. 594 and 608) which had been published in 1800 by Breitkopf and Härtel in four-handed arrangements. The first Fantasia starts and finishes with a Largo; a passionate Allegro, treated contrapuntally, frames a 'Tempo di Marcia' – 'Tempo di Marcia' because it is purely song-like in character and not in the least heroic. The piece gives the appearance of having been completed, although it begins in G minor and ends in D minor, and the last sixteen bars of the *primo* part are missing. It is instructive in that it shows first that, even as a boy, Schubert could write concentratedly; and, secondly, that he learned the art of counterpoint by imitation and had no need to wait for Salieri's instruction, which did not begin until nine months later, on 12th June, 1812. It is not in any sense animated counterpoint; but that is something which not even Salieri could have taught him.

The second piece is still longer but contrives a certain uniformity. It begins in C minor, and ends in B flat major, but it is built on a single chromatic, descending figure, treated once more in a contrapuntal, 'fugal' manner, which eventually develops into a true fugue, 'Allegro maestoso'. Only in a section marked 'Andante amoroso', and oddly enough also in B flat major, is there any thematic freedom. The influence of the polonaise is at work here and the whole section is modelled directly on the Andantino in Mozart's C minor Fantasia (K. 475). Both in its general and detailed construction, this second Fantasia is remarkable for its free-

dom and boldness. Small wonder that pupils and teachers
alike gazed in astonishment at the modest boy who was
capable of such things. In spite of its childish immaturity,
there is a direct link between this work and the 'Wanderer'
Fantasia and the superb F minor Fantasia for four hands
written in 1828.*

Schubert's other field of intimate music-making was the
string quartet. This was no doubt a favourite practice
ground with his fellow-pupils at the Convict, but more certainly in the family circle at home, where his father had to
take the 'cello part. He was the weakest member of the
family team, and the story goes that whenever he played a
wrong note it was not one of the older brothers, but Schubert, at the viola desk, who gave the sign to stop and who
observed, with great respect: 'Father, I don't think that was
quite right'. A string quartet dated 1811 and another dated
1812, both starting in D major, but modulating subsequently
into different keys, have been lost. But three quartets written
in 1812 have survived. The first of these (V, 1) however,
which begins in C minor and ends in B flat major, exactly
like the third Piano Fantasia, cannot possibly have been intended for the family circle, where they played Haydn,
Mozart and Pleyel. It is so completely unsuccessful and immature, that it is all the more difficult to explain the development which took place in Schubert over the next year or
two, and which leads from this attempt to a little masterpiece like the Finale of the C major Quartet, written in 1813.
In the first movement the introductory Andante is linked
thematically with the Allegro (G minor); in the Finale, too,
the same interval of a rising fourth plays its part, particularly in the 'contrapuntal' middle section (in C major!).
In the latter, however, the ambitious composer allows two
horrible octaves to creep in. The most successful movement
is the pleasant Minuet (in F) which is preceded by a simple
Andante (in B flat). Like the first Fantasia of 1810, this string
quartet is written, so to speak, in a state of innocence,
'before the fall'.

The second quartet in C major (V, 2) dated 30th September, 1812, consisting only of a first movement ('Presto')

* The influence of Mozart's C minor Fantasia is apparent also in a
newly-discovered Fantasia for piano two hands in C minor, written
about 1813 [manuscript in Malmö, Sweden] where themes from Mozart's
Adagio are textually quoted or elaborated (Otto Erich Deutsch).

and a Minuet, contains some brilliant writing for strings with
its humming rhythm and its violent unison passages, but the
form is not yet mastered. In the exposition Schubert falls
back too often on the tonic, and he is not yet capable of
writing a real development. The movement captures the
'spirit' of a quartet, but it is not a quartet movement. The
only striking feature of the Minuet is that it takes up the
main subject of the first movement in much the same way as
the Galliard takes up the theme of the Pavane in an old-style
suite.

Six or seven weeks later, on 19th November, Schubert
began a new quartet (V, 3) which he completed on 21st February, 1813, three weeks after his sixteenth birthday. There
is no mistaking the model – Haydn's Quartet op. 76, 2. It is
not in D minor, however, but in B flat major, and the main
subject is not so ubiquitous as in Haydn's case, nor is it so
animated by genuine counterpoint. A fanfare motive which
is announced loudly and yet unobtrusively in the exposition
becomes the accompanying rhythm in the development, and
the theme reappears in triple time in the recapitulation, with
the effect of increasing the volume of sound but not the
musical content. The Andante, in 6/8 time and likewise in
the main key of B flat major, is nearer to Mozart than to
Haydn, except that neither of those classical composers
would have modulated to C flat in order to achieve an enharmonic change of key, and neither would have been
capable of anything so daring as a passionate *tremolo* outburst after a *pp*. The *tremolo* is Schubertian, and does not
occur even in Beethoven in this particular form. The Minuet
('Allegro ma non troppo') is in D, with Trio in B flat major.
It is a good, honest Minuet, rather 'rustic' in character, and
full of surprises; the Trio already has the typical Schubertian
opening – unison, *pianissimo* and with a persistent rhythm;
even the return to the Minuet section is completely typical.
The Finale, with its 'short-legged' theme, harks back to
Haydn again – hyper-Haydn, one might almost say – with its
second leg shorter than its first, three bars as against four; it
is altogether freer and more personal than the first movement. Schubert is developing fast. Three months have
already brought a definite advance.

This rapid development (there may have been a connecting link in the shape of a lost Quartet in E flat) is most

clearly demonstrated in the next quartet (V, 4) in C, which was begun on 3rd March, 1813, the second movement being finished three days later and the remaining two movements on the following day. The first movement opens with a gloomy, chromatic Adagio, like Mozart's Quartet in C, and even the Allegro takes some time to arrive at the full brightness of C major; then, however, it slips immediately into an Italian style:

And in the development, the chromaticism of the introduction begins surprisingly to play a dramatic part. Indeed, the whole movement is full of contrasts. It deserves something better to follow it than the rather sentimental Andante in G after the style of Haydn, and the Minuet in B flat (!) before which the flag of Beethoven's First Symphony flutters all too clearly.

But there now follows the Finale, in which Schubert no longer concerns himself with Haydn, Mozart or Beethoven, and writes something in the nature of a little polka which is so gay and captivating that not even its conception as a piece of chamber-music nor its concessions to the incidental technicalities of quartet-playing can destroy its natural vitality. One might say that, while there is much here which is still the work of a boy, only a boy could have had the childish or divine courage to have written something like this, five years after the three quartets of Beethoven's op. 59 had appeared; in much the same way that only a boy could have written the Adagio of Mozart's A major Violin Concerto. The reference to the op. 59 quartets is not without reason; for in the first two, Beethoven uses two genuine 'Themes russes' as his 'primitive' raw material, without them thereby sounding any more 'primitive'. Schubert *fashions* his own raw material; he sits in that paradise to which others longingly aspire.

During his time at school or at the Convict, Schubert wrote a further three or four string quartets with which we can deal briefly, (V, 6, 7, 10). The first – in B flat major (8th June – 18th August, 1813) – lacks the two middle movements. The first movement derives from Beethoven's op. 18 rather than from Haydn or Mozart and vividly demonstrates Schubert's characteristic practice of combining punctuated subjects with triplet figures, while the other movement is a Rondo in the style of Haydn, once again with a 'short-legged', humorous first subject. The first movement of the D major Quartet, written between 22nd August and 3rd September, combines every manner of 'D major' reference – Mozart's K. 575 and 'Hoffmeister' Quartets, Beethoven's Second Symphony, and at the end there is even a hint of the *Zauberflöte* Overture. The movement is much too *cantabile*, monotonous and long-drawn out, and the recapitulation appears in the dominant, a convenience which we can forgive Schubert in so many other instances, but which is a definite offence in serious chamber music. The Andante reflects the mood of the Andante in Mozart's 'Prague' Symphony; even the Minuet and many passages in the Finale, with its fanfares and *tremoli*, seem to have been conceived more in a symphonic spirit than as chamber music.

There is an explanation for Schubert's reversion from Beethoven to Mozart. He wrote this quartet under the supervision of his new teacher Salieri, who, as an encouragement to his pupil, had arranged for it to be published, together with two others. Schubert did not follow this advice, but proceeded to dedicate it to his father on his name-day (4th October, 1813) for which occasion he also wrote the words and music for a cantata.* He must subsequently have been relieved that nothing came of this publication, for in July, 1824, we find him writing thus to his brother Ferdinand, who was still playing these early works in the family quartet. '. . . it would be a better idea if you were to concentrate on quartets other than mine, for there is really nothing in them. But then you like everything I write. . . .' In the intervening years he had written music of a very different kind!

The other quartet in D has a first movement which is still unbalanced – with a recapitulation in C! The three following movements (Andante in G, Minuet and final Rondo) have a

* Cf. O. E. Deutsch, *Music and Letters*, 1943, p. 27.

Haydnesque ring, but they are unfortunately both short and undeveloped. The Minuet is dated November 1813, and therefore falls outside the scope of this chapter, as do some other Minuets, Trios and Waltzes for string quartet which were written in this month (II, 8, 9, 10); but even if the three other movements are of an earlier origin, they would still be a retrograde step. And the same is true of a Quartet in E flat major, which the Collected Edition (V, 10) attributes to the year 1817, but which certainly was written quite shortly after the Convict period, in November 1813. It is Mozartian from beginning to end, only without the vigilance or alertness which Mozart contrived. Notice how schematic the recapitulation in the first and last movements is. The Adagio is actually an Andante; even the Minuet, entitled 'Scherzo', is not really Schubertian. The quartet was published posthumously as op. 125, 1, together with a second one, which differs from it in every possible respect.

The transition from chamber music to the works written for the school or family orchestra is marked by an Overture for string quintet, composed between 29th June and 12th July, 1811. It is not included in the Collected Edition, but it has equally good if not greater claims to publication than the first essays in the art of the string quartet. Greater, that is to say, because it is already a finished piece of work for a typically Mozartian combination with two violas – Largo and Allegro in C minor, which immediately emphasizes its serious character. The Largo, in 3/4 time, is mysterious and rather restless, like the beginning of the 'Leonora' Overture; and even the agitated, impassioned Allegro reserves a march-like, though calmer, contrast for its second subject, which appears in A flat major in the exposition and in G major in the recapitulation, nor is there any real spirit of optimism even in the major ending. The whole piece is treated more in the style of chamber-music, although by no means masterly in its execution, and is called an 'Overture' simply by virtue of its form.* But there dates from the end of this year or the beginning of the next a more ambitious Overture to the musical comedy *Der Teufel als Hydraulicus* (II, 1). This overture was written neither for the school nor the family orchestra, but for a somewhat unusual com-

---

* I am indebted to Mr. Otto Kallir of New York for his kindness in allowing me access to the manuscript.

bination which omits oboes, trumpets and side-drums – presumably, therefore, for some specific theatrical occasion. In this primitive piece, the musical curtain, so to speak, rises three times on a thrice-repeated statement of the key of D major. When at last the overture proper starts, it proves to be quite uneventful. It is lively, insignificant, and for the most part noisy. The whole piece has the obvious appearance of a suburban affair. Six months later on 26th June, 1812, there followed a new Overture in D, for full classical orchestra, even to the inclusion of trombones (II, 2). This added pretentiousness only results in an added pomposity in the Allegro section ('spiritoso'), the employment of trombones probably indicates that Schubert wanted to show that he too could write something which was far beyond the capacity of the Convict orchestra. We do not know the work in its original version. Schubert revised it, presumably not long after its composition, cutting out one episode, but expanding another section. The melodic material of the episode reappears in the fragment of an Octet for wind instruments (see below III, 2).

In direct contrast are the two Overtures in B flat (XXI, 1) and D (XXI, 2) which the Collected Edition places 'in the earliest period' and which were quite certainly composed before the autumn of 1812. The first, perhaps for *Der Spiegelritter*, written for the classical orchestra (without trombones), has a brooding Andante introduction, not unlike Beethoven's Fourth, but simpler and more rounded, and then a very personal and mysterious theme.

which, if it were anonymous, would probably be attributed to Anton Bruckner. But it is very Schubertian and the first inkling of such characteristic themes as that in the first movement of the Piano Sonata in A minor, op. 42; and it is likewise followed by its rhythmic complement. The second subject, which appears first in G minor, and then in D minor in the recapitulation, has a Haydnesque, military flavour. This work shows that, in spite of external influences and his dependence on past models. Schubert is already an individualist, even 'in the earliest period', and is gradually developing in a sphere from which he excludes all others.

The other Overture, in which the trombones reappear, proves this. It begins (Adagio) in a threatening minor key, like another, more famous Overture – that to *Don Giovanni*. But it changes to the major before the end of the introduction and leaves the transition to 'allegro spiritoso' to the wind instruments, led by the horns – with the same suggestion of yearning which occurs in 'Der Lindenbaum' in *Die Winterreise*. The Allegro which follows again shows the unmistakable influence of Mozart's overture, even to the extent of literal references. Young Schubert still finds it difficult to get away from the main key, so difficult that he keeps it for the second subject; to make up for this he introduces the latter in the dominant in the recapitulation! Beethoven could scarcely have suppressed a sympathetic grin at this. The trombones, used with impressive effect in the introduction, are merely noisy in the Allegro. It is worth noting that the overture as we know it today is the revision of an earlier version completed on 12th June, 1812. It is beautifully written, on good paper, and in his introduction to the revised Collected Edition Eusebius Mandyscewski explodes the sentimental story that the young Schubert always suffered from a shortage of music-paper. On the contrary, he was an extravagant individual, and it was only in later years that he became more economical with the expensive stuff – more economical, too, insasmuch as his handwriting grew continually smaller and finer.

On 28th October, 1813, Schubert finished his First Symphony in D major (I, 1), written not only for roughly the same orchestral combination as Mozart's last symphonies (the *single* flute is a clear indication) but also in the spirit of Mozart. Allusion has been made to the many affinities with Beethoven; that of the first subject with the *Prometheus* Overture, that of the second subject with the main, hymn-like melody in the *Prometheus* Ballet, or with the second subject of the Sonata 'Pathétique'. Reference has also been made to the similarity between the Minuet and the Scherzo of the Second Symphony, which also influenced the second subject of the Finale. But it lacks completely Beethoven's revolutionary orchestral crescendo. Schubert contents himself with a serenity that is typical of Mozart or – especially in the Andante, in spite of melancholy half-shadows – of Haydn. The delicate passage for wind instruments which leads back to the recapitulation in the first movement is completely Mozartian; the beginning of the recapitulation with the inclusion of the introduction in Allegro tempo is admittedly anything but classical, and a characteristic of Schubert's right up to the Octet. The Andante, in the perfectly normal key of G major, aims at achieving something different from the Andante of the 'Prague' Symphony, without completely freeing itself from its model, and consequently becomes uncertain and shapeless. The Finale proves that Schubert was well acquainted with the Finale of Mozart's 'Paris Symphony'. But there is no trace of Haydn's wit, of Mozart's occasional daemonic power, or of Beethoven's ferocity and violence; it is all superficial, musicianly, and festive, as becomes an uncannily gifted but inwardly healthy young man. The work is dedicated to the headmaster of the Convict, Dr. Franz Innocenz Lang, and is accordingly written in a most ambitious spirit. It must have caused some astonishment to teachers and fellow-pupils alike. It was his farewell present to the Convict, which he left during the course of this same autumn. On the last page of the manuscript there occur the following significant words: 'finis et fine'.

A few weeks previously Schubert finished a Minuet and Finale for four pairs of wind instruments, oboes, clarinets, horns and bassoons (18th August, 1813; III, 2): it is rather too pretentious an effort, in free form, like Mozart's 'Gran Partita'; the Minuet has two contrasting Trios, while the Finale is written in the spirit of one of Haydn's final Rondos. We do not know why Schubert wrote only the last two movements. All that is certain is that they were intended for the wind section of the school orchestra. At the end of the manuscript he added a burlesque postscript in which he signed himself as Imperial Chinese Director of Music at the Court of Nanking – perhaps by way of a joke at the expense of the legal style in which the affairs of the Convict were conducted. These two movements were followed by a short piece of funeral music in E flat minor for clarinets, bassoons and contra-bassoon, horns and two trombones, dated 19th September, 1813 (III, 3). The two horns intone a sustained

melody, 'grave con espressione', and repeat it with full ac-
companiment. O. E. Deutsch has made the plausible sugges-
tion that it was written in memory of the poet Theodor
Körner, who had died a few weeks previously in the War of
Liberation, and to whom Schubert had been introduced by
Spaun at the beginning of the year.

On 28th June, 1812, Schubert, the Convict pupil and chorister, started to cultivate the last field of music 'for special
occasions' – namely church music – exactly four weeks
before his voice broke. This necessitated his having to give
up his active role as a treble or alto, and over the alto part of
a Mass by Peter Winter, he wrote: 'Franz Schubert crowed
for the last time on 26th July, 1812'. This first essay in
church music is a setting of one of the four antiphons of the
Blessed Virgin Mary, a *Salve Regina*, of which he later
wrote many more, since there was a great demand for such
pieces in the daily office from Trinity Sunday until the end
of the Church year. There followed, three months later, a
Kyrie (XIV, 14) in D minor, for chorus and full orchestra. It
is very solemn, in spite of the quick tempo, for, after the
dignified, mysterious orchestral introduction, the musical
notation should really be written in 'allabreve' time. And
this solemnity is not colourless, but expressive, and even
works up to a number of explosive outbursts. It is written in
the traditional 'Austrian' form, with the 'Christe' in the relative major and including solo passages for soprano and
tenor. The 'Kyrie', however, is not simply repeated but is
enriched with new features. A severe critic would probably
have found fault with the homophonic treatment and with
an octave which has crept in, but he would scarcely have
suspected the hand of a boy of fifteen or sixteen in the
work.

In March, April and May 1813, Schubert wrote three
more *Kyries*. The first in B flat major (XIV, 21) is really only
a short *a cappella* movement, but written with a complete
mastery of every vocal medium – vocal suspensions and dissonances, and dynamic contrasts and shades. The April
Kyrie (XIV, 15) is set in D minor again, but is scored for a
different combination of wind instruments: oboes, bassoons,
trumpets and side-drums, with the addition of three trombones. With its flourish of trumpets in the first movement

and its rushing figures on the violins, it is much more superficial and ostentatious than the first, and, in spite of occasional suggestions of a devotional spirit, a true piece of 'baroque' church music. The May *Kyrie*, in F (XIV, 16), differs from it in its sustained tempo and its simpler orchestra which omits trombones. The first 'Kyrie' and the 'Christe' are song-like in character and intimate in the same sense as Mozart's *Ave Verum*, but the second 'Kyrie' is an orthodox Allegro fugue, with *stretta* and pedal point, and with violent, contrapuntal figures on the violins. It is academically so correct that one wonders what Schubert wanted or indeed was able to learn from Salieri in this style. (As a matter of passing interest, how did Salieri and Schubert understand one another? We are told that, even to the last, Salieri's German never advanced beyond the elementary stage, while the young Schubert certainly understood no Italian.)

One notices more readily that he has listened attentively to the Finale of the 'Jupiter' Symphony. It seems rather dangerous to join in the general chorus of opinion that Schubert never learnt anything – by which is always meant his lack of real instruction in counterpoint. Schubert lent colour to this opinion by having arranged, shortly before his death, to take lessons in strict counterpoint from Simon Sechter, who was some ten years older than himself. I have an idea that he would soon have given them up. For he is a contrapuntist in his own right and, so to speak, without knowing it, an instinctive polyphonist. A pious or archaistic text like Friedrich Schlegel's 'Vom Mitleiden Mariae' prompts him to the purest of three-part writing. And could not the following passage very well come straight out of J. S. Bach?

Ex.8

Yet it occurs in one of the Ossian songs of 1817 (XX, 305). Schubert thinks instinctively of things which other com-

posers, such as Brahms, only discovered by following the
path of historical experience. In his song 'Die Liebe' (XX,
291), composed in 1817 and written in 3/4 time, Schubert
ends with a device which was known as the 'hemiole' in the
sixteenth century – in other words, he changes to 3/2
time:

and by this means, he even succeeds in correcting the apparently false emphasis. Passages of genuine polyphony occur
where one least expects them, as, for example, in the Trio of
the Polonaise for piano duet op. 61, 4 (IX, 3 p. 151), and if
anyone were inclined to make a more exhaustive search, he
would find a rich polyphonic prize in Schubert's harmonic
store.

All this – the symphony, the duets, the chamber music, the
dances for piano or string quartet, the church music – is
'occasional' music, written for a more or less particular purpose.

But there is one sphere into which the boy was driven, not
by any practical demand, but by a daemonical urge to yield
to the power of his imagination and to pour out his feelings.
We recall the story that, while still a child, he wrote little
songs. The first of his efforts to have survived, however, is
dated 30th March, 1811, and it is not a song, but a long
lyrical *scena* – a setting of Schücking's poem 'Hagar's
Klage' (XX, 1), for which he had found the model in Zumsteeg's 'Hagar's Klage in der Wüste Bersaba', published in
1797. In order to understand the historical background to
such *scene* by Zumsteeg and Schubert, it is necessary to
know their source of origin. They are derived from the
melodrama for spoken narrative with illustrative orchestral
accompaniment, of which George Benda's *Ariadne* and
Medea (1775) were the first examples. These are passionately
dramatic *scene* – monologues, to which the orchestra en-
deavours not only to paint the scenic background, but to
illustrate the heroine's emotions the more impressively. The

opera put this new technique to good use. And it *was* a new technique, in spite of the 'aesthetically impossible' hybrid *genre*. For this 'melodrama' the opera not only furnished the model, but also owed to it its increasingly emotional *recitativo accompagnato*; and, largely by virtue of Zumsteeg's efforts, the song and the ballad owed to it a new and artistically more justified form – the dramatic, lyrical *scena*. From the spoken narrative there developed the more impressive vocal treatment, and from the orchestra grew the piano accompaniment – more artistic than the orchestra, because the purely suggestive power of the piano does not fetter the imagination, but sets it free and gives it wings. For this reason it is usually a mistake to orchestrate Schubert's piano accompaniments; the result is almost always a simultaneous coarsening and weakening of the original.

Now this *scena*, in which Abraham's rejected concubine laments over her dying Ishmael in the wilderness, rages, raves, calls upon Jehovah, curses the hard-hearted Patriarch and turns at last to prayer, is written precisely after the pattern of Zumsteeg's setting. It lacks any real form, alternating between 'arioso' and 'recitativo' and between an instrumental style and a true *espressivo* in the accompaniment, and ending on a hymn-like note. But it is much better and richer than Zumsteeg, and emotionally coloured rather than purely illustrative. There is nothing boyish about it except the choice of text.

One might suppose that Schubert also found the model for his next attempt 'Des Mädchens Klage' (XX, 2) in Zumsteeg – in the latter's third volume of songs, published in 1801. But Zumsteeg gives Schiller's poem the title 'Thekla, aus dem Wallenstein', and has set only two verses. His setting was clearly designed to be used in a performance of Schiller's drama (*Die Piccolomini*, III, 7); it is as simple as possible, even to the accompaniment, except for a suggestion of an arioso at the end. Schubert on the other hand set all four verses, and his only reference to the poem's dramatic context may perhaps be found in the arpeggios of the sonata-like accompaniment in which there is one distinct echo of the 'Moonlight' Sonata. His setting bears the same relation to Zumsteeg's as a finished picture bears to a sketch, this time in an illustrative sense as well. He clearly felt this setting to be a youthful lapse, for he twice returned to the text, in May 1815 (XX, 67) and in March 1816 (XX, 194). On both occasions he set it in simple strophic form, and both versions bear a direct relationship to each other. We can already see that, contrary to the widely-held view, he did not in any sense produce music 'automatically' like a spring. He was critical; he was conscious of his obligation towards the written word, and he did not rest until he had done justice to it.

The two next songs of the year 1811 – 'Eine Leichenphantasie', a poem by the young, highly-emotional Schiller of 1780 (XX, 3) and G. K. Pfeffel's 'Vatermörder' (XX, 4; 26th December) reveal once more the boy obsessed with the power of his own imagination. In this instance, at least, Schiller paid attention to form, and prepared the ground for the composer by repeating the first verse of the poem in a slightly varied form at the end and by including in the middle a kind of 'arioso' contrast, which presents us with an emotional picture of the dead youth. And Schubert has made excellent use of it, although he overdoes the gruesomeness of the tone-painting. For the 'bright' middle-section too, with its picture-book associations, he contrives a splendidly heroic climax in D major, in contrast with the key of D minor which 'frames' it. Pfeffel's piece of moralizing is a somewhat uncouth exercise in voluptuousness in C minor; but the emotion is genuine.

The next nine months produced no more songs by Schubert, and it is not until 24th September, 1812, that a new one appears – this time a setting of Schiller's little elegiac poem 'Der Jüngling am Bache' (XX, 5). Four verses of passionate longing, simple in style and free from Schiller's frequent classical allusions; and not merely four verses, but a genuine strophic song. And there arises at this point a problem which warrants a digression.

THE STROPHIC SONG

It was much more of a problem for Schubert, with his desire, even his sense of obligation, to exhaust the content, the heart, the innermost essence of a song, than for his Viennese and North or South German predecessors, who for the most part contented themselves with 'neutral' melody. If the reader wishes fully to understand this simpler and more formal solution of the problem, he need only refer to Goethe's comments on his studies with one of his domestic musicians, Wilhelm Ehlers, which appear in the *Tag-und Jahreshefte* of February 1801.

Ehlers was a useful and acceptable performer in many roles, both as an actor and a singer. In this latter capacity he was particularly welcome at social entertainments, for he sang ballads and other similar songs to guitar accompaniment quite incomparably and with the most precise regard for the words of the text. He was indefatigable in studying the correct method of expression, which, so far as the singer is concerned, consists of pointing the different shades of meaning in each verse, while repeating throughout a *single* melody. Thus he is able to fulfil the requirements of both lyric and epic poets alike. This approach to singing was so ingrained in Ehlers that, whenever I suggested it, he would cheerfully spend the evening, and even continue far into the night, repeating the same song over and over again with every conceivable shade of expression down to the smallest detail; for the success of such exercises convinced him that the so-called practice of 'Durchcomponierung' is thoroughly reprehensible, since the generally lyrical character is thereby completely destroyed and a false interest in detail is demanded and aroused.

This was written in 1822, and the above passage alone is proof enough that every approach made by Schubert and his friends to Goethe was doomed to failure. It cannot be said in Goethe's favour that he was inundated by the flood of Schubert's songs which poured in on him, but that he was bound, on principle, to find them 'reprehensible'. It was precisely this 'interest in detail' which concerned young Schubert, for he was a creature of fancy. But he was also concerned with the 'generally lyrical character', and so he set Schiller's four verses as a 'strophic song with variations', rather like a Rondo with instrumental interludes; for, driven irresistibly to find a means of expressing himself, he gives the second half of each verse a different treatment. The piece tends a little towards a cantata style, and the historian is involuntarily reminded of those Roman cantatas written by the Carissimi School in the middle of the seventeenth century, in which recitative passages invariably lead back to an arioso.

This problem obsessed and disturbed Schubert throughout his life. Sometimes he even contented himself with Goethe's solution. One such example is his setting of the poet's 'In-

dische Legende', written on 18th August, 1815 (XX, 111), in
which a *single* melody and a *single* accompaniment do duty
for nine long verses. The following note appears in the
manuscript: 'In these verses, as well as the others, the distinction between *piano* and *forte* must be determined by
their content'; and this corresponds exactly to the absolute
demands of the poet. But I do not believe, nor did Schubert
believe, that there was a single performer in the world who
would not have found this melody, with its nine-fold repetition, a hindrance rather than a help to his freedom of
expression. As a composer, Schubert is too rich. He has to
combine the fullness of musical expression with the adap-
tability of the melody He adheres to the strophic form where
there is good reason for it. We must put ourselves in his
place and try to imagine how his imagination and feelings
were aroused, when he read a poem; how he then set himself
to concentrate its whole essence in a single verse. Sometimes
he succeeded completely; sometimes he is fully successful
only in one single verse; and sometimes it is only the last
verse which reveals why it has been cast in this mould and no
other. The most extreme example of this is his setting of
Kosegarten's 'Mondnacht', composed at the end of July,
1815 (XX, 102). There are four verses; the key of B major
provides a general background for the landscape bathed in
silvery light:

> *Siehe, wie die Mondesstrahlen*
> *Busch und Flur in Silber malen!*
> *Wie das Bächlein rollt und flimmt!*
> *Strahlen regnen: Funken schmettern*
> *Von den sanft geregten Blättern,*
> *Und die Tauflur glänzt und glimmt.*
> *Glänzend erdämmern der Berge Gipfel,*
> *Glänzend der Pappeln wogende Wipfel.**

Neither the two last lines above, nor those of the next two
verses can justify ending a song which begins in B major
with a mighty crescendo in F sharp major. It is not until we
reach the last two lines of the final verse, with its Tristan-like

---

* See, how the moonbeams paint with silver wood and field! How the
stream rolls and sparkles! Moonbeams pour down, sparks fly from the
gently stirring leaves, and the dew-field sparkles and glimmers. Night falls
upon the sparkling mountain peaks, the billowing tree-tops sparkle.

atmosphere, that we discover the reason for this *fortissimo:*

> *Dich umschlingend, von dir umschlungen,*
> *Gar in Eins mit dir geeint—*
> Schon', ach schone den Wonneversunkenen.
> Himmel und Erde verschwinden dem Trunkenen.*

But to return to the subject of Schiller's Elegy. There is no more characteristic example of Schubert's artistic sense of responsibility than the fact that the four verses of this little poem allowed him no peace of mind. He wrote three more settings of them, each in strophic form. On each occasion, his treatment becomes simpler, more concentrated and, in consequence, richer. The setting of 15th May, 1815 (XX, 68), retains the melodic opening, but this time in F minor instead of F major; this strongly elegiac key colours the whole song. In April 1819 there is a completely new treatment in D minor, which is not only elegiac but plaintive, with a more animated accompaniment to the second half of each verse than to the first (XX, 359a). Yet it is precisely this animation that Schubert abandoned in the final setting in C minor (XX, 359b), which has certain less passionate features. It was this version which he published (op. 87, 2); it is, in fact, insusceptible of any further alteration.

At the stage with which we are here concerned, however, Schubert had not progressed so far. In the year 1812, there appeared 'Klaglied' (XX, 6) – a poem of four verses by Friedrich Rochlitz, who not only published the *Allgemeine Musikalische Zeitung*, but also fancied himself as a poet. Here Schubert quite simply set only the first verse, a little too much in Mozart's 'cantabile' style; and the 'sighing of the breezes' and the 'murmuring of the brook' tempt Schubert into a style of descriptive writing which is quite inapplicable to the last three verses; indeed, the words of the last two verses would need to be altered to make them fit the musical setting. His next song, too – a setting of L. H. Chr. Hölty's 'Totengräberlied' ('Dig, spade, dig!') (XX, 7) –

---

*Embracing thee, by thee embraced,
Once with thee, closely united,
Spare, ah! spare me, sunk in bliss.
Heaven and Earth vanish before my love-intoxicated eyes.

harks back to the eighteenth century. In those days, the Berlin or Hamburg *Lieder im Volkston* had started to specialize in particular classes of people. They no longer dealt with children, mothers and ladies of quality, but with individual professions which included not only such 'poetic' pursuits as those of huntsmen, fishermen, seafarers and millers but also the most prosaic callings of every kind. By virtue of his sombre occupation, the gravedigger is one of the more 'romantic' figures. Here he is a simple philosopher, an old man with a bass voice, who cheerfully sings the praises of his spade which provides him with never-ending work and bread in plenty. If it were possible to turn *Hamlet* into a ballad-opera, this would be the song to which the Clown would enter. Schubert also set his hackneyed text (there is a version by Ph. Em Bach, among others) for three male voices, in the same key of E minor and treated with the utmost simplicity (XIX, 20).

Between 12th April and 17th September, 1812, Schubert's output of songs travelled in a kind of circular, yet spiral, motion: he returned again to the point from which he started, but on a higher level. Once more, this period culminates in a large-scale ballad – a setting of Schiller's 'Taucher', but it is no longer an exercise in imitation. Schubert started, however, with Matthisson's 'Die Schatten' (XX, 8), four verses in classical Horatian metre, which he reduces to prose and accordingly treats with complete freedom (he begins in A major and ends in C). It is the hymnlike ending which induced him to set this song, with its retrospective atmosphere, its spirit of gratitude (to the 'honest Bonnet' among others) and its passionate longing; and what matters most to him is the modulation to C major by way of a restrained yet irresistible crescendo. Modulation is one of his most powerful means of achieving an outlet for his feelings. He then turned again to Schiller: 'Sehnsucht' (XX, 9: 'Ah, from the depths of this valley') on which he spent three days, 15th–17th April; and 'Thekla – Eine Geisterstimme' (XX, 11; 22nd–23rd August). The first is a bass song; the second has a striking accompaniment in the lower octaves throughout. At this stage, Schubert's only method of approach to both songs is through the medium of alternate passages of recitative and arioso; indeed, the heroic upsurge in the last verse of 'Sehnsucht' is almost operatic in conception. Schubert later rescued both songs – the first, by way of one of the most passionate songs of his development period (XX, 357), the second in the form of a mysterious strophic song (XX, 334); and in both, the expedient of using recitative has disappeared completely. Between these two settings of Schiller, Schubert turned his attention for the first time to English literature – Pope's 'Vital Spark' (XX, 10; 'Verklärung') in Herder's translation. Here, the interchange between recitative and arioso – accompanied by a kind of harp effect – is entirely suited to the ecstatic character of the text. It is a grandiose piece, which even fifteen years later Schubert could not have conceived differently.

The end of the spiral is reached with the setting of Schiller's 'Der Taucher' (XX, 12a and b). It need not concern us that the composition of this song lasted a little beyond the Convict period, for although the piece was started on 17th September, 1813, it was not completed until 15th April, 1814. A second version, started at the same time, was only completed in August 1814. For *only* a boy could have wanted to set to music this ballad of twenty-seven long verses, in the same way that only a boy could have wanted to set the 'Leichenphantasie'. Although we today find it difficult not to smile at this cruel king, with his thirst for knowledge, who must at all cost learn about the fathomless ocean-bed; at this 'bold and gentle' squire; and at this tenderly passionate princess, we should remember, however, that in 1813 the colourful picture which this ballad painted still exercised a powerful effect. And Schubert could not resist illustrating it in musical terms as well, with harmonic resources (an analysis of the modulations from C major to D minor would be most illuminating) which in their sheer boldness were far in advance of his time. There is nothing like them until we reach the Wagner of *Tristan* and the *Ring*. Albrecht Dürer demanded of a painter that he should be 'inwardly full of form'. Schubert is not only that, but, quite consciously, full of *new* form. This is proved by the second version, which discards some old-fashioned mannerisms and replaces them by a simpler style of expression; it is also significant that he translated several of the musical directions from Italian into German. For the transition to the D minor of the final section, a completely new passage has been interpolated, descriptive of the princess's emotional state:

From now on Schubert is equal to every descriptive demand, and never – or practically never – is it simply illustration for illustration's sake, but descriptive writing the sole function of which is to underline a state of mind.

From the time that the young Schubert began to receive instruction from Salieri, he led a double life as a composer, comparable in some respects to that more painful double life which he was forced to lead a little later, torn between the demands of schoolmastering and his creative urge. Naturally he could not show Salieri such things as his settings of Schiller's ballads, quite apart from the fact that Salieri would not have understood them. Salieri made his pupil persevere with settings of texts from Metastasio's operas and oratorios in different styles; there have survived eleven choral pieces and three arias, one for bass and two for soprano in which Schubert had to write out the voice-part in the old-style clef in strict accordance with the rules.* They are conventional, rhetorical pieces, but at the same time plain and straightforward. Naturally they are not to be compared with his later pieces in Italian, where Schubert parodies the Italian musical idiom a little and in so doing falls in love with it. Far from acting as a deterrent, this preoccupation with the Italian idiom encouraged him to write a genuine 'German operetta', as soon as he was released from the prison-life of school and from Salieri's supervision.

* These were among the papers left by N. Dumba, and were published only recently, in 1937: *Der Junge Schubert*, ed. A. Orel, Wien, Ad. Robitschek.

The choruses for three male voices, which he wrote between 15th April and 15th July, 1813, are far removed from Salieri. Were they written for his friends, these terzets, or do they owe their origin purely and simply to Schubert's enthusiasm for Schiller's lofty and philosophical poetry? For all of them (XIX, 9–14 and XXI, 37–43) are fragments from poems by Schiller – from 'Elysium' and 'Triumph der Liebe' in particular. It is not easy to find an historical explanation for these thirteen songs, one of which was left unfinished. They recall Mozart's 'Gesellige Lieder', with or without their accompaniment of wind instruments; or they remind us of Haydn's canons, and one of Schubert's terzets, based on an Epigram of Schiller's ('Zwei sind die Wege' – in couplets) seems to establish this link. But Haydn's canons and other part-songs of this kind are witty, moralizing, and pedantic; yet the one real canon among Schubert's pieces (Ein jugendlicher Maienschwung') is lyrical and passionate. Indeed, they all give the impression of vignettes by a talented youth, in free, declamatory style, with a range of dynamics that is always expressive and sometimes extreme, varying from *pp* to *fff*. The writing is for the most part homophonic but sometimes animated by counterpoint, and scrupulous attention has been paid to the choice of key. The Epigram is in C major; there is a Pastorale ('Hier strecket der wallende Pilger') in B flat, and the hymn-like piece ('Selig durch die Liebe') is in E major. On its own stands the setting of two verses from Schiller's 'Sprüche des Confucius' ('Dreifach ist der Schritt der Zeit'). It is treated almost entirely in free polyphonic style, full of shifting, even violent, contrasts of light and shade. The words 'eternally the past stands still' are symbolized by a change of time, from 4/4 to 4/2, and the effect is such that one might almost suppose that Schubert was familiar with *a cappella* works of the sixteenth century, and might hesitate to accept that the piece was written in the year 1813. But there is so much that is inexplicable in Schubert, who 'learnt it from God' and in reality had no need to learn anything, that we must of necessity let the question pass.

On the other hand, a short cantata for which Schubert wrote the words – in imitation of Schiller's style – and the music, at the end of September 1813, to mark his father's name-day, is an 'occasional' work in every sense (XIX, 4).

The male-voice trio – the three brothers Ignaz, Ferdinand
and Karl – is this time accompanied on the guitar (probably
by Schubert himself). It is a cheerful affair and a little exaggerated in a humorous way ('... May Father Franz's happiness last forever!') A two-verse 'Trinklied' (XVI, 16) in C
major for bass solo and four-part male voice chorus (29th
August, 1813) seems to have been written for his circle of
friends. The typically Schubertian feature of this song is that
instead of closing on a *ff* for the voices, it ends with a quiet
reflective postlude. There is a considerable number of drink-
ing-songs of this type.

Chapter Three

From Pupil to Schoolmaster

Autumn 1813–Autumn 1814

The period covered by this chapter is not an entirely arbitrary choice. For at the beginning of it stands the D major Symphony, with which Schubert bade farewell to the Convict, while at its close there took place the two performances of his Mass in F major (16th and 26th October) in the Liechtental and Augustine churches respectively; at the end of it, too, we come to the composition of two songs to poems by Goethe, which seem to mark not only the beginning of a new epoch in Schubert's own creative achievement, but in the history of song-writing in general.

At the time of leaving the Convict, Schubert was no longer quite the same excellent pupil that he had been in the early part of this five-year penance; for a penance it was, for all his good-natured patience. Had he stayed on he would have been awarded the so-called Meerfeld scholarship, on one condition, however – namely that 'he should take steps to bring himself up to the standard of the second form during the holidays'. This was obviously a prospect which did not appeal to him. Moreover, there hung over his head the threat of compulsory military service, which he had good reason to fear, and from which the teaching profession was exempt. No doubt, therefore, it was not difficult for his father to talk him into becoming a schoolmaster like himself and his other brothers. So Schubert returned home and started to attend elementary classes at the so-called 'Normal High School' within the city precincts. At the end of the school year he had not made particularly good progress; in theoretical subjects he still varied between 'good' and 'fair'; but among practical subjects, Divinity deteriorated from 'fair' to 'bad'. For all that, his diligence was acknowledged.

During this time, however, his talent for making friends

progressed. The circle of young people among whom he himself was later to become the focal point was a fellowship which was held together not by any articles of association, but by pure enthusiasm and mutual interest. The professions and aspirations of its members differed widely, but they all shared a common idealism, whether they were civil servants, scholars, poets, painters or musicians. In his autobiography, Grillparzer has admirably described a similar circle in which he himself moved, and had he not been too old – he was born in 1791 – he would very likely have belonged to the fellowship of 'Schubertians'. 'We founded an Academy of Science, which held meetings every week, at which lectures were read. But in order that the whole thing should not become too serious, we founded at the same time a comic journal in which we printed all manner of nonsense by our academicians or other members.'

There were also expeditions to the lovely countryside round Vienna, extravagant plans for the future, and at the end of the day a visit to some inn or coffee-house. Unfortunately Schubert's circle – Spaun, Senn, Mayrhofer, Schober and his other older or younger friends and companions – had no such written record of matters serious and frivolous. But the mixture was the same – only with this difference. With them, the emphasis was not on science, but on poetry and music.

It is characteristic of Schubert that no sooner had he left the Convict, and two days after completing the D major Symphony – that is to say on 30th October, 1813 – he started work on an opera. It is as if he had made up his mind from the beginning to register a success and thus to escape from the teaching profession. And only in the field of opera was a success possible. On the title-page of the manuscript, we find him still paying tribute to his teacher: '. . . by Franz Schubert, pupil of Herr Salieri, Principal Court Music Director, in Vienna'. The work was completed in exactly a year, on 22nd October, 1814. Since he was out to achieve success, he took no chances and seized upon the first, though not unfortunately the best, available libretto: *Des Teufels Lustschloss* with its sub-title 'Eine natürliche Zauberoper', by the notorious Baron August v. Kotzebue (XV, 1). 'A natural magic-opera'. In other words we can expect to find the whole paraphernalia of the fantastic pantomime. The parallels with Mozart's *Zauberflöte* are obvious; but at the last moment we are treated to a happy ending which is a masterpiece of sheer banality. The story runs as follows:

The bold and noble knight Oswald (=Tamino), in company with his less bold and less noble squire Robert (=Papageno) experiences the most singular adventures while spending the night in a castle which is by reputation as enchanted as it is unsavoury: and together with his faithful wife Luitgarde (=Pamina) he is subjected to a succession of utterly futile ordeals. In due course, the whole business turns out to be simply a complicated and expensive arrangement on the part of Luitgarde's father, who disapproves of Oswald having abducted his daughter and decides to put him through a test of character. In this mixture of chivalrous drama and pantomime, nothing is spared in the way of scenic effects and stage devices. It does not occur to the youthful composer that every theatre manager would shrink from such lavish expenditure on a beginner's opera, even though he must have had before him an example of modest stage requirements in Weigl's *Schweizerfamilie* or Gyrowetz's *Augenarzt*. And here at his first venture, Schubert submits to a text which, as a song-writer, he would not have touched with a barge-pole. About the time when he finished this opera, he discovered Goethe and wrote 'Gretchen am Spinnrade'. But in his opera, he is thinking purely relatively. He is out for success.

As was his usual practice, he wrote out the score in full, down to the last note. He even revised the work thoroughly as a result of the experiences he had had with his Mass. It is something of an embarrassment for us to see such a wealth of final detail lavished on a work which is in reality nothing more than an operatic exercise. But as an exercise-piece it is so good that it is frankly heart-breaking to see so much purely musical imagination coupled with so naïve a dramatic technique. At the outset the tempestuous Overture – which leads straight into the first scene and contains a 'preghiera' for the wind-section in the middle – gives one the impression of a stepping-stone between the Overture to *Don Giovanni* and one of the early Berlioz overtures. Anyone seeing the second subject might think that it was by the Berlioz of the *Corsair* or the *Franc-Juges* rather than by

Schubert. On the other hand, the models are unmistakable; *Don Giovanni* and, above all, *Die Zauberflöte;* and in a trio in canon and in the duet of the reunited couple, *Fidelio* (to hear which, Schubert sold his school books in May 1814, according to Schwind). But we must repeat again emphatically that Schubert acquired nothing of really intrinsic value from *Fidelio*. Beethoven's canon, or to be more accurate 'round', has a dramatic function; it indicates clearly, at the right moment, that we have here something more serious and more sublime than a purely middle-class ballad-opera plot. Schubert's canon remains nothing more than a canon, in a purely musical sense, and it occurs in the wrong place; admittedly, the dramatic duet comes at the right moment, but it is much too long-drawn-out. Even at the age of sixteen or seventeen, Schubert's inventive powers as an operatic composer are astonishing. One might well write an essay on his orchestral technique – for example the use of the horns in the duet (No. 19), like 'heralds of death'. But for all his youth, he is already a craftsman, only unfortunately a craftsman without practical experience of the stage. He writes at random; he no longer writes like all the great operatic figures from Monteverdi to Mozart for individual singers and for particular vocal peculiarities, and consequently his operatic roles lack a definite outline. In this dangerous freedom, he is already a 'Romantic' as an opera-composer.

In 1822, Joseph Hüttenbrenner, to whom Schubert had given the manuscript of the second version of his opera as security for a debt, was ingenuous enough to offer the work to the Director of the Kärntner-Tor Theatre and the Theater an der Josephstadt in Vienna, to Holbein, Director of the Prague Opera, and to the composer Peter v. Winter in Munich, for performance. Only Holbein showed any semblance of interest and involved Hüttenbrenner in the expense of sending him the score.

Apart from the opera, 1813–14 is a year of vocal music. For the time being, Schubert did not attempt any more overtures or symphonies, and the one instrumental work of any importance is a new string quartet, on which he did not start work until he had finished the Mass. This quartet (V, 8) was not written for domestic use, but in a much more ambitious style. For the family circle, he contented himself with an arrangement – if one can call the simple addition of a 'cello part for his father an arrangement – of a Nocturne for flute, viola and guitar (op. 2) by Wenzel Matiegka, who was one of the then fashionable composers in Vienna (1773–1830) and choirmaster at the church of St. Leopold and St. Joseph.* It is difficult to understand why Schubert copied out this work almost note for note, with the exception of two variations in the last movement (which he took over as they stood), for he could well have composed something of his own in the same time. But there was probably a virtuoso of the guitar staying with the Schuberts at the time for whom he did not consider himself competent to write a part. It is instructive and a little ignominious to think that this piece could have been accepted as an original work for so long. For it falls a long way short of the standard of a 'genuine Schubert' of 26th February, 1814, which was the date when he started to copy it out. In the first movement, which consists of pretty, Mozartian commonplaces, Matiegka admittedly takes a Schubertian liberty and begins the recapitulation in the dominant. But Schubert had long since ceased to write minuets as old-fashioned as this one, and the slow movement in B flat minor – 'Lento e patetico' – is completely un-Schubertian, for all its peculiar song-like quality. Yet it is significant that Schubert concerned himself with this quartet, for it includes, between the slow movement and the Finale, a 'Zingara', and this Finale consists of variations on a melody by Friedrich Fleischmann (1796) – a bud which is to blossom in due course.

On the other hand, the String Quartet in B flat major is 'genuine Schubert'. It was begun on 5th September, 1814, the second movement was written between 6th and 10th September, the Minuet on the following day, and the Finale completed on the 13th. Our view that Schubert could compose as fast as he could copy is confirmed when we read in the manuscript at the end of the first movement: 'Completed in $4\frac{1}{2}$ hours'. This was admittedly made easier for Schubert by the fact that he had already started this movement as a Trio and only needed to re-write it. We can perhaps best describe it as bucolic in a melancholy kind of way, but with a new and sustained inner agitation which is not to be found either

---

* The work was published by Georg Kinsky under Schubert's name in 1926 and 1931; once more we are indebted to O. E. Deutsch for establishing the true authorship.

in Haydn or Mozart. The development introduces an enharmonic change, but no 'dramatic' solution. The following quotation will show how close we have come to the elegiac mood of the 'Romantics':

Ex.6

That could well appear note for note in Mendelssohn twenty or thirty years later.

For the 'Andante sostenuto' the slow movements from Mozart's C major and 'Hoffmeister' Quartets together served as models, even to the extent of one literal reference; but there is an extravagantly cheerful theme, with an accompaniment in sextuplets, which is new and Schubertian. The Minuet – in E flat major instead of B major – is closer to the spirit of Mozart's symphonies; but for the 'presto' Finale – a 'scherzo' so bubbling over with wit and humour – it is almost impossible to find a model, unless one concedes the existence of a second, younger Haydn. All the themes of the Scherzo of the great C major Symphony are already present, but treated and animated in a chamber-music spirit.

THE MASS AND SCHUBERT'S RELIGIOUS FAITH

Between 17th May and 22nd July, 1814, Schubert wrote his first complete Mass, and where he had failed with his opera, he now succeeded. It was performed on 16th October at the Centenary celebration of the Liechtental church and repeated ten days later in the Augustine church, on both occasions under his own direction. And we at once notice a peculiarity in the *Credo* of the Mass, which recurs in all his Masses: the words 'Et unam Sanctam catholicam et apostolicam ecclesiam' are omitted. This means that, from a strict point of view, his Masses are not acceptable for lit-

urgical use, for the Church requires that the sacred text be
sung in its entirety and particularly those words on which its
spiritual and temporal authority rests.

How is this to be explained? Did Schubert wish, after his
own fashion, to make a silent protest against this authority?
We have already mentioned that the sons rebelled against
their father's bigotry. Ignaz, the eldest, seems in particular to
have suffered under it. In a letter dated 12th October, 1818,
he writes of his younger brother's good fortune in having
escaped from the bondage of school-teaching, while he himself must submit to the 'blockheaded Bonzes', by which he
means in particular the senior members of the clergy. 'It will
astonish you to know that things have come to such a pass at
home that no one dares to laugh any more, when I tell a
funny story about my Divinity lessons. You can well appreciate that, in such circumstances, I often feel like losing
my temper and that freedom is only a name to me.' Whereupon Schubert replies on 29th October from Zseliz that
brother Ignaz's hatred for the 'Bonzes' does him credit, and
goes on to paint a drastic picture of the priests where he is
staying – priests compared with whom their Viennese
counterparts are regular models of tact and culture. This
was one letter which his father was certainly never allowed
to see. But in a letter from Steyr dated 25th July, 1825,
Schubert freely expresses his opinion to his father, too. He
pokes gentle fun at his brother Ferdinand's morbid spleen.
'He probably still keeps crawling to the Cross; and he will
certainly have imagined himself to have been ill another
seventy-seven times and to have been on the point of death
nine times, as if death were the worst thing that could
happen to us mortals. If he could only take one look at these
divine mountains and lakes, whose aspect threatens to stifle
or devour us, he would not be so attached to this petty existence as not to think it a piece of great good fortune to be
confided once more to the incomprehensible power of the
earth to create new life.' His father must have opened his
eyes in astonishment when he read this, for it does not sound
much like the catechism. It was open rebellion. And expressions like 'the vanished power of the clergy' or 'Lord
Jesus Christ, to how many infamous deeds must Thou lend
Thine image?' (Letter to Ferdinand written on a journey to
the Salzkammergut, 12th to 21st September, 1825) are not

exactly indicative of respect for the Church. And is it not curious, when his friend or acquaintance Ferdinand Walcher begins a letter to Schubert dated 25th January, 1827, with a musical quotation of 'Credo in unum Deum', and then goes on: 'I know very well that you don't. . . .'? Surely that refers to a previous conversation about religion or the Church.

It would be wrong, however, to interpret this as a deliberate protest on Schubert's part. That might be the answer, if the omission occurred only in his later Masses, but it cannot be true of a youth of sixteen or seventeen. The simplest and most trivial explanation would be that he made a copy of the text of the Mass, in which he inadvertently omitted these seven words, and that he continued to use this copy whenever he sat down to compose a Mass. But it is also possible that there existed in the Vienna of the Emperor Joseph's time a liturgical edition of the text which set no great store by this particular part of the Creed. Qualified authorities on the period and on this problem tell me that the omission was actually not unusual at that particular time, and that the after-effects of this liturgical indifference continued to be felt during the years following, when the power of the clergy was restored under the Emperors Leopold and Francis.

It is not without interest to look at the manner in which Beethoven, who, typically enough, was both pious and critical, set this passage. In the C major Mass, the chorus declaims it briskly in unison and with a kind of cheerful indifference; in the *Missa Solemnis,* however, the seven words are practically inaudible, for they are rattled off at a great pace by the tenor alone in unison with the double-basses in the orchestra, accompanied loudly by the sopranos and altos of the chorus and by the trombones. Clearly Beethoven did not set much store by them either.

Another view is that Schubert either used two editions of the text of the Mass or was particularly 'critical'. For in the 'Quoniam tu solus sanctus', he sometimes sets the words 'Jesu Christe' to music, and sometimes omits them. In the two great Masses in A flat and E flat at any rate they are omitted.

However, Schubert's 'aesthetic' attitude towards the Church seems to me a more important question. In a letter (12th September, 1825) to his brother Ferdinand, he mentions how struck he was with the brightness of the interior of

Salzburg Cathedral – 'light in every corner'. He is no mystic. He loves brightness, colour and clarity. This passage throws much light on the nature of the man.

It is true that Schubert's Mass and his church music in general differ materially in style from Haydn's or Mozart's and quite definitely from Beethoven's. Haydn and Mozart write unsophisticated music, at least in their Masses. They never depart from the traditional church style. The only problem that faces them is a purely artistic one – namely how to treat the text with the most exact regard for detail, and clothe it in the most appropriate fashion, no matter whether they are writing a *Missa Solemnis* consisting of several sections, or a *Missa Brevis*, in which the numerous words of the *Gloria* and *Credo* have to be dealt with in a single movement. We have already mentioned in passing Beethoven's C major Mass, which is a work apart; the *Missa Solemnis*, the struggle of a true believer to comprehend God, had not yet been written in 1814. Schubert is neither so completely traditional and 'artistic' as Haydn and Mozart, nor so subjective or revolutionary as Beethoven. He is secular (in the nineteenth-century meaning of the word) in a different sense; he is more sincere, more personal, more carefree. Consequently the *Kyrie* of this first Mass (XII, 1), in 6/8 time, is neither a fervent prayer nor of a colourless solemnity, but meek and pastoral even to the use of the wind instruments to which the introduction is given and which figure prominently throughout the rest of the work. The second 'Kyrie' is a repetition of the first, only with fuller accompaniment; the soloists – all four in the 'Christe', but only the soprano in the 'Kyrie' – stand out from the chorus while it declaims and modulates in a melodious homophonic style. Was Schubert at that time already in love with the singer of this solo, or was it her singing which aroused his youthful passion? Her name was Therese Grob. She was a year younger than the composer, the daughter of a widow who ran a small silk-mill near the Liechtental church. Her father had immigrated from Switzerland. Schubert loved her with a quiet sincerity which was more than mere calf-love – as in his music, so in love and friendship alike he was neither fanatical nor immature. He dedicated songs and a few small pieces of church music to her, and only finally gave up hope of marrying her three years later, when his 'middle-class' prospects proved to be hopeless. In 1820, she married a master-baker and died childless forty-eight years after Schubert. The fact that he could not forget her and did not find a new object for his affections had unfortunate consequences for him when he once or twice sought 'love' the easier and more dangerous way in Esterhaz or in Vienna.

In the *Gloria* – in C major – side drums, trumpets and the trio of trombones are added to the orchestra as a matter of course. The movement is a succession of dignified, simple and powerful sections, in which the 'Gratias' alone is treated in a more intimate fashion, as a trio for the soloists. The *Agnus* vividly recalls the beginning of Mozart's *Requiem*, and not merely because of the similarity of key (D minor). The 'Quoniam' is somewhat thin and noisy, and was replaced later (at the end of May 1814) by a more refined version. The 'Cum sancto spiritu' is treated as a purely academic fugue, with a *stretta* and other sophistries. After all, Salieri was present in the audience. But at the same time there is no lack here of Schubert's own personal characteristics, such as the lovely enharmonic modulation at the end.

While this *Gloria* consists of separate sections, like the *Missae Solemnes* or *Missae Lungae* of the time, the *Credo* on the other hand is treated as a single entity, as was the practice in a classical *Missa Brevis*. The chorus quietly recites the words of the text and the only emphasis is provided by a solemn and yet dynamic theme on the wind instruments, accented in a stereotyped fashion. A new, flowery theme accompanies the tenor solo of the 'Qui propter nos homines'. At the 'Crucifixus' the re-entry of the chorus is accompanied by an agitated darkening of the harmony. With the 'Resurrexit' the wind instrument theme returns, broken only by the bass solo of the 'Et iterum', and leads to a quiet close, which is most unusual in a Festival Mass. The freedom and sureness of the transitional passages are remarkable.

The *Sanctus*, 'Adagio maestoso', which is prefaced by two introductory bars of mighty orchestral crescendo, is monumental or, to be more precise, a little theatrical. The *Benedictus*, 'andante con moto', for two solo sopranos and tenors, has a double link with Mozart, not only because of the choice of key, B flat major, in which the *Benedictus* of the *Requiem* is also written, but because it also takes the canon or 'round' from the Finale to the second act of *Così fan tutte* as its model. Had Schubert heard one of those Mass arrangements to which the most *buffo* of all Mozart's *buffo* operas had been subjected? At any rate this kind of canon, in which the first voice sings the melody right through before the second voice enters, is one of his favourite forms in his choral music and, above all, in his operas. After this, the 'Hosanna' dwindles away to a comparatively short final chorus.

In the *Agnus Dei*, there are clear indications of the influence of Pergolesi, the impression of whose *Stabat Mater* had been indelibly stamped on the whole of the eighteenth century. And in the 'Dona nobis', Schubert returns to the pastoral 6/8 of the *Kyrie*; it is a cradle-song, with varied repetitions in rondo-style. Schubert was later dissatisfied with this excessively lyrical treatment. At the end of April 1815 he substituted another version, written in a more lively polyphonic and chromatic style, with brisk alternation between soloists and chorus, and with a flourish of trumpets at the end. The Mass was no easy task for him, as is proved by the many changes in detail and in the manuscript as a whole.

We have attempted to describe this first Mass of Schubert's in some detail, because it illustrates one side of his Catholicism – the traditional, Austrian and (if the expression is not misunderstood) theatrical side. There is another side to his Catholicism, which has nothing to do with the Church: the fervent, ecstatic, Marianic side, which is to be found in his settings of Novalis' Poems, or in his setting of Sir Walter Scott's 'Ave Maria'.

There dates from the last days of June 1814 another *Salve Regina* (XIV, 9), in B flat major, for solo tenor and chamber orchestra (strings, 2 oboes, 2 bassoons and horns) which is described in a biography of Schubert as being 'without any distinguishing features' – a phrase which smacks of a description in a passport. On the contrary, it has some extremely distinguishing features, and if Salieri had been dissatisfied with the Mass, he certainly would not have been with this piece. It is written in a decidedly Italian, arioso style, with an almost burlesque accompanying theme; light and flexible in form and confidential in expression – an intimate prayer, which at the end becomes almost operatic in manner. The best explanation of it is that it was written as an exercise for Salieri.

Finally on 24th and 25th July, Schubert wrote a didactic, patriotic cantata for bass solo, four-part male voice chorus and orchestra (without flutes and clarinets) 'Wer ist wohl gross?' (XVI, Appendix 1), a straightforward piece, in spite of the persistent polonaise rhythm, and inspired perhaps by one of Mozart's Masonic Cantatas. Only his enthusiasm for some special occasion can explain why he should have repeated this music for seven verses.

Apart from the Mass, the important feature of this year 1814 is a number of songs in which the seventeen-year-old youth has already advanced far beyond all his contemporaries. At the head there stands – at least in the Collected Edition (XX, 13–15) – a cycle of three Romances, taken from Fr. de la Motte Fouqués novel *Der Zauberring* and entitled *Don Gayseros*. (For other similar examples, one thinks involuntarily of Mozart's songs from Hermes' novel *Sophiens Reise* or of Brahms' *Magellonen-Romanzen*.) The first of the Romances is a dialogue between the suspicious Christian Donna and the Moorish Knight, a dialogue strangely clothed in two melodies which appear in constantly changing keys: F – B flat; E flat – A flat; then by way of D flat to: G flat – B; G – C; F – B flat; E flat – A flat. In other words, a strophic song, entirely dependent upon a kaleidoscopic pattern of harmony. The second is also in the form of a dialogue, in which the Moor confesses his paganism. The atmosphere of a dialogue at night to the sound of strumming guitars is captured with astonishing accuracy; if the song had been anonymous, one would have said that the writer must at some time have visited Spain. But Schubert took his Sevillian style from Zumsteeg's *Der Mohrin Gesang* (Vol. II), in which the key also alternates between E minor and E major and in which the characteristic rhythm rises to the surface. The last Romance brings the tragic and Christian ending, heroic ('kraftvoll') rather than devout. Schubert never wrote anything like this again; the cycle stands like a foreign body among the rest of his songs.

In April he turned once more to Matthisson and never left him again. He wrote thirteen songs; and up to the middle

of October the remainder of his output consisted only of two
settings of poems by Schiller, which are of a kindred spirit.
Friedrich v. Matthisson (1761–1831) had collected his poems
in a 'complete edition' in 1811, but ever since the beginning
of the eighties he had been one of the most frequently set
poets of his time. Some of his poems have been set by more
than a dozen different composers. He was the man of the
hour.

Friedrich Matthisson, who was much esteemed as a poetic landscape painter of the sentimental school, and was praised even by
Schiller, followed resolutely in the footsteps of Klopstock,
Hölty and Ossian. His 'Elegie, in den Ruinen eines alten
Bergschlosses geschrieben' paints a picture of the days of chivalry, so that he may luxuriate in the memory of a past age. His
'Genfersee' celebrates in song the cradle of modern, romantic
nature-consciousness, with an evocation of distant times and
objects in Klopstock's manner. His 'Distichen aus Italien' are
more graphic and vivid, and are comparable with Goethe's
Roman Elegies or Venetian Epigrams.*

This, then, is what attracted the composers of his day and
also the young Schubert: the country scene set in a sentimental light, ecstatic love (which Schubert shunned
throughout his life), the emotional remembrance of the departed, the preoccupation with death and the grave. In April
he wrote five songs: the already hackneyed 'Ich denke dein'
(XX, 16), which he treats with gentle restraint rather than
impassioned fervour, 'Geisternähe' (XX, 17), seven verses
set to a single melody, with deep feeling and a wealth of
musical imagination; 'Todtenopfer' (XX, 18), four verses
in quasi-classical metre, delivered freely, yet with restraint;
and with a wonderful and exquisitely mysterious passage in
which he modulates from E minor to E major. The fourth
'Trost an Eliza' (XX, 19) is a masterpiece in every bar. Schubert no longer follows Matthisson's strophic form. He
reduces it to recitative prose and only when the intensity of
his emotions cannot be denied does he resort for a few bars
to an arioso style. And no one had previously written a song
quite like the fifth and last, 'Die Betende' (XX, 20: 'Laura
betet!'). It is not distinguished by any novelty of form. It is a
simple strophic song, with the same melody repeated four
times. But what a melody and how radiant the harmonic
background (B flat major)! One might almost call it a secular

* W. Scherer, *History of German Literature*, 9th Edition, p. 644

chorale. In October, Schubert varied and heightened this
colour still further in 'An Laura. Als sie Klopstock's Au-
ferstehungslied sang' (XX, 28) to a hymnlike, ecstatic fervour, with an incomparable wealth of harmony. I cannot
resist quoting one of Reichardt's settings of Matthisson, in
order to illustrate the change which had taken place in
twenty years and the difference between a composer who is
the poet's complete servant and who is unwilling to go
beyond the most meagre resources, and one like Schubert
who, with every stimulus that the poet gives to his imagination, yet remains so much his own master, and who is
so replete with music:

Ex.7 *Innig.*

Herr-lich ists im Grün-en! Mehr als O-pern-bühn-en ist mir

A-bends un-ser Wald, wenn das Dorf-ge-läu-te

dump-fig aus der Wei-te durch der Wip-fel Dämm-rung hallt.

followed by five more verses

Schubert never wrote a setting of this actual poem, although
at other times he was not in the slightest disturbed by the
fact that earlier settings already existed.

The Matthisson songs of July 1814 ('Lied aus der Ferne',
'Der Abend', 'Lied der Liebe', XX, 21–3) and one of uncertain date ('Erinnerung', XX, 24) are all free strophic songs,
and are curiously enough all in the same time, 6/8. They are
free because Schubert always has an eye to the possibility of
a change to recitative, and reserves to himself the use of a

surprising modulation as the means of emphasizing spiritual emotion. From the end of September there dates the Romance, 'Ein Fräulein klagt' im finstern Turm' (XX, 27), a macabre ballad, in which Schubert resorts to vivid musical illustration, and yet, in spite of a few episodes in recitative and in a comparatively free, declamatory style, achieves a symmetry of form by adhering to a narrative rhythm. This treatment and this wealth of harmonic resources remind one involuntarily of Pedrillo's Romance in Mozart's *Entführung*. A macabre ballad of a different kind is the 'Geistertanz' ('Die bretterne Kammer der Toten erbebt', XX, 29) of 14th October. It is the midnight hour, but the vivid description is unfortunately weakened by a sentimental twist at the end. Schubert illustrates it by the colour of the key, C minor, weird unison passages in dance rhythm, and little, suggestive touches of tone-painting. Early as it is, the song is the final outcome of two rough sketches written when he was fifteen (XX, 590), the first of which begins in F minor, with a 'symphonic' introduction, in the nature of a 'programme'. In the second, the final choice of key and time are already firmly established. Two years later, in November 1816 Schubert returned once more to the text, and set it as a four-part male-voice chorus (XVI, 32), delivered in a perfectly simple, homophonic style, starting as before in C minor, but ending broadly in A flat major – a triumph of feeling over tone-painting. This triumph is an important factor in Schubert's development.

When we said that Schubert does not mind about the existence of earlier settings – not even famous ones – the best evidence of this is to be found in the last of these Matthisson songs of 1814, 'Adelaide' (XX, 25). It is almost unthinkable that he was not acquainted with Beethoven's best-known contribution in the field of song-writing, which was published in 1796 as op. 46 and 'dedicated to the author'. The poet himself acknowledged that he was firmly convinced that 'no one' (of the many composers who had set his ode to music) 'had more completely eclipsed the words by the melody than that genius of Vienna, Ludwig van Beethoven.' This is true in a profounder sense than Matthisson imagined. For Beethoven simply used the test in order to produce something in the nature of an arioso or a cantata, an 'Andante con allegro'. In its respect for the poet's words and also from a purely musical point of view, Schubert's setting is far superior to Beethoven's. Admittedly, he does not pay any attention to Matthisson's four verses as such, except that in the fourth he repeats the music of the first in an extended form. But in the second:

> '. . . *im Gefilde der Sterne strahlt dein Bildnis,*
> *Adelaide*'*

there occurs an emotional outburst – illustrated musically by a modulation from A flat to G flat – which is echoed in the third verse so spontaneously, so enchantingly, and with such overwhelming effect that it would be futile to search for a model. There brims over here a spring of sheer exuberance which, for want of a more precise expression, we usually label 'romantic'. Between Beethoven's 'Adelaide' and Schubert's lies the dividing line between 'Classicism' and 'Romanticism'.

Schubert took great pains with Schiller's two poems, 'An Emma' (XX, 26; 17th September) and 'Das Mädchen aus der Fremde' (XX, 30; 16th October). Three versions of the first of these exist, in which the 'ternary' treatment – the first verse in F, the second modulating from D to A flat, the third returning uneasily to F again – is plainly established from the outset. But in each version the accompaniment becomes simpler, clearer and more sonorous, until Schubert considered the song fit for publication (op. 58, 2). 'Das Mädchen aus der Fremde' is the brighter counterpart to Matthisson's 'Romance', in the same time and with a similar accompaniment in chords, intimate and simple from beginning to end. Schubert, however, was not content with this kind of simplicity; a year later on 12th August, 1815, he set it once more in the form of an even simpler strophic song (XX, 108), with the direction 'langsam, lieblich' and with a beautifully-contrived accompaniment in three-part writing, and not simply in chords.

On 19th October, 1814, Schubert wrote his first setting of a poem by Goethe, and for the time being Matthisson and Schiller are forgotten. It was not his first masterpiece; that distinction had already been achieved by the 'Laura' songs and by 'Adelaide'. But for the first time he chanced upon a poet who was by nature as true, pure and great as himself.

*'. . . in the starry field thy likeness shines, Adelaide!'

He did not need to put any more into such poetry than it already contained. It was an event not unlike Gluck's chance meeting with Calzabigi; or, to take a purely musical parallel, like Mozart's introduction to certain of Bach's works. It is an example of one of those historical strokes of good fortune of which we have already spoken – a good fortune from which posterity has admittedly profited more than did Schubert himself. From a personal point of view Schubert was less lucky at this time; he had to become an assistant schoolmaster.

Chapter Four

The Assistant Schoolmaster

Autumn 1814–Autumn 1815

In the autumn of 1814, Schubert started work as his father's assistant at the school. We have only the scantiest of information as to how he carried out his duties and how he managed the young children of the Liechtental community – with occasional firmness, it would appear, when they were too naughty. But it was not in his nature to make any violent gesture of rebellion. His father must have noticed this, for he tried to better his own position and thereby that of his sons also; it was with a direct reference to his sons 'who already are all in the service of German education', and to Karl the artist and Franz the composer in particular, that he applied at the end of August, 1815 – unsuccessfully – for a vacant post at the 'German School' of the Schotten-Stift. But he obviously did not notice that Franz's mind was rarely, if ever, on his job and that he would have worked just as mechanically at the Stift as he did under his own supervision.

Love and friendship both made headway. We have already mentioned Therese Grob; and Anton Holzapfel, one of Schubert's fellow-pupils at the Seminary, has told us that Schubert confessed his love for the girl in a long, passionate letter, which prompted Holzapfel to offer him some discreet advice in an attempt to talk him out of his foolish infatuation. In the matter of friendship, Schubert fared better. At the beginning of 1814, he had set to music a half-pessimistic, half-patriotic poem by Johann Mayrhofer which Joseph v. Spaun had doubtless brought to his notice; and shortly afterwards Spaun arranged a personal introduction. Thus began a longlasting and fruitful association. Mayrhofer was ten years older than Schubert and a native of Steyr in Upper Austria. Since 1810 he had studied law in Vienna, and from 1820 onwards he was employed as a Censor, an occupation which, with his passionate longing for freedom, must have been mental torture to him. This is typical of the kind of fate that might befall an Austrian, and it is similar to that of a greater man, Franz Grillparzer, who also suffered throughout his life from the conflict between his poetic ambitions and his official duties. Mayrhofer was 'taciturn, sarcastic and a misogynist'.* He could not have been an easy person to get on with, particularly in the confined atmosphere of domestic life, and so, after ten years, this intimate association broke up. In 1831, after the fall of Warsaw, Mayrhofer attempted to commit suicide; five years later he made a second, and successful, attempt by jumping from an upper window of his office. He was fond of music (he himself played the guitar) and fully appreciated the greatness – one might even say the divinity – of his friend. As a poet, he followed in the footsteps of Schiller or of Schiller's imitators, only with this difference: he combined Schiller's enthusiasm for classical antiquity with all the gloominess of Ossian; Young's *Night Thoughts* was one of his favourite books. He had a profound influence on Schubert and we shall be much concerned with him in later chapters. In the autumn of 1815, another friend, Franz v. Schober, appeared on Schubert's horizon. He was born in Sweden the year before Schubert, but of German parents (his mother was Viennese). He was educated in Schnepfenthal and Kremsmünster and then came to Vienna to study law. He was an extremely colourful character, a little affected or theatrical, and, in contrast with Mayrhofer, anything but a misogynist. His subsequent history is most remarkable. He was for some time private secretary to Franz Liszt, chamberlain at the Court of the petty principality of Weimar, married a blue-stocking at the age of sixty, with the result that might have been expected, and died at the age of eighty-six. Although he lived to see Schubert's posthumous fame firmly established, he never brought himself to put on record his reminiscences of him. His counterpart is Schubert's schoolfriend, Albert Stadler, who came from the same district as Mayrhofer and who had been at the Seminary since 1812. It was he who, up to the year 1817, copied every one of his friend's songs that he could lay his hands on, and consequently rescued for posterity several which would otherwise have been lost. He was himself an

* Deutsch, op. cit., p. 44.

amateur composer of songs, became a government councillor, and died at a great age in 1888.

Although schoolmastering took up most of Schubert's
mornings and thus deprived him of the best time for composing, this first year of uncongenial employment was his
most productive hitherto. It is as if the pressure of circumstances caused the spring to bubble up all the more freely.
And it was in the field of opera that it yielded the fullest
measure, for reasons which are not difficult to understand.
During this year Schubert was gripped by a mania for writing opera, as soon as he realized that there was no success to
be had with *Des Teufels Lustschloss*.

Between 8th and 19th May, 1815, he wrote *Der
vierjährige Posten*. Between 27th June and 9th July he completed his serious one-act ballad-opera *Fernando*. Next we
find him busily engaged on *Claudine von Villa Bella* until
the end of August. And finally the remainder of this notable
year up to New Year's Day (which carries us somewhat
outside the scope of this chapter) was occupied with the
humorous ballad-opera *Die Freunde von Salamanka*. Such
an output exceeds even that of an Italian composer writing
to order. The only difference is that Schubert wrote without
being commissioned to do so, and merely shot his arrows
into the air. And one of these arrows at least would have
reached posterity, had we not been deprived of it by one of
those absurdities which recur throughout the history of art
and mankind alike. Only once in his life did Schubert
embark on one of Goethe's opera libretti, and the result was
Claudine von Villa Bella, which, so far as it goes, is his
operatic masterpiece. But today we possess only the first act.
In 1848, the score of the second and third acts, then in the
possession of Josef Hüttenbrenner, was used by his servants
for lighting the fires.

Of the remaining operas of this year 1815 which have
survived complete, the most successful is *Der vierjährige
Posten*. The libretto is by Theodor Körner (1791–1813) at
whose parents' house in Dresden Goethe and Schiller were
frequent visitors. After moving to Vienna in 1811, he was
appointed court poet at the Burgtheater in January 1813. He
was a third-rate imitator of Schiller; yet in the history of
German literature he enjoys an undeserved place of honour
for his part in the Prussian rebellion against Napoleon, and

as the author of the most celebrated war-poems of his day, which were collected under the title of *Leyer und Schwert*, and which fired the imagination not only of Carl Maria Weber and a hundred other composers, but occasionally of Schubert, too. Goethe, with typical benevolence, described Körner as 'a poet of decided ability, who in his youthful enthusiasm produces excellent, agreeable things with facility and freedom'. The libretto of *Der vierjährige Posten* (XV, 2) is certainly written with facility, if not with freedom; and although it is not particularly excellent, it is none the less very agreeable. Duval, a French soldier, is inadvertently left behind on sentry duty when his regiment leaves a German frontier village. He falls for the lovely daughter of the village judge and settles down to live there. The happiness of the couple is complete. Then, four years later, another war breaks out and the regiment returns. Duval finds himself in danger of being recognized and shot as a deserter. But, like a lesser forerunner of the cunning peasant lad in Smetana's *Bartered Bride*, he hits on an idea. He flings on his old uniform, returns to his sentry-post and explains that before he can be dealt with, he must first be relieved in the regulation manner. The uncompromising attitude of the captain leads to a threatening situation, but all ends in general rejoicing thanks to the over-riding decision of a humane general – apparently such phenomena existed in those days, at least in France. There is only the remotest echo of Kotzebue in this idyll; it is in better taste and more harmless than anything he ever succeeded in producing. The whole libretto is written in verse, and rhymed couplets provide a better link than prose between the musical numbers, although one wonders why these passages in verse were not treated as recitative. Schubert could have set much more than the existing eight numbers to music, particularly the final *dénouement*. Here, admittedly, he would have had to insist on the text being rewritten, even though the author was already dead.

But the opera, as it stands, provides a very attractive musical blend of pastoral and military, and this blend is at its most charming in the Overture. The 'preghiera' of the young wife whose happiness is threatened (No. 5) with its initial accompaniment of wind instruments only, like Elizabeth's 'preghiera' in *Tannhäuser*, is a little commonplace; but the dramatic ensembles (No. 4 and No. 7) are full of animation,

while in the quartet (No. 4) Schubert actually achieves a
canon which has a *dramatic* function and for which the
canon from *Così fan tutte* obviously served once more as a
model.

The serious or, rather, the melodramatic counterpart to
this unpretentious ballad-opera ('Singspiel') is *Fernando* –
similarly entitled a ballad-opera (V, 3). The libretto – seven
numbers linked by a spate of emotional verbiage in prose –
is the work of Schubert's fellow-pupil at the Convict, Albert
Stadler, who, although he was three years older, was if anything less experienced in the dramatic technique of opera
than Schubert himself. What Schubert clearly wanted from
him was a libretto which aimed at the utmost play upon the
emotions, and the most arresting dramatic situation. We
must not forget that he had heard Beethoven's *Fidelio* in
May 1814. So Stadler sets the introduction (Schubert inten-
tionally does not write an Overture) in a wild part of the
Pyrenees and presents before us a distraught boy who has
lost his mother in a thunder-storm. Hard on his heels comes
his father, who is leading a Cain-like existence in the wilderness as a result of having killed his wife's brother in a fit of
temper; he is dressed as a hermit. There follows a moving
recognition-scene between father and son. At this point the
mother arrives on the scene. A peasant has previously
brought news of her death, but it now transpires that a
worthy charcoal-burner saved her from being torn to pieces
by a wolf. The couple are reconciled and there is a final
duet, which is expanded into a simple, straightforward quartet when the peasant and the charcoal-burner (in unison) join
in. This *Fernando* is a 'horror-opera' after the style of Le-
sueur or Dalayrac, a *genre* with which Vienna was well acquainted, and if we had more precise information, we should
probably be able to establish the actual model which the two
young authors took. Schubert keeps strictly to the mechanics
of this *genre*, which one could compare with some present-
day horror-films, were it not for the fact that, at the beginning of the nineteenth century, the tendency would have
been towards undiluted excitement rather than undiluted
emotional sentiment. In the storm-scene he is blatantly theatrical, and at the same time sure in his touch; Fernando's
big entrance-scene (C minor) would do credit to a Parisian
romantic opera of the Hérold school in its utter emotional

emptiness; the mother's aria with its tinge of the heroic at least provides one surprising 'effect', for the middle-section is accompanied simply by the two flutes. Only in the duet of the reunited couple do we find one or two genuinely moving touches, such as the chord of a seventh at the word 'love'. The number which strikes me as being most significant of Schubert, the young operatic 'expert', is the boy's Romance (No. 3) in which a chapter of past history is related, very much after the pattern of the Opéra-comique. It is a song of two verses with a simple string accompaniment, *in D flat major*; but as a song-writer Schubert produced scarcely one other strophic song as monotonous and ordinary as this one. For in his operas, as we have said before, he contents himself with 'categories', with second-rate invention. Compare this Romance with the song from Friedrich de la Motte Fouqué's *Undine,* which Schubert set as a separate piece (XX, 184) on 15th January, 1816. It seems on the surface to be, if anything, still simpler in style, and yet it is much purer, deeper and more personal.

In *Die Freunde von Salamanka* he reverted once again to a cheerful, more pretentious subject. It is a 'comic ballad-opera', this time in two acts. The author of the libretto was his friend Mayrhofer. The connecting text has been lost and we do not even know whether it was written in prose or verse. But Johann N. Fuchs has not found it difficult to re-construct the plot (in the preface to the score in the Collected Edition, V, 4):

Countess Olivia, renowned for her wealth and beauty, is courted by many suitors. Count Tormes, attracted by tales of her beauty, aspires to win her hand, without having yet met her. Don Alonso also loves Olivia. In order to thwart the Count's designs and win her for himself, he agrees upon the following plan with his two life-long friends Fidelio and Diego. The latter is to disguise himself as a robber and fall upon Olivia while she is out walking by herself in the forest. When she calls for help, Alonso and Fidelio will appear and rescue her and thus introduce themselves to her in an advantageous light. Since Olivia, who has a dreamy nature, enjoys walking in the lonely forest, she consequently provides the friends with an excellent opportunity for putting their plan into operation, and the comedy is success-fully staged during one of these walks. Diego attacks Olivia. She calls for help. The two friends hurry to the spot and rescue her. Diego escapes and when she has recovered from the shock, she gazes with grateful emotion at her rescuers. Meanwhile Olivia's servants arrive on the scene with Eusebia and the

Alcalde. Eusebia recognizes in Fidelio her lover, introduces him
and Alonso as well to her mistress, and all repair to the nearby
castle in high spirits.

In due course, Olivia gets to know her alleged rescuer better
and falls in love with him; Alonso confesses that the whole affair
was a trick, begs her forgiveness and at the same time asks for
her hand in marriage. Don Diego has found his ideal in Laura,
the Alcalde's daughter. He woos her and, after having proved to
her father his fitness for a judicial office, he receives her hand in
marriage and also, with Olivia's consent, the post of judge.

When the happy couples have thus been paired off, Count
Tormes arrives in order to present himself to Olivia and to make
a formal offer of marriage to her. Fidelio, however, takes him to
Eusebia, who enters into the joke, and it is to her that the Count
makes his proposal. Through Olivia's intervention he learns that
he is too late and that she is already promised. He retires in a
rage and leaves the field to his lucky rival and his friends.

Johann Mayrhofer, we know, was an educated and well-
read man. But that profited him not at all. The name of the
heroine (and not merely her name) recalls another Olivia –
Shakespeare's; Count Tormes reminds us of Malvolio; the
setting and development of the plot, of Spanish comedies by
Lope de Vega or Calderón, and also of Goethe's *Claudine*.
The *buffo* scenes suggest partly the Italians and partly Kotzebue. Mayrhofer had to complicate matters with an intrigue in order to pair off the three 'friends' – two tenors and
one bass, each to some extent individually characterized (Alonso naturally as an ardent and aristocratic lover, Diego
more as *buffo*, Fidelio as a sturdy wag) – with the three
sopranos. Having contrived this intrigue, Mayrhofer was not
equal to the task of unravelling it. But at least he wrote a
libretto which up to a point avoids both the pure 'comedy of
situation' of the *opera buffa,* and the triteness of the Viennese ballad-opera. It is an attempt at a musical comedy,
and Schubert had no need whatever to be ashamed of having
set it to music.

Once more it is individual details rather than the opera as
a whole, the musical rather than the dramatic aspect, which
delight us. The Overture is a superficial affair, but nonetheless gay and lively; its most attractive feature is the light-
hearted Jodler of the second subject.

Ex.8

And this gaiety flares up in the Introduction where the three friends sit together and announce their recipe for a good life with all the effervescence of youth. It recalls in spirit the Introduction from *Così fan tutte*. Schubert moreover succeeds in all those other numbers which he can, so to speak, take by storm with that musical instinct which is innate in him and which is sustained by the existence of an opportune model. He even succeeds in some of the dramatic ensembles, such as the scene of the attack on Olivia, which is liberally sprinkled with Mozartian figures of speech; or a trio for women, in which two warning voices are prettily contrasted with the third – and predominant – voice; however, in its counterpart which follows – a trio for male voices – the same music occasionally has to sustain diametrically opposite sentiments. The weakest number is another trio in which the Alcalde challenges Diego to an examination in legal matters, while the candidate and his sweetheart add their anxious asides; it deals with this absurd scene (and perhaps rightly so) in the trite manner of a comic opera by Dittersdorf, Weigl or Wenzel Müller.

One is inclined to the view that Schubert is at his most successful when he forgets the dramatic aspect and simply writes 'interpolations'. The description of the vintage with which the second act opens, led by the bass in spirited fashion to the jubilant accompaniment of the chorus, is a sheer enchantment, and might be placed alongside the later 'Ständchen' of 1827 as its counterpart, if indeed this 'Ständchen' were not quite so unique. An extremely rambling duet between Diego and Xilo, the mule-driver, is a pure jewel from the orchestral point of view (a dialogue between bassoons and horns). A pastoral aria for Fidelio (No. 2), 'Man ist so glücklich und so frei', is inconsistent with his dashing character, but with its delightful touches of colour in the accompaniment it could well take its place with Schubert's best songs. There is a charming serenade for Diego (No. 15). Laura and Diego sing a duet which is entirely superfluous to the dramatic action (No. 12, 'Gelagert unterm hellen Dach'); but it begins with one of Schubert's most personal idioms, which reappears note for note in a later masterpiece, the 'Andante con variazioni' of the Octet of 1824.*

* I hope that the subsequent use of this 'interpolation' does not

But, quite apart from many such Schubertian characteristics of harmony and rhythm – or, to put it more clearly, characteristics of aesthetic expression, there are still occasions when Schubert shows that he is also a dramatist; that is to say, he sees deep down into the hearts of the characters. The duped tenor, the stupid, arrogant Hidalgo, Count Tormes, is brilliantly portrayed in a mawkishly affected aria (No. 10); in her first aria (No. 5) Olivia's character is not yet sharply drawn, but in her second (No. 13), in which she becomes aware of her irresistible love for her rescuer, she becomes a girl who is passionately in love, a human being.

If 1815 is indeed the correct year for the operatic fragment which has survived under the title of *Adrast* (XV, 14), then it is a fair assumption that Mayrhofer set out to provide his friend with an immediate tragic counterpart to *Die Freunde von Salamanka*. This seems quite logical, for *Adrast* has every appearance of being a forerunner of *Die Bürgschaft* of the following year, to which we shall come in due course. This is the 'classical' Mayrhofer, who here uses the operatic form as a medium for the same expression which he achieves in his poetry. It is not the Theban Adrastes whom he has chosen for his hero, but an extremely gloomy youth of the same name, who while visiting Sardis at the invitation of King Croesus, induces the latter's only son, Atys, to take part in a boar-hunt and thereby causes his death. It is obvious that the numbers which Schubert composed or which have survived do not appear in their proper dramatic sequence in the Collected Edition. Only the scenes for male chorus and the arias and the duet for Adrastes (Tenor) and Croesus (Baritone) seem to have been written.* There is no indication where the women's parts or voices fit in.

This time the model is Gluck. We know that Schubert had been conversant with Gluck's music since 1813. A performance of *Iphigenie auf Tauris* with Anna Milder and J. M. Vogl in the leading roles had made a deep impression on him. The Introduction, Shepherds' Chorus and Adrastes'

---

conflict with my view that there is no fundamental connection between Schubert's dramatic works and the rest of his music.

  *An introduction with an additional duet was recently discovered in the Vienna National Library.

solo are modelled on the 'Tombeau' in *Orfeo ed Euridice*, with incomparably richer musical resources and incomparably weaker dramatic effect, although Schubert could only have acquainted himself with Gluck's masterpiece from the score of the piano-edition, for it had not been performed in Vienna since 1781. But Gluck was a free model for Schubert. There is a prayer-chorus of Mysians in which they entreat Croesus to send Atys forth to kill the boar which is ravaging their land, and this seems to have been written with Gluck's Scythian choruses in mind. But it is fashioned in the form of a striking choral recitation, for which there is really no model. A scene for Croesus – recitative and aria – the aria accompanied by the strings alone with divided 'cellos, is a piece of the most exquisite and noble contrivance. If anyone wished to show how the 'classical' spirit was reflected in Schubert's imagination, he should not forget to put *Adrast* beside the 'classical' settings of odes by Schiller, Goethe, Mayrhofer and Jacobi.

Beside this noble experiment, there stands the less noble fragment *Der Spiegelritter* (XV, 12), another opera by our old friend Baron August v. Kotzebue, which Schubert unfortunately carried to a further stage of completion than he did *Adrast*. The libretto had already been set to music in 1791 in Frankfurt-am-Main by Ignaz Walter, and no one has summed it up better than Kotzebue himself in a 'preface':

People have often asked me to write an opera in the modern manner, and now at last I have done so. I trust that the reader will find it just as droll, romantic and silly as its older brothers and sisters on the German stage. Of all an author's works, this kind of opera is the easiest to write. May heaven grant me the same good fortune which it has granted to Herrn (Ferdinand) Eberl and Consorten. In other words, may it present my Looking-Glass Knight with music like Dittersdorf's, Mozart's Martin's or Reichardt's. Then the fellow will make his way in the world successfully.

Kotzebue could never have suspected that Heaven would grant him quite such good fortune, that a Schubert would one day stumble upon him. Yet it is some small consolation to us that Schubert on this occasion falls below his own operatic level. In the style of the *Zauberflöte* imitators he remains the complete expert; and in the ensembles he sometimes descends into the depths of vulgar comedy and perpetrates absurdities which as a song-writer he would not have taken seriously for one moment. The remarkable thing about this *Spiegelritter* is that it should have come from the same pen which shortly before had set Goethe's *Claudine von Villa Bella* (XV, 11) to music.

It has often been said that Goethe himself falls below his usual level in his ballad-opera libretti. But this is not true. He had very definite ambitions in this direction, and if his 'operettas', *Erwin und Elmire, Scherz, List und Rache,* and *Claudine von Villa Bella* do not scale the heights of 'eternity', the reason is that it was not his intention to write a *Faust* or a *Natürliche Tochter*, but to pursue one immediate object with them. That object was to raise the tone of the German ballad-opera and to breathe new life into it on the model of the *opera buffa*. If he had completed his last attempt, the *Zauberflöte* sequel (and had incidentally found the right composer for it), this 'work of lofty symbolism' would have provided just such a projection into the realm of artistic eternity. He lacked the appropriate composer and the suitable audience, and his friendship with Zelter did not blind him to that fact for one moment. He repeats this view in his *Annals*, in 1816, when he was thinking of basing an opera on Oriental material. 'It would in fact have been written ... had I only had a composer beside me and a great audience before me, so as to compel me to adapt myself to the capabilities of the one and the taste and demands of the other.'

Now, the young composer in Vienna who about this time was busily engaged on his *Claudine von Villa Bella* would not yet have been capable of doing justice to an Oriental opera of this kind, and the Viennese would not have been capable of providing Goethe's audience. (Yet is it not a curious fact that Schubert's last thoughts were of 'an opera based on Oriental material'?) But young Schubert was the ideal composer for *Claudine von Villa Bella*, and his work – at least in the one act which has survived – was the accomplishment of something which previous composers of the libretto, Ignaz van Beecke (Vienna, 1780), J. Fr. Reichtardt (Charlottenburg and Berlin, 1789) and J. Chr. Kienlen (Munich, 1810, Stuttgart, 1811), probably wanted in vain to achieve or, more probably, never even foresaw. The only unfortunate thing is that *Claudine* was no longer *à la mode*. Historically speaking, the hour of this type of opera had long since struck.

It was the second version of the opera, in verse-form, which Schubert set to music. The first version, written in 1775, links the songs, ariettas, ensembles and choruses by means of dialogue in prose, and clearly defines the characters of the three leading figures: Claudine 'a girl who is worshipped to the point of idolatory by all who know her, and whose childlike nature makes her doubly charming', and her two lovers in whom Goethe had personified his own double nature: the devoted youth and the headstrong (though at heart, noble) adventurer – rivals who in the end turn out to be blood brothers. The plot thickens when the adventurer, as leader of a band of vagabonds, abducts Claudine. In the second version, written in 1787 in Rome, under the direct influence of the Italian *opera buffa*, Goethe sees to it that Rugantino, the unruly brother, does not go away empty-handed either and wins as his bride a charming, capricious girl, more suited to his own temperament. Quite apart from the greater uniformity which the treatment in metrical verse-form achieves, every scene – Rugantino's quarrel with one of his more unscrupulous companions, the attack on the castle, and the rescue-scene – is much more alive. Goethe was justifiably proud of his work. 'Everything is calculated to meet the requirements of the lyrical stage, which for the first time I have here had an opportunity to study: to keep all the characters occupied in a certain order and for a certain length of time, so that every singer has enough rests ... there are a hundred things to be done and to which an Italian sacrifices the whole sense of the words; I can only hope that I may have been successful in satisfying those musical and dramatic requirements with a piece which is not too nonsensical.' (Rome, 10th January, 1788.) What a difference between Goethe and Kotzebue!

As we have seen above, the stupidest of accidents deprived us of the chance of discovering how Schubert dealt with the animated scenes of the second and third acts. Nothing of them has survived beyond the bare voice-part of the serenade 'Liebliches Kind', and one voice-part of the duet 'Mich umfängt ein banger Schauer', which Schubert jotted down for the singers at some time or other. The first act,

which has survived, remains idyllic in character until the
Finale, the robbers' quarrel. But in its idyllic vein, Schubert's
music is a sheer delight from beginning to end. The introductory Adagio of the Overture, in E major, is almost too
pretentious and serious, with its mysterious dynamic and
harmonic contrasts. Then, however, there follows a light-
footed Vivace which already imitates the Italian manner,
despite the fact that Rossini's successes in Vienna did not
begin until later. The development is *episodic* and even includes a short *stretta*, with the second subject in A and G,
instead of the orthodox B and E! On the other hand, the
vocal numbers are all completely German or, rather, Mozartian – perhaps too Mozartian, since in 1815 it was no
longer possible to write the kind of music that had been
written in 1788 or 1790. The Finale, in particular, with the
dispute between the two 'leaders', the knight and the bandit,
accompanied by interjections from the chorus, is lively
enough, but too 'four-square', too rigid in design, and too
stylized. On the other hand the description of Claudine's
birthday reception is charming, with its delicate shades of
contrast in the congratulatory remarks of father, cousin,
lover and chorus; the ensemble which follows this Introduction and in which the presentation of gifts is made is also
charming and was clearly influenced by the 'Giovani liete'
from Mozart's *Figaro*. If Pedro the lover's aria, with its
blend of the heroic and the idyllic, is weak, and Claudine's
first aria ('Alle Freuden, alle Gaben') rather conventional,
the effect is to heighten the beauty of her second aria, which
has become widely popular as a song with piano accompaniment. It cannot be fully appreciated in this reduced version,
which is usually transposed and which loses much by its
commonplace accompaniment; for Schubert represents the
ever-present Cupid by a tremolo on the strings – 'Liebe
schwärmt auf allen Wegen'. Lucinde's arietta 'Hin und
wieder fliegen Pfeile' shows us something which scarcely, if
ever, appears in Schubert's songs: a character like that of the
wanton Philine in *Wilhelm Meister*. The piece is a miraculous blend of 'classical', Italian and Spanish styles. The
robber's song 'Mit Mädeln sich vertragen' might offer a
point of comparison with Beethoven, who set the words for
bass-solo and orchestra during his Bonn period, had not
Schubert simply written a brisk solo with accompanying

chorus, while Beethoven instinctively produced a long solo in the form of a duel-scene.

A ballad-opera (?), *Der* (*Die?*) *Minnesänger*, written about this time and mentioned by Leopold v. Sonnleithner in his obituary notice of February, 1829, has been lost without trace, and we do not know who wrote the libretto nor whether it was merely a fragment or a completed work.

Chapter Five

The Piano and the Piano Sonata

If we ask ourselves which contemporary musical form Schubert left completely uncultivated, the surprising answer is: the concerto. There does exist a youthful essay in concerto form, written in 1816 – a piece for violin and orchestra or, to be more precise, an Adagio and Rondo in D, the Rondo constructed roughly on the model of the Rondo from Mozart's 'Haffner' Serenade, with two 'alternativi' in G and D minor. But one glance at the oddly reduced orchestra – strings, oboes, trumpets and side-drums – is enough for us to recognize it as a work which was probably written to order for some special occasion – in fact, as we now know, at the request of his brother Ferdinand; and the modest treatment of the solo violin part, without a cadenza – indeed, almost without any opportunity for a cadenza – proves that in this instance the problem of virtuosity was far from Schubert's mind.

But not only in this instance. It is one of the distinctive characteristics that he almost entirely avoided the display of virtuosity which is inseparably associated with the whole concept of the concerto. He was a piano-composer, yet he wrote no piano concerto, either in his youth or in his maturity. One might suppose that he could have carried on Mozart's idea of the concerto in which the piano was still treated as *primus inter pares*, an equal partner with the orchestra in an 'undramatic' sense, with perhaps the sole exception of the concertos in D minor and C minor. But that was no longer possible after Dussek, Hummel and Wölf (all three of them composers of concertos) and particularly after Beethoven, whose five piano concertos had all been published by 1809. Since Beethoven there existed only the dramatic relationship between solo instrument and orchestra and no longer the harmonious dialogue between the two; and to fit the piano for its dominating role, the solo part had been equippped with a virtuoso technique of which the pre-1800 generation had never even dreamed.

It does not follow that Schubert would have despised and rejected the fundamental principle of the concerto as such – namely pianistic brilliance as an end in itself. But he confined it to what we might call his 'sociable' pieces, to chamber music in a lighter or less serious vein, like the great Duos for violin and piano, the two Piano Trios, and the 'Trout' Quintet. When he really makes a concession to virtuosity, to *fioritura*, as for example in the Adagio in E written in April 1818 (XI, 11), he is scarcely recognizable any longer; it is more like one of the violinist Rode's sugary recital pieces or like an imitation of the slow introduction to a *coloratura* aria by a composer of the Rossini school. In his Variations for two or four hands, he naturally has to provide greater technical difficulties; the one major work for solo piano which can make some claim in the direction of virtuosity is the 'Wanderer' Fantasia. This is a fine work but not, to our mind, one of his most successful piano compositions and it has had the not unjustifiable fate to be recast in a symphonic arrangement by Liszt, with the virtuosity of the piano part heightened still further. Is it not significant that the composer himself was unable to play it adequately?

The piano is a very different instrument for Schubert than it is for Beethoven, or even Weber. For Schubert it is the vehicle of the most personal, intimate expression, and not merely in the smaller forms such as the Moment Musical, the Impromptu or the Scherzo, but also in the more ambitious forms of the Sonata and sometimes even the Variation. His personal opinion of his own piano-playing is contained in a letter dated 25th (28th?) July, 1825, in which he tells his parents that he had performed the Variations from his Sonata, op. 42 'not unsuccessfully, inasmuch as several people assured me that my fingers had transformed the keys into singing voices. If this is really true, then I am highly delighted, since I cannot abide the damnable thumping which is peculiar to even the most distinguished pianists and which pleases neither the ear nor the mind.'

Schubert was remarkably little influenced by Beethoven, not even by the latter's more intimate sonatas or sonata movements. He was a 'modern' composer, more 'modern'

than Beethoven, because he was younger. But at the same
time he was still fully conversant with the more conventional
eighteenth-century conception of the sonata, a conception
which had not yet been, so to speak, put out of joint by
Beethoven's violence. A clear indication that Schubert was
familiar with the intimate, eighteenth-century function of
the piano is shown in his setting of Schiller's 'Laura am
Clavier' (XX, 193), particularly the second version. He does
not translate the verbal exuberance of the poet's

> *Seelenvolle Harmonien wimmeln,*
> *Ein woolüstig Ungetüm,*
> *Aus den Saiten, wie aus ihren Himmeln*
> *Neugeborne Seraphim;*
> *Wie, des Chaos Riesenarm entronnen,*
> *Aufgejagt vom Schöpfungssturm, die Sonnen*
> *Funkelnd führen aus der Nacht,*
> *Strömt der Töne Zubermacht ...**

into a musical exuberance. Laura's piano is still the instrument of Mozart's day – a spinet rather than the more powerful instrument which Beethoven used or envisaged – and 'the
language of Elysium' is that of one of Mozart's A major
sonatas.† One of the most decisive influences on Schubert's
piano style can be traced back not to Beethoven, but to the
Haydn of the D major Sonata (No. 51 in the Collected Edition) which is generally held to have been written in England. The first movement of this sonata of Haydn's,
sauntering easily along with its melodic curves moving in
octaves over an animated counter-melody in triplets

Ex.9   *Allegro comodo.* *)

♦) In the original erroneously: Andante

* Rapturous harmonies swarm, in ecstatic profusion, from the strings,
like new-born Seraphim from their heavenly regions; as suns, loosed
from the giant arm of Chaos and aroused by the storm of creation,
emerge, blazing, from the night, so streams forth the melody's magic
power.
   † There is admittedly a fuller, more modern, more Schubertian flavour

will convince the listener that something, specifically Schubertian, is foreshadowed here, that there is a definite hint of
something which was later to become an entirely individual
and personal characteristic of Schubert's.* And it is a very
remarkable fact that the direct influence of this movement
does not emerge fully until Schubert's later piano works,
although by then it is strengthened and intensified by the
influence of the Rondo from Beethoven's op. 31, 1. Of all
Beethoven's sonata movements, it is this one which certainly
made the deepest impression on Schubert, for it is a pre-
Schubertian movement in the truest sense of the word, with
its cheerful lack of pathos, its complete avoidance of the
unexpected and its easy, sauntering gait.

Nevertheless, Schubert's general freedom from outside
influence is the more astonishing when one realizes that, at
the time he was writing his first two piano sonatas, the whole
of Beethoven's piano music up to Opus 90 – that is to say,
with the exception of the last five sonatas and the Thirty-
Three Variations – had already been published. He could
easily have become a second and better Ferdinand Ries, who
wrote a large number of piano works in the Beethoven
manner. It is all the more unjust and irrational to compare
Schubert with Beethoven as a sonata-composer, and then to
criticize him for his 'lack of conciseness', his 'aimlessness',
his 'deficient grasp of musical form' and so forth. It is much
the same thing as blaming Hölderlin for not being a
Goethe, or criticizing Shelley for not being a Shakespeare.
On the contrary, one cannot but admire the degree to which
Schubert managed to maintain his independence not only
from the overpowering model of Beethoven, but, in spite of
the large number of influences at work, from all models in
general. Mozart was no longer a force to be reckoned with,
for his sonatas had become, from a purely technical and musical point of view, too 'innocent' and too outmoded. But the
effect of this was to enhance the importance of Mozart's
pupil, Johann Nepomuk Hummel, who had been a disciple
of Salieri's as well, and who lived in or near Vienna until

to the A major in which he set Schubart's poem 'An mein Clavier'
shortly afterwards.
*The external evidence that Schubert could have been familiar with
this sonata is provided by the fact that it had been published by Breitkopf
and Härtel in 1804, and then reprinted in the collected edition (Vol. XI,
No. X) in December of the following year.

1816, although between 1794 and 1814 he no longer played in public. The high regard in which Schubert held him is shown by the fact that he wanted to dedicate his last three sonatas to him (they were in fact dedicated to Schumann by the publisher). A certain amount of Hummel's brilliance finds an echo in Schubert too, but not so much in the sonatas as in the 'sociable' pieces already mentioned above. In a certain sense Schubert was quite unable to compete with Hummel. For Hummel had been a pupil not only of Salieri's, like Schubert himself, but also of the stricter Albrechtsberger, and consequently there occur in his piano music things for which the listener would search in vain in Schubert's. Take the previous example from the last movement of a piano sonata, op. 13, which was dedicated to Haydn and written shortly after 1800.

Ex.10

Schubert disliked such discursive or sketchy developments, which have a joint origin in Mozart *and* Albrechtsberger; they were too lacking in colour for his taste. He could never forgo the richness, the sensuousness of harmony. And we do not know whether he was completely satisfied with the potentialities of the Viennese grand piano as illustrated by Hummel in his Piano School and Piano Exercises. Yet is this absence of 'severe' characteristics in Schubert's music something to be deplored? He often replaces it by contrapuntal inventions which we might call 'spontaneous' polyphony, and which are all the more enchanting by virtue of their spontaneity.

In its first movement Hummel's sonata contains one feature which provides us with a starting-point for the understanding of a further peculiarity not only of Schubert's sonatas, but of his entire instrumental music. The first subject of this movement – rather solemn, with a contrapuntal accompaniment – bears the inscription 'Alleluia'. It is a Gregorian plainchant and it is therefore clear that this movement, for all its spasms of 'galanterie', is conceived in praise of God. Of Schubert, on the other hand, one could say that all his music is conceived in praise of God without his having to draw attention to the fact. Sometimes we find a direction like 'Allegro patetico' (full of sheer musical enchantment, rather than pathos), but no 'Sonata pathétique', no 'Les Adieux', never a thought or indication of a programme. His ultimate object is *music*. When we find a piano-duet, which he wrote in his last year, labelled 'Storms of Life' by the publisher (not by Schubert himself), the effect is much the same as that of a bad illustration to a good poem, which detracts from its subject and which obscures rather than clarifies it. Moreover, Schubert not only avoids any suggestion of a programme, but at the same time he is never witty like Carl Maria Weber, for example, who is really his antagonist. Weber's piano sonatas, all four of which were written and published between 1812 and 1822 (which is admittedly no proof that Schubert was familiar with them), are always designed with an eye to virtuoso display. At the same time they are always based on a hidden programme – in spite of the fact that Weber hastened to suppress any such indication of a programme as the title 'L'infatigable' which originally prefaced the finale of the first sonata. All this is quite alien to Schubert: the melodramatic pathos of the first movements, the three whimsical minuets (none of which are really minuets in the true sense), the sensitive affectation of the slow movements, the applause-seeking brilliance of the finales. Take the first movement of Weber's E minor Sonata with its almost too ostentatiously weary first subject ('con duolo'), its agitated extension ('con agitazione') and climax

('pesante'), the exuberant, Lisztian second subject ('dolce'),
the transition to the terse, dramatic development, the major
section in the recapitulation, the resigned descent of the conclusion ('mormorando con duolo') – how elegant, how rhetorical, how theatrical it all is! It is not for us to decide
whether this is good or bad music. But it is at any rate music
which is drawn from a different, more arbitrary source of
feeling, which moves in a different sphere of expression from
the music of Schubert's piano sonatas. Schubert's music is
spontaneous. This does not mean that Schubert does not
sometimes have a common point of contact with Weber. In
the Finale of the E flat major Sonata, op. 122, at the beginning of the development there is a dialogue between
treble and bass, between, as it were, violin and violoncello,
which corresponds exactly to the dialogue of the song-like
subject in Weber's Rondo Brillante, op. 62. And in this instance, it is Weber who would have been the 'imitator' since
his Rondo only appeared in the summer of 1819, two years
after Schubert's sonata. And is it not Weber's own brand of
gaiety when, in the Finale of his artless Sonata in G minor
for violin and piano, Schubert writes:

However much contemporaries may be opposed to each
other, there are still occasions when they meet on common
ground. Weber's resources are admittedly much richer, since
he was a virtuoso. Schubert never exceeds his own, except in
a few instances such as the 'Wanderer' Fantasia. His character is such that he seems as a rule to be writing only for
himself and not for the world in general.

Moreover, Schubert does not experiment with the form of
the sonata. With him, there is no 'Sonata quasi una fantasia'
like the two which Beethoven combined in his op. 27 and
with which he began to sacrifice even traditional form to the
growing momentum of his musical inspiration. Schubert
adheres to conventional form, at least in his piano sonatas, in

his chamber-music and in his symphonies. He writes piano sonatas of four, or when he omits the Minuet, of three movements, and his three last sonatas, written in 1828, are, if possible, even more purely musical, even less influenced by mental reservations than his earliest examples which he wrote in 1815. And in 1828 the young Schumann's thoughts were already turning towards his own piano-music – music full of poetical 'programme', imbued with the spirit of Jean Paul and E. T. A. Hoffman. Nothing shows more clearly the extent to which Schubert is a romantic *Classicist*, and how little his 'Romanticism' is capable of being defined as an intermingling of music with poetry to the detriment – or enrichment – of the music. His 'Romanticism' is something far deeper. It is concerned with the mystery of melody, of harmony, of sound; it is the musical echo of the miracle of creation, as incapable of definition as the opening of a flower or the birth of a butterfly from its chrysalis.

Schubert's first two piano sonatas, written in 1815, the first (18th to 21st February) in E major (X, 1), the second (September) in Cmajor (X, 2), are in three movements. They are fragments, or, to be more precise, unfinished; the first ends with a Minuet in B major, the other also with a Minuet in A minor; and it is unthinkable that Schubert, the young traditionalist, would have ended with movements which are not in the tonic key. One must not be misled by the Collected Edition which has included them among the completed works, while at the same time relegating certain completed sonatas to the company of unfinished fragments. There exists an unfinished sketch for the first movement of the E major Sonata (11th February, XXI, 8) in which the *second* group of themes, but not the first, already appears in its final form. Schubert altered the first group because he felt that he must give it a less Mozartian, a more 'modern', more heroic treatment. The result is not completely successful; for this first group has a purely preparatory function. It is the gateway, as it were, to the lyricism of the second. Schubert is of a fundamental lyrical disposition. His instrumental music is conceived in the same spirit as that which animated the songs of his Anacreon, whose lyre was attuned to love and love alone, 'instead of the dark thunder of epic lays'. There is nothing 'discursive' in this movement and consequently it does not require a coda which is only called for when it follows on a detailed analysis of the themes. In this early sonata movement, Schubert is not yet capable of filling in the outline which he himself has drawn; but there is already abundant evidence of the full presence of his inventive powers. It is for this reason that his unfinished fragments give one as much pleasure as his completed movements.

The second and third movements present a very different picture. The second, an Andante in the minor of the main key, has all the immaculate finish of one of the great songs of this year of songs, 1815, and it contains one very singular stroke – namely, the return of the first subject in *simplified* form, over a halting bass figure which has already been anticipated in the theme itself. This is followed by a parenthetical section with a fresh subject in a new, more animated rhythm. And for the first time we discover the 'pattern' (it is not strictly a pattern at all) which is to remain a constant feature of many of Schubert's slow movements until we come to his last piano sonata: the agitated mood of the middle section persists into the repetition of the main section. At the same time, this pattern prevents him from writing broad Adagios; he contents himself with an Andante or an Adantino. A grandiose example of this peculiarity is also to be found in his songs – in the duet version of Goethe's 'Nur wer die Sehnucht kennt', written in January 1826 (op. 62, 1; XX, 488). Here, too, the repetition of the first stanza is not simply a repetition but a return on a higher level, transformed by a spiritual experience. And if the slow movement of our sonata is a prototype, so also is the Minuet. The main section states its turbulent, ringing proposition; the Trio ('sempre staccato' and *pp*) is a melodious murmur of chords, full of unexpected modulations. It is a singular fact that the main sections of Schubert's Minuets are for the most part full of that very 'method discursive' which his first movements lack, his Trios, on the other hand, usually have a spiritual affinity with the German Dances or Ländler of which he had written a considerable number since his earliest period.

The fragment of a Sonata in C major, written rather more than six months later, is in the nature of a backward step, if only because in the first movement Schubert involuntarily succumbed to the concept of the 'Grand Sonata'. The distinction between *tutti* and *solo* is clearly marked. The dimensions of the building have grown larger, without any simultaneous strengthening of the structure. The recapitulation appears in the subdominant – a practice which is admissible in 'Italian overtures' and similar works, but which is an unpardonable piece of laziness in a sonata. The slow movement derives from Haydn or the sentimental Beethoven of the Adagio from op. 2, 1; in the Minuet there occurs a literal reference to the virile Minuet in Mozart's G minor Symphony. Only the Trio of the Minuet (A major) is completely Schubertian and completely enchanting. There is no discernible model for this 'homely' flavour or for the unaffectedness of this rhythmic irregularity.

The negative proof that Schubert deliberately avoided any suggestion of 'virtuosity' in his piano sonatas is provided by his first set of Variations which, like the first sonata, were written in February 1815, and dedicated to Salieri (XI, 6). It is not without an element of comedy that these Variations, dedicated as they are to Mozart's adversary, should be fundamentally Mozartian in character, and when in Variation X the theme appears 'Allegro' and in triple time, the opening bars are indistinguishable from 'Se vuol ballare', even to the identical key of F major. It must have come as an unpleasant shock to Salieri. Schubert treats the Variation as a quite distinct musical form; in his sonatas he uses it only once, in op. 42, and then in an intimate, restrained manner and treated with great freedom. The same freedom is apparent here, to the extent that he even disregards the number of bars in the theme. But he still follows Mozart's pattern: a Variation in the minor, an Adagio profusely decorated with *fioritura*, and finally the Allegro with coda mentioned above. For the rest, he varies the tempo and indulges in some modest display which makes us smile a little, if only because it is so unostentatious. There was no touch of vanity about Schubert either as a man or as a composer; consequently he only resorts to exhibitionism of this kind against his own inclination.

Similar in character is an Adagio in G major (XXI, 22) written on 8th April, 1815. Its models are to be sought not so much in the literature of the piano as in the Romances and Airs for violin by Kreutzer and Rode, and the similarity of key also reminds us involuntarily of Beethoven's two Romances, op. 50. Schubert's Adagio is a lyrical recital piece with affected touches of virtuosity. But no sooner had he finished it than he wrote a second version which contains no trace of this virtuoso treatment, and in which the middle section (the first is repeated note for note) assumes the character of a kind of development, full of suspensions and full of harmonic surprises. He returns here to the simplicity of earlier piano pieces such as the little Andante in C major (XI, 9) of 9th September, 1812, which would not be out of place in a sonatina (just as the second version of the G major Adagio could well be the slow movement of a sonata). There are several more pieces of this kind – youthful exercises in sensuous piano-tone – which he left unfinished (XXI, 16, 17, 19). It is as if he wanted to unleash the physical powers of an instrument which in the eighteenth century was still so imperfect and inarticulate. In one of these pieces (XXI, 17) he quite literally never reaches the end. It is as if he is sitting alone at the piano with no one listening to him. Since we are constantly being told that many of his sonata movements are 'much too long', we may well ask: 'And why too long?' They are written for the pianist who need give no thought to anyone else; who, as he improvises, forgets himself and the world.

In his chamber music and symphonies of this year, 1815, Schubert is far less subjective. Take, for example, a string quartet in G minor (V, 9) composed between 25th March and 1st April, and written, one might add, under the influence of Beethoven's op. 18, 2, and of another famous work in G minor, Mozart's symphony. The theme of the first movement harks back to Beethoven's Finale, and the echoes of Mozart, particularly in the Minuet and again in the first movement, are unmistakable. The only difference is that Schubert takes a liberty in this movement which Mozart and Beethoven would never have permitted themselves: the development contains an extended *cantabile* subject over a mounting *tremolo* on the three accompanying instruments, while the recapitulation starts in the relative major. At this stage Schubert still makes concessions, and is not a fatalist like Mozart. The Finale employs another of those short-legged themes in the manner of Haydn, but, unlike Haydn, it remains throughout in the minor. The most characteristic movement is a very charming Andantino in Schubert's favourite rhythm, the sustained anapaest or dactyl, and with a genuinely romantic touch, when 'cello and first violin carry on a private conversation over a soft accompaniment in triplets by the two inner parts.

Schubert started work on the quartet after having completed a far more ambitious work – his Second Symphony in B flat (I, 2). The first movement had been written between 10th and 26th December, 1814, and it is uncertain whether it was intended originally as an overture and was only later expanded into a symphony. Whether that was so or not, this first movement also has a symphonic model. The introductory Largo, alternating between rhythmic phrases on the wind and supple string figures, is unmistakably a free imitation of the Introduction to Mozart's E flat major Symphony, while the Allegro contains a variety of allusions to Beethoven's *Prometheus* Overture, Second Symphony and Triple Concerto, also in free imitation. It is so broadly constructed that, without previous notice, one might well be forgiven for wondering, during the exposition, whether one was not already in the middle of the development when the first group of themes reappears. This development, when it does come, introduces a new interplay between widely different subjects – broad *cantabile* and sprightly *staccato*. Once again the recapitulation begins in the sub-dominant with the result that the second subject enters without further preamble in the tonic and the coda loses its air of finality. It is a favourite practice of Beethoven's to modulate 'off the rails' at the beginning of the coda and to make the return to the tonic the occasion for a new triumphant climax. Schubert dislikes this practice. In this broadly constructed movement, he deliberately avoids Beethoven's dynamic crescendo.

What Brahms, with his deep understanding of concentration, thought of such a movement is contained in the notes which he added to the commentary on the work in the Collected Edition. He is not merely tolerant of Schubert's complete lack of concern, but actually enamoured of it. While writing this movement, Schubert altered the rhythmic structure of the first subject.

This unimportant alteration [wrote Brahms] acquires a peculiar interest when one compares it with the equally insignificant-looking but far more important transformation which the first subject of the great C major Symphony underwent. The practice of altering themes in this fashion only after a large or small part of the movement has already been developed out of them is significant evidence of the freshness and unconcern with which Schubert planned and even wrote his works.

And later, on the question of an alteration in the second subject:

The fact that the theme has become twice as broad in this new version is again typically Schubertian. In contrast to Beethoven with his constant striving after an extreme conciseness of expression, the alterations which Schubert made in his works prove in almost every case the genuine delight he took in a broad, leisurely, musical means of expression which cannot dwell in sufficient detail on the material it contains.

Brahms, who revised his own B major Piano Trio with a critical eye, was clearly less stringent than many modern critics of Schubert.

The two middle movements are not drawn to the same dimensions as the first. It is generally true to say that, as a composer of slow movements, Schubert avoids the large-scale Adagio. The exceptions – in the 'Wanderer' Fantasia and the String Quintet – prove the rule. In this instance the Andante is a set of variations after the style of Haydn, with much prominence given to the wind instruments either in groups or individually, and with no complications whatever. The extremely vigorous Minuet (it has no title, but simply the indication 'Allegro vivace') is in C minor, which is certainly not typical either of Haydn or Beethoven. But the main section is a mixture of elements from the Minuets in Mozart's E flat major and G minor Symphonies. It is not until the Finale that we again find something of the first movement's substance. It is a piece of symphonic frivolity in sonata form, full of dynamic surprises, dropping off to sleep, as it were, and then waking up with a start. The second subject is a variant of the piquant main theme in the Finale of the First Symphony.

After finishing the string quartet, Schubert started work on another symphony (I, 3), written between 24th May and 9th July, 1815, which is a long time by his standards. It is as if he had wanted to rectify the 'faults' of the B flat major Symphony with this one. It reverts to the D major of his First Symphony. Although it employs exactly the same orchestral combination, it is far shorter and at the same time far more concentrated. The slow introduction, which bears some resemblance to that of its predecessor, is further removed from the Mozartian model and more agitated; the gateway of the dominant opens twice. Then follows an intensely Schubertian theme that anticipates a more famous successor which was to appear in 1828, particularly when one recalls the original form of the latter:

It is a theme which expresses nothing but rhythm and harmony, except that the famous later version is simpler and bolder and immediately adds the complementary metrical and dynamic contrast. Here, as an indication of increased concentration, Beethoven's orchestral crescendo also begins to play its part, culminating in an heroic *fortissimo*. The second subject again anticipates to some extent the *character* of the Ländler of the 'Unfinished', but in march tempo and with an excess of high spirits. The very short development which elaborates it is strongly reminiscent of Mozart's 'Haffner' Serenade. In the recapitulation, this second subject appears in the subdominant, which is again something that Beethoven would certainly have objected to as an unwarrantable convenience. One might similarly describe the Allegretto, which takes the place of the slow movement, as 'simplified Haydn'. It is even more guileless and elementary than an early Haydn movement of this kind. The third movement combines a Ländler and a Scherzo labelled 'Minuet', the chief feature of which is an exaggerated stress on the unaccented beat. But the most charming movement, as in the above-mentioned C major Quartet, is a Finale in 6/8 time and with a *buffo* flavour – an Overture rather than a Finale. It anticipates many later works – for example, the Finale of the D minor String Quartet.

Compared with the operatic output of this productive year, the sum total of instrumental music is insignificant. And it seems still more insignificant, in quality as well as quantity, if we add into the balance the rest of the vocal works of this period – the church music, the choruses for male and female voices and above all the songs. In contrast with Beethoven, Schubert is a composer whose centre of gravity rests on vocal music, or to be more precise, with whom the scales are much more equally balanced between vocal and instrumental music.

We will start with the Mass in G major (XIII, 2), written between 2nd and 7th March and begun the day after he had completed two settings of poems by Körner. He finished the second of these, which is comparatively long, 'in five hours'. Now, to write a whole Mass in six days seems a not inconsiderable achievement. It is more readily understandable, however, when one observes that this Mass, in the 'innocent' key, is scored for strings (and organ) only, and that it is predominantly a vocal mass, a typical *Land-Messe*. In the *Kyrie*, only the 'Christe' section is on a more serious and elaborate scale with alternating passages for chorus and soloists. In the very commonplace *Gloria*, too, the soprano part is treated in a different, more immature style than in the solos for Therese Grob. The *Credo* is a choral movement in simple, declamatory style, accompanied by alternate *staccato* and *legato* figures in the orchestra. Its *form* is purely instrumental in conception, in spite of the vocal medium. The *Sanctus* uses Mozart's stock direction of 'Maestoso', while the 'Hosanna' which follows it takes the form of a somewhat compromising *fugato*, as it also does in some of the early Masses of Schubert's great model. The *Benedictus* is pastoral in character, but its broad treatment in the form of a canon for three of the soloists tends to destroy the balance of the work. The most delicate and sensitive movement is the *Agnus Dei*, the opening of which once again recalls Pergolesi. The speed of composition betrays itself in certain omissions in the score to which Eugen Spiro has already drawn attention.* Once again Schubert's lack of rev-

* *Zeitschrift der Internationalen Musikgesellschaft V.*, pp. 51–4, 1930s.

erence for the Church makes itself evident. We are face to face, as it were, with a paradox. Here is youthful expertise, the product of an excessive tradition and a prodigious talent.

On 10th April and between 15th and 17th April two shorter liturgical works were written, an Offertory 'Tres sunt qui testimonium dant in coelo' and a Gradual 'Benedictus es Domine' (XIV, 4 and 5). Both are scored for an almost identical choral and orchestral combination (the addition of trumpets in the Gradual gives it a somewhat greater brilliance) and both were without doubt commissioned works. The first, which achieves a sonorous dignity by virtue of the almost continuous use of trombones, is part of the Office of the Ecclesia Triumphans; yet Schubert felt it necessary to symbolize the mystery of 'unitas in trinitate' by means of a sudden *piano*. The most striking features are a pedal-point on C against a background of vigorous harmony, the persistent rhythm in the *ritornello* and epilogue, and the use of Mozart's 'motto' of four notes. The Gradual, which was published as op. 150, has a superbly baroque opening ('Adagio maestoso') and an Alleluia fugue which might likewise be described as superbly baroque and at the same time academic. One thinks instinctively of the Church of St. Charles, Vienna, with its pillars and its dome. And again one wonders what more Schubert wanted to learn or indeed could have learnt from Simon Sechter at the end of his life, for even at the age of eighteen there was nothing he did not already know. In complete contrast to these two works is an offertory *Salve Regina,* written on 5th July (XIV, 2), for soprano and strings (without the violas), to which Schubert added clarinets, bassoons and horns on 28th January, 1823, when he was revising the work for publication as op. 47. It is a church-aria in the simplest 'da capo' form, but full of subtle and expressive detail, and full of devotion for the Blessed Virgin.

The choral and orchestral combination of the Offertory 'Tres sunt' is repeated in a *Stabat Mater,* written between 4th and 6th April (XIV, 12), and incomplete in that Schubert set only the first two verses. It is a simple and effective choral arioso, with a deep vein of pathos. A year later he returned once more to this subject and the result is one of his loveliest achievements.

The transition to the songs of this important year is marked by a number of secular choruses. One of these, Castelli's 'Trinklied', written in February 1815 (XIX, 8) for soloists, three-part male-voice chorus and piano, strikes a serious mood in the solo part; Schiller's 'Punschlied' (29th August; XIX, 7) is a typically spirited song for a convivial occasion, sung *fortissimo* throughout. With his 'Bardengesang' (20th January; XIX, 15) Schubert returns once more to the unaccompanied male-voice terzet form of 1813; it is a splendidly lively piece but not to be compared with the earlier 'Spruch des Confucius'. For the first time we find him writing two three-part songs for women's voices with piano accompaniment, 'Das Leben ist ein Traum', 25th August, and 'Klage um Ali Bey', both dating from about the same time (XVIII, 5 and 6). The former – a trifle of several verses – suffers from the pious triviality of its text. The latter, however, is a setting of a whimsical poem by Matthias Claudius, and in spite of its direction, 'klagend', and its key (E flat minor) it is full of grotesque humour, which expresses itself in an exaggerated range of dynamics. Such humour is rare in Schubert's piano songs. Then, on 11th July, 1815, he wrote for the first time a chorus for mixed voices with piano accompaniment, a setting of Schiller's 'Hymne an den Unendlichen', which was published posthumously as op. 112 together with two other choruses of a similar character – 'Gott im Ungewitter' and 'Gott der Weltschöpfer', both with texts by J. P. Uz (XVII, 6–8). The three pieces were all probably written about the same time. They are choral music in the truest sense, not quasi-solo quartets like Brahms' 'Liebeslieder' Waltzes and similar works, and the form was comparatively new. They indicate a fresh, 'romantic' approach to music-making, different in every way from Schubert's own 'quasi-solo' male-voice quartets, which we shall discuss later. The musical and spiritual starting-point for this kind of vocal music is Beethoven's setting of Gellert's 'Die Ehre Gottes in der Natur', which was at that time familiar not only as a song but also in its choral version. Schubert's second chorus has exactly the same hymn-like character. The first is a little bombastic and philistine in character. By far the most distinguished is the third and last – 'mit Majestät, sehr langsam'. Of the three verses, Schubert concentrated particularly on the second, with special emphasis on metrical accuracy. The piano accompaniment has the same independence that we find in his songs, and Schiller's 'organ-music of the thunderstorm' is transformed into a harp-like effect. If the Collected Edition is correct Schubert set a printer's error – 'Blitz' instead of 'Blick'.

A further stage in the transition to the songs of this year is marked by the unison or two-part choral songs with piano accompaniment, all of them naturally strophic in style and with short interludes or a brief postlude. There are two songs from Theodor Körner's *Leyer und Schwert* which date from the period of patriotic enthusiasm – 'Trinklied vor der Schlacht' divided between two choruses (XX, 53) and 'Schwertlied', for solo and chorus (XX, 54). We are positively thankful when the latter sings its 'Hurrah!' with a false accent. There followed, in May 1815, Schiller's Ode 'An die Freude' (XX, 66), a few years before Beethoven's lapidary setting. Schubert's treatment, in which the chorus answers the soloist in a different time and metre, is most impressive. Finally, there is Schiller's 'Punschlied, im Norden zu singen' (XX, 110), set for two-part chorus and appropriately cast in the form of a polonaise. And one wonders whether certain other songs of a 'convivial character' were not also intended for chorus: Goethe's 'Tischlied' (XX, 97) and 'Bundeslied' (XX, 115), or Gabriele von Baumberg's 'Lob des Tokayer's' (XX, 135). All of them are brisk, cheerful and answer the purpose for which they were written.

But it is the piano-song proper in which Schubert's creative activity reached its peak during this year. On some days alone he wrote six, seven, eight or nine songs. The process which led from the first reading of a poem to conception, shaping and the physical act of writing followed an uninterrupted course, in the same manner as a running jump. Occasionally – as, for example, after the composition of 'Gretchen am Spinnrade' – pauses of a few weeks occurred, in January, March or July 1815, but for the rest, scarcely a day passed *sine linea*.

The October day in 1814 on which 'Gretchen am Spinnrade' (XX, 31) was written has been rightly and wrongly called the birthday of German song – wrongly, inasmuch as it is not a song in the true sense, and because some songs of consummate perfection had already been written before

1814, particularly by Schubert himself. 'Adelaide' and 'Laura' are two such examples, the former of which is treated with the same freedom of form as 'Gretchen am Spinnrade'. But the author of those texts was Matthisson and on this occasion Schubert chanced upon Goethe. He chanced upon a poet who is not 'sentimental' but genuine (Schiller would have said 'naïve'), not stylish but simple, not profligate but powerful in his use of words. It is a scene from *Faust*, but it is clear from the outset that it cannot be sung on the stage, quite apart from the difficulty of orchestrating the piano accompaniment. (*Pizzicato* on violas, 'cellos and harp.) It is a transfiguration. The proper treatment for the stage would be a strophic song. Schubert, however, writes what has been called a lyrical monody, with a conventional 'da capo', it is true, and a melodic unity, but with a constantly changing, sensitive inflexion. And the accompaniment – is it painting, this humming of the spinning wheel, this sound of the foot upon the treadle? Or is it not rather the symbolic expression of spiritual unrest? It is emotional painting, feeling become as clay in the composer's hands.

A work of art of comparable significance – though it is a simple strophic song of no more than fourteen bars – is Goethe's 'Nachtgesang' (XX, 32), written six weeks later. It is no ordinary serenade and Schubert was quick to appreciate this fact. In his setting of the third verse

> *Die ewigen Gefühle*
> *Heben mich, hoch und hehr,*
> *Aus irdischem Gewühle;*
> *Schlafe! Was willst du mehr?**

he illustrates the poet's sense of universality by his choice of key (A flat major), and at the right moment he achieves his climax by a modulation to D flat. Voice-part and accompaniment end on an interval of a third, mystic, unresolved.

Between the extremes of these two songs come the following. 'Trost in Tränen' (XX, 33) is a simple strophic song, the question in the major, the answer in the minor, but with an iridescent ending in the major. 'Schäfer's Klagelied' (XX, 34) is another lyrical *scena*. The version which was

---

* The sense of eternity raises me high above the earthly tumult. Sleep in peace! What more dost thou wish?

published as op. 3, 1 at the end of 1821 is infinitely richer in detail and is transposed from E minor to C minor. This was the first of Schubert's songs to be publicly performed. Franz Jäger, who was then a singer at the Theater an der Wien, sang it at the *Römischer Kaiser* on 28th February, 1819, and the revised version was presumably written for that occasion. 'Sehnsucht' is admittedly a relapse into the style of Zumsteeg. Goethe's stanzas are divided between *recitativo secco* and descriptive arioso. The same applies to 'Am See' (XX, 36), a setting of a poem by Mayrhofer, which was instrumental in bringing about the first meeting of the two friends. Here we even find the direction 'taktlos' over an arioso passage – in other words, 'to be sung in free style'. It can only have been the rich pageant of imagery and feeling which prompted Schubert to set this sentimental elegy on the 'great German Leopold' of Brunswick to music.

In December 1814, Schubert applied his creative powers to a more worthy subject. This was the Cathedral Scene from *Faust* (XX, 37) in which the 'Evil Spirit' whispers his threats to the kneeling Gretchen while from choir and organ the *Dies Irae* echoes through the nave. It lends itself easily to orchestration and yet, in so doing, one would ruin it. It is, so to speak, a completed study of considerable boldness, and there even exists a preliminary sketch for it, in which, admittedly, such things as the anticipation of a Wagnerian 'question-formula' do not yet occur.

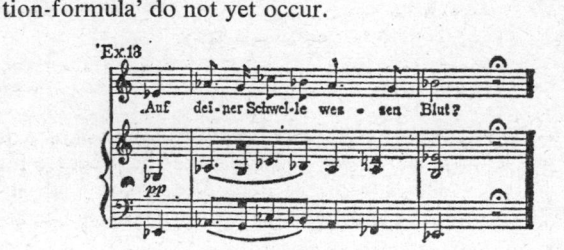

No contemporary composer except this eighteen-year-old schoolmaster in a Viennese suburb wrote anything like this.

This book is not a treatise on Schubert's songs. It is not the intention, nor indeed is it possible, to analyse and assess all the strophic settings of poems by Ermin, Matthisson, Hölty, Stolberg, Kenner, Kosegarten, Paumgartner, or his friend

Albert Stadler, which he wrote during this period, although almost every one reveals some individual feature or contrives its own highly sensitive modulation to the dominant or mediant and back, or harbours its own secret, as we have seen in Kosegarten's 'Mondnacht'. Schubert tries to make his intentions clearer by means of musical directions in German – an innovation for which Zumsteeg was chiefly responsible and which Schubert imitates. The Italian 'Andante con moto', 'Allegro moderato' and so on, which satisfy the requirements of his instrumental music, are no longer adequate for his songs. In their place we find: 'Lieblich, etwas geschwind'; 'Mit Liebes-Affect'; 'Wehmütig'; 'Sehr langsam, feierlich mit Anmut'; 'Erzählend'; 'Unruhig, klagend, im Zeitmasse wachsend bis zur Haltung (Fermate)'; 'Tändelnd, sehr leise'; 'Sehr langesam, ängstlich'; 'Etwas langsam, unschulgid'. And in the long, ballad-like songs with their constant change of expression, these indications become still richer and more individual. What Schubert is trying to prevent is a neutral style of delivery, the bare routine of singing. These are German songs, faithful to the text and to the poet. Schubert's feeling for the poet is as delicately balanced as a pair of jeweller's scales. In evidence of this one can quote two poems by Gabriele von Baumberg which Mozart had already treated in a purely sentimental fashion, but which Schubert set with a slightly archaic flavour, in the style of Haydn's piano sonatas ('Der Morgengruss', XX, 124, and 'Abendständchen', XX, 125).

We can best understand this rich output of songs if we accept it as a kind of return-journey – a return-journey by roundabout ways to Goethe. And in the ballad it represents an advance from a 'loose' to a 'compact' form, from Bertrand's 'Minona' (XX, 40) or Schiller's 'Die Bürgschaft' (XX, 109) with their constant alternation between recitative and arioso, to the compactness of 'Erlkönig' (XX, 178). Not only in his ballads but sometimes even in a strophic poem of a purely lyrical character, Schubert gets over a difficulty by setting 'descriptive' or less 'emotional' stanzas in recitative form. But this practice becomes more and more infrequent. His ideal becomes the strophic variation – that is to say, he takes each verse as it stands but allows himself complete freedom of treatment. A classic example, not entirely lacking in humour, is his setting of Goethe's 'An den Mond', a lyric at which countless composers from Kayser and Reichardt down to the twentieth century have tried their hand in vain. In the first version, written on 19th August of this same year, 1815 (XX, 116), Schubert treats the verses in pairs and separates them by an interlude or postlude; but since there are nine verses in all, the last one presents a certain problem. And he must very soon have realized that in spite of the 'fairly slow' tempo and the *pianissimo* delivery, he could never do justice to the profound magic of these words with his rather too prosaic melody. So, shortly before 'Erlkönig', he wrote another setting (XX, 176). This time he alters the key from E flat to A flat and adopts a resigned and delicate melodic treatment. He gives the sixth and seventh verses their own, more animated music and then reverts again to the peace and tranquillity of the opening in a slightly altered form. It has been claimed, with some justification, that it is physically impossible to set this poem of Goethe's to music on the grounds that it is already verbal music of the purest and profoundest kind, that it is itself instinct with music. If it *is* possible, then Schubert's second setting at least does justice to it.

Yet Schubert could write a good song without recourse to Goethe. Take, for example, the erotic hymn, 'Als ich sie erröten sah' (XX, 41) by a poet named Ehrlich about whom literary histories give no further information. This song, with its passionate freedom and its unity of melody and accompaniment, would defy any attempt to place it in its chronological context, if we did not know that it was written on 10th February, 1815; and it would be part of every singer's repertoire, if it had been included in *Die Winterreise* or *Schwanengesang*. 'Vergebliche Liebe' (XX, 58), by an equally obscure poet named Bernard – unless it is Josef Karl Bernard, who wrote the libretto for Conradin Kreutzer's opera *Libussa* – is a magnificently dramatic lyrical *scena*. Körner's 'Liebesrausch' resolves itself into a dithyramb by virtue of its extravagant accompaniment. J. G. Fellinger's 'Die erste Liebe' builds up to a passionately exuberant climax at the end. The Hölty songs of the spring of 1815 all have a peculiar charm, although 'Mainacht' (XX, 70) later inspired Brahms to a more successful setting. 'An den Mond' (XX, 69) is surprisingly reminiscent of the 'Moonlight' Sonata at the beginning and again at the end; and 'An

die Nachtigall' (XX, 72) is a glittering jewel – two short
verses of a few bars, and instilled with an intensity of feeling
and a descriptive power which are far in advance of the
period when it was written. Kosegarten's 'Die Erscheinung'
is the prototype of 'Die Forelle' and anticipates it quite literally both in the melody and the harmony.

When Goethe provided the purest stimulus to Schubert's
imagination, the latter does not always succeed in finding the
perfect setting for the poet's words at the first attempt, as we
have already seen. The D minor of 'Am Flusse' (XX, 47),
written in the present year (1815) and rather too Mozartian
('wehmutig') in conception, is transformed, at the end of
1822, into the major; the tempo becomes 'moderate', the
form more compact, and for the first time in the introduction and postlude there appears in the background the
river itself, which is conspicuous by its absence in the earlier
setting. The second version of 'An Mignon' (XX, 48), which
Schubert dedicated to the poet, is simpler in its choice of
key, in its dynamics and in its melody. The second setting of
'Ich denke dein' (XX, 49) includes an interlude and a postlude, but even in its original version it is a song of the most
intense emotional concentration, a truly miraculous achievement, when one compares it with such ineffective contemporary efforts as Zelter's songs of 1808. Admittedly
Zelter's 'Erster Verlust' is a song of singular beauty and
richness – possibly his most beautiful, with a genuine climax
at the end, and with interludes which anticipate Brahms.
And yet Schubert is far superior to him. He comes straight
to the point with the first three bars (Ex. 14).

In Klärchen's 'Freudvoll und leidvoll', from *Egmont*
(XX, 78), Schubert seems to be competing with Beethoven;
yet it is not competition in any real sense, for Beethoven was
writing for the stage, while Schubert's setting is a piano-
song, instinct with the most *personal* feeling. He is quite

Ex.14 *Sehr langsam, wehmütig*

Ach, wer brings die schö - nen Ta - ge.

certainly competing with no one in Goethe's 'Meeresstille' (XX, 82), in which he accompanies the 'anxious' delivery of the vocal line with gentle arpeggios in bold modulation, symbolical of the gentle rippling of the water. It is another impressionistic song, which Hugo Wolf was to imitate eighty years later in one of the Mörike songs. On the same level stands 'Wanderers Nachtlied' (Der du von dem Himmel bist') (XX, 87), treated with a simplicity and sensitivity of expression which makes every other setting seem ponderous and artificial. Goethe's 'Der Fischer' (XX, 88) is treated by Schubert not as a ballad, but as a Romance in strophic form. It is reminiscent of the Romances in the German ballad-opera, in which it was the usual practice to give a *résumé* of previous events leading up to the plot. The immortal counterpart to this song is 'Heidenröslein' (XX, 114) which had been published in 1773 in Herder's *Von Deutscher Art und Kunst* under the title of 'Fabelliedchen'. One cannot help comparing it with Reichardt's feeble setting, on which Friedrich Rochlitz, the critical *doyen* of Leipzig's musical life, had lavished his praise: 'In the true folk-song tradition, and for all its simplicity, masterly in its perfect accuracy of expression'; or with the setting, in 1820, by Wenzel Johann Tomaschek of Prague (op. 53, 1), who dresses it in Bohemian costume and lays particular stress on its 'traditional' character. Schubert does not imitate the folk-song tradition. He creates it or provides an occasion for it. Twelve years later we shall find him writing a song for *Die Winterreise* ('Am Brunnen vor dem Tore') – a pure 'art-song', which the 'people' – whatever may be understood by that word – have simplified and sentimentalized, and in this way appropriated to themselves.

Schubert's setting of Goethe's 'Der Rattenfänger' (XX, 112) misses the Mephistophelian spirit which Hugo Wolf captured so perfectly; but 'Der Schatzgräber' (XX, 113) is another incomparable song, and for the first time makes use of the magical change of the melody from major to minor, which is later to become one of Schubert's typical devices. For 'Wonne der Wehmut' (XX, 117) we have Beethoven's lovely, though much too 'stagy', setting from which to draw a comparison. Schubert is much simpler and more concentrated, and he provides against any possible sentimentality by the direction 'Etwas geschwind (rather quickly)'. 'Wer kauft Liebesgötter' (XX, 118) is full of playfulness; and 'Die Spinnerin' (XX, 119) is the strophic counterpart to 'Gretchen am Spinnrade', with the same underlying sense of tragedy. The counterpart to 'Heidenröslein' is the 'Schweizerlied' (XX, 121) with its gentle suggestion of a yodelling-song. It is yet another of Schubert's *unintentional* folk-songs.

In the middle of September 1815, Schubert discovered Klopstock and started to experiment with his free metrical forms, as Gluck had done forty years earlier. 'Vaterlandslied' or 'An Sie' (XX, 141, 142) are really very similar in style to Gluck, only with an added richness in both melody and accompaniment. 'Die Sommernacht' (XX, 143) is treated as a 'recitativo in tempo' with expressive piano interludes. 'Das Rosenband' (XX, 139), one of Schubert's purest and tenderest melodies, has an accompaniment which combines economy of treatment with an intense latent energy. The group ends with the hymn 'Dem Unendlichen' (XX, 145), the three existing versions of which are all essentially the same. It is one of Schubert's best-known songs (it has even had to suffer the misfortune of being orchestrated) and, with its direction: 'To be sung slowly, and with all possible vigour', it has become a show-piece for sopranos with a 'big' voice. In its simplicity, freedom and grandeur it is remotely reminiscent of Gluck's 'Divinités du Styx'.

During this year Schubert occupied himself only sporadically with Klopstock's pupil, Friedrich Schiller. He mastered 'Erwartung' (XX, 46) with its difficult alternating stanzas, by faithfully observing the interchange between recitative and arioso. He was dissatisfied with his first setting of 'Das Geheiminis' (XX, 105), even though it invests the four stanzas with a superbly harmonized melody, and he recast it later (XX, 431) in the form of a strophic song with variations. This is typical of Schubert's method, for he is determined to do justice to *each individual* verse. On the other hand, he found 'An den Frühling' (XX, 136) capable of only slight improvement two years later. As for a setting of Schiller's 'Hoffnung' (XX, 106), written during this year, it is quite obvious that he simply forgot that it existed, for it is far superior to the later version (XX, 358) which he published as op. 87, 2. The following anecdote is told of him. While in the company of his friends, he heard one of his own songs and asked in genuine surprise: 'That's rather a good song. Who wrote it?'

In the second half of the year 1815, besides other settings of lengthy poems by Schiller, such as 'Hector's Abschied' (XX, 109) or 'Klage der Ceres' (XX, 172), Schubert wrote 'Die Bürgschaft' (XX, 109), which he was later to use as material for an opera. This brings us to the lavish output of ballad music during this year, for which Schubert drew on Körner, Bertrand, Stadler, Kenner and, above all, Ossian. We can only touch briefly on these ballads, although they are of the first importance and notably rich, from the historical point of view, in surprising details of pictorial illustration (one might almost call it a concealed form of orchestral illustration) such as the use of the *tremolo*. This interest applies even to a 'murder-story' like Hölty's 'Nonne (XX, 77) or Bertrand's 'Adelwold und Emma', which now merely strike us as unintentionally funny. Consequently it is only today that we have begun to realize the singular fact that the settings of Ossian's ballads, in particular, contain musical figures of speech which one would not expect to find until Wagner's *Ring des Nibelungen*. Admittedly, the most arresting moments are the lyrical climaxes such as those in 'Ossian's Lied nach dem Falle Nathos' (XX, 147) or 'Das Mädchen von Inistore' (XX, 148). With the single exception of 'Kolma's Klage' (XX, 83), Schubert has to resort again and again to the expedient of recitative in his long ballads, to the detriment of their overall musical unity – until he discovers the solution in 'Erlkönig'. Here the two bars of recitative at the end are no longer a mere expedient, but an indispensable necessity. The unification which he achieves by means of the sinister, pounding triplets of the accompaniment is theatrical and 'physical'; the boldness and aptness of the modulation spring from the same source as the boldness and aptness of the declamatory style. In spite of the false accents – particularly in the second line – Schubert is a melodist, and when the correct delivery of the words comes into conflict with the inherent logic, the perfect shape of the melody, then he sacrifices the former to the latter. There are countless composers who pay more scrupulous attention to the matter of delivery in their songs than Schubert; yet that

has not made them greater than him. Carl Loewe's setting of
'Erlkönig', written about the same time (1817), is a much
more genuine ballad than Schubert's. It is treated and developed to its climax within the framework of a strophic
form, and is much more 'nordic' in its emphasis. It would
probably have given the poet greater satisfaction. And yet of
the two, it is Schubert's setting which proved the more triumphant success in the eyes of his contemporaries and of
posterity, by virtue of his direct, passionately dramatic descriptive treatment.

Even in the eyes of his contemporaries. His friends received the ballad with enthusiasm. The story of its
composition is well-known. 'We found Schubert in a state of
great excitement, reading "Erlkönig" aloud from a book,'
writes Spaun in his reminiscences. 'He walked up and down
several times with the book in his hand. Then suddenly he
sat down and in an incredibly short time – no longer than it
took him simply to write it down – the glorious ballad was
put on paper. As Schubert had no piano, we rushed to the
Convict with it, and there, that very same evening,
"Erlkönig" was sung and received with rapturous applause.
. . .' There exist today four separate manuscripts of the song
(XX, 178), one with a simplified accompaniment, and we
need not detain ourselves here with the question of their
chronology.* It was published as op. 1 and dedicated to the
'Hofmusikgraf', Moriz von Dietrichstein. The first edition
appeared at the beginning of April 1821, some six weeks
after the song had received its first public performance.

It must have been in the autumn of this memorable year
that Schubert read *Wilhelm Meisters Lehrjahre*, for it was
on 18th October that he wrote the first of his long series of
'Harper' and 'Mignon' songs. Throughout the rest of his life
these poems held him under their spell. And we must bear in
mind that throughout his life he never set to music a single
one of Philine's songs – that lovable and light-hearted
beauty, who writes with such frankness in praise of the
pleasures of night. It was scarcely the question of moral
considerations that restrained him. But there comes to mind
a question which he is reputed to have asked. 'Do you know

* Cf. Max Friedlaender, 'Die erste Form des Schubert'schen
"Erlkönigs,"' in *Vierteljahrsschrift für Musikwissenschaft* III, pp.
122–8, 1887.

any *really* cheerful music? I do not know any.' What he had in mind was the inherent sadness of music. He felt it too deeply to prostitute it in the name of wit. He is often graceful, even roguish, but never witty.

He wrote six settings of Mignon's 'Nur wer die Sehnsucht kennt'; two of the Harp-player's 'Wer sich der Einsamkeit ergiebt'; three of 'Wer nie sein Brot mit Tränen ass'; and it will be better if we start with the later versions and retrace our steps from them to the earlier ones. Mignon's 'Kennst du das Land, (XX, 168) is the only one of these songs which he did not attempt more than once; yet it must not therefore be assumed that he was satisfied with his first effort. Who could possibly be satisfied with any one setting? Certainly not even Zelter, who made six attempts at this most celebrated of all Goethe's songs. Schumann also set it to music twice, and twenty-six years after that day in May 1810 when Beethoven sang his own setting to Bettina Brentano for the first time, he wrote*

Apart from Beethoven's, I know no single setting of this song which can match in the slightest degree the impression which the poem makes without any music. Whether it requires different music for each verse is one thing; let Beethoven tell you whence he produced his music.

Now Beethoven produced his music out of the fullness of his heart. He wrote a song of unusual simplicity, each stanza a thing of metrical grace and each refrain full of exuberance; and naturally enough he could not bring himself to illustrate the second and third verses with any degree of liveliness. Goethe himself was far from satisfied. When W. J. Tomaschek played his own setting to him in Carlsbad in 1822, Goethe's first reaction was to pay him a somewhat ambiguous compliment. 'You have understood the poem'. Then he went on. 'I cannot understand how Beethoven and Spohr could have so completely misunderstood the song as to set each verse to a different melody. I should have thought that the same distinctive features which occur in the identical place in each stanza would be sufficient indication to the composer that what I expect from him is a song pure and simple. By her very nature, Mignon can only sing a song, not an aria'. Now Beethoven's setting is no more an aria than

*I quote from Max Friedlaender's *Das deutsche Lied im* 18. *Jahrhundert*, II, 187.

Schubert's. And since Schubert knew Beethoven's setting – it had been published in 1810 as op. 75, 2 – and imitated it, his freedom of action was restricted. We find the same choice of key, the same change of tempo (although not of time-signature), the same melodic idiom, Schubert even sets the second verse to the same music as the first; only in the third, with its graphic description:

> *Kennst du den Berg und seinen Wolkensteg?*
> *Das Maultier sucht im Nebel seinen Weg;*
> *In Höhlen wohnt der Drachen alte Brut;*
> *Es stüzt der Fels and über ihn die Flut....**

does he resort to the minor and to pictorial allusion. And – such is the curse of imitation – his refrain is even more exuberant than Beethoven's, and in fact approaches the style of an arioso.

With the remaining Goethe songs of this period Schubert makes amends. He set 'Geistesgruss' (XX, 174) three times; even then it required a fourth version, which he eventually published, and in which the introductory 'recitative' disappears and makes way for a style of delivery which is firmer (and at the same time more mysterious, due to the *tremolo* in the accompaniment). In this miniature cantata Schubert emphasizes that the tempo must be kept uniform throughout. 'Hoffnung' (XX, 175) which was first written in F major, evidently for a male voice, and subsequently transposed nearly an octave higher into the key of E, is a pure jewel. It is a song with a sustained melody over a staccato bass, and its effect is heightened by the knowledge that the prayer which it voices was not to be answered in Schubert's own case:

> *Schaff', das Tagwerk meiner Hände,*
> *Hohes Glück, dass ich's vollende!*
> *Lass, o lass mich nicht ermatten!*
> *Nein, es sind nicht leere Träume:*
> *Jetzt nur Stangen, diese Bäume*
> *Geben einst noch Frucht und Schatten.*†

* Knowest thou the mountain and its path among the clouds? The mule seeks its way in the mist; in caverns dwells the ancient blood of dragons; the rock falls sheer and over it tumbles the waterfall.
†May Fortune grant that I finish the day's work of my hands! Let, ah! let me not weary! No, these are not empty dreams: though they be but saplings now, these trees will one day yield fruit and shade.'

Fruit and shade enough for posterity, but not for Schubert himself. There remains 'Rastlose Liebe' (XX, 177), which was published among the songs dedicated to Salieri. It is full of youthful exuberance which reaches its climax in a post-lude marked *fortissimo*. For all its passionate declamatory style, it contrives a remarkable restraint and a perfect balance between melody and accompaniment.

Chapter Six

The Last Years of Schoolmastering
From 'Mignon' to 'An Schwager Kronos'

Autumn 1815–Autumn 1816

This period of Schubert's creative activity could well be given a negative title – the Year of Indecision. As such it is a faithful reflection of the mental state in which he lived. He must have felt far more unsettled than is normal for a youth of seventeen or eighteen. At the beginning of 1816, an opportunity occurred at least to exchange schoolmastering for a post as Director of Music, which had been advertised by the municipal authorities in Laibach, who were planning a public music school at the German Training College. Schubert submitted his application, accompanied by a testimonial as to his qualities from Salieri, as well as numerous other recommendations – and failed to obtain the post. The successful applicant was the Laibach 'Tonkünstler', Franz Sokol.

Documentary evidence of his spiritual *malaise* is provided by his diary, which he began in June 1816 and continued until the autumn. People who are completely happy do not as a rule keep diaries. The first entry is a hymn to Mozart and it goes on to mention a sentimental walk with his brother Karl, and the celebrations in honour of Salieri's jubilee; and on 17th June it records that on that day the writer composed for money for the first time – a cantata for the occasion of Professor Heinrich Josef Watteroth's name-day, with text by Philipp Dräxler. It bore the title of *Prometheus*, was performed five weeks later and has vanished almost without trace, although we know that Schubert wrote out not only the full score but also the orchestral parts in his own hand. Money, however, was not the only thing which

this work produced. It also resulted in Schubert's introduction to Leopold v. Sonnleithner, who was subsequently
to become one of his best friends. At this point the diary
breaks off and is only resumed again in September with a
series of more general entries, before being finally laid aside.
These observations, which sometimes read like selections
from different authors, are for the most part eccentric and
unhappy, and are the product of a spiritual *malaise*. A letter
from Johann Mayrhofer to Schober (7th September, 1816)
probably has some connection with the origin and character
of these observations. He writes that he is expecting a visit
from Schubert and several friends in the Wipplingergasse,
and that 'Schubert's melodies will disperse the gloom which
at present surrounds us in these somewhat difficult days'.

Schubert's depression must have been increased by his disappointment over Goethe's failure to reply to a letter of
Joseph v. Spaun's which had been accompanied by a
number of Schubert's finest settings of Goethe's poems (including 'Gretchen am Spinnrade' and the version of
'Erlkönig' with the simplified accompaniment). The sense
of disappointment was made all the more acute by the fact
that the songs were returned – we do not know when – but
without any observation whatever on the part of the celebrated poet, a single word from whom would have made the
modest composer happy. Spaun's letter (dated 17th April,
1816) was certainly a model of tactlessness. He explained
that he and his friends were planning to publish Schubert's
songs and ballads, followed by his instrumental works as
well. The songs would appear in eight volumes, the first two
devoted to Goethe, the third to Schiller, the fourth and fifth
to Klopstock, the sixth and seventh to Matthisson, Hölty,
Salis, etc., and the last two to Ossian, 'which latter are far
superior to the rest'. He went on to say that the whole collection would be dedicated to Goethe and added that the
settings of poems other than Goethe's were equally good and
perhaps even better, and that 'the pianist who performs them
for your Excellency must not be lacking in skill and expression.' All this could only be calculated to frighten his
Excellency out of his wits. Goethe, as usual, ignored both
the letter and the songs which accompanied it, and it is con-
sistent with this fact that Schubert's name never once occurs

in all the voluminous correspondence between Goethe and Zelter, not even during the four years after Schubert's death.

A survey of Schubert's music during this year leads one to the conclusion that only in his songs did he show a steady development towards the culminating achievements of the 'Harper' and 'Mignon' songs and 'An Schwager Kronos', and even then the course he followed was not entirely straight. In every other field he seems to have had scarcely any fixed objective. He even became an 'occasional' composer, not in the same sense as he had been during that earlier and still comparatively recent period when nearly everything he wrote was an 'occasional' work, but in the nineteenth-century sense, when this description was applied only to those works which – to put it unkindly – were not written at random or which were not the product of spontaneous inspiration. The most important of these works would appear to have been the *Prometheus* Cantata which he 'wrote for money' and about which Sonnleithner gave us a certain amount of information fifty years later, including a few musical quotations which unfortunately tell us very little.* It lasted for three-quarters of an hour without a break and was written almost entirely in accompanied recitative, after the style of the Ossian songs. The one 'compact' number was a duet between the Goddess of Earth (Gaea) and Prometheus. The dialogue was framed between three choruses, the last of which was a triumphal chorus for mixed voices and orchestra. Of more modest proportions is the musical 'Contribution to Herr von Salieri's fiftieth jubilee ... by his pupil Franz Schubert' (XVI, 44), written on 16th June, 1816, for unaccompanied male-voice chorus, to the composer's own words. O. E. Deutsch has described the festivities of that Sunday when, in the evening, each of Salieri's pupils arrived with a gift for his master. Schubert's contribution begins with a four part 'apotheosis' or apostrophe to the 'kindest, best, wisest and greatest' of all teachers, which he later rewrote as a trio with piano accompaniment. Then follows a 'da capo' Arietta in miniature for the first tenor, and the work ends with a cheerful three-part canon

* O. E. Deutsch, p. 67.

Unser aller Grosspapa
Bleibe noch recht lange da!*

A similar but somewhat earlier work, dating from the end of September 1815, is *Namensfeier* ('Erhab'ner, verehrter Freund der Jugend') for solo trio, chorus and orchestra. It was intended for Franz Michael Vierthaler, Director of the Imperial Orphanage, and was written at the request of his brother Ferdinand, who had his eye on promotion (XVII, 4).

His instrumental music also included 'occasional' works. One of these is the Adagio and Rondo Concertant in F (VII, 2), written in October 1816 for Therese Grob's brother Heinrich who, among other things, played the 'cello. This instrument is not, however, given any noticeable prominence. In conception and execution it has much of J. N. Hummel's sunny disposition and gentle brilliance, with a few charming Schubertian modulations and enharmonic changes. The Rondo is really constructed in sonata-form, and consequently Schubert once more allows himself the convenience of beginning the 'recapitulation' in the subdominant and so brings the movement to a leisurely conclusion. The three sonatas – or to be more precise, sonatinas – for violin and piano (VIII, 2–4) must also have been 'occasional' works. The first and second, in D major and A minor respectively, were written in March, the third, in G minor, in April. They are 'sonatas' in the eighteenth-century sense. In the artless, conversational relationship between the two instruments, in the terseness of form, and in their amateurish treatment they seem to hark back to Mozart or to the pre-Mozartian period. The model for the first movement of the G minor Sonata is palpably obvious: the Allegro from K. 379, in the same key. And, as was the old practice, the first of these sonatas has no Minuet. In the Finale of the third there occurs the passage suggestive of Weber's brilliance to which we have already drawn attention. It is as if Schubert had ignored the existence of Beethoven's op. 12, 23, 24 or even op. 47 and 96.

Except for a number of dances and smaller pieces, these three sonatas represent the full extent of Schubert's interest in the piano during this year. Not until the following one did

* 'Long life to our Grandpapa!'

he feel the inclination to let his imagination range once more over this field. For the time being he had no such ambition. This is also true of one of the two chamber-music works without piano of this period, a String Trio in B flat, written in September 1816 (VI, 1). It consists only of a first movement, very charming, rather Mozartian, fluent and melodious, but no more than that.

The second movement, an Andante sostenuto in E flat major, stops short at the thirty-ninth bar, and Schubert probably broke it off at that point because he was not clear in his mind about the form and found himself returning far too soon to the beginning. Another String Trio, again in B flat major, was actually completed and a very charming little work it is with its remarkable mixture of an Italian style in the first two movements and a Haydnesque one in the last two.

The second of these works of 1816, a String Quartet in E major which the Collected Edition (V, 11) erroneously places 'about 1817', is a very different proposition. It is the first one to have been written without any reference to the domestic quartet at home, and it stands exactly midway between these 'domestic quartets' and the last great representatives of the series which starts with the Quartet Movement in C minor of December 1820. It is much more difficult to play, and at times even tends towards those spasms of virtuosity which Schubert later avoided so scrupulously. Only the final Rondo is faintly reminiscent of its Haydnesque origin, but it is more compact in design than the earlier 'imitations' of this kind. The first movement, an 'Allegro con fuoco', is terse and quite novel, in so far as it employs a subsidiary and second subject with a carefree, Italian flavour. If there existed a chamber-music movement by one of the great Italians, this is the form and appearance it would surely take. Cherubini is much more 'German' in his quartets, and one thinks involuntarily of Giuseppe Verdi's much later quartet. The Andante, with its 'horn' fifths in the theme, is at once 'Viennese', rich and mysterious, and has an expressive coda which soars upwards like a lark ascending. Contrasted with the main section of the Minuet and its successions of sixths is a terse, duet-like Trio in C. Schubert still cherishes his secret ambition. Later, as we already know, he repudiated this string quartet, too; but for us it contains much of interest.

A much less ambitious work is the little Overture in B flat (II, 3) written in September 1816, and modestly scored for horns, trumpets and side-drums, but without flutes and clarinets. The role of the clarinet is taken by the bassoon. An unostentatious 'Adagio maestoso' is followed by an Allegro which is treated in a discreetly military style and which runs its uneventful course without any distinctive features either of harmony or modulation. This time the recapitulation appears in the tonic, but modulates to E flat so that the second subject can enter quite naturally in B flat. It is all a little naïve, pre-Revolutionary and straightforward. One would like to think that the Overture was written for some mildly farcical little comedy at a suburban theatre. O. E. Deutsch has advanced the very plausible theory (p. 107) that it served as the overture to a cantata with text by Johann Baptist Hoheisel, which was written about this time in honour of Joseph Spendou (XVII, 2). Both the orchestral combination and the similarity of key fully support this view. A year or two later, on the occasion of a prize-giving ceremony, Schubert's brother Ferdinand, who had been employed as a teacher at the Training College of the Imperial Orphanage since 1816, arranged a second performance of the work, which was received 'with enthusiastic applause'. Spendou, a canon of St. Stephen's, Chancellor of the University and a great patron of the Schubert family, was on the point of retiring from his post as Inspector-General of elementary schools. It was quite natural that the most gifted member of the Schubert family should write something in his honour, and not, on this occasion, for money. The cantata itself, for all its pretentious vocal complement of soloists, three-part boys' choir and mixed chorus, is extremely simple in design and consists of a series of bass recitatives in the nature of *obbligati,* which link a motet-like dirge for soprano and boys' choir, a duet, a 'chorus of widows', and finally a hymn in the tonic. One can only admire or deplore the scrupulous care with which Schubert set this pathetic farrago of moral dialectics to music.

The most considerable instrumental work of this year is the so-called 'Tragic' Symphony in C minor, for full orchestra, including two pairs of horns, which was started in April 1816 and finished on the 27th of that month (I, 4). The title 'Tragic' was a belated addition on Schubert's part, probably on the occasion of a later, though unauthenticated, performance in the so-called Gundelhof, under the direction of the violinist Otto Hatwig. It is a work which betrays the disturbing influence of Beethoven – the Beethoven of the C minor works, particularly the String Quartet op. 18, 4, and the *Coriolanus* Overture. It comes as something of a shock when we find that the excessively Beethovenian opening of the 'Allegro vivace' is quite out of character with the original, highly concentrated and genuinely powerful Introduction ('Molto adagio'). For this Allegro is not 'tragic' but merely emotional, with a second subject in A flat, a harmonic surprise in E, and the conclusion of the exposition in A flat, which is no less a liberty than the beginning of the recapitulation in G minor. The dualism of the style is apparent in the dynamic range of this movement which, in its simple interchange between loud and soft, is not yet typical of Beethoven, but rather of Haydn and Mozart. There follows an Andante (not an Adagio) in A flat (without trumpets, side-drums and the second pair of horns), whose 'dolcezza' one can dismiss as a piece of affectation. It includes an 'alternativo' in the minor, as in the slow movement of Mozart's E flat major Symphony. It is broadly constructed and much too lyrical, but for all its breadth and weakness it anticipates the slow movement of the great C major Symphony. The Minuet, 'allegro vivace', is in E flat and suggests Beethoven with its rhythmic uncertainty, hovering between 2/4 and 3/4. The second part of the Trio is introduced by this enchanting figure, so characteristic of Schubert:

Ex.15

The movement which is most strongly suggestive of Beethoven – or, in other words, full of Beethoven's rhythms and emphatic orchestral crescendi – is the Finale, and the introductory bars which, so to speak, ring up a sombre curtain correspond to the four opening bars in Beethoven's Piano Trio, Op. 1, 3, which have a similar function. But the tragic catharsis, the change to the major, is no real solution; for all its lofty idealism, it is still conventional. Here are the first signs of Mendelssohn's Romanticism, with its facile accept-ance of a legacy too easily acquired. It is characteristic of Schubert's greatness as a romantic Classicist that he later renounced this legacy and chose an independent course.

It is as if Schubert was conscious of this danger during the composition of his next symphony (I, 5). Written in Sep-tember and October 1816, it stands at the end of this period. Alternatively, it is as if he had wanted to give practical proof of his estrangement from Beethoven which he had recorded in his diary on the occasion of Salieri's jubilee. It is written in the cheerful key of B flat major and scored for a small orchestra without trumpets and side-drums. The orchestral combination is exactly the same as that in the original ver-sion of Mozart's G minor Symphony, without clarinets. The only remaining reminiscence of Beethoven is the four-bar 'curtain' in the first movement, but this time it rises quietly; and it is one of the delicate refinements of this movement that this 'curtain' reappears in the development, but not in the recapitulation. The dynamics are pre-Beethoven. The 'Andante con moto' hovers between Haydn and Mozart and its loveliest passage is reminiscent of the Garden aria from *Figaro*. The Minuet is so Mozartian that it would fall into place quite naturally in the G minor Symphony. The Finale, on the other hand, is once again pure Haydn. And yet this chamber symphony is more harmonious and in many re-spects more original than its predecessor, and from the point of view of form the Finale is perhaps the purest, most pol-ished and most balanced piece of instrumental music that Schubert had yet written. The work was performed for the first and also the last time during Schubert's life in the autumn of 1816 – once more under the direction of Otto Hatwig. It was not given in the Gundelhof, but in the Schot-tenhof, since the orchestra at these domestic concerts was not yet at full strength. This also explains the intimate character of the work.

In this year, too, the vocal music outweighed the instrumen-tal. And it also outweighed it in quality, without taking into account Schubert's songs which were his own particular *métier*, and in which he was already without a rival. He wrote a great deal of church-music and moved with a surer step because he was deeply rooted in the tradition of the

eighteenth century and simply carried it on. Evidence of this
is provided by an Offertory, 'Totus in corde langueo'
(XIV, 1), which is simply a soprano aria with clarinet *ob-
bligato*, flutes, horns and strings (less the violas as in
Mozart!) and written in a baroque, Italianate style. For
some inexplicable reason, Schubert published it in mid-Sep-
tember 1825 as op. 46, and dedicated it to Ludwig Tietze, a
singer in the Chapel Royal and his favourite tenor. As
further evidence, there is a duet 'Auguste iam coelestium'
(XIV, 10) for soprano, tenor and small orchestra, written in
'da capo' form and completely in the jesuitical style of pastoral chamber-music of the previous century. Finally, there
is a German *Salve Regina* in F, for chorus and organ, written on 21st February. It is entirely homophonic in style after
the model of Mozart's *Ave Verum* with almost an excess of
modulation. Another *Salve Regina* in B flat, written in the
same month, for four-part mixed chorus (XIV, 20), is, if
possible, still more homophonic and simple in treatment,
since it completely dispenses with all orchestral interludes.

In contrast to these works, and more pretentious in its
scope, is a *Tantum ergo* in C for soloist, chorus and church
orchestra – that is to say, for strings less violas, oboes, trumpets and side-drums – dedicated to his revered teacher
Michael Holzer and written throughout in the florid, eighteenth-century Viennese style. The violins, in ornamental contrast to the chorus's homophonic declamation, are figured
throughout in semi-quavers, and one cannot help thinking of
the *Credo* in Mozart's Coronation Mass, with which Schubert must certainly have been familiar. One month later, on
25th September, 1816, he wrote a *Magnificat*, treated on a
more lavish scale for soloists, chorus, and orchestra (strings
including violas, oboes, bassoons, trumpets and side-drums:
XIV, II). It is in three sections, with a middle movement in
F for the soloists in the nature of an Andante, flanked on
either side by a majestic and sonorous movement. The whole
work is hymn-like in character, theatrical and solidly constructed – a noble and satisfying piece of traditional baroque
church-music.

The most ambitious liturgical work of this year is a Mass
in C major (XIII, 4), for soloists, chorus, strings (without
violas) and organ, and completed in July 1816 (not 1818, as
Nottebohm assumed). It is a *Missa Brevis*, in exactly the

same sense as the short masses of Mozart and Haydn, in which everything is reduced to the most concise formula and in which the *Gloria* and the *Credo* are treated as symphonic musical entities. Only the section from the 'Et incarnatus' to the 'Resurrexit' is given special prominence as a separate episode. There is no fugue, no 'erudition', only occasional animated imitations in the solo parts. The traditional influence reveals itself in the *Gloria*, particularly in the symphonic correspondence between the 'Quoniam' and the opening section, precisely after the model of Haydn or Mozart. Schubert must have been particularly fond of the work for its simplicity and spontaneity. He would not otherwise have published it (op. 48) two or three years before his death, with a dedication to his teacher Michael Holzer, choirmaster in Liechtental, 'in friendly remembrance', and with the addition of woodwind, trumpets and side-drums; nor would he have replaced the original setting of the *Benedictus* as a soprano solo by a new one in the form of a solo quartet in 1828. The whole work is an example of that *second* simplicity which a great composer normally achieves only at the end of his life. In its original form (?) the Mass was performed on 8th September, 1825, in the Church of Mary the Comforter, together with the above-mentioned tenor aria for Tietze, a *Tantum Ergo* (XIV, 6) and an Offertory. It was given in the critical presence of Schubert, which explains the alterations.

All this is 'traditional' music. But the most important of these liturgical works (if one can call it a liturgical work) is something other than 'traditional'. It is a setting of Klopstock's free adaptation of *Stabat Mater* (XIV, 13), for soloists, chorus and orchestra (two flutes, two oboes, bassoons, horns, three trombones). The date on which the work was started, 28th February, 1816, suggests that Schubert hoped to have it performed on Good Friday of that year. There is no record, however, of any such performance. Even in its Latin form, the *Stabat Mater* was not a liturgical, but simply a 'devotional' work for use in side chapels or at private prayer. Accordingly it had become since Agostino Steffani, Emanuele d'Astorga and particularly since G. B. Pergolesi, an occasion for a more subjective expression of feeling than the other forms of sacred music permitted. Small wonder that the 'most sensitive' of all German poets, the bard of the

Messias, was attracted to the text. His paraphrase, written in 1767 and published in 1771, was intended from the outset to be set to music and was sometimes printed as an explanatory text for performances of Pergolesi's setting. Klopstock replaced the quatrains of the original by freer stanzas of unequal length, varying between three and seven lines. For the most part, Schubert adhered to the poet's metrical scheme, but towards the end he omitted two quatrains.

It is clear that he was familiar with Pergolesi. Like the latter, he begins in F minor and ends in F major; he gives an added emphasis to two sections (1–7) (8–12) by ending them with fugal movements, and he mixes the archaic element, in the form of academic (though not entirely orthodox) fugues, with sections treated in freer style. And these 'free' sections are quite enchanting in their conciseness and simplicity, in their melodic splendour and in their harmony. The combinations of soloists and chorus, the subtle changes in the instrumentation, are unique in their exquisite charm and inventive power. Of the twelve numbers it is difficult to single out the best: a double chorus in G minor and a tenor aria in C minor; a bass aria *à la* Sarastro in E minor; a chorus in E major. The excessively 'conscientious' Amen-fugue is the only movement with which one might dispense. The problem of a subjective or objective approach in church-music becomes quite immaterial here; in religious devotion of this sort, every kind of direct approach to feeling and musical freedom is permissible.

Although it was not written at the same time, there is a spiritual affinity between this *Stabat Mater* and a setting for mixed chorus of Klopstock's Easter Hymn ('Uberwunden hat der Herr den Tod', XVII, 17). On the other hand, J. P. Uz's hymn 'An die Sonne' (XVII, 12), a rich and dignified piece of the same type, was definitely written in June 1816 about the same time as the *a cappela* setting of the angels' Easter Hymn from Goethe's *Faust* (XVII, 15). In this latter instance Schubert has written a setting perfectly suited to the requirements of the stage – which, of course, is sufficient reason why it is never used.

This should have brought us naturally back to the question of opera. But after the completely ineffectual activity of the previous year, Schubert was disheartened. We know of only one operatic venture during 1816 – a fragment at that, but at least a fragment which stopped not far short of completion: *Die Bürgschaft*, an opera in three acts (XV, 13). The practice of expanding Schiller's ballads into operas was nothing new. In his *Briefe eines aufmerksamen Reisendun*, J. Fr. Reichardt tells us on 8th January, 1809, of an opera by Conradin Kreutzer based on Schiller's 'Taucher'; and there are several other versions of *Die Bürgschaft*, including one by Schubert's friend Franz Lachner (1828). Schubert himself had set the ballad to music a year previously. The dramatic adaptation is ostensibly the work of 'an anonymous student', and we would suspect this student to have been the librettist of *Adrast* without further argument, if we were prepared to hold Mayrhofer responsible for such lines as those which occur at the opening of one of the choruses:

> *Es lebe, es lebe der meutrische Thor,*
> *Er ziere das Kreuz mit dem schönen Leib* . . .*

or in the middle section of one of the arias:

> *Feste gibt es heute wieder*
> *Bei dem König, an dem Hof,*
> *Uebermuth singt üpp' ge Lieder,*
> *Bei dem Prasser, zu dem Soff.* . . .†

Only two very young, inexperienced people could have conceived and carried out the idea of using as the basis for an opera for the Viennese stage Schiller's ballad about the conversion of a tyrant through the example of two friends' loyalty to each other. How utterly ingenuous to imagine that the story of an attempted assassination of a tyrant (and even a tyrant was still a potentate in the opinion of the Hapsburg censor), that an opera which opened with a chorus of subjects bemoaning their oppressed state, could possibly hope to be produced in the capital of the Emperor Francis! Schubert's belated realization of this fact probably explains why his manuscript was never completed.

---

* 'Long live the mutinous fool!
   Let his fair body adorn the cross. . . !'
† Today the king holds high revel again at his court. Wantonness sings licentious songs at the drunken orgy!

Yet, purely from the point of view of operatic technique, the anonymous student set about his task in no unskilful fashion. The first act, in two scenes, opens with a description of the oppressed condition of the Syracusans, and the broodings of the would-be assassin, Moeros. Then, in the midst of a general tumult, follows the unsuccessful attempt on the tyrant's life. Moeros requests that his friend, whose name is Theages, be held in custody as a hostage for his own return, and the scene ends with an aria for the tyrant, Dionys, in which he expresses his evil doubts: 'Ob er wohl wiederkehrt?' ('*Will* he come back?') The second scene takes us to Theages' home and introduces his wife and children. With the Finale comes the moment of farewell – the anguished wife, the prayers of the children, the two friends' expressions of mutual confidence, and in the background the warning voice of the guard urging them to make haste. The second act is divided between Moeros's adventures on his homeward journey and the despair of the hostage's waiting family. The third describes the mounting anxiety of the hostage himself as he languishes in prison. At this point the manuscript breaks off.

The music is partly cast in the same noble, classical mould as *Adrast*. If the model for the latter was Gluck, that for *Die Bürgschaft* is to be found in the somewhat tawdry French school of Gluck's imitators, although I cannot say for certain which example Schubert took. The orchestral 'descriptions' of the second act – Moeros's struggle with the elements, the thunderstorm and rushing torrent; the robbers' attack and Moeros's fight with them; blazing sun and gushing spring – this is all typical of Parisian Opéra-comique of the revolutionary period, imitated or rather taken over *en bloc* by an indescribably gifted composer, who does not paint artificial scenery but Nature herself. Sometimes, admittedly he tends to see Nature in the light of Gluck's Elysium, as for example in the oboe solo during the scene at the spring. In its mixture of the heroic and the emotional, the sentimental and the idyllic, almost all the rest is purely conventional, at least in its conception if not in its execution. But almost every number is striking and concise, which is something quite unusual. Perhaps the most striking are the choruses. One of these (No. 3, 'Wie dürster der Aetna') is not in a classical, but a brilliant, Sicilian style; the chorus which follows it is superbly descriptive of the rough, apathetic crowd. The quartet of robbers (No. 13) has the same flavour of simple, grotesque humour as a similar quartet in Verdi's *Macbeth*. Schubert often achieves the naïve simplicity of the latter, but without his powerful dramatic instinct.

In the songs of this year of indecision and disquiet, Schubert seems to have returned to his starting-point, to the pre-Goethe period of 1813 and 1814. They have all the appearance of a return in two senses – in the choice of texts and in the almost exclusive preference for the strophic song. But appearances are deceptive. For at the same time, this year marks Schubert's growing interest in the deeply philosophical poetry of his friend Johann Mayrhofer, and eventually leads back to Goethe, to 'An Schwager Kronos' and to the renewed interest in the *Wilhelm Meister* songs, on a more impressive level. And it was precisely this more intensive preoccupation with the strophic song which prepared the way. For the concentrated form of the strophic song necessitated a refinement of harmony, and it is this which was the real outcome of this year of apparent stagnation. He became not only richer as a composer, but he also became more sensitive in his relationship to the poet. He acquired a more delicate sense of appreciation for each one and for his individual peculiarities. It would otherwise be difficult to account for his returning again to the older generation of Klopstock, Uz, Stolberg, Matthisson and Salis, after having once experienced the spontaneity, warmth and greatness of Goethe's poetry. (Admittedly, he discovered and mastered the most delicate and charming of that older generation, Ludwig Heinrich Christian Hölty.) This does not mean that Schubert himself was any less warm, spontaneous and sincere than before. On the contrary the deepening and refinement of his harmony developed out of a profounder feeling for the spiritual content of the poems, and this profounder feeling in its turn was closely connected with all the human experiences and secret sorrows of his second year of schoolmastering.

SCHUBERT'S HARMONY

If, while we are discussing the songs of this year, we digress
for a moment on the subject of Schubert's harmony, it is
with the full knowledge that it is inseparable from his
melody and rhythm. But while it is perhaps sufficient to refer
to his melodic wealth and to his rhythmic methods and idio-
syncrasies as occasion demands and in specific detail, his
harmonic achievement was epoch-making not only in the
historical sense, in that he was the protagonist of what we
call the 'Romantic' Movement, but also because the living
expression of harmony belongs to the very essence of the
man himself.

Here, too, he followed old paths and at the same time
discovered new ones. He was, in fact, the 'Romantic Classicist'. He found in Mozart, his real predecessor in that direction, overwhelming beauties of sound and of harmonic
progression, and one can often put one's finger on the precise
context. One such example is to be found in the first movement (bars 57–63) of Mozart's so-called 'Hoffmeister' Quartet K.499, where the tension of a passage in F sharp minor
resolves itself into the felicity of a fourth/sixth (6/4) chord
of A major. Schubert imitated this frequently, but at the
same time 'sharpened' the effect by a chromatic descent in
the bass to the fundamental of the 6/4 chord – or, to keep to
our example, from F sharp by way of F natural to E. In
Beethoven he discovered – apart from many half-accidental
passages of harmony (if such things exist in Beethoven) – the
elementary interchange between minor and major, of which
the most impressive instance occurs in the Allegretto of the
Seventh Symphony. There is a characteristic example of the
profound impression made on him by one of Beethoven's
most euphonious movements. It is the Minuet from the
Piano Sonata in D major, op. X, 3. In the supplement to the
Collected Edition (XXI, 24) there appears a Minuet of Schubert's in A major, which originally belonged, without any
shadow of doubt, to the A minor Sonata of 1817 (X, 6).
Schubert rightly removed it from this work, since three
movements is the ideal form for a sonata which is relatively
modest in design, and because its inclusion would have advertised too clearly the Beethoven original on which it was

modelled. But in fullness of sound this little piece is far superior to Beethoven, both in the Minuet section and in the Trio. The fifth and ninth of a set of variations on a theme of Anselm Hüttenbrenner's (XI, 7), written in August 1817, will serve as a further example. From the rhythmic point of view they are an echo of the Allegretto from Beethoven's Seventh Symphony, but for the rest they depend entirely on harmony. One might almost say that in both instances the major mode opens like a flower in a tropical night. In his piano movements Schubert's writing is always as full as possible just as his quartet movements constantly tend towards an orchestral style (as Mandyczewski has already justly observed). In comparison with Schubert, Beethoven seems sparing of sheer sound as a piano composer, and sketchy and dry as a writer of quartets. Take another A major work, the Finale of the A minor Quartet op. 29 which, for all its Hungarian colour, has a mysterious affinity with the quartet movement of Mozart's mentioned above. The triplet runs which precede the recapitulation are finally concentrated into compact *harmonic* masses of a completely novel kind:

One of the greatest miracles of harmony in Schubert, universally known and frequently imitated since 1865 – for example, by Brahms in the slow movement of his First Symphony – is the second subject in the 'Andante con moto' of the 'Unfinished'. We start in the relative minor of E major, in C sharp minor, but proceed to modulate, over a background of shifting rhythm filled in with a harmonic texture of suspensions and retardations, by way of D and D flat to F, D minor and A back to our starting-point of C sharp minor, which in its turn becomes D flat major when the oboe answers the clarinet's enchanting melody. The whole seems not to have been consciously thought out but simply to have *happened,* to have grown out of the depths of despair and happiness. Yet Schubert knew exactly what he was doing.

Up to this point we have mentioned only instrumental works, and the few examples we have given could be multiplied many times over. But it is in his songs that Schubert's harmonic invention really reveals itself, when the text guides his imaginative powers irresistibly into completely new channels. It has been said with some justification that, as a harmonist, Schubert is not only richer in his songs than in his instrumental music, but a fundamentally different person. Nor is this fact contradicted by the mysterious affinity that exists between many of his instrumental works and songs. In his instrumental music, a movement or a cyclic work always ends in the tonic, no matter how remote the key relationship of the individual movements may be, as, for example, in the B flat major Piano Sonata with its slow movement in C sharp minor. But there are dozens of songs – quite apart from the long ballads and the Ossianic lays – which do not return to the key in which they start. Sometimes – and particularly during the period with which this digression deals – Schubert was frightened by his own boldness. In September 1816 he set J. G. Jacobi's 'Lied des Orpheus, als er in die Hölle ging' (XX, 250a). He begins in G flat major and ends in D major. The Thracian singer's appeal to the Underworld takes the form of a kind of arioso with an enchanting second section in C sharp minor, and the song ends with a *stretta* that achieves two separate climaxes. The second version (XX 250b), however, is infinitely weaker since Schubert transposes this second section into F sharp minor, and modulates to the chord of G major before B flat, instead of G major before D major.

But such second thoughts are rare. Take, as an example from this period, the setting of Fr. L. v. Stolberg's 'Stimme der Liebe' (XX, 210), written in April 1816. It is one of those songs which cannot do themselves justice in the fullness of their accompaniment – in this case, resonant chords in triplets – and which build up to a climax from *pp* to *ff,* only to die away again. It begins like an ultra-romantic symphony with a bare, suspended chord, the third and fifth of the D major triad, and the entry of the bass of the accompaniment no less indeterminate. But after two bars of the voice-part we find ourselves in E flat, after eight in D flat, and after eleven, by enharmonic modulation, in C sharp minor. The return to D major is – to use a paradox – dictated by the same natural force. The exuberance of the poem, which is in itself absurd, is – if we may borrow a Wagnerian expression – 'redeemed' by the music, and is transformed into something true and genuine.

Another example of harmonic exuberance from this period (April 1816) is the A flat ending (the beginning is in F minor), of A. W. Schlegel's 'Die verfehlte Stunde' (XX, 206). Here, both the chromaticism and the use of the 6/4 chord are typical:

The sharp distinction between keys becomes more marked, as for example in the short prelude to Hölty's 'Auf den Tod einer Nachtigall' (XX, 218), written on 13th May, 1816:

Or take another prelude, this time to 'Der Harfenspieler, II' (XX, 255a), in its original form of September 1816 in which we are not far removed from another, more famous prelude:

It must not be thought that these are all spontaneous discoveries, like that of a child who finds a rare flower, for
which botanists have long hunted in vain. Again, Schubert
knew what he was doing. Sometimes his sense of humour
betrays itself. In September 1816 he set to music Mayrhofer's 'Alte Liebe rostet nie' (XX, 253). The 'old love' that
never grows rusty is Mozart, and as its symbol he uses
Mozart's favourite 'motto' phrase:

It was during this year of the concentrated strophic song that
Schubert 'found' himself as a harmonist; his 'discoveries'
naturally increased in number during his later years, and
would provide endless examples. We will merely mention
the extraordinary progression of chords in 'Prometheus'
(XX, 370: 'Hat mich nicht zum Manne geschmiedet'), while
there is a further example from one of the ecstatic Novalis
songs (XX, 372: 'Nachthymne') which we will take the liberty of quoting:

When he wishes to illustrate a fleeting image such as the 'war-bling birds' in 'Die gefangenen Sänger' (XX, 389) or the 'crowing cock' in 'Frühlingstraum' from *Die Winterreise*, he does not shrink from a glaring discord:

This brings us to what might be called the problem of Schubert's 'key characteristic'. In considering it, we must naturally discount all those cases in which Schubert himself changed the original key or allowed it to be changed for external reasons. The best-known example is the Impromptu in G flat major, op. 90, 3, which was published in G major, with a different time-signature into the bargain. It is difficult to say why Schubert himself transposed the Sonata, published as op. 122, from D flat major (XXI, 9) to E flat major (X, 7); once anyone has played the Andante (Andante molto) in C sharp, he will never want to play it in G minor again. With his songs, the reasons for transposing them are easier to understand: for the most part, publishers or singers found them pitched too high. The modulations from G flat to D flat in the original version of Mayrhofer's 'Iphigenia' (XX, 325), written in July 1817, became F to C in the publisher's transposition. The original setting of Schiller's 'Thekla' (XX, 334) is in C sharp, the published version in C. On the other hand there seems to have been an internal reason which influenced Schubert to alter the E major of Mayrhofer's 'Alpenjäger' (XX, 295) to F major for purposes of publication, for F Major is the pastoral key.

Be that as it may, one must admit that Schubert's range of keys is infinitely richer than that of any earlier or contemporary composer, and that it is not only richer but also quite different. This richness makes it more complicated to lay down 'categories' as one can always do in the case of Mozart, Haydn and Beethoven. Here, too, a distinction must be drawn between the instrumental works and the songs. In his symphonies, overtures, quartets and sonatas, Schubert apparently keeps within the pattern set by Beethoven. Admittedly there is an 'unfinished' in B minor, but no piano sonata in F sharp major and no string quartet in C sharp minor. The greater freedom of modulation certainly invests Schubert's keys with a more variegated, kaleidoscopic, iridescent quality than those of any of the three classicists. But in the songs one seems to be able to detect a system governing the choice of key. The Ossian songs and the long ballads are probably most qualified to follow this system, and it is this very fact which prompts one to note once more how far the key of Schubert's 'emotional' choice is forced off its straight course by his pictorial or descriptive urge. But this urge is itself for the most part 'emotional'. We will again choose an example from the present period; Ossian's 'Der Tod Oscar's' written in February 1816 (XX, 187). It begins in C minor and ends in E flat major (consequently, with the same key-signature), and in keeping with the gloomy nature of the poem, the main body of the song moves in the region of B flat. But with the description of Dargo's daughter – 'lovely as the morning, gentle as the glow of evening' – we find ourselves in B flat major, and with a youth's declaration of his passionate and hopeless love, in E major. A duel is fought in C minor; a self-accusation is in A flat.

The very fullness of this system invests each harmonic change with a fresh clarity. Naturally enough, in his youthful period, Schubert is more extreme in his choice of key and in his modulations than during his later years. One can practically determine the degree of subjectivity of song from its key. 'Heidenröslein', which is a short ballad, is in G major; Claudius's 'Am Grabe Anselmo's' (XX, 275), a most intimate and personal expression of feeling, in E flat minor. An extreme case is the chorus for four male voices, 'Der Entfernten' (XVI, 38), which is in C sharp major. The poet, Salis, tells of a vision of his loved one which hovers over him 'in the deep gold of morning, in the rosy light of evening'. Schubert insists on reproducing this ecstatic colouring, even though he creates difficulties for the singers in so doing. Yet how simple are the choice and sequence of keys in *Die schöne Müllerin* or *Die Winterreise*! (They are at the same time extremely free.) Nor should they be altered, just as the individual songs should always be entrusted to the proper voices for which they were intended. It does not greatly matter whether a soprano or a tenor sings them. But an alto song is an *alto* song, and a bass song can be sung only by a *bass*. Those who do not know Schubert's songs in their original keys and registers, and have not heard them performed by the voices for which they were intended, know them only partially. And no singer really knows them who treats them merely as vocal exercises.

But to return to the songs of this year. Although we said earlier that they seem to represent a return to the strophic song and to the poets of the sentimental, Anacreontic school, we must emphasize once again that it is a return on a higher level. And Schubert has not only become more sensitive in his harmony. His renewed and heightened simplicity is different from that of his predecessors. Of all the many possible comparisons, we will choose 'Daphne am Bach', written in April 1816 (XX, 209) to a text by Stolberg, and already set by Zumsteeg in 1783. In their simplicity the two songs look exactly alike. But Zumsteeg heads his setting 'Im Volkston' – a direction with which Schubert dispenses, since he never imitates the folk-song manner. Zumsteeg does not give a separate line to the voice. Voice-part and right hand of the accompaniment are almost identical. The 'Brook' is missing; in Schubert's setting it is present and sets the scene for all four verses. Zumsteeg ends each couplet with a meaningless flourish in the bass. Schubert repeats the last line and adds a charming postlude. The difference is as imperceptible as it is infinite. There is something paradoxical in the fact that only a few weeks earlier, on 13th March, he had written a second setting of Schiller's 'Ritter Toggenburg' (XX, 191) based on Zumsteeg's, in which he followed his model as slavishly as a child traces a drawing.

Another mark of refinement is his new feeling for the conventional limitations which governed this sentimental poetry of an older generation – poetry, moreover, which had just received its *coup de grâce* at the hands of Goethe. He is never archaic, as Mozart was to some extent in his humorous parody of Hagedorn's 'Die Alte'. He still has a real affection for this sentimental or cheerful poetry. He even set to music a few of the 'occupational songs' which were fashionable around 1780, such as Salis's 'Pflügerlied' (XX, 197) and 'Fischerlied' (XX, 204) or Hölty's 'Erntelied' (XX, 226). This latter, especially, is a little masterpiece. Yet it is no longer an 'Arbeitslied' designed for a particular purpose, but a song raised to the highest level of art. Perhaps the best example of his new approach to these poems is 'Die Liebes-götter' (XX, 231) by J. P. Uz, a poet to whom the young Mozart had already been attracted:

> *Cypris, meiner Phyllis gleich,*
> *Sass, von Grazien umgeben. . . .**

It is Anacreontic doggerel, full of pastoral conceits, and Schubert set it as such – not as a parody of the eighteenth century, but with the most delicate feeling for the musical graces of a past age. Of all these songs, the best known or perhaps the *only* well-known example is Hölty's 'Seligkeit (XX,) which is widely favoured as a short and safe encore by sopranos with a 'roguish' sense of humour. But Schubert heads it 'lustig'. It is a simple little waltz – not a Viennese, but a Schubertian waltz. Once again we are forcibly re-minded how little Schubert is capable of being classified as a 'Viennese composer'. Again, is he 'Viennese' in his songs – in that field where he is at his most independent? One would like to know what there is Viennese about 'Erlkönig', *Die Winterreise* or the Suleika songs.

But it would be far from true to say that he was exclus-ively preoccupied with the strophic song, even during this year. His setting of a psalm-like hymn by Uz, 'Der gute Hirte' (XX, 234), is treated in the style of a cantata and

* Cypris, like my Phyllis, was sitting, surrounded by Graces. . . .

reminds one of Beethoven's 'Adelaide'. The Ossianic songs
'Der Flüchtling' (XX, 192) and a fragment called 'Lorma'
(XX, 592) are *durchcomponiert*, as are Schiller's 'Laura am
Clavier' (XX, 193) and Klopstock's 'Edone' (XX, 230),
which Mozart had earlier parodied, but which becomes
in Schubert's hands an absolute masterpiece of melodic line.
The settings of Mayrhofer's poems, on whom he concentrated his full attention for the first time, are also *durchcomponiert*. At the end of 1815 he had tackled a ballad
entitled 'Die drei Sänger' (XX, 591) – a kind of song-con-
test, the anonymous author of which was probably Mayrhofer; but in September 1816 he set Mayrhofer's
'Liedesend' (XX, 249), a somewhat sentimental ballad of a
very similar type, in the echo-song 'Abschied' (XX, 251),
'Rückweg' (XX, 252) – a strange complaint since 'the road
home' leads to 'dreaded and hated Vienna'! – and the little
strophic song about the 'old love', mentioned above. And
Mayrhofer led him back to Goethe. For there then followed
new settings of the Harper and Mignon songs from *Wilhelm
Meister*. Schubert not only *regarded* these settings as final
and published some of them as op. 12. They *are*, in fact,
final. He had already written a simple, lyrical setting of 'Wer
sich der Einsamkeit ergibt' (XX, 173) in November 1815. In
the meantime he had read the novel again, and he now
understood not only the character but also the situation. He
now grasped the sinister significance of the phrase—

> *Es schleicht ein Liebender lauschend sacht*
> *Ob seine Freundin allein. . . .**

in other words, whether she is in the company of another
lover. This phrase has been completely misunderstood by
every other composer of the song. In 'Wer nie sein Brot mit
Tränen ass' (XX, 256) he makes of the indictment of the
godhead something horrible though without pathos. All
these songs, even the 'Tristan-like' setting of 'An die Türen
will ich schleichen' (XX, 255) mentioned earlier, are in A
minor, and in this last and saddest of them the harp-effects of
the first two disappear. This is Schubert's first great song-
cycle.

It was followed by two of the five existing settings of one
of the Mignon songs, 'Nur wer die Sehnsucht kennt' (XX, 259,

*A lover comes stealthily, listening to discover if his lady is alone. . . .

260) to which we shall return later; then came 'Der König
in Thule' (XX, 261) and 'Jäger's Abendlied' (XX, 262).
Both are strophic in form and the latter, in particular, can
only be properly understood if the singer concentrates on the
last verse. To this September there also belongs a fragment
(XX, 594) from Goethe's 'Gesang der Geister über den
Wassern', the only *song*-setting of this 'highly symbolical'
poem, which so occupied Schubert as a composer of choral
music. It was followed, however, by 'An Schwager Kronos'
(XX, 263) in which Schubert reached the second culminating point of his artistic achievement. He himself was
perfectly aware of this. In June 1825 he published the song
as op. 19, together with 'An Mignon' (XX, 48) and 'Ganymed' (XX, 311) and dedicated them 'to the poet, in respectful admiration', although once again without any result.
'Schwager' was the early nineteenth-century name for a pos-
tillion; 'Schwager Kronos' (not Chronos) is the demon-pos-
tillion on the journey through this world of a reckless
adventurer who, having tasted life to the full, determines to
drive triumphantly out into the night, even though it be the
night of Hell. Schubert's imaginative power and unity of
purpose in handling the changing imagery, and the delicacy
of feeling which underlies the passionate ardour of his conception are unique. The song was far beyond the capabilities
of the singers of that time. It is, in fact, 'timeless'. Schober-
lechner, it is true, sang it in public on 11th January, 1827, at
a meeting of the Society of Friends of Music, but there is no
known contemporary review either of this concert or of the
song's first publication. Mayrhofer probably understood it.
It was about this time that he wrote his apostrophe 'to Franz
Schubert' under the title of 'Geheimnis:

>   *Sag an, wer lehrt dich Lieder, so schmeichelnd und so*
> *zart?*
>   *Sie rufen einen Himmel aus trüber Gegenwart. . . .*
>   *Den schilfbekränzten Alten, der seine Urne giesst,*
>   *Erblickst du nicht, nur Wasser, wie's durch die Wiesen*
> *fliesst.*
>   *So geht es auch dem Sänger, er singt, er staunt in sich;*
>   *Was still ein Gott bereitet, befremdet ihn wie dich.**

---

*Say then, who teaches thee songs, so caressing and so tender? They
call forth a Heaven out of the clouded present. Thou see'st not the

It was the unconscious simplicity, the divine spark in his friend that – rightly and wrongly – astonished Mayrhofer. Schubert accepted his tribute, in so far as he set it to music in October 1816 (XX, 269) in his freest style and full of melodic and harmonic symbolism, beginning in B flat major and ending in F major. Some months later he set two verses of 'An die Musik' (XX, 314), a more 'objective song of thanksgiving, by another friend, Franz v. Schober, 'to music', that is to say, 'which leads to a better world' and opens the way to 'better times' for Schubert and his friends. The setting is simple and exquisite with prelude and postlude and symbolical imitations between the voice-part and the bass of the accompaniment. It has been regarded as a 'motto' for all Schubert's music and used accordingly. But music meant much more to Schubert. It is probable that the setting in D minor of Schober's 'Trost im Liede' (XX, 313) which was composed about the same time, with its emphasis on the intimate relationship between sorrow and happiness and with its dissonances, expresses Schubert's attitude to music much more faithfully than the other somewhat 'homely' thanksgiving-song in D major.

---

ancient one with his crown of reeds who pours out his urn; thou see'st only water, as it flows through the meadows. So is it with the singer, too. He sings and marvels to himself. The silent handiwork of the gods amazes him and thee alike.

Chapter Seven

Freedom: the Return to the Piano
The Italian Style

Autumn 1816–Autumn 1818

In December 1816 Schubert twice recorded on the manuscript of a pair of songs ('Lebenslied' and 'Leiden der Trennung', XX, 284 and 285) the comment: 'At Herr v. Schober's lodgings' just as Mozart had earlier noted on the manuscript of one of his songs (K. 520): 'In Herr Gottfried von Jacquin's apartment in Landstrasse'. But Schubert's remark indicates a different, less fortuitous circumstance. Schober had recently returned from a visit to Sweden and had taken lodgings in the Landskrongasse, where Schubert had joined him, perhaps only temporarily for the Christmas holidays. 'It looks, however, as though he had already at that time escaped from his teaching duties and had found his first refuge here, from the autumn of 1816 to the autumn of 1817'*

It was a decisive step. It has already been said elsewhere that Schubert was the first 'free' composer of the nineteenth century after Beethoven who had paved the way, and in a different sense from Beethoven. He still composed 'occasional' works, but he no longer wrote to order. Beethoven's *Missa Solemnis* had been a commissioned work; Schubert's last two Masses were the outcome of the same spiritual impulse which inspired his songs and quartets, though they were probably also written with an eye to practical use. He no longer depended on patrons but on publishers – a tragic dependence, to which we shall have to devote particular attention in due course. The spiritual urge to write in complete freedom became so irresistible that, in spite of violent opposition from his father, he cast off every shackle of middle-class security. But since he was not a dis-

*O. E. Deutsch, op. cit., p. 73.

tinguished writer like Beethoven and did not share Beethoven's characteristic rudeness, he became a Bohemian and remained one to the end of his life, in spite of several attempts to find a middle-class retreat as a conductor or a music director or an assistant Kapellmeister. We will not commiserate with him. He would have been miserable in any post. At least the knowledge that he was a free agent must have made him happy, even though he paid a high price for his freedom.

Hand in hand with the dissociation from his middle-class environment went a growing sense of artistic responsibility towards himself. That is the reason why he turned once more to the piano sonata which Beethoven, whom he secretly admired and secretly feared, had raised to such a pinnacle of achievement. And it is as if he had wanted to contradict his plaintive conviction: 'After Beethoven, who can do anything more?' He *had* to do something different from Beethoven. While the year 1816 had produced only a number of lesser piano pieces and dances and the three innocent sonatas for violin and piano, Schubert returned in the spring and summer of 1817 to wrestle once more with the cyclic form, with the sonata, with the *piano* sonata, pure and simple. This can only be explained as a deliberate effort on the part of the twenty-one-year-old Schubert to symbolize his coming of age.

We will take first of all the four completed works; a sonata in B major, written in August (X, 5), and published by Diabelli as op. 147 with a dedication to the virtuoso Thalberg (1843); a somewhat later sonata in A minor (X, 6), written, however, in March, according to the manuscript, and published as op. 164; one in E major (XI, 14, No. II–V – here the Collected Edition is extremely confusing), and one in E flat major which was certainly composed after June 1817 – *after* June, since an earlier sonata in D flat major (XXI, 9), which has already been mentioned and which is complete except for the Minuet and the conclusion of the Rondo, bears this date.

Before and between these four works, however, a number of extremely interesting experiments were written. From May there dates a sonata in A flat major (V, 3) which lacks the Finale, unless one prefers to accept that Schubert simply forgot to transpose the final movement in E flat major into

the tonic. There is also a sonata in E minor (June), of which
only the first movement is to be found in the Collected Edition (X, 4). The slow movement, an Allegretto, was published by Erich Prieger and the Scherzo (A flat major)
appeared in *Die Musik* (XXI, 1, 1928);* finally there is the
fragment of a first movement in F sharp minor (XXI, 10),
written in July 1817.

The A flat major Sonata is very immature and contents
itself with the dimensions and breathes the spirit of a Haydn
piano sonata. Above all Schubert avoids competing with
Beethoven. One might say that this sonata was written after
playing Haydn's works or under the influence of them. This
is clearly illustrated in the Andante, which is a modified
version of a famous symphonic idea of Haydn's.

It adds, however, a parenthetical section of its own in the
minor which bears a genuinely Schubertian stamp. In spite
of the influence of Haydn, the piece is so Schubertian and so
perfect that the composer could have included it among his
Impromptus or Moments musicaux, and if it bore no date,
there is not a single musicologist who would be able to place
it in its chronological context. This is what is doubly miraculous about Schubert; he could yield to a strong influence
with a completely feminine lack of concern yet without
losing his own individuality; and even in his youth he could
contrive a masterpiece in conventional form, which has the
appearance of having fallen from Heaven. What makes the
E flat Finale (if it is a Finale) that follows so remarkable is

* In the meantime (1949) the whole sonata (i.e., the first three movements to which, quite arbitrarily, the Adagio and Rondo of op. 145 are
added) has been published: British & Continental Music Agencies Ltd.,
London; edited by Kathleen Dale.

the fact that it states and varies a typical Schubertian Rondo subject, in 6/8 time. It is not in fact a Rondo, but is constructed in sonata form.

Schubert himself apparently attached particular value to the first movement of the Sonata in E minor, for he wrote it out twice, with very slight variants. It is easy to understand why. The movement is not merely short, but also concentrated. Here, in this sequence of blossoming musical ideas, so lovely in the very nature of their existence that one accepts them without asking whence they come, Schubert achieved his early sonata ideal. It is true that another composer would have speculated quite differently from Schubert with this melodic 'capital', which again and again passes gradually from the heroic to the lyrical or alternates between the two in sharp contrast; but it depends entirely whether one chooses to be disappointed by this uninvested wealth, or prefers to accept Schubert at his face value. The Allegretto in E major is followed by a Minuet in A flat major – a most unusual key, since Schubert generally chooses a more closely related key for his Minuets. There are admittedly other comparable instances, such as the Scherzo (E major) in an unfinished F minor sonata (XXI, 12). It is a very serious and extended Minuet, so serious that one could well take it to be the Finale of a sonata in A flat major. Finally there dates from July 1817 the above-mentioned fragment of a highly promising first movement of a sonata in F sharp minor (XXI, 10), full of pianistic delicacy such as the Barcarolle theme of the opening. Schubert accentuates the development section not by any thematic tension, but by a darkening of the modulations. We travel from C sharp major to C flat minor. This is the 'Romantic' Schubert, who avoids the discursive, dramatic conflict of themes and takes refuge instead in a mysterious abyss of harmony. Here too one must either apply to Schubert the sort of criticisms Beethoven would have made, or accept him heart and soul as he is. This fragment is without any doubt the immediate forerunner of another sonata in the same key (XXI, 20), the first movement of which he also left unfinished, though in a more advanced state. The Scherzo, however, was completed. Both the unfinished first movement and the Scherzo are utterly lovely and enchanting.

Before we discuss the four completed sonatas of the summer of 1817, Schubert's first piano works in cyclic form (for the experiments of 1815 were never carried beyond a fragmentary stage), we should first perhaps have a clear idea in our minds of what the word 'cyclic' means in relation to his sonatas. This involves the question of unity in a work of several movements, and it is therefore important to note that of these four sonatas, three have four movements, and one – the Sonata in A minor – only three.

We are faced by a difficult problem. Who can determine with any certainty the germ of such a work? Who can say which movement was written first? Who can prove that the specific character of such a germ has inevitably determined the form and content of the whole work? One treads cautiously and uncertainly, and thinks, for example, of Beethoven's 'Waldstein' Sonata, the middle movement of which was originally a broadly constructed 'Andante favori'; or of the Kreutzer Sonata, the Finale of which was taken from the Violin Sonata op. 30, 1 – 'because it is too brilliant for this sonata'. Beethoven, of course, was perfectly right, particularly in the case of the 'Waldstein' Sonata, and succeeded in strengthening the unity of this work. But we would of necessity accept it without demur, if he had retained his 'Andante favori', ended his op. 30, 1, with the Finale of the 'Kreutzer' Sonata and written for the latter a new Finale more in keeping with the incomparable first movement. Nevertheless, his alterations prove that he had in mind a spiritual and stylistic balance between the individual movements, a balance of which we are immediately conscious and which we immediately acknowledge. But the unity of a cyclic work can only be 'proved' when there is a thematic relationship between the individual movements. Schubert has something of this sort in mind in his A minor Sonata when he varies a harmonic idea from the major in the first movement to the minor in the third movement:

It is quite possible, however, that this is accidental, or unintentional, an instinctive passion for a particular nuance, a passion with which every composer is familiar. For elsewhere, in Schubert's early works, the relationship between movements is more tenuous than it is in the works of the 'classical' masters, though it is almost always justified by an instinctive feeling. The older he grew, the more this changed, as we shall see in due course, particularly when we come to consider such works as the E flat major Trio or the great C major Symphony.

However uncertain we may be about the germ of a cyclic work, the fact remains that the character of the whole is usually determined by the character of the first movement. A distinctive feature of these four sonatas – and of Schubert's music in general – is the moderate tempo in each of them; twice 'Allegro non troppo', once 'Allegro moderato', and once, it is true, 'Allegro', but for a movement which would lose its lyrical quality if it were in a really quick tempo. Throughout the whole of Beethoven's piano works, the expression 'moderato' never once occurs.

'Lyrical quality' – therein lies the answer. The musical propositions which Schubert usually states in that section of the sonata movement which we call the 'exposition' are all lyrical. And consequently they require no 'trial of heart and reins' in the form of a strict development. To resolve them into their thematic components would result not in their intensification but in their destruction. It is usually sufficient to lead them along a few byways of modulation and to surrender them to that impulse towards the major with which Schubert is utterly absorbed, as a lover is absorbed with the desire to see his beloved again. The length of a first movement, such as that in the A minor Sonata, is the result not so much of a particularly rich development section as of a repetition of *both* sections (which embrace the development).

A first movement of this kind does not need the counterbalance of a Finale, which 'resolves every conflict'. In three instances they are movements in sonata form; the fourth is a Rondo. But this particular Rondo (in A minor) is more passionate and more serious than the movements in sonata form. Even though the Finale of the E major Sonata bears the title 'Allegro patetico', it still leaves us on a note of exuberant triumph. And between first and last movements of this kind there is no need for long, heavy, profound Adagios. Schubert writes Andantes, and when he in fact heads the slow movement of the E major Sonata 'Adagio', it is simply an oversight. These Andantes are all extended songs, in which melody, harmony and sound spring from a state of spiritual happiness. There is no model for the harmonic exuberance of the Andante (in E major) of the B minor Sonata and the only counterparts are to be found in Schubert's own music. And only in Schubert's own Impromptus are there counterparts to the 'Allegretto quasi Andantino' of the A minor Sonata which is a modification, in E major, of one of Schubert's favourite musical ideas.

The three Minuets, two of which are marked 'Scherzo', spring from the same source as the slow movements. The pearl among them is that from the E major Sonata which, with its comical obeisances and with the addition of the title 'Pierrot', would not disgrace Schumann's *Carnaval*. Another of the Trios, that in the Minuet of the E flat major Sonata, proves that there is here a direct relationship with the living dance. It appears note for note among the Schubert's Dance Minuets (XI, p. 196). Here we have another distinctive feature of his sonatas: he introduces genuine dances into them which is something that Beethoven never did and never would have done. Admittedly we find in the latter such things as the good-humoured parody of an old-fashioned Minuet in the Eighth Symphony, and a movement in one of the last string quartets with the direction 'alla danza tedesca'. But Beethoven stylized the 'traditional' spirit. He was a Viennese by adoption, while Schubert in his Minuets and Ländler was a genuine one. (That much we concede.)

None of these sonatas contain Variations either as middle movements or Finales. With regard to the use of Variations as Finales, Schubert, unlike Mozart or Beethoven, generally speaking considered them to be no longer a suitable form for the purpose. Instead, in August 1817 he wrote thirteen Variations on a theme from a string quartet op. 3 by his friend Anselm Hüttenbrenner (XI, 7) – a theme, as we have already mentioned, which was modelled on the slow movement of Beethoven's Seventh Symphony. These Variations alternate between A minor and A major and are full of remarkable harmonic effects (a particular case in point is the Variation in F sharp minor); some are more melodically inclined, but unfortunately the conclusion lacks a final climax. In November he wrote two Scherzi in B flat major (XI, 15) which are too elaborated for inclusion in a sonata. The latter may originally have belonged to the E flat major Sonata, op. 122 (since it uses as a Trio the Trio from the Minuet of this sonata), and have been removed by Schubert at a later date. The first Scherzo has a typically South-German sense of humour and a leisurely and distinctive charm; the second, alternating between D flat major and E major in the main section, is full of underlying restlessness and passion with which the pure 'Minuet' character of the Trio (in A flat major) contrasts very happily. If these two Scherzi were included among the Impromptus or Moments musicals (why not keep to Schubert's inaccurate French!), they would be universally familiar.

There is no basis for comparison, either, between the three earlier sonatas or sonatinas and a Sonata for violin and piano in A major (VIII, 6), which was written in August 1817 and published as op. 162. It is 'sociable' like all Schubert's (and not only Schubert's) chamber-music works in which the piano figures, although the sociable mood later reaches the point of virtuosity. And a slight, purely superficial tendency towards virtuosity is already noticeable here. But Schubert's growing sense of responsibility is reflected in the fact that in the first and last movements he does not 'relax' when he reaches the recapitulation nor, as a result, in the development sections either. The Scherzo is a genuine, sparkling Scherzo (in E major, 'presto'), and even the Finale has the character of a Scherzo. The slow movement, an Andantino in C major, is a little too light-weight, but it contains a mysterious middle section in A flat major ('dolce'). This is Schubert's last contribution in the sphere of violin and piano sonatas. Later he either wrote technically more ambitious music for both instruments in the form of the Rondo or the Fantasia, or he wrote for a larger combination.

In the year 1817 there appeared three overtures. The first in D major (11, 4) was written in May, and is scored for full orchestra, including side-drums but curiously enough without trumpets. It has a most unusual Introduction – not the normal Adagio, but an 'Allegro maestoso' and an 'Andante sostenuto'. It is as if a curtain were suddenly raised to reveal an unexpected scene painted in pastoral, idyllic colours. Even the 'Allegro vivace' which follows is unusual; the clarinet seeks to establish this pastoral atmosphere, though not without the peace and tranquillity being disturbed once more by the return of the noisy clamour of the Introduction. In spite of its concise form, the work is more a potpourri than an overture, with delightful melodic alarums and excursions; before the noisy ending, the 'Andante sostenuto' returns once more in a broader and richer treatment. One could not find a more perfect introduction for one of Ferdinand Raimund's fairy plays than this overture.

But at any rate it is still a 'German' overture in contrast to its two later companions 'in the Italian style'. Both bear this specific title, although it is only in the second of the two that we can be certain that the title was of Schubert's own making. In the Italian style? That seems to contradict our view that Schubert had grown more 'serious', more responsible, more conscious of himself, for in the eyes of many German composers the Italian style was synonymous with facile invention, with superficiality and with seductive or coarse sensuality. But Schubert's inclination towards this style only proves his independence, and the fact that he approached purely artistic problems without any consideration of the moral or nationalistic issues involved. The forbidden style attracted him; he liked it, although his sense of humour was strong, enough for him to realize that he himself was far superior to it.

Now, the style which attracted him in 1817 was not the one in which he had been educated by Salieri and in which he had written his academic exercises. On the contrary it was a new – one might almost say, a racy – style, although this 'racy' quality was simply the personal speciality of one man: Gioacchino Rossini of Pesaro.

ROSSINI

Vienna quickly got to know Rossini. The acquaintanceship began at the end of November 1816 with the one-act opera *L'inganno felice*. One month later, on 27th December, there followed *Tancredi* in the original Italian (in German on 12th March, 1818); on 15th February, 1817, *L'Italiana in Algeri* (in German in January 1821); in June, *Ciro in Babilonia*, followed, in September 1818, by *Elisabetta; Il Barbiere di Siviglia,* in German at the end of September 1819 and in Italian in April 1823; in March 1820 *Il Turco in Italia*. It was a regular invasion.

We know how the real victims of this invasion, the German composers, reacted to it. When later the Rossini mania reached its climax, between 1821 and 1825, under the aegis of Domenico Barbaja, Beethoven was unsparing in his caustic comments on the Viennese public. At the same time he was by no means disposed to underestimate Rossini, as witness a conversation of his with the Breslau music-teacher Karl Gottlieb Freudenberg (1825): 'I rather imagined that Beethoven would scoff at Rossini, who was the idol of Vienna at that time. But not a bit of it. He conceded that Rossini was a talented and melodious composer, that his music was in keeping with the frivolous, sensual spirit of the times, and that his output was so prolific that he could write an opera in as many weeks as it took the Germans years.' In the case of Carl Maria Weber, the reaction took the form of violent hostility on national grounds – not so much against Rossini as against the most powerful representative of the pompous new *opera seria*, Spontini. We know that *Freischütz*, performed in 1821, was accepted as a specifically 'German' opera, at least by Weber's supporters, and that Weber himself carried his German *opera seria, Euryanthe*, right into the enemy's camp by getting Barbaja, of all people, to produce it in Vienna. The most amusing evidence of antagonism towards Rossini is to be found in the diary of Louis Spohr, who became acquainted with this new, revolutionary style about the same time as Schubert – in other words, at the end of 1816. During his journey to Italy, he heard *L'Italiana in Algeri* in Florence, and this is what he had to say about it:

This opera . . . did not entirely come up to my expectations. In the first place it lacks what all other Italian music lacks—namely, purity of style, delineation of the characters, and reasonable calculation of the proper duration of music for the stage. I had not expected for one moment to find these qualities which are indispensable to any opera, if it is to be called 'classical', because one does not feel their absence in the slightest in an Italian opera. But I certainly did expect to find qualities which would distinguish Rossini's work from that of his colleagues, such as novelty of ideas, purity of harmony, and so forth; but here too I did not find much. What strikes the Italians as novel in Rossini's operas is not new to us, since it consists for the most part of ideas and modulations which have long been common currency in Germany. Equally, one looks in vain for purity of harmony in Rossini, as in every other modern Italian composer. But in his observance of rhythm and in his full use of the orchestra he distinguishes himself from his fellow-countrymen.

Later, in Rome, when he had made himself more fully conversant with Rossini's style, he criticized his 'flowery melodies', his *parlando* in staccato recitative-style, his orchestral crescendi and stretti. He summed it up thus:

My final verdict on Rossini amounts to this. He certainly does not lack imagination and spirit, and with these qualities he could easily have become one of the most outstanding vocal composers of our time, if he had been methodically instructed in Germany and guided on to the one and only right path through the medium of Mozart's classical masterpieces. But if he continues to write as he does now, he will not advance Italian music by one single step. In fact he is more likely to bring it low.

Schubert was far removed from this kind of bad-tempered criticism. Naturally enough he, too, saw the comic side of highly emotional recitative and the exaggerated pathos of Italian opera and made fun of them. In January 1822 Matthaeus v. Collin, to whom Schubert had been introduced by Spaun, wrote a reproachful letter in verse ('Und nimmer schreibst Du?') to his poor correspondent of a friend in Linz, and invited Schubert to set it to music. This Schubert proceeded to do (XX, 588) in the form of a recitative and aria in the most exaggerated burlesque style – 'Allegro furioso', with wild figures, unison passages, terrifying *tremoli*, a vocal cadenza, and an aria in C minor which modulates to the major and does not shirk even a high C for good measure. The parody is so good that it almost ceases to be a caricature. Schubert enjoyed himself in this style. We know that he heard a performance of *Tancredi*; in May 1819 he heard *Otello*, and wrote to Anselm Hüttenbrenner on the 19th: 'This opera is far better, that is to say more characteristic, than *Tancredi*. You cannot deny that he (Rossini) has extraordinary genius. The orchestration is highly original at times, and so, occasionally, is the vocal writing, except for the usual Italian gallopades and several reminiscences of *Tancredi*.' Extraordinary genius! There must obviously have been heated discussions among his friends as to Rossini's merits and demerits, and, as was his usual practice, Schubert the composer took the line of least resistance. From now on he absorbed the Italian idiom with more conscious emphasis into his own musical vocabulary, where previously he had already used it in simpler form, as, for example, in the second subject of his early String Quartet in C major. He wrote, as we shall see, operas in the Italian style, canzonettas and *buffo* arias which are direct, and German 'Refrain-Lieder' which are indirect, imitations. The 'Italian' idioms recur right up to the last, as, for example, in the much-criticized passage in the slow movement of his F minor Fantasia for four hands. And there is much that is accepted as purely Schubertian which would be better described as pseudo-Rossini.

The first 'Italian Overture', in D major (II, 5), begins with a world-famous introductory Adagio which Schubert used again for his *Rosamunde* Overture. Everything about it is Italian – the beginning of the theme in B minor, the modulation to D major, and especially the modulation to F major which Spohr would certainly have criticized as too 'flowery'.

The 'Allegro giusto' is less characteristic. It is superficially 'military', and only Italian in so far as it is quite unambitious in its construction. In the middle section, in F minor, the best-known melody from *Tancredi* ('Di tanti palpiti') appears almost note for note, and a *stretta* in different time, and as one might expect, with crescendi and *fortissimi*, accentuates the conclusion.

The Overture in C major (II, 6) is of a quite different racy, Italian calibre. Here we have precisely the opposite. The Adagio, for all its light treatment and delicate orchestration and notwithstanding its slightly theatrical, 'Empire' style, could well be the introduction to a 'German' Allegro. But when the actual Allegro begins, we are left in no shadow of doubt:

With its sustained second subject, crescendi, rollicking double-basses, and *stretta*, it is the most cheerful kind of imitation imaginable – *imitation,* not parody; and one would have to be very pedantic and 'Germanic' not to be exhilarated by so much charm and good humour. Nothing is missing; the lyricism, the strings of triplets, the sentimental use of thirds and sixths. The two overtures seem to have given Schubert himself so much enjoyment that he transcribed them for piano-duet (IX, 10 and 9), the D major Overture in December 1817 and the C major some time before March 1818, for during that month it was publicly performed 'in an eight-handed arrangement', i.e., on two pianos, with Schubert and Josef Hüttenbrenner at one and the two sisters Therese and Babette Kunz at the other, during 'a private concert and recitation held by the retired Imperial Court actor Karl F. Müller' at the *Römischer Kaiser*. On 17th March there was a rehearsal at the Kunzs' house, to which Schubert had to summon Hüttenbrenner urgently by letter. This marks the return, after a long interval, to music for four hands.

Schubert's acquaintance with Rossini's operas also influenced to some extent the character of the so-called 'Little' Symphony in C major, which was written between October 1817 and February 1818 (I. 6). It is curiously unpopular with those same conductors who readily condescend to play the 'Tragic' and the intimate B flat major Symphonies. It is not surprising that they find it strange. It does not fit into any accepted pattern. On the one hand it abounds in Italianisms (Ex. 27), and the second quotation is enough to suggest that a thorough study of its thematic material and

its modulations would produce anticipations of the great C
major Symphony. The rising interval of a third which is later
to become the warning-call of the trombones, or the enthusiastic 'reveillé' of the Finale is already present note for note.
The introductory Adagio could well preface an 'Italian'

overture, but it is more delicate in its treatment and, in its
use of modulation to establish the key, it is modelled to
some extent on Beethoven's First. The woodwind opening of
the Allegro reminds one involuntarily of Haydn's 'Military'
Symphony; but the extravagant leaps of ninths and sevenths
which follow are completely 'unclassical'. The whole movement breathes an atmosphere of almost completely unruffled
cheerfulness in the interplay of its themes and ends with a
'piu moto' that is in no sense a *stretta*, but Schubert's first
coda. The delicately constructed Andante is also playful,
with the recapitulation of the main section enriched by the
rhythmic subject of the middle section. The beginning of the
Scherzo is suggestive of Beethoven. Schubert knew the
Scherzi of both the First and the Seventh a little too well,
and just as in the Seventh the relation of the Trio to the
Minuet is that of A major to F major, so here it is E major to
C major, and Schubert's 'piu lento' corresponds exactly to
Beethoven's 'Assai piu lento'. The Finale is playful and 'sociable', with a graceful main theme which Schubert loses
sight of for a long time in the spirit of a Rondo. The movement is much less a 'Finale' than a 'Divertissement', full of
the most carefree Schubertian fancies. The most characteristic of these is when the woodwind move or saunter along
in consecutive thirds over a tremolo on the violins and a
rhythmically accentuated subject on the double-basses,
punctuated by flourishes on the horns. Schubert is still sus-
ceptible to any influence, but already each influence is firmly

transformed at his hands into something essentially personal. Nevertheless it was not until he began to sketch the great E major Symphony some years later, in 1821, that he set foot again on this dangerous ground.

The work was performed at the beginning of 1818, once more by Hatwig in the Gundelhof. Not one word on the subject of this performance has survived, while the Italian Overture in C major was repeated on 1st March of this year at the violinist Eduard Jaell's academy together with an overture by Riotte, and was favourably received by the critics. Schubert's friend Franz v. Schlechta even used the occasion, in the *Wiener Theaterzeitung*, 'to call particular attention to this young artist and his wealth of talent'.

The influence of Rossini is also noticeable in the songs of this period, between 'An Schwager Kronos' and 'Einsamkeit', written in July 1818. We will try in due course to explain our reasons for choosing this particular song. We do not even need to quote as evidence of this the arietta 'La pastorella al prato' to a poem by Goldoni, which Schubert wrote in January 1817 (XX, 574) and which he also set as a male-voice quartet (XVI, 19) with fuller text in the old A–B–A 'da capo' form. It is no longer an exercise-piece and its Italian manner is quite different from that of the arias and ariettas which he wrote for Salieri. It has Rossini's sweetness and 'solmizating' extravagance and it is the true forerunner of the four unpretentious Canzones to texts by Metastasio and Jacopo Vittorelli, written for Fraülein v. Roner in 1820 (XX, 575–578), and the three grand pieces 'in the Rossini manner' written for the singer Lablanche in 1827 (XX, 579–581).

Scarcely less obvious and still more astonishing is the effect of the Italian style upon the songs and choruses of this year, in which Schubert seems to have been no longer concerned with the problem of 'song-form' as such. He set to music whatever chance or his Viennese environment (and particularly his association with Mayrhofer) brought his way. He returned once more to the gloominess of Ossian ('Die Nacht', XX, 305). But it is symbolic that he apparently never completed this long piece. At any rate, it has survived without an ending. In Diabelli's first edition of 1830 and also in the Collected Edition it has been quite arbitrarily coupled with Zacharias Werner's 'Jagdlied' (XX, 290) which is as different from it as chalk from cheese. And it is moreover ironical that, as O. E. Deutsch has pointed out, the text is not the work of Macpherson, and is therefore, so to speak, a forgery of a forgery.

At no time had Schubert's output been more uneven, and between November 1817 and March 1818 five or six months passed without the composition of a single song – a hitherto unprecedented state of affairs. He set two songs ('Der Sänger am Felsen' and 'Ferne von der grossen Stadt', XX, 264, 265) by the Viennese writer Caroline Pichler – both strophic in form, the first 'theatrical', with a *ritornello* for the 'flute'; the second containing an echo of Haydn's Emperor Hymn, which is quite in keeping with the product of so patriotic a lady. He set a song and a duet ('Leiden der Trennung', after Metastasio, and 'Licht und Liebe' XX, 285, 286) by the Viennese poet Matthäus v. Collin, the tutor of Napoleon's son, the Duke of Reichstadt. He set his patron Anton Ottenwald's 'Der Knabe in der Wiege' (XX, 335), in strophic form, but with the stanzas treated in pairs throughout. He set two songs by Graf Ludwig v. Szèchényi which he published as op. 7 and dedicated to the poet ('Die abgeblühte Linde', 'Flug der Zeit', XX, 300, 301) – the first in straightforward recitative and arioso form, and the second, also superficially 'Italian' in form, melody and rhythm. The last stragglers of the period of the strophic song and of Hölty and Salis are not lacking; the most striking is Matthisson's 'Skolie' (XX, 283), which is almost identical with Zumsteeg's setting of 1796. Hölty himself has admittedly vanished. But in his place Schubert discovered Mathias Claudius, the charming, simple, humorous editor of the *Wandsbecker Bote*, who had died in 1815. Of all the poets of the North-German school he is the only one who did not merely profess 'simplicity', but actually experienced it and imbued it with the purest and deepest feeling. Even Claudius sometimes tended to lapse into the Anacreontic style, for which Schubert himself still felt a certain sympathy, as for example in 'An eine Quelle' (XX, 273); not written in 1816, as the Collected Edition suggests, but in February 1817; in fact Claudius tempted him into occasional flights of roguish humour, in much the same vein as the earlier 'Klage um Ali Bey' for women's voices; 'Phidile' (XX, 279), for example,

or even 'Ich bin vergnügt', of which he wrote two completely different settings (XX, 280, 281). The most perfect
result is achieved when Schubert captures the simplicity of
Claudius. Strangely enough he misses the mark with his setting of the poet's loveliest lyric ('Der Mond ist aufgegangen',
XX, 278), which is too 'melodic' in treatment and too formal
in its accompaniment. He probably knew J. A. P. Schulz's
incomparable setting and wanted to try a different approach.
Neither 'Am Grabe meines Vaters' (XX, 274) nor 'Am
Grabe Anselmo's' are simple enough, and it is as if Schubert
was influenced here by Beethoven and by the sentimentality
and arioso-style of many of his songs. But on the other hand
there is the well-known 'Wiegenlied' (XX, 277) which Richard Strauss used in his *Ariadne auf Naxos*; 'An die Nachtigall' (XX, 276), a 'Mädchen-Lied' in which the fashionable
Anacreontic style is completely ousted, and which is the prototype of some of Hugo Wolf's loveliest Mörike songs.
There is the 'three-part' song, 'Täglich zu singen' (XX,
304). And finally there is the most famous of all the
Claudius songs, 'Der Tod und das Mädchen' (XX, 302),
written in February 1817 – a short, deeply moving reconcili-
ation scene from a *danse macabre*, which establishes D
minor as Schubert's own key-symbol. We shall see how it is
later to become the germ of a string quartet; but the bud is
already as perfect as the full flower. It must have been immediately after the composition of this song that Spaun
wrote a counterpart, 'Der Jüngling und der Tod' (XX, 312),
in which Death comes as a welcome redeemer; and while in
the first version (which begins in C sharp minor) Death
appears in G minor, in the second setting (beginning as
before, in C sharp minor) he appears in D minor, with a self-
quotation. How exactly Schubert's imagination worked
becomes evident when we recall his settings of Salis's 'Grab'
for unison chorus with piano accompaniment (or perhaps a
four-part chorus? – XX, 182), the one written at the end of
1815, the other (XX, 186) in February 1816; here, too, Death
appears as a guide along the path to peace. Throughout,
even in the later setting for bass (XX, 323), there is the same
measured tread in the rhythm and the consoling ending in
the major. The same exactness marks the song 'Trost' (XX,
292), a setting of an anonymous poem, composed in January
1817. The inevitability of death is symbolized in the same

solemn rhythms; the verse begins in G sharp minor and ends in E major.

In October 1816, one of Schubert's most famous songs was written. It appeared in the manuscript as 'Der Unglückliche – Gedicht von Werner', but was published as op. 4, No. 1 under the title of 'Der Wanderer – Gedicht von Schmidt von Lübeck' (XX, 266). In the first version, Schubert seems to have given scarcely any thought to the question of performance, for the voice part, a powerful alto, ends with a repetition of the last words in the lowest bass register. There are other instances where he lost sight of the practical purpose of a song, as for example in Mayrhofer's 'Antigone und Oedip' (XX, 309, March 1817) which was published as op. 6, 2, and dedicated to Michael Vogl, the singer; but Vogl would have needed to be an alto to have performed the piece. 'Der Wanderer' is in the form of a short cantata, even to the recitative opening, and the 'somewhat quicker' middle section recalls Mignon's 'Kennst du das Land?' But it contains two unforgettable phrases. One, at the words:

> Die Sonne dünkt mich hier so kalt,
> Die Blüte welk, das Leben alt*

in Schubert's favourite rhythm and in his favourite harmonic idiom. The other, at the words:

> Ich wandle still, bin wenig froh,
> und immer fragt der Seufzer wo?†

The song captured the youthful, romantic pessimism of the time. Schubert used the first of these two phrases as the central point of his most 'brilliant' piano work, the 'Wanderer' Fantasia, op. 15.

Some twelve months later there appeared a second famous song, and like 'Der Wanderer' it was to become the focal point of an instrumental work, the 'Trout' Quintet, although again in a simplified, and not in its original, form. It was not self-glorification which led Schubert to choose his own melodies for his instrumental works, and particularly for his variations, but merely the simple or naïve knowledge of

---

* Here the sun seems to me so cold, the flowers faded and life old.
† I wander silently and know but little happiness, and ever the sigh asks: 'Whither?'

how good those melodies were and of the harmonic wealth
they contained. He felt the need to spin out a concentrated
musical idea which was, so to speak, fettered by the text, to
make it a plaything for his imagination, to demonstrate how
far he could elaborate it. 'Die Forelle' (XX, 327) is a simple
strophic song, but its form, as such, is 'deranged', since Schubert found it impossible to do justice to the third verse,
which describes the catching of the fish, within the framework of the melody. He therefore treated this verse as a
'scena', a 'recitativo in tempo'. Has anyone noticed that
there is here a connection with Mozart's 'Veilchen'? Without
this 'derangement' it would be a pure folk-song, which is
precisely what Schubert made it again in his variations.
There exist four versions of the song, which differ from each
other in minor respects, but the characteristic, graphic, accompanying figure remained unchanged throughout. In the
final version of 1821 (XX, 327 d) Schubert added a five-bar
prelude which is not to be found in the Collected Edition, but
which should never be omitted in performance. He completed
the copy dated 21st February, 1818, 'at midnight' in Anselm
Hüttenbrenner's house and sent it to the latter's brother 'in
earnest of my sincere friendship', although in a fit of drowsy
absent-mindedness he had poured the contents of the ink-pot
instead of the sand-box over it.

The variations of style in the songs of this period are apparent not only when one compares a German 'folk-song'
like 'Die Forelle' with 'La pastorella', but even in his output
of purely German songs. The outward signs of Italian
influence are the numerous repetitions of words and the
arioso passages which Schubert resorted to more frequently
in 1817 or 1818 than at almost any other time. The three
verses of Schober's sentimental poem 'Am Bach im
Frühling' (XX, 272), which would be best set in the form of
a simple song, are treated as a kind of 'da capo' aria. The
third verse – a 'recitativo in tempo' – is followed by a repetition of the first two. The same applies to Mayrhofer's
'Auf dem Strome' (XX, 306). It is as if Schubert had made it
his deliberate intention to depart from the principle of the
strophic song. Friedrich Rochlitz's 'Alinde' (XX, 280) is
treated as a Romance and has the same close affinity with the
stage as the same author's 'An die Laute' (XX, 288), a little
jewel with 'realistic' accompaniment. It could well serve as a

nocturnal serenade for any Don Juan. Out of Schiller's 'Elysium' (XX, 329) is fashioned a great cantata-like work, and from his 'Kampf' (XX, 333), a 'scena' for a powerful bass, with a 'fiery' beginning and an ending full of pathos. A whole series of songs written about this time are deliberately set for bass voice: Schubart's 'An den Tod' (XX, 326), a mighty outcry; Salis' 'Das Grab' (XX, 323), already mentioned above and treated this time not as a choral song (XX, 186) but in an entirely individual style; Stadler's (?) 'Der Strom' (XX, 324), written 'as a souvenir for Herr Stadler', a grandiose and tempestuously emotional piece, with an almost Schumannesque accompaniment. Above all, however, there are the settings of poems by Mayrhofer: 'Die Fahrt zum Hades' (XX, 297), in the same Italian manner as the somewhat later 'Kampf'; the three songs which Schubert collected together in op. 21 and dedicated to Mayrhofer himself – 'Wie Ulfru fischt' (XX, 296), 'Auf der Donau' (XX, 317), a melancholy song with an accompaniment of extraordinary imaginative power, and 'Der Schiffer' (XX, 318), composed in one *single* passionate stroke. And whatever one may think of Mayrhofer as a poet, there is no denying that he occasionally provided Schubert with something as absurdly emotional and sentimental as the long 'Olympian' narrative 'Uraniens Flucht' (XX, 319). Yet side by side with this we find effective classical 'scene' or ariosi such as the forsaken 'Philoctet' (XX, 307) or 'Iphigenia' in alien Scythia (XX, 325 – 'Blüht denn hier an Tauris Strande), two songs which are both distinctly superior to the somewhat Romance-like 'Atys' (XX, 330). And Mayrhofer inspired his friend to a lovely and sensitive pastoral outpouring like 'Erlafsee' (XX, 331; the first of Schubert's songs to be printed and published), and to a splendid vision like 'Memnon', a poem which is in itself not unworthy of Shelley, and which Schubert set in a manner fully worthy of him – 'very slow and passionate', with a depth of feeling and a perfection of form. No wonder that this song is amongst the five which were orchestrated by Brahms.

Eventually Mayrhofer led Schubert back to Schiller and Goethe, along paths far removed from all Italian influence. In Schiller's grandoise 'Gruppe aus dem Tartarus' (XX, 328) the repetitions of the text are not formal or purely lyrical, but grim, spiritual climaxes. It is a song of a declamatory and harmonic boldness and power which Schubert's contemporaries failed utterly to comprehend and which are, in fact, timeless. On the same level stand the Goethe songs of this period: 'Auf dem See' (XX, 310), with its unity of feeling and scene-painting, and the free-metrical stanzas of 'Ganymed' (XX, 311) with their fusion of a hymn-like style and heart-felt emotion. It was about this time (March 1817) that Schubert also ventured upon Goethe's 'Mahomet's Gesang' (XX, 595) but came to a standstill before the final climax; four years later (March 1821) he made another attempt, in a setting for bass voice and in C sharp minor instead of E major. The design is so grandiose that in this instance it can only have been external reasons which prevented him from completing it. In contrast to this he laid aside the setting of Gretchen's scene from *Faust* ('Ach neige, du Schmerzensreiche', XX, 596; May 1817) after completing only forty-three bars – despite wonderful touches in each of these bars – because they struck him as being too lyrical, and because they reminded him too much of the theatre.

This feeling of spiritual crisis is perhaps the reason why only three songs were written during the period after the great 'lyrical pause', between March 1818 and the start of the journey to Hungary in July. So much so, that one might almost say that Schubert lost interest in song-writing. The first of these is a cantata-like setting of Theodor Körner's hymn to his native land of Saxony, 'Auf der Risenkoppe' (XX, 336). In June there appeared 'Grablied für die Mutter' (XX, 338), which begins in B minor and ends *pianissimo* in the transfiguring key of B major. It is, as it were, an echo of the Hölty-Salis period. The finest of the three songs is a setting of Alois Schreiber's poem 'An den Mond in einer Herbstnacht' (XX, 337), written in April. This lengthy song provides a magnificent ending to the period with which this chapter deals, since it blends with absolute purity the 'Italian' style – that is to say, the aria-form with occasional recitative passages – with the 'German' which follows the poet's every shade of feeling with the utmost sensitivity and yet preserves the seraphic pattern of sound. The main section takes the form of a dialogue between voice-part and accompanying melody which one might easily quote as an example of Schubert's instinctive contrapuntal skill.

Last, but by no means least, there remain three or four

compositions for male-voice chorus written during these years 1817 and 1818, for they are among the most remarkable of Schubert's achievements during this period – the most remarkable because they are among the most independent. The models are to be found only in Schubert's own works, in those 'motet' settings of Schiller and Ossian which he wrote in 1813 and 1815. They contain no vestige of any Italian influence, for in Italy, the land of opera, the practice of male-voice ensemble singing had died out several centuries earlier; a probable – if facetious – explanation of this may be that no Italian would have condescended to sing second tenor. Had these songs been composed in Berlin, they could be explained at least from an historical point of view as having been written for Fasch's and Zelter's *Singgesellschaft* which consisted solely of professional musicians and is not to be confused with the great *Singakademie*. The *Singgesellschaft* would probably have appreciated the artistry of these songs of Schubert's – even their artistry as convivial pieces. For two of these choruses deal with convivial subjects, 'Lebenslust' (XVII, 13) written in January 1818, and an adaptation of Bürger's 'Das Dörfchen' (XVI, 46). An *adaptation*, since Schubert shortened Bürger's idyll, and specifically omitted the somewhat lascivious passage about the shepherdess 'slipping off her skirt' before bathing. In his later version of the work which he published with the addition of a dubious piano or apocryphal guitar accompaniment (XVI, 4), he also omitted all reference to the poet's Elise, who is so 'lightly clad' in the morning. The pastoral description assumes the character of a hymn, treated in the form of a 'canon'. It is this form which links a work of this kind with the convivial canons and epigrammatic quartets and terzets of Joseph and Michael Haydn, Nägeli, Zelter and their generation.

The settings of Salis's poem 'Lied im Freien' (XVI, 34) written in July 1817, and Goethe's 'Gesang der Geister über den Wassern' (XVI, 33), written in March, are of a different character. In spite of its title, 'Lied im Freien' is no open-air song, like Mendelssohn's 'Wer hat dich, du schöner Wald' or his 'Jagdlied' which were designed to be sung by nature-loving bachelors, old and young, but a large-scale motet in which Schubert tried to achieve by the choice of key, harmony and time-changes, and by the freedom of

his modulation, that 'emotional painting' which the piano
provided for him in his accompanied songs. The finest of
these pieces, commensurate with the greatness of the text, is
undoubtedly the setting of Goethe's ultra-symbolical nature
study. It belongs in the same category as 'Ganymed', 'Prometheus', 'Mahomet's Gesang' and 'Grenzen der Menschheit', except that here the problem of reproducing the
emotional and pictorial atmosphere of the poem in one
single lightning stroke was infinitely more difficult than in
these piano-songs. If one looks for parallels – not for
models, since they do not exist – one will find them only in
the madrigals of Marenzio or Monteverdi, yet with this
difference. Schubert does not simply illustrate, nor, for all
his boldness, does he merely experiment with harmony, like
the old Italians. No one can have any real conception of
Schubert's greatness unless he knows these works. There is
clear proof of his greatness and his seriousness in the fact
that this poem, originally written in antiphonal form, never
lost its hold on him. He realized that a bare four-part treatment did not do justice to the poet's mysticism; so in December 1820, he wrote a second attempt for male-voice
chorus alternating with strings; and eventually, in 1821, he
found the solution in a large-scale setting for soloists, chorus
and string orchestra. We will return to this in due course.

Chapter Eight

Zseliz and Steyr

The Hungarian Influence and the Piano Music for Four Hands

From the Autumn of 1818
to the Quartet Movement in C minor and *Lazarus*

In July 1818, on the recommendation of J. K. Unger, the father of the celebrated singer Caroline Unger-Sabatier, Schubert went as domestic music-teacher to the two daughters of Count Johann Esterhazy at the latter's country seat at Zseliz in Hungary, and his salary for the first month, including travelling expenses, amounted to 200 gulden.* Now, after a lapse of two years which had been particularly unproductive of personal correspondence, we once more have a few letters from him: to Schober and the rest of his friends, and to Ferdinand and his other brothers and sisters, all written between the beginning of August and the end of October. At first he was in the best of spirits – 'I live and compose like a God.' 'Thank God I *live* at last, otherwise I should have become a frustrated musician.' But after four weeks, we already find him writing: 'Happy as I am and well as I feel and kind as the people are here, I still look forward, day in day out, to the moment when I can say: "To Vienna To Vienna!"' He hankered after news of his friends Schober, Mayrhofer, Spaun and Senn, and greeted the arrival of their letters with cries of joy. He poured out his heart to his friends and assured them that he would not stay away one moment longer than was absolutely necessary. 'Not a soul here has any feeling for true art, except the Countess occasionally (if I am not mistaken). So I am alone with my beloved, and have to hide her in my room, in my piano, and in my heart. Although this often makes me sad, it also helps

*At that time 1 gulden was equal to 10p. approximately.

to inspire me the more.' He then goes on to describe his surroundings in greater detail: his room, of course, was not in the castle but in the inspectorate with the rest of the household staff. Listen to his own description:

It is fairly quiet, except for 40 geese which sometimes set up such a cackling that one cannot hear oneself speak. The people round me are all, without exception, very nice. It isn't often that a Count's household staff gets on so well together as this one does. The Inspector, a Slavonian, is a nice fellow and prides himself a great deal on his former musical talents. He still blows two German dances in 3/4 time on the flute with commendable virtuosity. His son is studying philosophy and is here on his holidays at the moment. I hope I shall get on very well with him. His wife is a woman like all women who want to be called ladies. The steward fits his office perfectly, a man with an extraordinary insight into his pockets and money-bags. The doctor, who is really clever, ails like an old woman at the age of 24. All very unnatural. The surgeon, who is my favourite, is a much-respected old man of 75, always bright and cheerful. God grant to each of us so happy an old age. The magistrate is a very honest, decent sort of man. A companion of the Count, a cheerful old soul and an excellent musician often keeps me company. The cook, the chambermaid, the housemaid, the governess, the butler, etc., and the two grooms are all very nice. The cook is a bit of a rake, the chambermaid 30 years old, the housemaid very pretty and often my companion, the governess a good old thing, the butler my rival. The two grooms are more at home with the horses than with human beings. The Count is rather rough; the Countess is haughty but more refined; the two little girls are nice children. So far I have been spared the ordeal of dining with the family. . . .

It is amusing to note that Schubert, characteristically enough, only introduces the main personages in the household at the end. The 'very pretty' housemaid – we know her name – who also encouraged the attentions of the butler, was possibly the cause of the serious disease which attacked Schubert a few years later and which weakened his physical resistance when the final illness came. And consequently this first Hungarian visit was not perhaps so happy or auspicious after all. Towards the end of it he began to see things a little more clearly. 'I should be as happy as I was when I first arrived here, were it not for the fact that I get to know the people round me better every day. But I now see that I am really lonely among them, except for a couple of really nice girls. My longing for Vienna grows daily.'

This longing was no longer clouded by the thought that he would have to return to the hated duties of schoolmastering. It is quite certain that Schubert no longer lived with his father in the Rossau after November 1818. He went to live with Mayrhofer, with the same landlady, Frau Sanssouci (what a charming name!), with whom Theodor Körner had formerly lodged, and shared one and the same room with him. As O. E. Deutsch has very plausibly suggested,* Schubert's father made one final attempt a year later to compel his son to return to schoolmastering by means of a petition to a high church dignitary. But the petition was never sent and exists to this day in the torn state to which it was reduced, probably after a violent argument between father and son. In August 1819, Schubert still ranked officially as an assistant schoolmaster in the Rossau in the eyes of the Inspectorate, but only in a nominal capacity.

At the beginning of July 1819, Schubert was free to accept an invitation from Michael Vogl to spend the period of the Opera closed season at Steyr, Vogl's birthplace, in Upper Austria. Early in July the two odd companions set out. At Steyr, Schubert stayed with a Dr. Schellmann, and was highly delighted by the spectacle of eight young girls in the house – the daughters and their friends – 'almost all of them pretty'). He asked Ferdinand to send him the manuscript of one of his settings of *Stabat Maters* which he wanted to perform; celebrated Vogl's fifty-first birthday on 10th August with a cantata; made an excursion to Linz, where he wrote a short letter to his roommate Mayrhofer; planned another trip to Salzburg, which, however, came to nothing on this occasion; and returned to Vienna during the latter half of September.

This is perhaps a suitable place to give a brief character-sketch of Schubert's travelling-companion, who played so great and benevolent a part in his life. Johann Michael Vogl was nearly thirty years older than Schubert. He had been a singer at the German Opera since 1794, where his performances had filled Schubert with enthusiasm as a boy, and it must have been a great moment for him when he was introduced to this important and imposing figure by Schober at the latter's home in February or March 1817. Vogl, at first a little condescending towards the shy and awkward young

* Op. cit., p. 120 ff.

man, grew warmer, more appreciative and more enthusiastic with every new song. He developed more and more into the ideal interpreter of Schubert's songs – that is to say, the first representative of a class of singers whom one could call the great 'diseurs', and who remained rare enough phenomena even in the nineteenth and twentieth centuries. He still retained a sufficient link with the eighteenth century to indulge in occasional vocal 'conceits' even in Schubert's songs and to 'adorn' Schubert's simplicities with embellishments, sustained notes and cadenzas. This is a little surprising, for he was an extremely unusual type of singer, a man with a classical education, who read Greek and Latin, and was also at home in the English language. It was not until late in life that he renounced his bachelor's existence, at which even the kindly Schubert could not resist poking a little gentle fun. As a performer on the stage, Castelli has given us the following description of him:*

... Vogl, the great Schubert singer and the latter's first apostle, whose whole physical appearance—movements of hands, feet and the whole body—was angular and ugly; who was anything but an actor, but who produced such extraordinary effects by the power of his singing and by the perfect accuracy of its colouring that he entranced his listeners and they forgave him everything else. ...

One of the features of the Hungarian period is that Schubert turned once more to the composition of music for four hands, long after the experiments of the Convict period and shortly after the arrangements of the two Italian Overtures. It was the most convenient and friendly way of keeping the two young Countesses occupied musically, and of teaching them in a practical manner a feeling for melody, good time-keeping and a certain virtuosity. Early in his stay at Zseliz or perhaps before setting out on his journey, Schubert wrote a number of vocal exercises for soprano with figured bass (XIX, 36), much as Mozart had previously done for his Constanze. But since they were extremely difficult, he clearly had not struck the right medium. Piano duets were the answer.

From now on, however, Schubert was constantly occupied with music for four hands, right up to the last year of his life, and for different reasons. He used it as his stock-in-trade

* *Memoiren meines Lebens* I, 148; 1861.

for publishers, for four-handed pieces were easier to sell than symphonies and quartets and even songs – easier, at any rate, than *his* songs. He used it as the medium for works which are really orchestrally conceived, for instead of sketching them in outline, he preferred to write them down in this finished form, and in fact did so with equal ease. It was then left not to him but to posterity to orchestrate them, particularly his marches. And finally he cultivated this form for its own sake. One can say that he really created it, in spite of Mozart's splendid models, which he certainly made the young Countesses play or himself joined them in playing: the great sonatas (K. 497 and 521), the charming G major Variations (K. 501), and even, perhaps, the early sonatas (K.381 and 358). There is a very late Fugue for four hands in E minor by him, written on 3rd June, 1828, at Baden (IX, 28), to which we shall return in due course and which seems to be directly modelled on a fugue of Mozart's (K. 401). But there is this difference. Mozart achieved his ideal of music for four hands in his Sonata for two pianos (K. 448), and all his other four-handed pieces were written, as it were *faute de mieux*, with this ideal in mind. Schubert, on the other hand, established the *genre* and by the end had almost exhausted it again.

We will begin with the Sonata in B flat major, wrongly dated 1824 in the Collected Edition (IX, 11), because it corresponds most clearly to the three-movement model of the eighteenth century, or rather of Mozart. It begins with a movement in sonata-form followed by an Andante con moto and an Allegretto in song-form which, if it did not offend against the key, one could well interchange, particularly since the turn to the major at the end of the Andante is so beautiful. There is much in this sonata that is Italian and 'virtuoso'. The 'virtuoso' character is particularly noticeable in the repetitions where a melody is given to the left hand of the *primo player*, and overlaid with figurative ornamentation. Impressive *cantabile*, passages lend themselves readily to treatment in octaves, as anyone will know from the piano part of the 'Trout' Quintet. Throughout there is a light, graceful interplay between *primo* and *secundo*, and everything sounds full and yet transparent. There is as yet nothing really Hungarian about this sonata, unless one deliberately reads such a construction into it, but when it was published as op. 30,

Schubert dedicated it to a Hungarian, Count Ferdinand Palffy d'Erdöd.

With the Introduction and Variations on an Original Theme (IX, 18) we need not concern ourselves, since they are not by Schubert. When a Hamburg publisher reissued Schubert's eight variations on a theme from Hérold's opera *Marie*, op. 82, he added to them as op. 82, 2 these variations, the theme of which is almost indistinguishable from that of Beethoven's 'Danse russe' from the ballet *Das Waldmädchen*. They would be much too brilliant for the Schubert of 1818, and he would never have contented himself with four variations followed immediately by a Finale; and, as the composer of these variations, he would have been a far too faithful imitator of Hummel.

In his letter of 8th September, 1818, to his friends in Vienna, Schubert asks Spaun to give his kind regards to 'Herr Gahy', a Hungarian acquaintance who had been introduced to him by Spaun and who was a favourite partner of his when playing his piano-duets. It was probably Gahy to whom Schubert dedicated the Rondo in D major of January 1818 (IX, 14), one of the forerunners of the 'Hungarian' piano-duets. The printed copies bear the motto: 'Notre amitié est invariable', and this friendship is in fact perfectly symbolized in the balance of the partnership. It is typical of Schubert's sly sense of humour that he set this Rondo for Gahy – who liked to play Schubert's dances in a manner calculated 'to galvanize the dancers'* – in the form of a true Polonaise, with a middle-section which later reappears more or less faithfully in the Finale of the G major Piano Sonata op. 78.

This brings us to Schubert's 'military dances' which play so great a part in his music: his Marches. They owed their origin naturally enough to the warlike and – even after the 'neutralization' of Napoleon – militaristic period which also prompted Beethoven to make such frequent use of martial rhythms, not only in his *Marcie funebre* and other Marches, but less blatantly in a whole series of other works – as, for example, in the first movements of all his piano concertos. Now, Schubert was as little 'patriotic' as Beethoven. On no account is he ever Prussian or 'Potsdamian', and no Prussian regiment could drill to his marches. Schubert himself pro-

*O. E. Deutsch, op. cit., p. 102.

vided the 'programme' for the first of the three marches, in B minor, C major and D major (IX, 1), which were later (1824) published as op. 27 under the title of 'Heroic Marches'. It served as a prelude to a large-scale choral-cantata setting of Schiller's 'Die Schlacht', which Schubert sketched in March 1816 (XXI, 44); it is sombre and rather 'nordic'. But the third is an unmistakable French quick-march – the real heroes of the Napoleonic period were after all the French – and only the second, gay and slightly jaunty, with its rocking Trio in A flat major, could be called 'Austrian'. Of the other six marches written in 1818, and published as op. 40 in 1825 in two volumes dedicated to Dr. J. Bernhardt, the doctor who was treating Schubert (IX, 2), the second and fourth in particular are characteristically Austrian, while the third is already typically Hungarian. Schubert certainly did not need to go to Zseliz in order to make his first acquaintance with the Hungarian style in all its various forms. He found it, among other things, in Haydn's chamber music. The fifth, in E flat minor, is a *Marcia funebre* which naturally enough derives from Beethoven and is modelled to some extent on the Funeral March in the latter's Piano Sonata, op. 26; the last of the six again tends towards the French style. Throughout, the 'military' orchestration of these marches is implicit, and nowhere is there any doubt where the oboe, the clarinet or the trumpet would be included.

It is significant that even the Variations on a French song (the Romance 'Le bon chevalier' [Reposez vous, bon chevalier] of Queen Hortense), written in 1818 and dedicated as op. 10, to Ludwig van Beethoven 'by his devoted admirer Franz Schubert' (IX, 15), are based on a march-theme in E minor, and develop into a regular March-Fantasia. This is a mark of homage to the heroic composer Beethoven, to whom a devoted admirer like Schubert should really have dedicated a string quartet, a symphony, a piano trio – or an assortment of songs. According to Schindler's account Beethoven does not seem to have behaved particularly well, when Schubert personally presented him with a printed copy of these Variations.

Schubert had an unhappy experience when, in 1822, he presented to the master a copy of his Variations for four hands which he had dedicated to him. The shy and speechless young composer contributed to his own embarrassment, in spite of the fact that he was introduced by Diabelli, who interpreted for him his feelings towards the great man. The courage which had sustained him as far as the house forsook him completely in the presence of the prince of composers. And when Beethoven expressed the wish that Schubert himself should write down the answers to his questions, his hand was as if paralysed. Beethoven ran through the Variations and discovered a harmonic inaccuracy. He gently drew the young man's attention to this, but at once added that it was not a mortal sin; whereupon Schubert completely lost control of himself, perhaps as a direct result of this kindly observation. He rushed out of the house and bitterly reproached himself. He could never again summon up the courage to present himself before the great man.*

Was Schindler present at this meeting? Did he, like Diabelli, accompany Schubert to the house? The whole anecdote is probably nothing more than another attempt on Schindler's part to give himself airs and to associate himself with episodes in the 'great man's' life. Be that as it may, it is quite incomprehensible what he meant by the 'harmonic inaccuracy' which Beethoven criticized. On the contrary, Beethoven would have been much more likely to have expressed his dissatisfaction at Schubert's lack of boldness, his indeterminate wavering between old-fashioned variations in the manner of Hummel and greater freedom, as, for example, in the C major of the third and in the C sharp minor of the sixth and one from the last variation before the Finale. What superb models of legitimate boldness Beethoven himself had established with the op. 34 Variations, the 'Eroica' Variations op. 35 or the XXXII Variations in C minor (1807)! (Schubert could not yet have known the Diabelli Variations, on the theme of which he later contributed a variation of his own.) In the first two variations, Schubert begins quite traditionally with figuration and a *staccato* bass; then admittedly there follows a genuinely Schubertian alternation between a lyrical and a martial mood, and a genuinely Schubertian fullness of sound. And after the last variation in which the lyrical (*primo*) and the martial (*secondo*) moods are combined, there comes a Finale which in its dynamics – the crescendi and explosive outbursts – reveals the affinity to Beethoven. But this probably made little impression on Beethoven, since he knew more about this kind of thing than

Life of Ludwig van Beethoven, 3rd ed., 1860, p. 522 in Kalischer's new impression.

anyone else. Again, how much wiser it would have been to dedicate three, or even half a dozen, songs to him!

It is with some embarrassment that one finally mentions the Overture in F minor or F major (IX, 8) which Schubert himself published with Cappi in 1825 as op. 34. It was written in November 1819, and was completed, as Schubert noted on the lost manuscript, 'in three hours in Joseph Hüttenbrenner's room in the Bürgerspital and as a result missed my dinner'. The Introduction in the minor is a completely unceremonious piece of work in the Italian or pseudo-Rossini manner, but the Allegro in the major would be better suited to one of the naturalistic French operas of the Hérold school in its theatrical emotionalism, particularly in the *stretta* with its fanfare flourishes. Nowhere is Schubert less 'romantic' and nowhere is he more a child of his time. But should we blame him for writing and publishing such works, in order to earn a little money?

A March for piano solo (XI, 16), the date of composition of which is difficult to determine, provides the transition to the remaining piano works of this period. It is in E major, with a Trio in A flat major, and reveals the same variety of harmonic colour and the same affinities as the 'Beethoven' Variations; from a dynamic and rhythmic point of view there is something almost wild and barbaric about it. When writing it, Schubert must have had something particular in mind. Perhaps it is a sketch for some Entr'acte or for a piece of incidental music for some theatrical work or other. But the setting is for piano, and justifies our turning once more to Schubert in his capacity as a composer of piano sonatas.

We last left him as a sonata-composer in the year 1817. The Collected Edition jumps from this year (from the Sonata in E flat major, op. 122) to the year 1823 (to the A minor Sonata, op. 143). And it therefore looks as if there was a period of five or six years in Schubert's short life during which he no longer concerned himself with the piano sonata. In actual fact the Sonata in A major, op. 120, which the Collected Edition attributes 'to the year 1825' was written in the summer of 1819 (the credit for being the first to establish this fact is due to Ludwig Scheibler, *Zeitschrift der Internationalen Musikgesellschaft*, VIII, 485, 1907), and it was preceded by a whole series of the most remarkable experiments. These experiments prove that the problem of the piano sonata not only occupied Schubert incessantly, but irritated him profoundly. There is the fragment of a Sonata in C major written in April 1818 (XXI, 11) and consisting of a first movement (Moderato) and an Allegretto in the form of a Siciliano, which must be considered as a Finale. The first of these movements breaks off in the middle of the development, the second immediately before the recapitulation. Not only are both movements written out without that scrupulous care which elsewhere – even in his sketches – is a characteristic of Schubert's, down to the clear indication of the articulation, but both in their form and melody, too, they provide documentary evidence of the spiritual confusion which he must have experienced about this time. Once again it is as if he had wanted forcibly to break away from Beethoven. The themes are Mozartian and classical, but in their treatment – melody, figuration, modulation – Schubert slips almost accidentally into a Romantic, and, in the second subject of the first movement, an operatic style. Still more revealing is the fragment of an F minor Sonata written in September 1818. The first movement breaks off at the recapitulation; the second (a Scherzo in E major) is complete, as is the Finale, except for a few bars in the recapitulation (XXI, 12). In this fragment it is as if Schubert had wanted not to break away from Beethoven, but, in a fit of despair, to outrival the composer of the 'Appassionata'. The choice of an identical key is evidence of this. Schubert lapses into a naturalistic ferocity. The first movement is purely spectacular, and the Scherzo and Trio are equally sketchy in their pianistic design. The most remarkable movement is the Finale with its blustering theme. In place of the development there blossoms a melodic flower of the most exquisite, compelling charm, as if to compensate for a slow movement which has been lost or which was never even planned. No contemporary wrote anything like this and Schubert, after his own fashion, did indeed outrival Beethoven.

As for a fragment of a first movement in C sharp minor, written in April 1819 (XXI, 13), one can accept it both as a completely unsuccessful experiment and as a miracle of Schubertian harmony. The movement is completed only as far as the end of the exposition and the theme resembles the *preliminary* to a theme rather than a theme itself. It leads swiftly to pure lyricism in E major and to a wealth of modulation to B major, at which point Schubert recalls the theme to mind and retraces his steps to the dominant in G sharp minor by way of the most astonishing bypaths. It is a fantastic and, so to speak, aimless, wandering exposition. How far Schubert had strayed from the other, 'virtuoso' path is shown by the Adagio in E major of April 1818 (XI, 11), which we have already discussed.

It is therefore not surprising that, after all these efforts to find himself, he returned to the pure lyricism of his A major Sonata (X, 10) – a lyricism which is hardly disturbed even in the development of the first movement and which, in the second subject, culminates in his favourite rhythm. The Andante in D major is little more – and yet so much more! – than a song with a concealed text of happy resignation, which later found its explanation, both in spirit and in key, in a setting of Caroline Pichler's poem 'Der Unglückliche' (XX, 390) which he wrote in January 1821:–

> *Die Nacht bricht an, mit leisen Lüften sinket*
> *Sie auf die müden Sterblichen herab...**

A Minuet or Scherzo is missing. In key, in time and in its childlike spirit, the Finale also recalls a song – 'Hänflings Liebeswerbung' (XX, 316), written in April 1817 – and alternates throughout between seriousness and good humour. Schubert wrote the sonata at Steyr for the daughter of one of his hosts, Josephine v. Koller, who, as he informed his brother Ferdinand on 19th July, 1819, 'is very pretty, plays the piano well and is going to sing some of my songs'. She was then eighteen years old, and we shall hear more of her in due course. The fact that it was written for a young girl, who played the piano 'well' but not perfectly, naturally accounts to a large extent for the character and style of this sonata.

Schubert's visit to Steyr produced another work in A

*The night draws on, and falls with gentle breezes upon the weary world. . . .

major, probably the most popular of all his instrumental compositions – the so-called 'Trout' Quintet, which was published as op. 114 by Joseph Czerny a year after his death (VII, 1). It was commissioned by the musical patron of Steyr, Sylvester Paumgartner, manager of a mine and an amateur performer on wind instruments and the cello, who entertained at his house the kind of select little music club which the Italians would have called an 'Accademia'. Schubert continued to enjoy his hospitality during subsequent visits. Now this delightful work, for which Schubert there and then wrote out the parts, conforms exactly to this period of music for four hands: the piano is contrasted with the string-group – violin, viola, 'cello and double-bass – like one player with the other, and the atmosphere of lively conversation persists throughout. If one looks for a model or a counterpart one would find it in Hummel, who published as op. 87 a 'Grande Quintuor' for precisely the same combination of instruments. It is a serenade for chamber ensemble. In the first movement Schubert introduces the recapitulation in the sub-dominant and dispenses with a coda. The movement simply comes to an end after a well-ordered sequence of pleasant and increasingly richly figured Schubertian ideas. One of these ideas, the last in the 'angular' rhythm, dominates the contrasting section of the following Andante, with its lyrical opening. It has a faint Magyar or Slav ring about it. And the Finale practically dispenses with fancy-dress, and advertises itself as *all' ongarese*. The first subject dominates the movement, which is a rare occurrence with Schubert, and the melodic ideas and rhythms which compete with it are taken from the first movement (the 'Trout' Quintet is a very homogeneous work). But Schubert is at his most Schubertian in the concise and stormy Scherzo and Trio, in his contrast between rhythmic emphasis and lyricism, and in the movement which has given the work its name and which gives it its 'serenade' character: the variations on the simplified melody of 'Die Forelle'. The model was provided by Haydn's variations on the Emperor Hymn. The strings alone announce the theme; then the melody is given in turn to the piano (in its characteristic high octaves), the viola, and the double-bass and 'cello together. With the fourth and fifth Variations there follow, admittedly, somewhat un-Haydnesque excursions into the realm of D minor and B flat major, and the B flat major Variation serves as a bridge-passage to the Finale in which the melody of the song at last appears in all its charm with the original accompaniment. It is as if a roguish beauty were to remove the veil which has hitherto made her features only a subject for speculation. The Schubert of this quintet is not the great Schubert, but the one whom we cannot help but love.

This brings us to the two instrumental works of 1819 and 1820 which no longer have anything to do with the 'sociable' or the Italian or Hungarian style, nor with the influence of Beethoven or Hummel, and which play a similar role in the field of Schubert's instrumental music to that played by 'Adelaide' or 'Gretchen am Spinnrade' in his songs. For they represent the break-through to complete independence. It is noticeable that this break-through takes place at different stages in the various fields of creative achievement. It occurs first in the songs and then in the instrumental music. It never materializes in the operas, but does so at least in the quasi-operatic field of oratorio. The first of these two works, an Overture in E minor written in February 1819 (II, 7), is scored for a new orchestral combination which includes two pairs of horns and – for the first time – trombones, and for the first time it dispenses with the conventional slow 'Intro-duction', though not with an Introduction 'in tempo', which, in its powerful 'attack' and crescendo, establishes the rhythm and heroic character of the work. The theme, however, does not appear until the forty-second bar. How should one de-scribe this overture, with the simultaneous dynamic *and* har-monic tension of its crescendi and with the halting dialogue-style of its musical texture – an overture which has no model and no contemporary counterpart? The rhythmic main theme reveals itself as a triumphal fanfare subject, par-ticularly when it changes at the end to the major, but fun-damentally it symbolizes a nameless sombre power, for which the trombones provide the colour. The whole melodic pattern, particularly a dialogue between oboe and bassoon, is a vain attempt to break this power. In the Collected Edi-tion this overture follows after the 'Italian' Overture in C. Between the two there lies a gulf which seems to be un-bridgeable. This is the Schubert who is to write the B minor Symphony and later the great C major Symphony. In the

diary of theatrical and musical events in Vienna of a certain
Matthias Franz Perth there is an entry under 14th March,
1819, recording the performance of an overture of Schubert's by his brother Ferdinand. (Ferdinand had become an
honorary member and conductor of an amateur Society of
Friends of Music, which gave its twelfth concert on this
date.) O. E. Deutsch suggests that it may have been this
overture, since it was the most recent that Schubert had written. If this is correct, then Ferdinand was a better musician
than we have given him credit for, and it is quite understandable why no critical notice of the performance has survived. Even today there might well be conductors – and
audiences – who would not be able to make head or tail of
this overture.

The second of these two epoch-making works is the String
Quartet Movement in C minor, written in December 1820
(V, 12). There is no bridge leading to it from the earlier
quartets – not even from the E major Quartet of 1816 (which
only stands between it and the 'domestic quartets' in a chronological sense), nor even from Beethoven's Quartet in C
minor, op. 18, 4, or any other of *his* quartets. Schubert's C
minor is not emotional but weird, and this weird atmosphere
is increased by the almost continuous tremolo in the 'accompaniment' or in the theme itself. The contrast or complement to this C minor is not C major or E flat major as it
would be with a 'classical' master, but A flat major, the key
of the 'lyrical' ('dolce') second subject. There is no recapitulation after the 'veiled' development; instead the beginning of the movement reappears towards the end, as if to
destroy its rapturous ecstasy and quench its bright radiance.
Schubert started a second movement, which unfortunately
appears only in the appendix to the Collected Edition, where
scarcely anyone notices it. It is an indescribably rich and
tragic Andante in A flat major in 3/4 time, modulating ab-
ruptly to C flat major, with an 'alternativo' in F sharp minor.
Mandyczewski has suggested that it was purely accidental
that this quartet remained 'unfinished' like the B minor Symphony two years later. We will leave that open to question.
At any rate it is a major misfortune for our musical heritage
that this movement at least was never completed.

It is not without reason that, in considering the vocal works of this period, we begin this time with the songs. For in his songs Schubert had become fully conscious of his own powers. In the choice of his texts he had become by now a 'modern', nineteenth-century composer. He turned his back on Matthisson, Salis and Uz, and permitted himself only an occasional 'relapse', as for example one or two reminiscences of Stolberg shortly before *Die schöne Müllerin*. Schiller and, more especially, Goethe still remained the brightest stars on his poetical horizon, while the Viennese poets and his own literary friends in Vienna, from Collin to Seidl, Castelli and Grillparzer, still held a special place in his affections. But after 1818 he turned his attention almost exclusively to the constellations of Romanticism in the North and in the South – to the two Schlegels, Novalis, Rückert, the North-German Zacharias Werner, the Swabian Ludwig Uhland, to Ernst Schulze and Wilhelm Müller, until at the end of his life he discovered a new, iridescent variant of Romanticism in that of Heinrich Heine. It was pure chance that limited his horizon, as for example in the case of Eduard Mörike or Joseph v. Eichendorff.

At the same time he now chose many of his texts with particular regard to so great a singer, original an interpreter and singular a personality as Johann Michael Vogl, although one can almost say that even the earlier songs and ballads had been written, as it were, for a pre-existent Vogl. In the first letter which he wrote to his friends from Zseliz (3rd August, 1818), he asked Schober to pay his respects to Vogl and to suggest to him that he might like 'to sing one of my songs – *whichever he likes* – at the Kunz's concert in November.'

In the same letter he wrote: 'Mayrhofer's "Einsamkeit" is finished and to my mind, it is the best thing that I have done'. When the composer of 'An Schwager Kronos' says that, then there must be something in it, even though he is mistaken. He could not publish the piece (XX, 339) since no publisher would have accepted it. It is too long – 'a philosophical' song, and clearly written with Vogl in mind. Mayrhofer describes the life of a profoundly dissatisfied man, who is driven forth by an irresistible urge from the quiet retreat of a monastery into a violently active life, to innocent country pleasures, to the cheerful society of his friends, to 'the constellation of Love', into the horror of battle, until as an old

man he finds the fulfilment of his boyhood longing in
Nature. For Schubert this ballad or this cantata – call it what
you will – becomes the 'fulfilment' of everything that he had
tried to achieve in his Ossian and Schiller ballads. The recitative sections which introduce each individual 'scene' here
have a legitimate function; the scenes themselves are painted
with a wealth of musical imagination and a depth of feeling
which make Schubert's pride understandable. The piece is
written with complete disregard for the opinion of others.
One might compare it with *Tristan* which, though originally
planned as a practical, practicable opera, developed involuntarily into its composer's most uninhibited and personal work.

Apart from 'Einsamkeit', the visit to Zseliz produced only
a few songs. The author of the text of three of these – 'Der
Blumenbrief', 'Das Marienbild' and 'Das Abendrot' (XX,
340, 341, 344) – was Alois Schreiber, who was probably also
the author of the anonymous 'Blondel zu Marien' (XX, 343).
For the text of the most famous of them, 'Litanei auf das
Fest Allerseelen' (XX, 342) Schubert went back to
J. G. Jacobi. As poetry, 'Der Blumenbrief', 'Das Marienbild' and 'Blondel' all bear certain traces of the affected
style of Nazarenism.* There is nothing child-like, however,
about Schubert's simplicity. On the contrary, it is deeply
emotional and animated by delicate shades of harmony
which do justice to every change of mood even in the two
strophic songs. 'Das Abendrot' stands on its own, not only
because it is written for a bass voice, but because the text is
worthy of a greater poet than the obscure Schreiber:

Du heilig, glühend Abendrot!
Der Himmel will in Glanz zerrinnen;
So scheiden Märtyrer von hinnen,
Hold lächelnd in dem Liebestod.

Des Aufgangs Berge still und grau,
Am Grab des Tags die hellen Gluten;
Der Schwan auf purpurroten Fluten,
Und jeder Halm im Silbertau—

* The cult of pious, simple-minded conduct, the return to an imaginary
pseudo-Mediaevalism, was one of the growing pains of Romanticism.

O Sonne, Gottesstrahl, du bist
Nie herrlicher, als im Entfliehn!
Du willst uns gern hinüberziehn
Wo deines Glanzes Urquell ist.*

In Schubert's hands this has become a magnificent show-piece, the second verse in C sharp minor contrasting with the hymn-like mood of the first and the passionate fervour of the last ('Feurig, doch nicht zu geschwind'). It is full of varying degrees of lyricism, utterly exquisite and yet not superficial. 'Litanei', on the other hand, is a strophic song of that intimate and simple devotion to which the poets and painters of the day aspired in vain.

In November 1818 (after his return from Hungary), Schubert turned his attention to the elder of the two Schlegels, August Wilhelm, particularly in his capacity as the translator of Petrarch. (He had, admittedly, already set Schlegel's playful 'Lob der Tränen' (XX, 294) to music in 1817.) The rediscovery of the Italian (and Spanish) literature of the Middle Ages and the Renaissance was one of the intrinsic achievements of the Romantics, and consequently Schubert is very 'modern' in these three Petrarch sonnets (XX, 345–347). (The author of the third of them was also Petrarch, although the Collected Edition ascribes it to Dante. Incidentally, this one is not in Schlegel's translation, but in J. D. Gries' highly accomplished version.) They are, in the original Italian: 'Apollo, s'ancor vive il bel desio', 'Solo e pensoso i più deserti campi'. 'Or che'l ciel e la terra e'l vento tace'. Of these three sonnets, the last two, in particular, had been set to music dozens of times in the sixteenth century, but always in two parts, with the octet and the sextet treated as separate entities. For a sonnet virtually defies musical composition as a single whole. Schubert mastered the

---

*Thou holy, glowing sunset!
The sky dissolves in splendour;
Thus go martyrs from hence,
Gently smiling in love-death.

Silent and grey the eastern hills,
Bright the glow at the grave of day;
The swan floats on crimson waters,
And every blade of grass is bathed in silvery dew.

O Sun, Light of God, thou art
Never more glorious than in thy departing!
Fain wouldst thou draw us
Whither the source of thy splendour lies.

form by a mixture of eloquent recitative and arioso, although the last and latest of the three sonnets makes only the slightest use of recitative, treats each section in a melodic, hymn-like style and approximates to a 'da capo' aria. They present three solutions – and probably the *first* solutions – to the problem. Anyone who wishes to approach the subject of Schubert by comparing his settings with those of other composers (and thereby to appreciate what is in most cases his incomparable superiority) has always been able, up to this point, to find examples among his predecessors or contemporaries – Reichardt, Zelter, Beethoven, Tomaschek and many others. But not one of these set a sonnet to music. From now on the material for comparison must be sought in the period that followed, and so far as sonnets are concerned, in the works of Franz Liszt, long after Schubert's death.

From December, January and February 1818–1819, there date several settings of poems by A. W. Schlegel's younger brother Friedrich, which clearly illustrate Schubert's new 'Romantic' manner. The first, 'Bianka' (XX, 348) is an empty poetic trifle, which Schubert contrives to invest with a deeper shade of melancholy by means of the most delicate *pianissimo* and an iridescent interplay between major and minor. The second (XX, 349), 'Vom Mitleiden Mariae', a modern *Stabat Mater* in three verses, is a unique example of pure three-part writing and – as we have already mentioned – a monument of contrapuntal writing. One might almost say 'Bach-like' writing, for several times Schubert uses, as did Bach in similar cases, the melodic symbol of the Cross, more visible to the eye than audible to the ear. Schubert knew hardly a single note of Bach and still less of the music of the sixteenth century, in which this kind of symbolism was an integral part of the aesthetic equipment. It is a minor miracle of musical history which cannot be explained simply by attributing it to Schubert's genius.

The first song composed by Schubert in 1819 was a setting of Friedrich Schlegel's 'Gebüsche' (XX, 350), the last four lines of which can serve as a motto for the whole Romantic movement:

> *Durch alle Töne tönet*
> *Im bunten Erdentraume*

> *Ein leiser Ton gezogen*
> *Für den, der heimlich lauschet.**

(Schubert emphasizes: 'ein – *nur ein* leiser Ton . . .', as if he wished to stress something esoteric, something audible only to himself and his friends.) Does the reader recall that Schumann used these same four lines as a motto for his C major Fantasia op. 17? And is it not the purity of harmony in rich modulation with which Schubert illustrates the 'leiser Ton'? In spite of the slight difference of tempo, there is a fundamental connection between this song and the Impromptu op. 90, 3:

The biographical background is quite unmistakable in Schlegel's 'Wanderer', which Schubert himself published as op. 65, 2 in 1826 (XX, 351). Is this not Schubert speaking from the bottom of his heart and in profound sympathy with some of the emotional utterances in his diary?

> *Wie deutlich des Mondes Licht*
> *zu mir spricht,*
> *mich beseelend zu der Reise;*
> *'Folge treu dem alten Gleise,*
> *wähle keine Heimat nicht.*
> *Ew'ge Plage*
> *bringen sonst die schweren Tage.*
>   *Fort zu andern sollst du wechseln,*
> *sollst du wandern, leicht entfliehend*
> *jeder Klage'.*
> *Sanfte Ebb' und hohe Flut*
> *tief im Mut,*
> *wandr' ich so im Dunkeln weiter,*
> *steige mutig, steige heiter,*
> *und die Welt erscheint mir gut.*

---

* In this earth's motley dream there echoes through the maze of sounds, one faint sound for him who listens closely.

Alles Reine
seh' ich mild im Widerscheine
nichts verworren
in des Tages Glut verdorren:
*froh umgeben, doch alleine.**

Every word here is full of associations and symbolical, and Schubert set it like a motto of twenty-seven bars in melodic declamation or declamatory melody against the golden backcloth of a ringing D major, as a most intimate confession of his happiness and his resignation. With 'Das Mädchen' (XX, 354), a tender love-song on a somewhat archaic text (Schubert, however, ignores the archaism here), he abandoned Freidrich Schlegel for the time being. A year later he returned to him with a group of six songs (XX, 373–378), some of them trivial ('Die Vögel', 'Der Knabe'), some graceful and dreamy, like 'Der Schiffer' with its vocal echo – a song with which one could start an opera-act, if it were not written with such delicate and intimate detail; and some in a hymn-like style, as for example, 'Der Fluss' – a sublime 'barcarole' of two stanzas – the visionary 'Abendröte' and 'Die Sterne'. These are all songs which he could never publish and which did not enjoy any subsequent popularity either, since they are too personal and subjective and because the poet for his part follows paths that are too remote and steep. During this period Schubert was particularly attracted by metrical problems. He would not otherwise have set, in February 1819, the trivial jingle of 'Abendbilder' (XX, 352) by an obscure poet named J. P. Silbert – one of his greatest songs in the uniformity and delicacy of its accompaniment, in its mastery of form and in its inspired sound-painting ('des Abendglöckleins Töne'), and a complete contrast to a second setting of Silbert ('Himmelsfunken', XX, 353), a simple yet highly sensitive strophic song. Even Mayrhofer's 'Beim Winde' (XX, 365; October

---

* How plainly the moonlight speaks to me, heartening me upon my way. 'Keep firmly to the old road, and look not for a place wherein thou mayst abide. Else the dark days will bring eternal troubles. Forth to others must thou go, must thou fare, free with ease from every plaint.' With gentle ebb and rising flow deep in my heart, thus I go forward into the darkness, climbing upwards in bold heart, climbing upwards in high spirits, and the world seems good to me. All that is pure I see in soft reflection, nothing disordered, nothing withered in the heat of the day; in cheerful company, yet alone.

1819), treated in 'da capo' form, presented its metrical problems which Schubert solved without difficulty. In February 1819, he turned from Schlegel and Silbert to his intimate Viennese friends, Grillparzer and, once again, Mayrhofer. Grillparzer, who had just achieved his first great success with his tragedy *Die Ahnfrau*, is represented by a setting of 'Bertha's Lied in der Nacht' (XX, 355) – a poem which he had written in 1816 and which he had probably intended to include at the beginning or end of an act for the leading actress in this same *Ahnfrau,* Sophie Schröder (it was, however, never used). Schubert starts in E flat minor and ends in F sharp major, and it is as if he had tried to capture all the sultriness of a fateful night in the harmonic richness of the accompaniment. Moreover, it says much for his acute ear that he set to music so little of Grillparzer and so much of Mayrhofer, whose poetic gifts overshadowed the insignificance of his personality. For Grillparzer was one of those not unusual German poets who are incapable of writing verse, and in whose poetry the ideas scarcely ever achieve complete purity of form. Schubert quite obviously felt this to be a serious shortcoming. A poem like Mayrhofer's 'An die Freunde' (XX, 256), an exhortation to his friends to think of life after he is dead without forgetting the bonds of friendship, is certainly obscure in its thought, but simple and beautiful in its form, and is treated by Schubert as a study in minor and major, in economy and richness of harmony, and in *staccato* and *legato*.

It is strange that his thoughts turned once more to Schiller during this period, after which he returned to him on only one subsequent occasion, in 1823. It is as if he had wanted to solve once and for all a problem which he had previously failed to solve adequately; for he had earlier already set to music not only 'Sehnsucht' (XX, 357) but also 'Hoffnung' (XX, 358) and 'Der Jüngling am Bache' (XX, 359). Like the 1812 version of 'Sehnsucht' the 1819 setting was also originally designed as a bass song, and only transcribed for soprano for the purpose of publication as op. 39 (1826). Schubert made of it a recital piece, full of enthusiasm in the true Schiller manner, and probably intended for the 'philosophical' Vogl; and it is somewhat incomprehensible to us today how the guitar, for which 'this vocal piece was arranged' in 1826, managed the sonorous and substantial accompaniment. The two other songs, both treated strophically, are examples of Schubert's new, sensitive simplicity.

Quite on its own stands the fragment from Schiller's hymn or elegy to the vanished and happy world of the gods of Greece ('Die Götter Griechenlands'; XX, 371) which exists in two almost identical settings. It is the twelfth verse which Schubert removed from its context simply to give expression to a purely personal mood, and to which he gave its *musical* form by repeating the first couplet at the end. It becomes a romantic lament for a lost world, the only remaining trace of which survives 'in the fairyland of song', and the distinction is symbolized in the contrast between A minor and A major. Later, in the Minuet of his A minor Quartet op. 29, Schubert alluded to the beginning of this song, and in the first movement of the same work he used the contrast between minor and major as the basic principle governing its form and content. Thus, in the instrumental work, he gave full expression to something at which he could only hint in the song. It is not a 'programme', however, but a symbol. Precisely the same symbolism permeates his later setting of Zacharias Werner's 'Morgenlied' (XX, 379: 1820), in order to convey the contrast between the joyousness of Nature and the vanished 'freshness of life'.

It must have been in May 1819 that Schubert came across a copy of the poems of that arch-Romanticist, Friedrich v. Hardenberg, better known as Novalis, who had died in 1801 in his late twenties. I cannot better Wilhelm Scherer's description of his *Geistliche Lieder,* of which Schubert set five to music:

... noble expression of love for Christ, no mere reminiscence as in Hölderlin's poetry, but the mood of child-like faith in its full presence, in full possession, without a definite confession, now catholicizing, now completely individual; ideas akin to those of Goethe developed in a Christian spirit, in part profanity made sacred, in part links from the spiritual chain which unites him with Paulus Gerhardt (the greatest evangelical lyric poet after Luther in the seventeenth century); in rhymed stanza form, but including one hymn in blank verse. ...

It is this very hymn in blank verse, on the mystical sacrament of the Last Supper, with which Schubert began. He fashions a cantata from the text, with an arioso opening in C major, a solemn middle-section in A flat major, and a sacred, dithyrambic ending in F major. A similar ecstasy informs the somewhat later 'Nachthymne' (XX, 372), written in January 1820, which ends with a true 'Liebestod' and an ascension. In contrast to the former hymn (XX, 360), the four other hymns or songs are extremely simple. Indeed, the hymn to the Virgin ('Marie', XX, 364) has a certain cloying sweetness. Two (XX, 361, 362), with the same change from B flat minor to B flat major, belong together. All these songs provide the most striking documentary evidence of Schubert's mystical creed, which has only a superficial connection with his Catholicism. For here he is a free artist, while as a Catholic church-composer he is bound and sometimes restricted by tradition.

After this period of Christian mysticism, there began what might be described as Schubert's 'classical period' as a songwriter, for which Mayrhofer was once more the principal source for his texts. Schubert re-created for his friends and himself that world of classical antiquity, the loss of which he lamented in 'Die Götter Griechenlands'. Even those songs of Mayrhofer's which are not 'classical', such as 'Im Winde' (XX, 365), 'Sternennächte' (XX, 366) and 'Nachtstück (XX, 368), fall into this same category. All are marked by a flight from the present into the 'sacred fervour' of the soul, by cosmic meditation, and by a longing for death. 'Sternennächte' is a pure jewel in the richness of its accompaniment and in the simplicity and spiritual fervour of its melody. The shimmering splendour of night is symbolized in the key of D flat major (subsequently cheapened to B flat major in the posthumous First Edition) in the upper register of the accompaniment. 'Nachtstück' becomes a magnificent hymn with 'harp' accompaniment, after a cantata-like introduction, while 'Trost' (XX, 387), which was written at the same time and in which Mayrhofer and Schubert make a little romantic play with the sound of horns and the thought of the loved one's grave, is a simple strophic song.

The 'classical' spirit finds its noblest expression in the setting of Goethe's 'Prometheus' (XX, 370; October 1819), in extreme contrast with which is the pleasant, almost too lyrical setting of Goethe's 'Die Liebende schreibt' (XX, 369) which preceded it. This 'Prometheus' is the counterpart to 'An Schwager Kronos' – not so uniform in its tempo and its mastery of the free metrical form, but still bolder in its interchange of description and gesture, and its combination of recitative with exalted declamation, from its portrayal of the thunder-storm at the beginning to the triumphantly defiant and yet restrained close. It is the most powerful piece at the disposal of a bass, provided that he is a concert performer and not an opera-singer, who could ruin the whole song by adopting a theatrical style.

Later in this year, between September and December 1820, the 'classical' spirit finds a somewhat more archae-ological expression in Mayrhofer's 'Orest auf Tauris' (XX, 382), 'Der entsühnte Orest' (XX, 383), 'Freiwilliges Ver-sinken' (XX, 384) and 'Der zürnenden Diana' (XX, 387), of which two different versions exist. Only this last song could be published. It would be more accurate and less misleading if its title were 'The dying Endymion', who expires in a frenzy of ecstasy at the sight of the chaste goddess in her nakedness. In Schubert's hands it becomes a superb achieve-ment – a passionate recital-piece for a tenor, with lyrical repetitions of the text and a completely homogeneous, 'sym-phonic' accompaniment. But the three other songs – es-pecially the beautifully conceived hymn of Apollo in 'Freiwilliges Versinken' – are even finer and more 'timeless' in conception and execution. If they had survived as the work of an anonymous composer, they would probably be dated not 1820 but 1900 – if there had still existed in 1900 a German composer of such abandon and freedom as Schubert.

From 1819 and 1820 onwards, there is scarcely a single song of Schubert's that is not stirring, not even among those strophic songs which are outwardly least pretentious. 'Frühlingsglaube' (XX, 380), written in 1820, is a strophic song of this kind, and at the same time one of his most popular. It was his first and unfortunately his only encounter with the Swabian poet Ludwig Uhland, and it is the best possible proof of his alert self-criticism. In the autumn of 1822 he had given his friend Josef Hüttenbrenner three songs to deliver to his new publishers, Sauer and Leidesdorf. These songs comprised his op. 20 and consisted of the above song, 'Sei mir gegrüsst' (XX, 400) and 'Hänflings Liebeswerbung' (XX, 316). But on 31st October he begged Hüttenbrenner to return the manuscripts, 'as he had im-portant alterations to make in them'. These 'important alter-

ations' consisted, in the case of 'Frühlingsglaube', of the
transposition of the song from B flat into the darker, more
intimate key of A flat, and of a more precise indication of
the dynamic light and shade of the accompaniment. He
made no alterations in the voice-part, which, as was his usual
practice, he left to the singer's intelligence and feeling. Even
when, towards the end of 1820, he set his friends' poems to
music, as for example Fr. X. v. Schlechta's somewhat childish 'Liebeslauschen' (XX, 381) which illustrates a painting by
the 'Nazarene' artist Ludwig Ferdinand von Schnorr and
provoked Schubert to one of his rare excursions into the
realm of waggish humour, or Heinrich Hüttenbrenner's
sentimentally extravagant 'Der Jüngling auf dem Hügel'
(XX, 385), he did so with an intense spirit of devotion. When
he returned once more to Mayrhofer's 'Sehnsucht' (XX,
386), which paints in the manner of Petrarch the contrast
between Nature's awakening ('The cloud-nigh songs of the
larks echo their rejoicing at Winter's flight') and the 'storm-
tossed soul' of the poet, the result was one of his most remarkable songs. It begins in a completely 'Italian', almost
pedantic and superficial, style, and then develops, without
change of time, into a free and sensitive description of a
state of mind. One is involuntarily reminded of Monteverdi
and his setting of Petrarch's 'Zefiro torna', a five-part madrigal which paints the same extreme contrast. December
1820 marks the beginning of a succession of Schubert's
greatest songs, starting with Schlegel's 'Im Walde' (XX, 388)
for which these ambitious and powerful songs paved the way
and which in its turn paved the way for the songs from
Goethe's *West-östlicher Divan*. It is consequently difficult
to interrupt our survey at this point. But it is unfortunately
one of the inevitable evils of historical biography that the
historian has to stop and then re-start the current of events,
in order to satisfy the requirements of logical presentation.

We will turn now to Schubert's church and choral music,
and to the opera and the oratorio of this period.

On 24th August, 1818, he wrote to Ferdinand from his
Hungarian exile: 'It is half-past eleven at night and your
Requiem is ready. Believe me, it made me sad, for I sang it
from a full heart. Please fill in any gaps, i.e., write the text

under the music and the expression marks over it. If you want to make some repeats, do so without troubling to write and ask me here in Zseliz. . . .' Ferdinand, who in all innocence considered his younger brother's store of ideas as a family possession – he borrowed a short *Kyrie* which Franz had written in 1813 (XIV, 21) for a Pastoral Mass of his own – performed this short Requiem the following September in the Orphanage Church, apparently as his own work, and duly confessed his guilt, for on 29th October Schubert replied as follows: 'I had already forgiven you the sin of appropriation in my first letter, so you had only your tender conscience as an excuse for not having written for so long. So you liked the Requiem; you wept over it and perhaps at the very word at which I wept. My dear brother, that, to me, is the finest reward for this present.' Ferdinand also proceeded to publish the work in 1825–26 with Diabelli, and it was accepted as being his until O. E. Deutsch returned it to its proper author and published it in 1928.* The author of the text was probably Joh. George Fallstich, Assistant Director of the Orphanage from 1816 to 1829. We could wish that we knew as much about some of the larger and more important works as we do about this series of ten short pieces, the most notable feature of which is the limited key-range (the main key is G minor), and in the 'Memento', the seventh number, the suggestion of the Three Boys' music in *Die Zauberflöte*.

The 'transubstantiation' chorus ends symbolically in G major instead of the original key of B flat major. It should be noted here, as O. E. Deutsch has pointed out in the postscript to his edition of the Requiem, that in May 1822 Schubert started work on a Mass in A minor 'for his brother Ferdinand', which was not however carried even as far as the end of the *Kyrie*. From November 1819, there dates a *Salve Regina* for soprano and strings which was published by Diabelli fifteen years after Schubert's death under the title of 'Third Offertorium, op. 153' (XIV, 3). I do not know for what occasion it was written; but the piece, in a seraphic, one might almost say Lohengrin-like, A major, is also 'sung from a full heart', and in its song-like and yet sensitive handling of the long text it is a little masterpiece, of scarcely less

---

* *Deutsche Trauermesse für gemischten Chor und Orgel*, Schubert-Erstdrucke II, Wien, Strache.

significance than Mozart's *Ave verum,* from which it derives. Shortly afterwards he wrote six Antiphons for the consecration of palms on Palm Sunday (XIV, 18), likewise intended for his brother and designed for performance at the Orphanage. This time the setting is for four-part chorus without organ accompaniment, and once more in a very restricted key-range, but with lively expression within the framework of a most simple homophonic style. In particular the words of Jesus on the Mount of Olives – desperation and resignation – are rendered with the simplest harmonic and dynamic symbolism. Not one of these short works is a routine composition. Each is the product of a profound personal interest. We of the troubled twentieth century are ill-fitted to do justice to the innocent sentimentality of the early Romantic or pre-Revolutionary period. Our poets no longer sing of love and spring, of rose-petals and nightingales – and yet a rose-petal and the song of nightingales are still things of beauty.

It is no great step from such works of intimate devotion to the setting of Psalm 23 for two sopranos and two contraltos with piano accompaniment which Schubert wrote at the end of 1820 for the musical *soirées* of Anna Fröhlich's pupils in the Conservatorium of the Society of Friends of Music (XVIII, 2). Anna was the eldest of these four delightful creatures, who, according to the *Allgemeine Wiener Musikzeitung* of 1841, did more for art in general and for the art of singing in particular in Vienna than many a vocal gymnast. They were the daughters of a merchant; they lived by themselves in the Spiegelgasse and enjoyed the best kind of society; their names were Maria Anna, Barbara, Katharina and Josephine. They were all four trained singers, three of them in a professional capacity for a time. Only Barbara, the most gifted of them, married, and her husband, naturally enough, was a musician. Katharina, the most charming, has taken her place in literature, beside Goethe's Lotte or Frau von Stein, as Grillparzer's 'eternal bride' (in his constant state of morbid depression, he could never make up his mind to marry her). It was probably Grillparzer's cousin, Leopold v. Sonnleithner, who introduced Schubert to the sisters. And Schubert presented them with a precious gift – an enchanting piece in its inspiration (A flat major), its wealth of harmony and modulation, and its climaxes. Dare one say that it provides us with the key to the harmonic exuberance of the first Impromptu of op. 90?

The modulating repetition which follows emphasizes the clearness of the parallel still more forcibly.

To a purely 'occasional' work of this kind (in Goethe's sense of the word), Schubert added during these years one or two genuine occasional works which testify not so much to his artistic ability as to his friendly nature. One of these was the cantata for Johann Michael Vogl's birthday on 10th August, 1819, which has already been mentioned above. It was written at Steyr, to a plain, straightforward poem by Albert Stadler in rhymed couplets, and was performed by Josephine v. Koller, Bernhard Benedict and Schubert himself with Stadler at the piano. The poem is full of references to Vogl's most celebrated roles, asks naïvely whether he does not want to return home to Steyr some day,

Wenn dich einst in greisen Tagen
*Deines Lebens Mühen plagen.**

and suggests that his 'spirit will sing on' after he is dead. Not a very encouraging suggestion! From the biographical point of view, the most notable feature, so far as we are concerned, is the part which Schubert wrote for himself. According to this, he had a good bass voice with a compass extending from low G to E in the baritone register. The terzets, the last of which is a 'canon', frame two solos and an antiphonal duet between soprano and tenor; Schubert, modest as usual, provided no solo for himself. The solos are in a markedly Italian style; Schubert does not treat them very seriously. For the soprano, Josephine v. Koller, Schubert wrote a cantata or rather a two-stanza arioso in Vienna in March 1820, likewise to some verses of Stadler's, which she sang on her father's name-day (XX, 586). It is a simple and charming little work.

Of a quite different calibre are the part songs for several voices which Schubert wrote during these years. Even the male-voice choruses among them only partially belong to the type of 'convivial songs' which were cultivated by the Berlin choral societies, and to which Schubert also paid a modest tribute in May 1815 with his semi-patriotic duet-settings of poems by Körner and Hölty. The Viennese were certainly no less patriotic; but choral singing in the service of patriotism and loyalty was not one of the permanent features of choral singers' programmes, as was the case in Berlin. Even when such songs are 'convivial', as, for example, the rondo-like four-part choral setting of Fr. Haug's 'Wein und Liebe' (XVI, 37), with its slight 'choral society' flavour, Schubert does not write for a massed choir, but for musically enlightened soloists who are capable of doing justice to his modulations and enharmonic changes. Three of these choruses are strophic songs – a free setting of Schiller's 'An den Frühling' (XVI, 40) with a fa-la-la at the end as in the 'ballets' of G. G. Gastoldi, 'Die Einsiedelei' and 'Der Entfernten' (XVI, 39 and 38) both to poems by Salis and the latter in C sharp major with an astonishing harmonic modulation at the end. Only the two finest, the settings of Goethe's 'Ruhe, schönstes Glück der Erde' (XVI, 36) and

* When in hoary old age life's troubles beset you.

Mignon's song 'Nur wer die Sehnsucht kennt' (XVI, 35),
bear a date (April 1819). One might describe the former as a
cosmic cradle-song in motet form. And even Mignon's song
provides an unintentional parallel with the sixteenth century: it is a five-part setting (two tenors and three basses) like
a madrigal by Rore, Marenzio or Monteverdi, and its
middle-section ('Es schwindelt mir') is full of the naturalistic
tone-painting of the old art-form. Is it not strange that Schubert should put into the mouths of a chorus – and a male-
voice chorus at that – this intensely subjective confession of
a girl, which he set so frequently as a song – in much the
same way that one of the old madrigalists treats a ballad
from the *Decameron*? But his intention is clear: he wanted
to invest the text with the intensest expression by means of
an extreme purity of sound, boldness of harmony, and
exactness of dynamics. In its painful harmonic tension, and
particularly in the new treatment of the first couplet each
time it occurs, the piece is unique, even for Schubert. It is
precisely what a great painter would call a studio-piece: 'not
for sale' and to be appreciated only by the artist and a few of
his friends.

On 19th November, 1819, a male-voice quartet of Schubert's with piano accompaniment, 'Das Dörfchen' (XVI, 4),
was performed for the first time at Ignaz von Sonnleithner's
house by Josef Barth, Josef Götz, Wenzel Nejebse and
Johann Karl Umlauff. It was a work which was repeated
many times elsewhere and with a different combination of
singers. The applause was always so great that Schubert
wrote two more similar quartets: 'Die Nachtigall' (XVI, 5)
to a text by Joh. Karl Unger, expressly composed at the beginning of 1821 for a concert at the Kärntnertor Theatre
(and sung on that occasion without piano accompaniment),
and a setting of Matthisson's 'Geist der Liebe' (XVI, 6). We
will take them together, although in so doing we go a little
beyond the chronological limits of this chapter, since the last
of the three pieces was not written until January 1822. Schubert himself combined them in his op. 11 which he dedicated
to the first tenor of the quartet, Josef Barth, who (like
Götz) was an official in the household of Prince Schwarzen-
berg and at the same time a singer in the Chapel Royal.
Nowhere is the 'solo' character of such songs more noticeable than in these pieces, and their inclusion in the Col-

lected Edition under the heading of 'Male-voice Choruses' could not possibly be more misleading. With this 'solo' character, however, there goes hand in hand a convivial spirit, which is emphasized by the apocryphal addition of a guitar accompaniment ad libitum. A quartet of this kind could well be sung in the open air. Schubert showed a little favouritism in the part which he wrote for Barth; but all three pieces end with a canon or 'round' which gives each of the soloists his due. The first two are without any kind of harmonic surprises, and only in the last of the three did Schubert forget his middle-class audience and his middle-class singers by allowing 'Geist der Liebe' (in C major) to work its way down to the depths of C flat major. The four singers sometimes joined forces with four more of their friends to perform Schubert's eight-part setting of 'Gesang der Geister über den Wassern', and on one occasion a member of the audience, the secretary to Count Karl Esterhazy, noted in his diary (77th March, 1821) that the piece 'foundered completely', i.e., was not even remotely understood. No wonder. 'Geist der Liebe' fared no better.

Throughout this period, Schubert was constantly preoccupied with thoughts of opera, even during his stay at Zseliz. In their letters to him in his exile, his friends must have spoken highly of Rossini's Elisabetta, which had been produced on 3rd September, 1818, at the Theater an der Wien, for on 8th September, he replied as follows: 'That the opera people in Vienna should be so stupid as to perform all the best operas now, while I am away, makes me really rather angry.' And behind this humorous disappointment over his inability 'to be there,' there naturally lay his concern over not being able to write a great opera of his own, the success of which alone could have rescued him from poverty. If he could have written such an opera, he would certainly have offered a formidable challenge to Rossini.

Nevertheless, in January 1819 he began, with an eye to 'practical considerations', an opera which still kept completely to the lines of the German ballad-opera or his own earlier experiments in this field, such as Der vierjährige Posten or Claudine. Its title was Die Zwillingsbrüder, the libretto 'adapted from the French' by Fr. v. Hoffmann – a 'ballad opera in one act', as the manuscript of the full score described it. In the programme, however, it appeared as 'a farce with music'; for something unusual happened. The work was accepted and was also produced, after a long delay, at the Kärntnertor Theatre on 14th June, 1820. At the first performance it was given in a double bill with a two-act comic ballet, *Die Zwey Tanten, oder: Ehemals and heute,* with music by the prolific old composer Adalbert Gyrowetz.

Schubert probably completed it by January or February 1819. It was at any rate ready before May of that year, for on 19th May he wrote as follows in a letter to Anselm Hüttenbrenner: 'In spite of a man like Vogl, it is difficult to out-manoeuvre riff-raff like Weigl, Treitschke, etc. – That is why, instead of my operetta, they give other *trash*, which makes one's hair stand on end.' The explanation of this is given in a letter from Anton Holzapfel to Albert Stadler, written about the same time (24th May): 'Schubert ... writes at Vogl's instigation and therefore not without reason, operettas for production, operas and other big works. ...' Vogl himself had apparently suggested the adaptation of the libretto from the French (*Les deux Valentins*), because he wanted to play the double role of the elderly Bramarbas and the latter's good-natured twin brother. (How he managed to do this without the help of a dummy or 'double' is a little puzzling, for in the final scene both brothers are on the stage at the same time.) And it was thanks to his influence that the work was not only accepted but also performed.

It met with a mixed reception. 'Schubert's friends made a lot of noise and the rival faction hissed', writes an eye-witness of the first performance in his diary. '... At the end there was quite an uproar until Vogl appeared and said: "Schubert is not present. I thank you in his name." '* The press notices both in the Viennese and foreign (i.e., Dresden and Leipzig) papers were more or less unanimous in their condemnation of the piece. According to these, Schubert had no talent for comedy; he shot at sparrows with cannons; he 'pursues the listener restlessly by means of modulations

---

*Anselm Hüttenbrenner gives a slightly different version of what happened. In actual fact, Schubert was sitting in the gallery as usual with Anselm Hüttenbrenner, but could not be prevailed upon to exchange his old frock-coat for Hüttenbrenner's tail-coat, so as to be able to take a curtain. He listened smilingly to Vogl's apology and then celebrated the evening with his friends over a bottle of light Hungarian wine. (O. E. Deutsch, p. 135.)

and allows him no respite'; in the ensembles 'the voices seem
to be treated too individually (!)'; 'little of the real essence of
song'; '... whereas a confused surfeit of instrumentation,
and anxious striving after originality by persistent modulation allows hardly a moment's rest'. Mozart's son, Wolf-
gang Amadeus, jun., also happened to hear the first
performance, and he, too, thought that the music contained
some quite pretty things but that it was treated a little too
seriously. The notice in *Der Sammler* did not even mention
Schubert's name, although it dismissed his music by and
large as a childish experiment. Only Baron Schlechta's notice
in the *Conversationsblatt* gave him some degree of credit.
Nevertheless the critics as a whole foresaw a not altogether
hopeless future for the young composer. We do not know
what Schubert's reaction was to all this rubbish, in which the
critics who wrote for 'foreign' consumption excelled even
their Viennese colleagues. The work survived only for six
performances, and was withdrawn once and for all at the
end of July. Even Gyrowetz's ballet was of no assistance;
Gyrowetz himself in his autobiography did not number it
among his 'successful ballets'.

One of these Viennese critics expressed himself in the following superior terms: 'We can conveniently ignore the contents of the libretto', and thereby set the standard for much
of the subsequent biographical writings about Schubert. We
can in fact do no such thing, any more than could Schubert,
who had put himself in the place of his characters. A worthy
village mayor had promised his daughter's hand in marriage
to one of his neighbours – Franz Spiess – when the latter was
about to leave for the wars with his twin brother – Friedrich
Spiess. After eighteen years the girl has naturally long since
found another bridegroom, at which juncture the two
brothers, the one rough and the other good-natured, unex-
pectedly return as one-eyed wrecks, each without the other
knowing. And out of this *quid pro quo* the not particularly
exciting development proceeds.

Now Schubert could have retorted to his critics that he
had done complete justice to his characters: in the ariettas,
one of which – the good-natured brother's greeting to his
native land – was praised even by these severe critics; and
particularly in the ensembles, an extremely lively quartet
consisting of short motives, and a still livelier trio, in which

the two lovers stand their ground against Bramarbas' blustering insistence on his old rights. What put the critics out of joint was probably the wrong classification of the piece as 'farce'. As a result they completely misjudged the loveliest thing in the score, Lieschen's aria 'Der Vater mag wohl immer Kind mich nennen'. They found it simply 'too long'. But here the audience – particularly the professional members of it – *must* have noticed or felt something: the suppressed excitement, the enchanting *concertante* treatment of the wind instruments, the clean contours of the form. As a character sketch *in nuce*, it is a counterpart to Cherubini's 'Non so più', only the end is perhaps a little coquettish. The Introduction of the opera, a charming serenade or, rather, aubade for solo and chorus in Schubert's favourite rhythm, which had to be repeated at the first performance, deserves our special attention, as do the two duets for the pair of lovers, the concluding quintet with chorus, and the homely final chorus. The overture is a thing of grace and in it – in a mysterious key and a mysterious *pianissimo* – there is already a hint of the trombone motive in the first movement of the C major Symphony.

Schubert must have been disgusted by this first experience of a public performance of one of his operas, not merely because of the reactions of the critics but because of the intrigues which delayed the production. He therefore started work secretly on a subject for which he had no need of the theatre and in which he did not have to take 'practical considerations' into account – his *Lazarus*. It bears the title: 'Religious Drama in three acts'. But Schubert himself described it as an 'Easter Cantata' and could never have hoped to put such a work on the stage, least of all in Vienna, particularly since the author of the libretto was a Protestant theologian and pedagogue named August Hermann Niemeyer (1754–1828), who was a senior Ecclesiastical Commissioner in Halle and who was viewed with suspicion not only by the Imperial police but also by the Prussian authorities. Schubert accordingly wrote a 'sacred opera', in which imagination at its most vivid had to take the place of visible action, and in which he could devote to the vocal writing and orchestral accompaniment a delicacy of treatment which would not have been legitimate in the more 'drastic' field of opera.

Lazarus, oder Die Feier der Auferstehung is one of Niemeyer's early poetical works. It was published in 1778 and it
is a little puzzling how a copy happened to come into Schubert's hands.* It is also a little depressing, for chance might
have led Schubert to something better. Imagine that Goethe
had carried out his project of an opera or an oratorio based
on the story of Samson and Delilah on the lines that he had
once tried to explain to Zelter, and that such a libretto had
fallen into Schubert's hands. As we have mentioned, *Lazarus*
is no poetic masterpiece. The first 'act' contains the death-
scene of the sick man. His sisters, Maria and Martha, carry
him into the open-air, where he exhorts them to be resigned
to the inevitable – an exhortation which the pious Maria
accepts more readily than the despairing Martha. His brother
Nathaniel then brings from his Master and Saviour the assurance of eternal life and finally, as the embodiment and
living evidence of the miracle of resurrection, Jairus's daughter appears. And so, at the last, the sick man dies, in the arms
of his sisters and surrounded by his friends. The second 'act'
is set in 'a verdant meadow, full of gravestones and surrounded by palm-trees and cedars' close by Lazarus's house,
and introduces, as a contrasting character, the sceptical
Simon the Sadducee, who shrinks back from the yawning
grave. Nathaniel comforts him and invites him to attend the
burial of Lazarus. . . .

> *Vielleicht, dass dir im Liede der Freundschaft*
> *süsse Andacht der Unsterblichket herüberlispelt!*†

The fragment breaks off with the double choruses of this
burial-scene and with Martha's outburst of lamentation. As
poetry, it is all a peculiar mixture of Klopstock and Metastasio, only without Klopstock's power and Metastasio's
grace.

If we say that, from the point of view of the historical
development of opera towards the music-drama, Schubert's
fragment far surpasses *Tannhäuser* and *Lohengrin*, we are
not making too great a claim. Schubert was free of every
consideration of operatic convention, and here attempted
something which he only occasionally achieved in his operas:

* Johann Heinrich Rolle, 1718–1785, was the first to set this text to
music.
† Perhaps, in the song of friendship, sweet thoughts of immortality will
whisper to you!

the blending of recitative and aria. The long first 'act' contains only four arias, which grow directly out of the recitative and which are treated with the greatest possible freedom. And the recitative is accompanied throughout in the orchestra with a fullness and delicacy of treatment which, of their period, are quite unique. A detailed analysis would require a far greater space than is possible in this book. There occur in this sacred opera sublime things which are not to be found even in Schubert's songs, such as Jairus's daughter's description of her death, her glimpse of the heavenly paradise and her return to earthly life. Over the whole 'act' there lies a shimmer of transfiguration – the outcome of an intense enthusiasm, a purity of soul, and an astonishing creative power. Simon's aria in the second 'act' and Martha's grief-stricken outburst tend rather towards an operatic pathos; the former, written a few years before *Euryanthe* and several years before *Lohengrin*, anticipates everything that Lysiart or Telramund have to say; and this drift into a theatrical style may have been the reason why Schubert never completed the work. He felt that he could not surpass the first 'act' or it may even be that he realized in the end that he was wasting his efforts on a hopeless undertaking. But this first 'act' is a perfect work of art, and as *The Death of Lazarus* it could testify in our concert halls to Schubert's dramatic and musical greatness.

Chapter Nine

From *Die Zauberharfe*
to *Alfonso und Estrella*
The Mass in A flat. From the E major
to the B minor Symphony

End of 1820 to 1822

The excursion into the field of oratorio availed him little, and from now on Schubert was more than ever preoccupied with thoughts of opera. This particular episode must have convinced him that an operatic success offered the only possible solution to his problem of dependence or independence. He therefore probably jumped at the opportunity when in the summer of 1820 he was commissioned to write the music for a 'spectacular piece', which was planned as a benefit for the scene-painter, the stage-manager and the costume-maker of the Theater an der Wien – *Die Zauberharfe,* with a libretto by the secretary of the theatre, Georg Ernst Hoffmann. So far as the material and treatment of this work were concerned Schubert, with the experience of *Des Teufels Lustschloss* behind him, was on familiar ground. One of the critics who attended the performance, Baron Schlechta, has admirably formulated the recipe for a magic-play of this kind:

Take one good and one evil magician, who are at loggerheads with each other; then take a lunatic young lady of noble ancestry living in the ruins of a castle, a blubbering father and a spellbound son; add a few absurd knights who must make themselves quite ludicrous; and finally ten or twelve monsters, the more fantastic the better. Mix these ingredients with a bucket of tears, a handful of sighs and a solid lump of ridiculous magic. Stew the concoction until it is completely unintelligible—and the dish of nonsense is then ready to serve.

Die Zauberharfe is a piece which makes lavish demands on *décor* or scenic effects after the style of *Die*

Zauberflöte, but without that 'profound meaning' which in
this case even a Mozart could not have provided. Schubert
was therefore quite right in keeping his music on the same
'theatrical' level. One piece of this music – the Overture –
has survived to the present day, although only under the
name of 'Overture to *Rosamunde*' or even 'Overture to the
opera *Alfonso und Estrella*', under which title it was published. But it belongs to *Die Zauberharfe* since its themes,
both in the Introduction and at the opening of the 'Allegro
vivace', reappear throughout the work as a melodramatic
background. This opening section, varied in 'leitmotiv'
fashion, is used to illustrate the character of the sentimental
heroine Ida. Now, this overture is an awkward piece, in spite
of or rather because of its popularity. The Andante, familiar
to us as being identical with the Adagio which introduces
the Overture for four hands of December 1817 (IX, 10) –
this Andante is pseudo-Romantic, because it is semi-Italian
in style. The Vivace – a sonata-form movement without a
development section and with a *stretta* – is trivial in its harmony and noisy in its orchestration. One might say that
Schubert is here imitating or popularizing himself. According to Schwind (letter to Schober dated 23rd December,
1823) Schubert himself later summed the overture up perfectly when he described it as 'too homespun', i.e., too swag-
gering, too cheap (always assuming, of course, that Schwind
had not got his overtures confused). And the contemporary
critics were rightly surprised at the Overture to the third act
which is nothing but a March-Divertissement in rondo-
form.

For the rest, Schubert had to write a series of striking
choruses for knights and squires and for troubadours or for
all of these together, with or without solo, in march tempo or
in 3/4 time, accompanied by the full orchestra or by the
wind section alone. Occasionally, in some of his 'knightly'
music, he anticipates the C. M. Weber of *Euryanthe*

and he also competes with him elsewhere, as for example in a 'chorus of Genii' for women's voices ('Schlafe, Liebliche'). But above all, in five of the thirteen numbers in the score, he had to contend with one of the most unfortunate forms of dramatic music – the 'Melodrama'; that is to say, he had to provide the orchestral background to and link between empty emotionalism and hollow bombast in their extremest forms. He did it, so to speak, with practised skill. The score would provide a regular mine of information for a history of orchestration before Berlioz. Schubert here puts to theatrical use the intimate discoveries which he had made for *Lazarus*. One of the 'Melodramas' employs only a wind-orchestra off-stage. And in keeping with the title of the work, Schubert brings into action not one, but *two* harps. Next to the horn the harp is the 'Romantic' instrument *par excellence*. But our view that he is nowhere more un-Romantic or more superficially Romantic than in his stage-works still holds good. The miracle of the harp, which resolves the conflict at the most critical moment, is Schubertian in its modulation from B flat minor to E major, but from the melodic point of view it is pure Rossini. And one is doing the work no injustice if one describes it as a whole as 'melodramatic' in both senses of the word.

It must have been about the same time that Schubert turned his attention to a more serious operatic project – a version of *Sakuntala* based on Kalidasa's Indian drama, two acts of which were sketched for him by Johann Philipp Neumann. Neumann had been Professor of Physics, Secretary and Librarian at the Polytechnic Institute in Vienna, and was a man of considerable culture. Whether he was a good librettist is open to argument. The sketch remained a sketch, and the project no more than a project.

Kreissle v. Hellborn has given us a detailed account of the plot, which makes it clear – at least from the dramatic point of view – that Schubert was deterred from completing the opera by 'the covert suggestions of some of his friends to whom the poem did not appeal as suitable material for an opera libretto'. This Indian magic-opera, half fantasy half burlesque, which still belonged to the current *genre* of Viennese magic-plays, could never have been effective on the stage, and would never have repaid the expenditure of Schubert's creative genius. In the manuscript 'the voice-parts and

the text have been written out in full; the greater part of the
bass of the accompaniment has been filled in, and here and
there individual bars or figures of the violin and flute parts
have been noted down; the final chorus (Heavenly choir) is
the only fully completed number.' (It is a chorus with wind
accompaniment, probably for women's voices, in F major
and 3/4 time, and with the following words:

> *Lieblos verstossen – Ohne Erbarmen,*
> *Bist du von frommen – Liebenden Armen*
> *Gern aufgenommen – Sakontala!**

Schubert sketched the first two acts, but did not touch the
last, which would have contained a succession of large-scale
choral numbers. Unfortunately not a single note of the work
appears in the reprint of the Collected Edition – not even the
one completed number.

The year 1821 produced only a single contribution from
Schubert in the operatic field. This took the form of two
interpolations for inclusion in Louis Jos. Ferdinand Hérold's
comic opera *La Clochette*, which naturally enough became a
Zauberglöckchen in the process of adaptation for the Viennese stage. These interpolations consist of a highly
emotional aria for tenor, and a *buffo* duet for tenor and
bass. Just as Mozart was never prepared to descend below
his own level when he wrote interpolations for the operas of
his contemporaries, so Schubert here wrote two numbers
which were far superior to anything that Hérold was capable
of. The duet was particularly well-received, even by critics.

The following year, however, produced another fully-
fledged stage-work, the 'opera in three acts', *Alfonso und
Estrella*. This time the author of the libretto was once again
Schubert's friend Franz v. Schober. The two 'heavenly
twins' worked on it together at St. Pölten, where they were
enjoying the hospitality of Bishop Johann Nepomuk v. Dan-
kesreither in the autumn of 1821. They 'had great hopes of
it' (Schubert's letters to Jos. v. Spaun of 2nd November,
1821) and the reason is obvious. The title itself is most
significant, and shows that what mattered to the two friends
was to win at a single stroke and with the most modern
weapons that success for which they longed so much and

---

* Harshly, pitilessly rejected, Thou art tenderly received by gentle,
loving arms, Sakontala!

which was so vital to them. Titles consisting of the names of two lovers had fallen somewhat into disuse since *Orfeo ed Euridice*, but had become fashionable again with Rossini's *Torwaldo e Dorlisca, Ricciardo e Zoraide, Eduardo e Cristina,* Mercadante's *Elissa e Claudio*, Morlacchi's *Tebaldo e Isolina* and even *Zemire und Azor* by Rossini's arch-opponent, Louis Spohr. This work marks Schubert's departure from the ballad- and magic-opera to the Italian-style 'grand opera'. One must not allow oneself to be deceived by the German libretto, which often reads like the bad translation of an Italian original:

TROILA:
> *Was kann Dir Teurer fehlen,*
> *Von Lust bist Du umringt . . .*

ALFONSO:
> *Dir kann ich nichts verhehlen,*
> *Dich lieb' ich unbedingt.**

or:

TROILA:
> *Erkennst Du jene Menge?*
> *Dein Heer in Siegsgepränge*
> *Kehrt aus der Schlacht zurück.*
> *Mein Sohn hat sie geführt.*

MAUREGATO:
> *Wie tief bin ich gerührt,*

ESTRELLA:
> *Alfonso triumphiert.†*

Nor should one be deceived by the superficially 'Romantic' colouring of the plot in which, characteristically, a golden

---

* TROILA:
  > What can ail thee, my beloved son?
  > Pleasure and delight are all around thee . . .
  ALFONSO:
  > I cannot conceal aught from thee.
  > I love thee unfeignedly.
† TROILA:
  > See'st thou yonder host?
  > Thine army returns from battle
  > In all the pomp of victory.
  > My son led them.
  MAUREGATO:
  > How deeply am I stirred!
  ESTRELLA:
  > Alfonso triumphs!

chain is not a 'magic chain', and has no magic function, but
is simply a talisman and a sign of recognition. All the ingredients of the latest fashion in Italian opera are present
here: the arias, which even include the inevitable 'vengeance
aria'; the love-duets; a conspirator scene – as involuntarily
funny as all such scenes, which, though the situation
demands an atmosphere of hushed secrecy, can never avoid
a *fortissimo* outburst; the large-scale Finale for soloists and
chorus – in this particular case a *double* chorus. (The con-
sistent use of the double chorus suggests perhaps that Schober and Schubert had an immediate model in mind, unless of
course it was simply Schubert's own *Lazarus* or *Zauberharfe*.) The only number which has any claim to being 'Romantic' (in the most superficial sense) or 'German' is the
orchestral Ballade with harp which opens the second act.
Schober, who had provided Schubert the song-writer with as
happy a text as his poem 'An die Musik', built his plot
around a highly dramatic situation in precisely the same way
as his contemporary librettists. Troila, the deposed king, a
new Sarastro or Prospero, has lived for twenty years in a
pastoral retreat behind rocky walls, the revered sovereign
lord of his son Alfonso and a few faithful followers. The
usurper, Mauregato, is the father of a charming daughter
Estrella, a ray of light in the darkness of his brooding spirit,
who, losing her way while out hunting, meets Alfonso with
the inevitable operatic result: love at first sight. Adolfo, the
usurper's victorious general, and a sinister character, asks for
Estrella's hand as a reward for his military services, and
when he is rebuffed or discouraged by both father and
daughter, he turns conspirator. The conspiracy is on the
point of succeeding when Alfonso comes to the rescue and is
recognized as the legitimate heir and rightful bridegroom.
Troila-Prospero extends a general pardon, the villain is
whisked away to prison and after all this excitement the
opera ends in general rejoicing. There is nothing 'Romantic'
here. The whole work is 'theatrical' in the purest sense of the
word as applied to the Italian opera of the day.

Schubert accordingly does not hesitate to imitate the
Italian manner, although he abides by his principle and
avoids 'the usual Italian gallopades' and *fioritura*, since he
was not writing for Italian singers. When one studies the
Introduction in B flat major ('Still noch decket uns die

Nacht'), one is involuntarily reminded of a very similar Introduction, this time in B major: 'Posa in pace', from Verdi's *Un Ballo in Maschera*. Troila's first utterance is a large-scale *scena*, the arioso section of which is purely Italian in its vocal line and ornamentation:

The Verdi of *Ballo in Maschera* appears as large as life in the duet between Estrella and Alfonso (No. 12):

Occasionally one can still recognize the 'German' Schubert, as for example in Alfonso's *scena ed aria* (No. 5), an exquisite lyric piece for tenor, or in the Hunting Chorus for women's voices with solo. And throughout he is still recognizable in the warmth of the modulations and in the richness (though not the delicacy) of the orchestration. Liszt, who produced the work at Weimar in June 1854 as an act of piety, was quite right in emphasizing the reverse side to this richness (*Collected Papers*, III, 73):

> The orchestration plays a very subordinate role and is really nothing more than a piano accompaniment arranged for orchestra. Two particularly tiring features are the repeated use of arpeggios on the violas (so-called 'batteries') and the monotony with which he doubles chords, figures and passages on different instruments, without the slightest relief or variation on the part of the other instruments. . . .

So far as the general style of this opera is concerned, Schubert resorts too often to the use of arioso in a stereotyped rhythm which he elsewhere avoids, and to an illustrative symphonic technique such as the description of the battle (No. 23) which is not sufficiently positive, since it could equally well represent a storm. Everything is theatrical in the extreme. But – and here once again is evidence of his incomparable talent – it is a theatrical technique which points to the future. Adolfo's passionately sombre courtship-scene, with its powerfully rhythmic orchestral accompaniment, could well have been written by Verdi, and by the mature Verdi at that. The repentance scene of the usurper finds its first counterpart in *Don Carlo*. Even the overture in D major, with an introduction in the minor, and with a violent octave figure, is magnificently passionate; and I cannot possibly believe that it was this overture which Schubert himself found 'too homespun'.

We are probably being unjust to Schubert. We expect from him, even in his operas, an enchanted or enchanting world of romance, whereas he sought to provide nothing more than a German counterpart to the Italian *opera semi-seria* of 1820. And in one respect he went far beyond this *opera semi-seria*. The first four scenes of the third act are no longer individual numbers linked by recitative, but treated, from a dramatic musical point of view, as one great single scene which rises to a tremendous climax – a climax, that is, in the purely theatrical sense. And this was conceived and written *before* Weber's *Euryanthe*.

Here again, as in *Die Zwillingsbrüder*, the part of Troila was obviously written expressly for his friend and champion Vogl. But Schubert was unlucky, even though for once he had based an opera on practical speculation. On 7th December, 1822, he wrote to Spaun: 'I had no luck with the opera in Vienna. I asked to have it back and have now received it. Vogl has left the theatre, too. In the near future I shall send it to Dresden, whence I have received a very promising letter from Weber, or to Berlin.' And he added: 'I should be quite well, if only this wretched business of the opera were not so mortifying.' – clear evidence of how much he took these repeated disappointments with his operas to heart. We do not know how the correspondence with Weber ended; it is significant that Schubert's name is not mentioned even *once* in Weber's writings, although it occurs a few times in his letters. It is clear, however, that after Schubert's clash with Weber over the merits or demerits of *Euryanthe*, there was no longer any hope for him in Dresden. It appears that Weber maintained an unbroken silence after this, for on 2nd December, 1824, Schober wrote to Schubert as follows: 'Have you had absolutely no word from C. M. Weber? Write to him again and if you do not get a satisfactory reply, ask him to send it back (the score of *Alfonso und Estrella*).' Schubert probably did this, for about the same time the prospect of a performance of the work presented itself in Berlin. Anna Milder-Hauptmann, a pupil of Vogl's, whose name has gone down to history as the first Leonore in Beethoven's *Fidelio*, had become a successful interpreter of his songs in Berlin, and towards the end of 1824, she asked him to send her one of his operas, since 'she gathered he had written several'. One can imagine the excitement and the high hopes with which Schubert carried out this request. But on 8th March, 1825, she wrote to him thus: 'With regard to your opera *Alfonso und Estrella*, I am extremely sorry to have to say that its libretto does not correspond with the local taste. People here are accustomed to grand tragic opera or French comic opera. The popular taste being what it is, you will yourself realize that *Alfonso und Estrella* would not stand any chance whatever of success here.' This was simply an excuse, of course. She looked for a part for herself in the score, and when she did not find one – the part of Estrella is what one would call a 'lyric soprano role' – she had no further use for it. For in the following sentence she let the cat out of the bag. 'If I am to have the pleasure of being able to appear in one of your operas, it would certainly have to be suited to my personality – including, for example, a role for a queen or a mother or a peasant woman. I would therefore advise you to write something new, in one act if possible, and preferably on an oriental subject with a leading role for the soprano. You certainly ought to be able to make a first-rate success of this idea, judging from Goethe's *Divan* [she meant Schubert's setting of poems from the *West-östlicher Divan*]. With three characters, i.e., soprano, tenor and bass, and a chorus you could be sure of a good performance here. . . . Please let me know what I am to do with your opera *Alfonso*.' Schubert apparently asked her to send it back, the richer by one more disappointment, and for the time being it lay forgotten in his desk. It was not until the

late summer of 1827, on the occasion of a visit to the Pachlers at Graz, that it was mentioned again, and Schubert sent
first the libretto and then the manuscript of the full score to
Karl Pachler, who wanted to show it to the Graz theatre
manager Stöger. Once again nothing came of it, and Schubert would have had to wait until 1882 to hear a performance in his own native Vienna.

We have already mentioned 'Gesang der Geister über
den Wassern' and with it we will return to February 1821
and to a work in which Schubert did not feel himself
bound by convention. It is the second setting of the poem
for male-voice chorus (XVI, 3), and we hesitate to say that it
is superior to the earlier setting of March 1817. It owed its
composition partly, no doubt, to Schubert's determination to
do complete justice to an 'ultra-symbolical' text of this kind,
but partly, too, to his desire to provide his interpreters with
something 'practicable' and to simplify the difficulties of in-
tonation for them by the addition of an instrumental accompaniment. This second setting is for two groups of four
tenors and four basses, which Schubert keeps strictly separate from each other, and for an instrumental combination
of two violas, two 'cellos and a double-bass. It would be
sheer murder to perform the work with chorus and string
orchestra. But once again it says much for his uncompromising artistry that the second setting became no simpler
or more easily accessible in the process. We can judge how
seriously he approached it from a sketch in the form of a
Particella (XVI, 45) which has clearly not survived in its
entirety. It begins and ends in the slowest tempo, in reflective
mood and with an accompanying string figure in Schubert's
favourite dactylic rhythm. It gradually becomes more animated until it reaches the dramatic climax ('Ragen Klippen
dem Sturz entgegen'), in which the voices join in unison and
in thirds. It then calms down to a Pastorale and finally dies
away in the softest *pianissimo*, all passion spent and every
outline softened. As in an old motet, the harmony conforms
like a flash to each change of mood, except that in a motet of
this kind the double role of the instrumental accompaniment
as a connecting link and a supporting commentary was something as yet unknown. This second setting, like the first, is
one of Schubert's greatest works.

Schubert now approached his songs, if possible, in an even more serious frame of mind than before and the group-system of composition became as increasingly rare as the return to the strophic song. In the previous chapter we left Schubert, as a song-writer, at his 'classical songs', and we have confessed how arbitrary our method was to pick up the thread again with the setting of Friedrich Schlegel's 'Im Walde' (XX, 388). But this song, or, rather, this pantheistic hymn of over two hundred bars is no less epoch-making than 'Gretchen am Spinnrade', in its power of melodic expression and its ability – while still preserving throughout the unity of the rustling accompaniment – to transform this expression from a mystical to a heroic mood, to a piece of striking imagery ('Herrlich ist der Flamme Leuchten', 'Rasch die Flamme zuckt und lodert'), and thence to an atmosphere of idyllic calm. And he devoted no less creative energy to the next two songs, which he wrote in January 1821 – the settings of A. W. v. Schlegel's 'Die gefangenen Sänger' and Caroline Pichler's 'Der Unglückliche' (XX, 389, 390). We have already referred to the symbolism of one particular D major passage in the latter song while we were on the subject of the sonata which he wrote for Pepi v. Koller. But when Schubert dreams of the lost paradise

> *Woraus in deiner Jugend goldnen Zeiten*
> *Die harte Hand des Schicksals dich verstiess,**

we are reminded no less of the B minor Symphony.

Ex. 84

It is in keeping with this increased seriousness that Schubert turned once more to Goethe at the beginning of 1821, and to those poems where Goethe is at his greatest and most thrilling. We will begin with 'Grenzen der Menschheit', written in March (XX, 393), since there is a demonstrable connection between this song and the 'Prometheus' of October

---

* Whence in the golden days of thy youth
the hard hand of Fate cast thee forth.

1819. The poem is the counterpart to 'Prometheus'; in the latter there is the fiercest defiance of the arbitrary will of a tyrannical deity, while here there is a reverential shudder of awe at its power. Both poems open with the rumbling of a majestic thunderstorm, but in 'Grenzen der Menschheit' Schubert disregards the scenic background. He borrows from 'Prometheus' the iambic motif of defiance ('Ich dich ehren? Wofür?') and makes it the symphonic basis of the whole song. The manuscript reveals that at one point, in the fifth bar, he inserted the up-beat as an afterthought, as if he had forgotten something important and essential, as if he did not want the song to depend entirely on its harmonic power, ranging as it does between C major and E major. Like 'Prometheus', 'Grenzen der Menschheit' is also a song for bass. The manuscript shows that this, too, was an afterthought. Nothing proves better than this song how mistaken it is to imagine that Schubert simply sat down at his desk after reading a poem that had happened to catch his eye, and covered a few sheets of paper with notes. Must we repeat yet again that in this song, as in many others, Schubert anticipates Wagner's principle of unification by symphonic means?

One month later, in April, Schubert turned his attention to two of Mignon's songs from *Wilhelm Meister* (XX, 395, 394), and these would rank as the most perfect settings of them, had not Schubert himself surpassed them five years later. Both are in B minor. In both the accompaniment is pitched in so low a register that the voice-part seems to float above it, and in both Schubert aimed at a very simple and intense treatment. In 'So lasst mich scheinen, bis ich werde' there seems to be a melodic connection with the first movement of the last piano sonata, and the elementary contrast between minor and major here plays its most elementary role. The emotional intensity is best illustrated in the two-bar postludes:

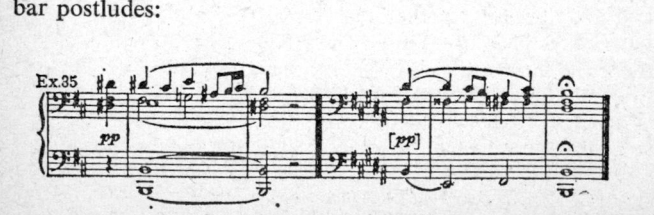

In January 1821, however, Schubert had discovered a new Goethe, just as the aged Goethe had rediscovered himself a few years earlier. The *West-östlicher Divan* had been published in the early autumn of 1819, and in it Goethe, the 'Greek', could express himself under the oriental cloak of the Persian poet Hafiz on light-hearted matters, on wisdom and on love with a depth and passion such as he had never before achieved. It is a coincidence that the idea of this disguise had its origin in Vienna – in the admittedly inadequate translations of the Viennese orientalist Josef v. Hammer-Purgstall who for his part was anything but pleased with 'Hatem'-Goethe's transformation and transfiguration of Persian poetry. Schubert was not in the slightest interested in orientalism. The only things that mattered to him were humanity and nature. Consequently in the very first poem of his selection ('Versunken', XX, 391), in which the poet toys in raptures with the curls of his beloved's hair, Schubert omitted the last two lines.

> . . . . *So hast du, Hafis, auch getan;*
> *Wir fangen es von vornen an.* . . .*

He was quite certainly unaware that the next poem, 'Geheimes' (XX, 392) has a literal origin in one of Hafis' love-poems, and equally unaware that the remaining two, 'Suleika I und II' (XX, 396 and 397) were not actually written by Goethe, but by his *inamorata*, Marianne Willemer, *née* Jung. She was an Austrian, so that here, too, there is a connection, so to speak, with Vienna, a return to Vienna. Of the four songs, the first two have a common key (A flat major), and the second two, to the East and West Winds, a common thought. Though they belong together, the first two are in fierce contrast to each other; the first depicts an ecstatic eroticism in its tempestuous accompaniment (Schubert could not publish it); the second, the most loving confidence, with its melody floating over a reassuring accompanying theme in the middle register. Brahms, who understood such things and who wrote what is probably an imitation in his 'Von ewiger Liebe', declared that 'Suleika I' was the loveliest song that had ever been written. It is not only in B minor,

---

* So hast thou also done, Hafis;
We will begin at the beginning.

but also anticipates the rhythm and figuration of the beginning of the 'Unfinished' – so literally that the underlying connection can hardly be denied. But it has little or nothing to do with the melancholy mood of the Symphony. It is a song, in which the state of suspense between description and feeling is as complete as it is in the setting of Schlegel's 'Im Walde' and which cannot do justice to itself after the powerful climax of the last verse, culminating as it does in the aching solace of the major key. 'Suleika II' is cast in the same mould with a middle-section full of exquisite modulations:

> ... Blumen, Auen, Wald und Hügel
> Stehn bei deinem Hauch in Tränen. . . .*

The last two verses build up to an animated climax and end on an intensely intimate *pianissimo*. When Schubert returned to the sensitive Anacreontic Salis in 'Der Jüngling am Bache', which follows the Suleika songs in the Collected Edition (XX, 398), he did so on a new level. The song is an early example of musical impressionism – one might almost say musical pointillism. The accompaniment lies throughout in the alto register while the melody has both the supple grace of a dance, and a dreamy, visionary quality. One no longer thinks of Salis' sentimental Louise, but of the god Pan, sleeping in the hush of noon-day.

It was not until some time later, probably 1824, that Schubert returned to the *West-östlicher Divan* with a song for male voices and piano (XVI, 15) of such deep significance that there is scarcely anyone who knows or performs it.

In a letter to Josef v. Spaun, dated 7th December, 1822, Schubert wrote: 'My Mass is finished and is shortly to be performed. I still have my old idea of dedicating it to the Emperor or Empress, as I think it a success.' Since he could make no headway with his operas, he was compelled to work towards the other possible method of establishing himself – towards the hope of being appointed to a choirmaster's post as a result of writing a large-scale liturgical work and getting it performed. The composition of the Mass was started after his return from Steyr in November 1819. The second and

***

* . . . Flowers, meadows, woods and hills
Weep at thy breath. . . .

final version, entitled *Missa Solemnis*, was not finished until September 1822 – an unusually long period of time for Schubert. It was not published until four years after Ebenezer Prout had written his articles or analytical studies on Schubert's Masses for the first year's issue of *Monthly Musical Record* (1871).

During the same period, 1818 to 1822, Beethoven was engaged upon his *Missa Solemnis*.

In the year 1822 Schubert had also contributed to the field of church music two shorter works, a *Tantum Ergo* in C major for chorus and orchestra (without flutes and without violas) and only twenty-three bars in length; it is written in a completely eighteenth-century style and is rather too lacking in solemnity for the particular solemn occasion – the Exposition of the Blessed Sacrament – for which it was written. The other work is a second *Tantum Ergo* in D major, dated 20th March, for full orchestra, the sole unusual feature of which is the inclusion of only *two* trombones. It is a dignified piece rather in the style of a Mozart *Sanctus* or *Magnificat* and this time Schubert set to music not merely the fifth verse of the hymn, but also the last ('Genitori, genitoque') on which the church ritual insisted.

But these occasional works scarcely bear consideration beside the great Mass (XIII, 5) which Schubert thought worthy of dedication to the highest authority, and which he hoped so much to have performed. It was not often that he expressed his satisfaction with a work on its completion. The degree of importance he attached to it is shown by his revised version of the fugue at the end of the *Gloria* ('Cum sancto spiritu') and by his replacement of the original 'Hosanna' by a new one. He recognized that these were two weak points without being able fully to correct them. The A flat major Mass is, in fact, one of his greatest works, even though it is not completely 'successful'. It is not altogether unprofitable, perhaps, to compare it with his great rival's work, which was written about the same time. Beethoven chose one of the few keys which were traditional for the Mass and keeps strictly within its limits; even his 'Gloria' is in D major, and his 'Gratias' and 'Domine' do not venture beyond B major and F major respectively. The 'Credo' is in B flat major and turns simply to D minor for the mysticism of the 'Incarnatus', and to F major for the 'Ascendit'. The

'Sanctus' is in B minor, the 'Benedictus' in G major, and the 'Hosanna' in D major. The 'Agnus Dei' reverts to B minor, and the 'Dona', quite naturally, to D major. Schubert chose a key which is extremely unusual for a Mass. And what variety of colour he achieves in his key-relationships! The 'Gloria' is in E major and the 'Gratias' in A major; the 'Credo' in C major and the 'Incarnatus' in A flat major, the 'Sanctus' and 'Hosanna' in F major. Not until the 'Benedictus' does the main key return, in a more than episodic way; the *Agnus Dei* begins, as one would expect, in F minor. In his harmony, Schubert is either looser or bolder than Beethoven. Beethoven wrote a commissioned work; Schubert wrote his Mass in the same way that he wrote his operas – 'at random'. What he did not and could not have was Beethoven's spirituality, acquired during and after a severe crisis in his creative development – that crisis in which Beethoven had fashioned for himself a purer, less emotional, more spiritual 'contrapuntal' language. In his church music, as in his operas, Schubert thought too much in terms of categories. His Mass suffered from the same dualism from which all eighteenth-century church music suffered – the dualism between 'erudite' and spontaneous expression. He realized this and consequently wrote only *one* long fugue, that at the end of the *Gloria,* and feeling that in spite (or because of) all his efforts it was too academic in conception, he recast the theme in a nobler mould and wrote a new fugue, which is both shorter and freer. In later years he made a large number of other detailed alterations and corrections in the Mass.

But in other respects he had the courage to be himself. If Beethoven is 'contrapuntal' throughout in his new sense, Schubert is a 'Harmonist' throughout in his. One might say that, from the outset, the gentle *Kyrie*, with its mood of pious resignation rather than prayer, simply emphasizes the key of A flat major, dissolved into *melismata* in free interplay between chorus and soloists. The effect of the E major of the *Gloria* after this is as if one were to reveal a flaming red in a green and purple church window. Schubert here added not only trumpet, side-drums and the trombone trio to the orchestra, but also the flute which elsewhere in his church music he uses only sparingly. Not even a pedant could find any fault with the construction of the movement. The closely-knit unity of the Allegro section (3/4, Maestoso e vivace) is no less pure than that of the 'Gratias' (2/4, Andantino) which includes the 'Domine Deus' as a contrast. It is repeated in a richer form and returns to E major with the 'Miserere' – with a mysterious ending. Then follows the 'academic fugue', interwoven with the fugal Amen, with *stretta* and pedal-point, and Schubertian enough by virtue of its modulations.

The beginning of the *Credo*, with its bright chords on the wind instruments and the archaic *a cappella* treatment of the voices, is so characteristic that it deserves to be quoted:

Like Beethoven, and like Mozart in his *Missa Brevis* in F major (K. 192), Schubert repeats this 'Credo, credo' in a new form each time and with added richness. The choral movement is set for double-chorus, in eight parts, and the trombones reveal their full power not only in a liturgical but also a mystical sense, in the dynamic and harmonic outbursts of the 'Et incarnatus'. For both here and in the 'Crucifixus' which follows, Schubert reveals himself as a true mystic. This 'Et incarnatus' is in 3/2 time, the same symbol of the Trinity which one finds in a fifteenth or sixteenth century Mass; and in the 'Crucifixus' each voice carries the following figure once:

– familiar from Bach's Passions and elsewhere as symbolizing the Cross, and a confirmation of our view that the
use of this same symbol in Schubert's songs is no 'accident'.
This time he does not end the movement with a piece of
'erudition', but with a powerful and thrilling hymn in C
major ('Et vitam venturi saeculi – Amen').

The beginning of the *Sanctus* has always ranked as one of
Schubert's boldest strokes. The sense of awe before the
Infinite expresses itself in the tremolo on the strings and in
the extreme tension of the harmony. There are three distinct
'starts' and in the space of a few bars we travel from F major
to F sharp major – C sharp major, from D minor to G flat
major – B flat major, from B flat major to C minor – G
major. The movement then proceeds devoutly, as if it were
traversing a heaven of dancing angels. The first 'Hosanna'
breathes a pastoral atmosphere, with a strong suggestion of
Zauberflöte. And here there occurs an example of Schubert's self-criticism, for in the second version, it is not the
suggestion of *Zauberflöte* with which he dispenses, but the
pastoral time-signature. The 'Benedictus' is a superbly animated movement with a striding bass and a floating accompaniment, while soloists and chorus alternate or mingle
with each other. In this Mass the solo passages are allowed to
emerge only briefly from the balanced pattern of sound.
There is no longer any place for 'display', no longer any
opportunity for indulging a secret passion. In the *Agnus Dei*
the 'Miserere' is introduced twice by way of a strange modulation from A flat major to E major and from E flat major to
C flat major, after an arioso beginning which suggests Pergolesi; the 'Dona nobis pacem' is like a procession, a
confident farewell.

It is obvious that so spontaneous and subjective a work
could not make any real impression on Schubert's contemporaries. It appears that Josef Eybler, who succeeded the
ailing Salieri as Court Music Director in the autumn of 1824,
considered the question of a performance in the Chapel
Royal, but eventually laid the work aside again on the
grounds that it was too difficult. In his celebrated application
of 7th April, 1826, for the post of Assistant Court Music
Director, Schubert mentioned 'five Masses ... which have
already been performed in various churches in Vienna'. But
the Mass in A flat cannot have been one of them.

If the small number and great importance of the vocal works of this year is evidence that this was a period of a new self-consciousness and sense of responsibility, the same is even more true in the instrumental field. Schubert became cautious and followed new paths. The unfinished string quartet was followed by two unfinished symphonies. The only completed works are the 'exceptional' 'Wanderer' Fantasia, and a short occasional piece, a Variation on a Waltz by Diabelli, written in March 1821 (XI, 8 – the Collected Edition wrongly dates it two months later).

We will begin with the latter. It must have been early in 1821 that the publisher Diabelli invited a number of Viennese composers to write one variation each on a Waltz in two parts which he himself had composed. Beethoven declined to join their ranks, and although he rightly thought very little of the theme, he privately contributed the XXXIII Variations, which Diabelli published as op. 120 on 9th June, 1824, as the first publication of the new firm of Diabelli & Co. Beethoven's arrogance compelled Diabelli to issue the publication in two parts; the first contained the XXXIII Variations of 'the musical Jean Paul of our day' (such was the description of Beethoven in the bombastic announcement of the enterprise), and the second, the fifty Variations by various 'national', i.e., Austrian, composers. The work was also published in due course under the title of *The National Society of Artists*. The fifty contributions included among others the last composition of Emanuel Förster and the first of Franz Liszt.

Almost three-and-a-half years elapsed before all the contributions reached Diabelli, and even then not all since there are several names missing which one would definitely have expected to be among them. The first to submit his contribution was Schubert. His variation is in the minor and is full of those little Schubertian harmonic touches which one would recognize as characteristic and personal in any surroundings. How simple and stylish this variation is becomes abundantly clear when one compares it with the harmonic posturings of Gottfried Rieger's contribution, which Heinrich Rietsch printed in the Beethoven Yearbook, Vol. I (1908).

But at the same time it is more refined and polished than the majority of Schubert's Dances – 'Germans', Waltzes,

Ecossaises, etc. – which must be regarded as improvisations committed to paper. This must have been the way he played when he provided music for his friends to dance to at parties. Towards the end of 1821 he published a number of dances of this kind with Cappi and Diabelli as op. 9 (XII, 1), under the title of *Original Dances for Pianoforte*. These were the first of his instrumental works to be published, since op. 1–7, which all appeared between April and November of this year, were songs, and op. 8, which also consisted of songs, did not appear until 1822. A number of them are dated in the manuscripts; Nos. 5–13, 12th November, 1819; Nos. 29–31, July 1821 when Schubert and his friends were staying with Schober's uncle, Jos. Derffel at Atzenbruck; Nos. 32–6 (with which the opus ends), 8th March, 1821. All of them follow a planned sequence. The first thirteen dances are all in A flat major, then by way of D flat major (14, 15) to A major – D flat is after all the same as C sharp – G major (19–21), B major (22–4) E major (25–7), A major (28), D major (29), A major (30), C major (31), and F major (32–6). The atmosphere throughout is genial, with the Ländler predominating. Schubert keeps almost exclusively to the simplest eight-bar form for each half of a dance. But the harmony is free and Schubertian, and one often has a sudden feeling that one is in the cultured and aristocratic company of young men and well-bred girls. The second dance is comically entitled 'Funeral Waltz', but it is no more 'funereal' than all the rest. Some of the twelve Waltzes of op. 18, which were published in two volumes at the beginning of 1823 (XII, 2), were also written in 1821 at Atzenbruck, and two of the Ecossaises date as far back as 1816 and 1820. They are more pretentious and their types more varied, and one can see more clearly the difference between Waltzes and Ländler. In the Ländler, it is almost always the alpine Jodler or Schuhplattler which determines the melodic and rhythmic invention. The Ecossaises are mostly of a more delicate type and are, without exception, written in sixteen-bar form. One cannot compare these Schubertian dances of op. 9 and op. 18 with those of Chopin. Once, while discussing Chopin's Waltz, op. 42, Schumann wrote that, if one wanted to play it at a dance, the majority of the ladies taking part would have to be at least countesses. The aristocratic nature of Schubert's dances lies in their spontaneity and charm. Nor do they lose this spontaneity and charm when this ambition rises to greater heights, as in the Ländler of 1823 – which, admittedly, he could not publish.

In complete contrast to these trifles or 'bagatelles', but of the same stature as the great songs of the first half of the year 1821, there stands the sketch of the great Symphony in E major, on which Schubert started work in August. He must have been determined to achieve in the symphonic field the same stature and complete independence which he had achieved in his songs. When, on 31st March, 1824, he wrote to Leopold Kupelwieser in Rome informing him that he had 'written few new songs', but that he had tried his hand at a number of instrumental works 'in order thus to pave the way towards a grand symphony', he could well have pointed to his 'experiments' of 1821 and 1822. This Symphony in E major provides a suitable opportunity to clear up once and for all the confusion surrounding the sequence and number- ing of Schubert's symphonies. Schubert wrote ten sym- phonies. There is no uncertainty about Nos. I–VI: the D major (1813), the B flat major (1814–15), the D major (1815), the C minor (the 'Tragic', 1816), the B flat major (1816), and the C major (1817–18). The correct sequence of the remain- ing four is as follows: No. VII, this E major Symphony; No. VIII, the 'Unfinished'; No. IX, the 'Gmund-Gastein' Sym- phony (1825), the existence of which is now generally ac- cepted; and finally the great C major. It is most confusing to find the 'Unfinished' correctly, if fortuitously, numbered the 'Eighth' in the Collected Edition, while the great C major Symphony, written six years later, appears as the 'Sev- enth'.

There is a story attached to the manuscript of the Sym- phony in E major. In 1846 Ferdinand Schubert gave it to Felix Mendelssohn, who apparently declined to complete the sketch, although he would probably have done so had he lived longer. In 1868 Mendelssohn's brother, Paul, presented it to Sir George Grove, and today it is one of the priceless possessions of the Royal College of Music in London. In 1882, John Francis Bennett published with Breitkopf and Härtel 'a completed version of the orchestral score in a pianoforte arrangement for two hands', and in 1934 Felix Weingartner reconstructed the score with a delicate sense of style, leaving the second and third movements untouched, and 'tightening up' the first and last movements, i.e., shortening them a little. Schubert completed the introductory Adagio and the first 110 (34+76) bars of the Allegro in detail. 'As for the remainder, it is sketched without a break down to the last bar of the Finale, not merely at those points where the orchestral parts carry the melody, but frequently, too, where they are harmonically and rhythmically important' (Weingartner). With the 'Unfinished', Schubert adopted a different method. There he wrote out the first two movements and the Scherzo, as far as the opening bars of the Trio, on two staves, before starting work on the detailed scoring, and it is not difficult to guess the reason. For in the method of scoring that we find in this E major Symphony, a composer – and particularly a composer of such exuberant invention and facility as Schubert – easily loses his sense of proportion. The difference between this 'sketched symphony in E major and the 'Unfinished' is simply one of extreme breadth and extreme concentration. There is a contrast and a mutual affinity between the two. Schubert was consciously striving after a concentrated style.

In the Symphony in E major, too, he was striving after a more closely integrated form. A theme which is, so to speak, born in the mysterious slow Introduction in the minor, and later begins to speak through the trombones (for this is the first instance in his symphonies where Schubert uses the trombone trio)

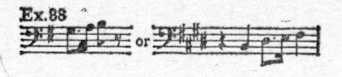

Ex.88

reappears again in the Finale. The foreshadowing of the C major Symphony is quite unmistakable. The Introduction is followed by the Allegro in E major. Here the invention is far removed from Beethoven and completely Italian in style, but the treatment is German and Schubertian in its striving, if not after compactness, at least after thematic untiy; the second subject is in G major and the beginning of the coda in C major. The whole movement alternates between an agitated and a lyrical mood. The Finale 'Allegro giusto' hovers between a lyrical rather than a humorous Haydnesque style and a faintly Italian flavour. The Scherzo in C major, 'allegro deciso', with a Ländler-like Trio in A major, is the 'tautest' movement of the symphony. But the crowning beauty of the work is the slow movement, an Andante in A major, in 6/8 time, with a middle section in F sharp minor, smooth-flowing as a barcarolle, with halting themes, magical in its harmony and full of melancholy happiness. It is a movement to which there is scarcely any counterpart and with which the Andante from the Octet alone is in any way comparable. The whole symphony is, as it were, a half-way house. It looks back to the Italian Overture, and forward to the great symphony which was to follow it six or seven years later. But in the same way that the String Quartet Movement in C minor has a closer affinity with the last three quartets, this symphony stands nearer, in its new, monumental mould, to the great C major than to any of its predecessors.

It is worth mentioning as a matter of interest that Brahms knew about the presentation of the manuscript to Sir George Grove, and was furious about it (letter to Jos. Joachim of December 1868). He was afraid that some mediocrity such as Costa or Benedict might take it upon himself 'to complete the score', and begged Joachim to prevent this 'prostitution'. Such a situation luckily never arose.

The symphony known as the 'Unfinished' had an even stranger fate than the Symphony in E or the great C major Symphony. It had to wait more than forty years before receiving its first performance, on 17th December, 1865, at a concert of the Philharmonic Society under the direction of Johann Herbeck – several months after the first performance of Wagner's *Tristan und Isolde*. On 10th April, 1823, Schubert's friend, Johann Baptist Jenger, had proposed him as an honorary member of the Styrian Music Society at Graz, 'because, although still young, he has already proved by his compositions that he will one day rank high as a composer.' The proposal was accepted the same day (or shortly afterwards). Some time elapsed before Schubert wrote to express his appreciation (20th September). 'May it be the reward for my devotion to the art of music that I shall one day be fully worthy of this signal honour. In order that I may also express in musical terms my lively sense of gratitude, I shall take the liberty, at the earliest opportunity, of presenting your honourable Society with one of my symphonies in full score.' Since the B minor Symphony was begun on 30th October, 1822, it cannot possibly have been written 'for the Styrian Music Society,' as local patriotism would have us believe, and it is also quite unthinkable that Schubert, with all his tact and discretion, would ever have presented the Society with an unfinished fragment. Josef Hüttenbrenner, who gave the Viennese music-director Herbeck the first information of the existence of the manuscript in his brother Anselm's possession (8th April, 1860), simply explained that Schubert gave it to him 'as a present for Anselm in token of his appreciation for having sent him, through me, the Diploma of Honour of the Graz Music Society'. Anselm never delivered the manuscript but kept it himself. In his biography of his father (Vienna, 1885, p. 164) Ludwig Herbeck has given us an interesting description of how on 30th April, 1865, Johann Herbeck visited Ober-Andritz near Graz, whither Anselm Hüttenbrenner had retired. There, in a drawer stuffed full of papers, he discovered the manuscript and rescued it from the suspicious old man, a curious character, who laboured under the conviction that he was an unappreciated genius. Since then it has become probably the best-known symphonic work in the world.

A study of the two completed movements provides the probable explanation why Schubert let matters rest at that point. Unlike the C Major Symphony, they have never been criticized for their 'heavenly length' – that much-quoted expression of Schumann's. (Schumann's unhappy phrase may have been meant either as a tribute or as an affectionate criticism.) Schubert wrote a superbly integrated sonata movement of extraordinary tension, which, for sheer concentration, can only be matched by the first movement of Beethoven's Fifth Symphony. But so far as this movement is concerned, any comparison with Beethoven is misleading. Among the characteristic features of the 'Unfinished' are its dynamics, but they are fundamentally different from those of Beethoven, the great master of dynamics. Beethoven's mighty orchestral crescendi always culminate in correspondingly mighty outbursts. With Schubert these outbursts are shorter, as it were, more dangerous, and the contrasts are sharper and more clear-cut. Beethoven is full of pathos; Schubert possessed of a demon. And the same contrast is apparent in both harmony and melody. Why B minor? It has been suggested with some justification that the answer is to be found in a number of Schubert's B minor songs, all filled with a mysterious or uncanny sense of power – the first Suleika song, for example, or 'Der Doppelgänger'. But this first movement springs from a more fathomless source; and the expression of poignant melancholy and the outbursts of despair could be answered only by the innocence of the Ländler-like second subject, which blossoms like a flower and yet ventures with such a brave show of courage into the development. Here once more is a sonata-movement that is not simply a 'framework' but, within the letter and spirit of conventional rules, a masterly renewal and vindication of the form.

The second movement, an Andante (with the subsequent addition of 'con moto') in the simplest binary form with coda, is not, as might be expected, in D major or A major, but in the key of E major which is lifted far above 'normality' and beyond traditional *emotion*. One might here suppose the influence of Beethoven to have been at work, in the shape of the Larghetto of his Second Symphony, and once again any comparison would be inadmissible. A better parallel would be the Andante of Schubert's own B major Sonata (X, 5). Here there is no longer any crescendo or diminuendo, but only the dynamic contrast between loud and soft; no melodic 'development', but only the interplay of small or large melodic groups of magical charm and magical euphony. Reference has already been made to the boldness of harmony in the so-called second subject and in the modulations in the coda. The whole movement, in its mysterious and unfathomable beauty, is like one of those plants whose flowers open only on a night of the full moon.

It is obvious why Schubert abandoned work on this symphony. He could not finish it, in any sense of the word. The Scherzo, which is fairly completely sketched, though in less and less detail (it breaks off after the first section of the Trio), and even orchestrated for its first nine bars, comes as an anti-climax after the Andante. In an article entitled 'The Riddle of Schubert's Unfinished Symphony'*, Hans Gal has made it abundantly clear that nothing could ever have been fashioned from the material of this Scherzo which could have approached the originality, power and skill of the two

* *The Music Review*, 1941, II, 1.

preceding movements. It is exactly what happened in the case of *Lazarus*. And are we to believe that Schubert was not fully aware of this power? He had already written too much that was finished, to be able to content himself with anything less or with anything more trivial. The one large-scale instrumental work of the year 1822, which was completed (in November) is the so-called 'Wanderer' Fantasia (XI, 1), and in fact it *had* to be finished, since Schubert had reason to hope that he might earn some money with the dedication which appeared on the published copy. On 7th December he wrote to Spaun in Linz, sending him at the same time three songs which he had dedicated to his friend (op. 13) and mentioning two further volumes of songs: 'Apart from this I have written a Fantasia for pianoforte solo which is also about to appear in print and is dedicated to a certain wealthy gentleman.' The wealthy gentleman was Emmanuel Karl Edler v. Liebenberg, a baptized and ennobled Jewish landowner who had been a piano-pupil of J. N. Hummel's. This largely explains the character of this Fantasia which – while not forgetting the exceptions – differs so greatly from the essentially intimate character of the rest of Schubert's piano music. It is brilliant; it had to provide something for the fingers, in the same sense as Hummel had done, and it does, in fact, provide much in the way of difficulties and technical problems. Is it not a moving and significant fact that Schubert wanted to dedicate to Hummel his last three sonatas, in which he is once more completely himself, as if to apologize for this incursion into Hummel's territory? But he would not have been Schubert if he had not preoccupied himself with other problems besides technical brilliance – in this case the problem of unity, clear and unmistakable, in a work of several movements. As we have already seen in the Symphony in E major, his preoccupation with the problem of unity is a distinguishing feature of this period and it continued to obsess him more and more frequently, in the Piano Trio, op. 100, and in the great C major Symphony. For this Fantasia consists of four movements, like a great sonata, Allegro – Adagio – Scherzo – Finale. The only difference is that they are directly interlinked or grouped round a focal point. This focal point is the slow movement, consisting of variations on that C sharp minor passage from 'Der Wanderer'

Die Sonne dünkt mich hier so kalt. . . .

which modulates with such overwhelming effect to E major. The song had been published at the end of May 1821 as part of op. 4 and had made a profound impression with its Byronic gloominess. For the first time Schubert included an Adagio as the centre-piece of a work. He preferred Andantes and Andantinos, because he disliked pathos, and therefore aimed at a different equilibrium between three or four movements from Beethoven. The dactylic-anapaestic rhythm of these variations which constantly recall Beethoven's Arietta in the richness of their figuration (op. 111, however, was not published until *after* the Fantasia had been completed) determines the basic rhythm of all the other movements and becomes purely dactylic in the Scherzo, as it does in the Scherzo of Beethoven's Ninth Symphony. The first movement, at least, has an underlying and undivulged 'programme'. It illustrates a 'storm', the clearest indications of which are the *tremoli* and the chromatic surge of the first subject; but there is also an atmosphere of happy calm in the E major section and in the second subject. The Finale uses the same themes in a kind of fugal development. It contrives to be both brilliant and somewhat ponderous since this fugal development very soon loses its breath. Without a doubt the most charming section is the Scherzo and Trio, which has an exquisite elegance throughout, both in its moments of brilliance and in its lyrical passages. This Hummel-like Schubert is not quite our favourite Schubert; we prefer the Schubert of the sonatas, the Moments musicals and the Impromptus. Yet just how utterly delightful Schubert can also be on his excursions into the world of virtuosity, or into the atmosphere of the drawing-room, is shown by an Adagio and Rondo in E major, the date of which is uncertain, but which was definitely written somewhat later (XI, 5; published as op. 147). The Adagio has a slight flavour of Rossini. The Allegretto consists of a lyrical theme over precisely the same staccato bass which Schumann used for the Fandango of his C sharp minor Sonata, and which also plays its rattling or tinkling role here. We have already mentioned (p. 150) that it existed in a different form and key, and that it was added – quite erroneously – as a finale to the fragmentary Sonata in E minor of 1817. It stands on its own.

Chapter Ten

Between the B minor Symphony and
Die Schöne Müllerin

1822–1823

Between the 'Unfinished' and *Die schöne Müllerin* there were written only a few works which are still familiar today – little more, in fact, than a piano sonata and a number of important songs. And for Schubert himself these were incidental works. For, in the larger sphere, he made another assault upon opera the weight and persistence of which recall the assault of 1815, except that on this occasion his whole approach was much more serious and deliberate. The parallels are quite unmistakable. Just as he had previously followed Kotzebue's 'natural magic-opera' with *Fernando*, so he now followed a kind of musical comedy with a 'grand heroic, Romantic opera'; and there is unfortunately a further parallel in that both assaults proved completely abortive.

We left Schubert as an opera-composer at *Alfonso und Estrella*. From this unsuccessful sortie into the field of the 'durchcomponiert' *opera semi-seria* in three acts, he turned once more to the one-act German ballad-opera with spoken dialogue. At the end of April 1823 he completed – if one can call an opera without an overture 'completed' – *Die Verschworenen*, or as it was re-titled in deference to the Viennese censors, *Der häusliche Krieg* (XV, 6). This time the author of the text was another of Schubert's Viennese acquaintances, the local writer Ignaz Franz Castelli (1781–1862), who was on friendly terms with Beethoven and Weber; he was Court Dramatist at the Kärntnertor Theatre from 1811 to 1814, librettist of Weigl's homely *Schweizerfamilie*, patriot and witty critic of the Viennese bureaucracy and above all of the Viennese stage-censorship. In the history of literature he has a reputation as the author of a number of poems in lower-Austrian dialect; he is known today almost solely by his shallow, though lively and amusingly written *Memoirs* (1861, reissued by Bindter in 1912), which provide us with a great deal of information about Schubert's Viennese milieu, but practically none about Schubert himself.

In *Die Verschworenen*, which was written in 1820 and published in February 1823, Castelli revealed himself as a successor of Kotzebue pure and simple. The whole nightmare of operatic convention, of the ballad-opera, becomes obvious when one realizes that the material for this one-act opera originated from Aristophanes' *Lysistrata*, which was produced in Athens in the year 411 B.C., as an ultra-political, topical comedy – brilliant and fearless in every sense. The primitive phallic type of humour of the old Athenian was as unthinkable in the Vienna of 1820 as was its political topicality. It must not be imagined, however, that topicality is always impossible in opera; it existed at every period throughout its history, disguised or undisguised. It was present in *Die Zauberflöte* and in *Fidelio*. But in pre-Revolutionary Vienna, it crept into the darkest corner. Aristophanes' Acropolis therefore becomes a mediaeval castle at the time of the Crusades; Lysistrata becomes a dignified German baron's wife; Myrrhine and the amorous Kinesias, a sentimental young married couple no sooner wed than parted. For the comic roles, which a ballad-opera demanded, Castelli introduces a lady-in-waiting and a squire, after the model of Mozart's Blonde and Pedrillo. Before the arrival of the knights, the squire, dressed in female clothes, overhears the women agree to refuse to sleep with their husbands, until the latter promise solemnly not to take the field against the infidels again. He reveals the plot, whereupon the husbands pretend to be completely indifferent, discuss new martial projects and then force their wives to equip themselves for a military expedition, firmly intending that they shall accompany them. This is all conducted in the most childish fashion and not without a certain amount of innuendo and lewdness in the dialogue; that much at least was permitted in Vienna in those days. Even Schubert contributed a little to this lewdness by writing the squire's part for a woman in man's clothing; only in the first duet is there an alternative version for tenor.

The big moment of the ballad-opera is the conspiracy-scene, the central figure of which is the heroic yet homely baron's wife (soprano) with an answering chorus of women. With its tremoli on the strings and its crescendi and decrescendi on the trombones, it smacks a little of a parody on similar scenes in 'grand opera'. A less lively counterpart is the choral scene in which the squire divulges the wives' plan of action and in which his story is answered throughout by bass-solo and chorus. The ceremonial greeting between the knights and their wives takes the form of a large-scale Polonaise, with a march-like ending. For the rest, there is the inevitable sentimental Romance, two pleasant duets and an extended Finale. But once again there is a little too much of ballad-opera convention throughout; and in an arietta for the baron, to which his wife replies in a similar vein, Schubert actually anticipates the spirit of the operetta, which was not to achieve its full splendour until long after his death. Again we have to emphasize how much Schubert depended on conventions in his operas – the same Schubert who as a song-writer was so fastidious in his choice of texts, so inventive and bold in his forms.

This contrast between the song and opera texts becomes positively grotesque when one turns to the last operatic experiment which Schubert completed – the 'heroic, romantic opera' *Fierabras* (XV, 10), begun on 23rd May and finished on 2nd October, 1823, three weeks before the first performance of Weber's *Euryanthe*. In the same year, and during precisely the same period, Schubert touched one of the highest points in his songs with *Die schöne Müllerin* and the lowest depths in his operas with this work – the more so since *Fierabras* cannot be classed as one of his *juvenilia*. It suffers from a fundamental inconsistency in that it employs all the forms of the latest *opera semi-seria*, yet unlike *Alfonso und Estrella*, returns once more to spoken dialogue – and what dialogue!

This time the libretto was provided by Schubert's friend Josef Kupelwieser, a brother of the painter and Secretary of the Kärntnertor Theatre, and when one looks at the *dramatis personae*: Charlemagne, his daughter Emma, her lover Eginhard, the hero Roland and the other Paladins, his companions; Boland the evil Moorish Prince who contrives – Heaven knows how! – to be the father of a noble son

Fierabras and a daughter Florinda who is, if anything, even more noble; in addition, Frankish and Moorish Knights and warriors, maidens and the general populace – when one looks at this, one realizes that one is in for something uncommonly 'Romantic' in this opera – 'Romantic', that is to say, in the manner of Walter Scott and his imitators. But this was not Schubert's kind of Romanticism, and it is a source of endless amazement that he should have taken so seriously something which must have left him in his heart of hearts quite unmoved, and that he did not throw his pen away at certain points. One scene, in fact – the third of the first act – seems to be missing in the score, but it may well have been a dialogue-scene.

The plot, which is borrowed from the old French 'romance' *Fierabras* (*The Braggart*) and the German legend *Eginhard und Emma*, is based on two suppositions. First, Eginhard, a knight (though not of princely blood) has fallen in love with Emma, the Emperor's daughter, is loved by her in return and has secret and anxious meetings with her. Secondly, however, Emma has also made a deep impression on Fierabras, the noble Moorish prince, whom she had previously met in Rome – where apparently she was staying incognito as a kind of guest in a boarding-house, she with Sir Roland and Fierabras with his sister Florinda. It goes without saying that Florinda has simultaneously fallen in love with Roland. As so often happens with tourists, the two couples have since lost sight of each other for a number of years. Then, during one of Charlemagne's battles with the Moors, Fierabras is defeated by Roland and brought to the Emperor's camp as a prisoner. There he recognizes his beloved again, but immediately renounces her. In spite of this he is suspected of being too intimate with Emma, when he rescues the young lady and Eginhard from an awkward situation after a nocturnal rendezvous. Charlemagne, who constantly judges by appearances like a perfect fool, has him put in chains, and sends Eginhard and the other Paladins, headed by Roland, to the vanquished Moorish prince, in order to negotiate a final peace settlement.

That is the first act. In the second, which is devoted to the fortunes of the Frankish embassy in the camp of the treacherous Boland, Eginhard appears again with his justifiable pangs of conscience (for at the end of the first act he has

behaved like a schoolboy), but Fierabras, the nominal hero
of the piece, and Emma vanish completely from the scene.
The knights start by singing a devout chorus and then leave
Eginhard alone with his sorrow, whereupon he is promptly
taken prisoner by a crowd of infidels who carry him off,
before a blast on his horn can summon the knights back.
The latter, it transpires, are in no hurry to rescue him, although they constantly repeat the refrain:

> *Verfolget die Spuren in hastigen Lauf.*
> *In Tälern und Fluren schnell suchet ihn auf.**

But this is just so much talk. For it is by pure chance that
they rediscover their comrades in Boland's camp, where they
proceed to surrender their arms and allow themselves to be
captured like sheep. It is inevitable that the closing scene of
the act takes place in prison, and opens with a short male-
voice chorus of prisoners *a cappella*; inevitable that Florinda
appears on the scene to set her Roland free; inevitable that
the attempted escape, melodramatically described, miscar-
ries, else what would become of the third act? 'Dumb show
of horror and despair.'

Nevertheless, Emma's unsuspecting companions, who had
started the first act with a spinning-song, now open the third
with a chorus to the effect that 'sorrow now must cease'.

> *. . . es weicht der Schmerz,*
> *Bald tönet der Reigen, die Lust füllt das Herz.*†

Charlemagne does not share these optimistic sentiments and
his anxiety over the ominous failure of his knights to return
eventually compels Emma to confess her indiscretion. Papa
rebukes her roundly, releases Fierabras immediately and in
answer to Eginhard's request for help, informs him that he
can only redeem himself by bringing back his colleagues
alive, even at the cost of his own life. This he achieves in
company with Fierabras in the nick of time, when the unfortunate Roland can already see the flames licking round
the stake. Finally we have not only the political reconcili-
ation between Charlemagne and the Moorish prince, but

---

* Follow his footsteps with all haste. Search for him in valley and field
without delay.
  † Grief gives way; soon the sound of singing and dancing will be heard,
joy will fill the heart.

also two happy couples, Eginhard and Emma, and Roland and Florinda. The noble Fierabras goes empty-handed, and appears to be perfectly satisfied to be accepted into the ranks of the Paladins and to be allowed in due course to fight against his own compatriots. The author, Kupelwieser, submitted the libretto in manuscript to the stage censors at the end of July 1823 and received it back with their approval on 19th August. The Imperial Censor had raised some objection to what he alleged to be a number of doubtful passages from a political point of view, but fortunately for the author he was not called upon to concern himself with the artistic merit of the piece.

Schubert, we must repeat, was twenty-six years old when he set this wretched and at the same time pretentious nonsense to music – pretentious, since each of the three acts demands three changes of scene and the resources of opera are strained to the limit throughout. And we do not rightly know whether to praise or blame him for having produced so bad a musical score. It is no sacrilege to say that this, his last completed opera, is also his most indifferent, empty and conventional one. It is difficult, too, to find even one number which one could readily accept as utterly charming; nor any number which would force us to confess that this is no longer operatic currency or stage technique, but Schubertian melody, Schubertian euphony and Schubertian modulation – modulation, that is to say, that is born of a full heart. Of the Overture, too, there is nothing more to be said than that it is passionate and conventional. The only noteworthy feature is the fact that the lavishness of the musical resources matches the lavishness of the stage requirements. For *Fierabras* is a very 'modern' opera, in the twentieth-century sense of the word. This modernity is most clearly illustrated in Schubert's almost complete avoidance of the aria. Florinda alone has one savage outburst in this form in the second act (No. 13). Almost all the 'arias' and duets have choral background. They are so to speak given a choral padding, as in the later instances of Bellini's *Norma* and *La Sonnambula*. And the ensembles are governed throughout by a contrast of which Schubert was only just master from a musical, though certainly not from a dramatic, point of view. The characters sometimes express the most contrasting sentiments in full harmony. There are operatic

conventionalities of which one would not have thought
Schubert capable, such as the repetition of the text in a
chorus of Franks (p. 507 in the full score) – leaving aside the
utter absurdity of the subject matter:

> *Nie soll der Schwache mit dem Glücke rechten*
> *Denn jede Schuld zahlt,* er, er, er *mit seinem Blut**

Naturally enough the opera was never performed. By the
beginning of 1824 Schubert had given up all hope, for on
31st March he wrote to Leopold Kupelwieser as follows:
'The opera of your brother (who did not do particularly well
in leaving the theatre) has been declared unusable and consequently my music has not been called upon. Castelli's
libretto *The Conspirators* [*Die Verschworenen*] has been set
in Berlin by a local composer and received with applause. In
this way I would appear once more to have composed two
operas all to no purpose.'

The year 1823 was none the less to provide Schubert with
one more approach to the stage, more 'immortal' than all his
genuine operatic experiments put together. After completing
Fierabras and *Die schöne Müllerin*, he wrote, between
30th November and 18th December, the incidental music to
Helmina v. Chézy's four-act play *Rosamunde, Fürstin von
Cypern*. Frau v. Chézy, *nee* v. Klencke, was a blue-stocking
from Berlin with a hereditary literary streak. She was married for a short time to the orientalist Antoine Leonard
Chézy in Paris and had by him two sons, Wilhelm and Max.
The former became a writer, the latter a painter, and both
came in close contact with Schubert's circle. This lady, who
was described by Bauernfeld in 1825 as 'extremely good-
natured, a little ridiculous and not particularly distinguished
for her cleanliness', made her mark in the history of music
when she became acquainted with C. M. Weber as a member
of a literary circle in Dresden and provided him with the
unfortunate libretto for *Euryanthe*. The preparations for the
first performance of this work (25th October) had brought
her to Vienna, where she at once gave full vent to her literary ambition. She presented to the management of the
Theater an der Wien a 'new drama with choruses', to which
according to *Der Sammler* of 18th December, the well-

---

* Never shall the weakling remonstrate with fortune, for every debt
shall *he, he, he* pay with his blood. . . .

known and talented composer, Herr Franz Schubert, had written the incidental music, and the first performance of which had been set aside for the actress of this theatre, Mlle Emilie Neumann. The story goes that Josef Kupelwieser, who was in love with this flighty lady and insignificant actress, persuaded Schubert to write the music. The first performance took place on 20th December. It is only from the reviews that we can learn something about the intricate plot of this piece – one of them in particular from the pen of the notorious, though on this occasion very benevolent, Siegmund Saphir, nephew of the equally notorious Moritz v. Saphir. We need not, however, concern ourselves with the plot, despite the fact that Schubert wrote to the authoress on 5th August, 1824, saying that 'he had been convinced of the merit of *Rosamunde* the moment that he had read it.' He was none the less delighted that she had condescended to remove certain 'unimportant faults' which an unsympathetic public had so clearly criticized.

Be that as it may, certain individual pieces of the incidental music which he wrote for the work (XV, 8) (there are nine in all) are among his greatest inspirations. For his overture he used the one to *Alfonso und Estrella* (the overture which is universally known as the *Rosamunde* Overture has nothing whatsoever to do with the real *Rosamunde*), and its orchestration and its somewhat 'homespun' grandeur make it admirably suited as an introduction to a solemn, emotional, Romantic affair. (Once again I cannot help feeling that Schubert used the overture to *Die Zauberharfe* and that Schwind made a mistake. He quotes a theme which is 'partly entrusted to the flute'; and that could only fit *Die Zauberharfe*.) At all events, Schubert did not write a new overture to *Rosamunde*. As regards the Entr'acte after the first act, 'Allegro molto moderato', Schwind was of the opinion that it was too sober for its context and too repetitive. Schwind, however, was very young and no particular connoisseur. The piece is a symphonic march of the largest dimensions, consisting of a constant interplay of the various groups of wind-instruments with each other and with the strings, of dynamic contrasts and strange episodes. Here, if anywhere, is the symphonic link between the 'Unfinished' and the C major Symphony. And if a conductor really wished to add a Finale to the two movements of the

'Unfinished', he could without much hesitation turn to this movement in B minor.

Continuing his account, Schwind tells us: 'A ballet passed unnoticed.' Schubert uses the Entr'acte as a 'Divertissement' and expands it with new ideas and a modulation to B major. It obviously accompanied the 'solemn procession' at the beginning of the second act, which Saphir mentions in his review. But at the end comes the Andante ('poco assai') in G major, probably intended for a girls' dance – one of those pieces of Schubert's which fascinate one by their very musical presence, by their very melodic and harmonious existence. According to Schwind the second and third Entr'actes also 'passed unnoticed'. The second has a direct bearing on the plot, with its atmosphere of excitement, its Bruckner-like double-basses, its tremoli on the strings, and its powerful crescendo; it probably illustrates Rosamunde's state of mind in prison. 'The song at the beginning of the third act and the chorus in the same are both excellent,' says Saphir; the former is a three-verse stage-Romance for alto with a rich accompaniment on wind instruments; it is in F minor but with a *ritornello* in the major, and could well take its place among Schubert's piano-songs; the chorus is a chorus of Spirits for male voices in D major, off-stage and naturally sung *pianissimo* with an accompaniment of horns and trombones. 'In the fourth act Rosamunde is discovered in an idyllic valley with her flocks' – and as an introduction to this scene Schubert wrote that Andantino, the theme of which he used both for the slow movement of his String Quartet in A minor and for the Variations of one of his most famous Impromptus. It might well serve as his motto, in the same way that the four-note subject in the Finale of the 'Jupiter' Symphony was Mozart's motto. Schwind calls it 'a short Bucolic' and mentions that it was greeted with applause. In this orchestral version it has a section in the minor in which the woodwind make charming conversation – including a phrase which later recurs note for note in 'Standchen'. 'In the fourth act there was a chorus' (we should add that it was preceded by 'shepherd melodies' for clarinets, bassoons and horns) 'of shepherds and huntsmen, so beautiful and natural that I do not remember ever having heard anything like it.' (Schwind); it, too, had to be repeated. The huntsmen's chorus – a double chorus – is typical; but the shepherds' chorus has a melancholy innocence which one might describe as the apotheosis of 'the pastoral mood in music'. Schwind hoped that it would 'deal the chorus from Weber's *Euryanthe* the sort of blow it deserves'. Not one of the reviewers mentions the ballet at the end, unless it was this that the critic of *Der Sammler* had in mind on 30th December when he wrote that Herr Schubert showed originality in his music, although unfortunately eccentricity as well. It is a Divertissement *all' ongarese*, but *alla tirolese*, too, in a Trio for clarinet, flute, oboe and bagpipe; but above all it is Schubertian in its teeming wealth of invention, in its rhythmic and harmonic ideas. It has rightly become, after the above-mentioned 'Bucolic', the best-known piece in the score.

After two performances of the work, the orchestral parts of Schubert's music were laid aside and it was not until the year 1867 that they were taken up again by two English Schubert enthusiasts, Sir George Grove and Sir Arthur Sullivan. Schubert himself, however, could justifiably have said that he had once again written a work for the stage 'to no purpose'.

It is as if, a few months after completing the 'Wanderer' Fantasia, Schubert had himself realized that he had taken the wrong road and determined to revert from Hummel and the virtuoso manner to his own individual style. In February 1823 he wrote a Piano Sonata in A minor (X, 8), which was published posthumously (1839) by Diabelli as op. 143 and dedicated to Mendelssohn. Diabelli gave it the title of 'Grande Sonate', yet it is anything but a 'grand sonata' in the Beethoven sense of the word. In spite of its strange manner and its explosive outbursts, it is an intimate sonata, contenting itself with three movements and modest dimensions. Not without justification reference has been made to its orchestral colouring – the dark accents of the 'trombones', which start to accompany it, the drum-roll before the recapitulation, the woodwind for the second subject; in the second movement, an Andante, the contrast of the theme, played by 'clarinet' and 'bassoon', with the whispered litany of the 'violas'. In the third movement, admittedly, this 'orchestration' ceases, and it becomes purely pianistic in its passage work, its chords and its accompaniment of the melody. But a much more important feature of this sonata is its concentration. The thematic material is concise, the treatment dramatic and intense. The second subjects stand quite on their own, like visions of paradise, and play no part in the development sections of the first and last movements, in complete contrast to Schubert's usual practice. The Andante is quite unique. Only once did he himself surpass it, in the Andante of his A major Sonata of 1828. One might say that Berlioz must have known it when he wrote his 'Marche des pélerins' in *Harold in Italy*. The work as a whole is really an isolated landmark, standing midway between the three-movement sonatas of his early period, particularly the A minor Sonata of 1817 (X, 6), and the two last groups of 1825–26 and 1828. It looks forward and it looks back. If one seeks a spiritual – not an *historical* – affinity, it is to be found, if anywhere, in Mozart's 'Paris' Sonata in A minor (K. 310). For Schubert's A minor is as fatalistic as Mozart's. The major close of the first movement signifies rather that no end has yet been reached; the second subjects bring no comfort, and the conclusion is without consolation. One is again reminded of Schubert's remark: 'Is there really such a thing as cheerful music? I do not know of any.'

That is true even of the Twelve Ländler which Schubert wrote in May 1823 and which were published as op. 171 by Spina in Vienna in the year 1864 (XII, 9). It is obvious why Schubert never found a publisher for them. They no longer have anything whatever to do with improvisation, and were much too ambitious for potential purchasers and for practical use. The harmonic richness, the wealth of melody, the originality of the modulations and the different types, are all quite unique. No. 1 is like an introduction, an 'Invitation to the Dance'. No. 3 could well be included as it stands in Schumann's *Carnaval*, while No. 8 (in A flat minor) could equally have been written by Chopin. No. 5 is one of those dances in which only the middle parts seem to be in motion and whose 'mute happiness' we shall encounter in a few more instances – for example in Schubert's most perfect and most individual sonata, the G major, op. 78.

One of these dances, No. 2, is identical with No. 1 of the 'German Dances and Ecossaises' (XII, 3), which Schubert published as op. 33 with Cappi early in 1825 – sixteen Ländler and two Ecossaises, a few dating from July 1824, of which No. 2 in D major is the most beautiful. No. 10 is an infinitely more primitive version of the Chopinesque Waltz from op. 171. They are generally speaking much slighter and were therefore that much more 'saleable'. The same is true of a collection (11) of Ecossaises written in January 1823 (XII, 25), the direct successor of two similar collections – one written in May 1816 (XII, 27) and the other in May 1820 (XII, 28). Of later origin is another, consisting of eight numbers, to which we will return in due course for a particular reason. Short pieces of this kind served Schubert as dedicatory pieces. Just as in February 1818, he had 'copied out expressly for his beloved brother' a 'Trio' (XII, 31) 'to be considered as the prodigal son of a minuet' ('the son of a prodigal minuet' would have been more accurate), so one of these Ecossaises of 1817 (XII, 2, No. 2) was copied into Fräulein Seraphine Schellmann's album accompanied by a facetious verse.

The second of two German Dances (XII, 18 and without a doubt wrongly dated January 1824 in the Collected Edition) is included in a 'Collection of new Piano Compositions, Songs with German, French and Italian texts, and Dances' which was published by Sauer and Leidesdorf at the end of 1823 under the title of *Album Musicale*. But this 'Collection' contains another contribution by Schubert of a quite different calibre, an 'Aire (!) russe for the Pianoforte', identical with the Moment musical in F minor which Schubert later included as No. 3 in his op. 94. It is a 'Divertissement' and the exact pianistic counterpart to the final Ballet-Divertissement in *Rosamunde*, irresistible in its piquancy and in the melancholy smile with which it closes in the major key. It serves to emphasize two things. First, how difficult it is to date Schubert's works, since it could equally well have been written in 1827 or 1828. Secondly, how careful one must be in the matter of 'national' classification; for what we might take to be 'Hungarian', was 'Russian' in Schubert's or the publisher's eyes.

SCHUBERT'S ILLNESS

On 8th May, 1823, Schubert wrote a poem entitled 'Mein Gebet', which attempted to put into words what the A minor Sonata had expressed in a more perfect form: his deep de-

spair, his longing for death, for a new and completely transformed existence:

> Sieh, vernichtet liegt im Staube
> Unerhörtem Gram zum Raube,
> Meines Lebens Martergang
> Nahend ew' gem Untergang. . . .*

He was ill. As his physical condition varied, so his mood
changed accordingly; thus on 14th August he wrote to Schober from Steyr, saying that he was quite well, but adding
immediately: 'I almost begin to doubt whether I shall ever
be completely well again.' He avoided company, as a reference by his nephew Karl in Beethoven's *Conversation-
shefte* suggests: 'Everyone speaks very highly of Schubert,
but they say he seems to have gone into hiding.' He did
not even take part in the drunken orgy with which his friends
celebrated the departure of the painter Leopold Kupelwieser for Rome on 8th November – 'we all dined there,
except Schubert, who was confined to his bed that day,'
wrote Schwind. He went on as follows: 'Schaeffer and Bernard, who visited him, assured us that he is well on the way
to recovery. They already speak of a period of four weeks,
by the end of which he will probably be completely restored
to health.' Schubert, in fact, wrote a letter to Schober himself on 30th November, in which he deplored the social and
intellectual decline of their circle and went on to say that his
'state of health (thank God) seems at last to be completely
restored'; and on 9th December Johanna Lutz wrote to her
fiancé Kupelwieser in Rome: 'Schubert is now quite well and
already shows a desire to stop keeping to his strict regimen.
If only he does not do himself harm. . . .' The strict regimen
apparently consisted of a regulated mode of life, plenty of
exercise, baths, moderation in eating and abstention from
alcoholic drinks. On 26th December we find Schwind writing
thus: 'Schubert is better, and it will not be long before he
once more has his own hair which had to be cut off because
of the rash. He wears a very cosy wig.' And on 13th February, 1824: 'Schubert is now keeping a fourteen-day fast
and is confined to his house. He looks much better and is
very cheerful, very comically hungry and writes innumer-
able quartets and Germans and variations'. 'Schubert is very

* See, my tortured existence lies shattered in the dust, a prey to
terrible affliction, nearing eternal destruction. . . .

well. He has given up his wig and reveals a pretty head of short, curly hair. ...' (22nd February) 'Schubert is now quite well. He says that after a few days of the new treatment he could feel his complaint lose its grip, and everything was different. ...' But Schubert's cheerfulness at this time was only a pretence. This is proved not only by some fragments from a lost diary of March 1824, but particularly by the beginning of a letter to Kupelwieser in Rome, who seems to have been one of his most understanding friends and to whom he 'could at last pour out his whole soul once more', (31st March, 1824):

I feel myself to be the most unhappy wretched creature in the world. Imagine a man whose health will never be right again and who, in his despair over this, constantly makes things worse instead of better; imagine a man, I say, whose brightest hopes have come to nothing, to whom the happiness of love and friendship offer nothing but pain, whose enthusiasm (at least the stimulating kind) for beauty threatens to vanish; and then ask yourself if he is not indeed a wretched unhappy creature?—'My peace is gone, my heart is heavy, I shall find it never and nevermore.' Thus indeed can I now sing every day, for each night, when I go to sleep, I hope I will not wake again, and each morning reminds me only of yesterday's unhappiness. Thus, joyless and friendless, I should pass my days, if Schwind did not visit me occasionally and bring me a breath of those sweet days that are past. ...

There is scarcely any doubt about the character of his illness. It was a serious venereal disease – untreated syphilis, to be more precise – for which there was no real cure in those days. Consequently the improvement in his condition at the beginning of March was also deceptive: 'Schubert is not very well. He has such pains in his left arm that he is quite unable to play the piano. Apart from that he is in good spirits[!] . . .' (Schwind to Schober, 14th April, 1824.) Later, however, in the summer, his second visit to Zseliz had a salutary effect, and in the autumn he wrote to Schober that he had been in good health 'for five months' (21st September). His friends also remarked how well he looked at this time. But at the end of 1825, a relapse set in and his friends had to spend New Year's Eve without him. During the following years he was a chronic sufferer from excruciating headaches, about which he himself complained on one occasion to his friend Marie Leopoldine Pachler (on the manuscript of a Children's

March for the little Faust Pachler): 'I hope that you are in
better health than I am, Madame, for my usual headaches
have started to attack me again.' Schubert never completely
recovered. And people who are conscious of their desperate
condition usually take that much less care of themselves.
Quite apart from his condition, Schubert was habitually inclined to neglect himself – Schubert, the 'homeless', given
over to every irregularity in his way of life, not un-
favourably disposed towards wine, a vessel of the strongest
artistic emotions. It is very probable that the malignant disease which attacked him in November 1828 found a body
sapped of its full powers of resistance and consequently an
easy prey.

Even during the period of his serious illness Schubert
wrote, in addition to his operas, works 'for convivial occasions'. In particular there are four settings for male-voice
chorus of poems by Matthisson ('So lang im deutschen Ei-
chenthale'), Schiller ('Liebe rauscht der Silberbach'), Salis
('Auf! es dunkelt' – a strophic song) and F. A. Krummacher
('Die Nacht' – 'Wie schön bist du'), which were published at
the beginning of October 1823, as op. 17, and in which Schubert struck the keynote for the male-voice chorus for the
whole hundred years that followed. Neither the patriotic
song, nor the lyrical nature-scenes nor the dance-song are
missing; the only style that is not represented is the humorous and jaunty, for which the North Germans, Zelter,
Ludwig Berger and their successors, had a special liking.
There is throughout a fullness of sound that the North
Germans – with the exception of Mendelssohn – never
achieved. But Mendelssohn must certainly have known these
particular four songs well.

In addition there dates from 22nd November, 1822, a quartet for mixed chorus with piano accompaniment (XVII, 11)

> *Schicksalslenker, blicke nieder*
> *Auf ein dankerfülltes Herz. . . .**

by an unknown poet. It is a lovely and gentle Larghetto in A
flat major, yet it is certainly not a personal confession, but
rather a work written expressly to celebrate the recovery of a
dear member of the family ('Liebevoll nahmst du der Leiden

*Disposer of Fate, look down
  upon a heart filled with gratitude. . . .

– Herben Kelch von Vaters Mund').* Then there is his op. 16, published at the beginning of October 1823, and consisting of two quartets for male-voices and piano – an earlier piece written in May 1816 'Naturgenuss' (XVI, 8) and Schober's 'Frühlingsgesang' (XVI, 7), an imitation of Schiller; here, too, the convivial character is emphasized in the direction that the piano may be replaced by an apocryphal guitar. The first tenor is given the predominant part, and the cheerful, homophonic beginning is followed on this occasion not by a 'round' but by a freer form of treatment. In another setting for unaccompanied male voices this treatment is replaced by a purely *choral* homophony, and one is inclined to prefer this latter setting (XVI, 31) to the one for a quasi-solo quartet.

On the other hand, however, the piano accompaniment to the setting for women's voices of J. W. L. Gleim's hymn 'Gott in der Natur', written in August 1822 (XVIII, 3), is a completely intrinsic part of the work – an accompaniment which is nothing other than the piano arrangement of an imaginary full orchestral score, with trombones, trumpets and drums. The chorus, too, requires the greatest possible volume of sound. It is one of Schubert's most theatrical choral pieces. The final 'allegro giusto' ('Lobt den Gewaltigen') reminds one of Handel, and in the 'orchestra' we seem to hear the sound of harps.

We left Schubert as a song-writer in the autumn of 1821, and we now turn our steps towards the year 1823, towards the landmark of the 'Miller' songs, which have an epoch-making significance quite apart from Schubert's music. One might well call the chapter dealing with the songs written between these two dates: The Unknown Schubert. For of the three dozen pieces of this period, only a small number have survived to the present day. This is partly due to the fact that, during this period, Schubert was too concerned with the poetry of his friends – Mayrhofer, Senn, Schober, Bruchmann, Leitner, Collin and other poets like Graf Mailath or Richard Roos – and was so attracted by the subject-matter that he overlooked the poetic weaknesses. Yet at the same time he discovered a pure lyric poet like Friedrich Rückert and found two genuinely passionate pieces in the

* It was a Herr Ritter, and the composition was commissioned, through Anna Fröhlich, by Frau Geymüller.

otherwise marble-smooth poetry of the classicist Graf
Platen. Suddenly, in the midst of this preoccupation with
'Viennese' poetry, he turned once more to Goethe with a
group of five songs, of which three at least are 'immortal',
and in May 1823 he again took Schiller as his inspiration for
two no less immortal pieces. Not one link in this chain is
insignificant and even where the motives which actuated
his poets are of the feeblest, most sentimental and most
affected, it is worth while seeking the motives which prompted *him* to set them to music. In almost every case it was his
feverish state of mind which made him receptive to a heart-
felt expression of suffering or hope.

This applies particularly to the first of these songs, a setting of Johann Graf Mailath's 'Der Blumen Schmerz' (XX,
399) to which one could equally give the title of 'Longing for
Death', and which is a piece of sickly sentimentality. Yet
Schubert brought out all its underlying delicacy and neutral-
ized its sentimentality by the simplicity of his treatment. It is
in E minor like the later 'Trockene Blumen' of *Die schöne
Müllerin*. He countered the exuberance of Rückert's love-
song 'Sei mir gegrüsst '(XX, 400) by keeping to the quietest
pianissimo throughout and allowing himself only two
emotional outbursts. He ensured for the song, or rather for
the melody, a double popularity by using it for the Variations in his Duo, op. 159, for violin and piano. In 'Wach-
telschlag' (XX, 401) he once more entered into competition
with Beethoven (unconsciously, since he obviously found the
poem elsewhere), and used in his accompaniment the same
figure as his great predecessor, the dactylic call of the pious
bird. It is difficult to decide whether his setting is superior to
Beethoven's. Beethoven set every verse to different music
and paints or reproduces every nuance of the text, particularly the allusion to war and to the thunderstorm. Schubert simply suggests this by a modulation to the minor key.
He is simpler, more lyrical, more 'undramatic'; he has no
need to emphasize the details.

Once again it is not possible for us to deal with each individual song in detail nor even to mention each individual
song, and an author writing exclusively about Schubert's
vocal music would be quick to criticize us for what we
had omitted. We, on the other hand, could with equal
justification accuse posterity of indifference towards the

small handful of songs from this group which have survived. Mayrhofer's 'Nachtviolen' (XX, 403), full of the most sensitive harmony and with its accompaniment lying almost entirely in the resonant middle octaves, is a masterpiece of mysterious intimacy. The same poet's 'Heliopolis II' (XX, 405), written in April 1822 for a bass voice, is an intensely passionate and powerful piece and counter-evidence against the stupid representation of Schubert as 'a feminine nature', as is the defiant piece which followed it, 'Selige Welt' (XX, 406), a setting of a lovely poem by the sensitive Johann Senn. If sentimentality is a trait of 'femininity', then Beethoven is much less 'masculine' than Schubert. Even 'Die Rose' (XX, 408), with which he turned once more to one of the Schlegel brothers, Friedrich, is a masterpiece in its archaic harmonic colouring and in the symbolic interplay between major and minor. The exactness with which Schubert's imagination worked is shown in his setting of Schober's 'Schatzgräber's Begehr' (XX, 412) which exists in a second version enriched with delicate little touches. It is in the same key as 'Der Tod und das Mädchen', and the rhythmic figure of Death, in all its different versions and variants, permeates the whole song, which ends in archaic fashion with hollow fifths. 'Schwestergruss' dates from November and is a setting of a poem by Franz Bruchmann, written 'after the death of the poet's sister' (XX, 413). It, too, begins with the rhythmic figure of Death and hovers between F sharp minor and major. It is one of those ecstatic Adagios which Schubert avoided for so long in his instrumental music, and foreshadows the slow movement of the String Quintet. Even in pieces like Schober's long 'flower' ballad 'Viola' (XX, 423), or his 'Pilgerweise' (XX, 429) and 'Vergissmeinnicht' (XX, 430; May 1823), where his choice of text was sadly at fault, there are touches of exquisite poetic fancy. 'Pilgerweise' provides what may be the key to the slow movement of his A major Piano Sonata of 1828, to which we shall return in due course; and 'Vergissmeinnicht' contains in one passage

> *Tränen sprechen ihren Schmerz nur aus,*
> *Und ein unergründlich Sehnen*
> *Treibt sie aus sich selbst heraus. . . .**

> ** Tears express but their grief,*
> *and an unfathomable longing*
> *drives them forth from itself. . . .*

what is perhaps not only a literal echo of the 'Unfinished' in rhythm and key, but an interpretation.

Nevertheless we would not insist that posterity has been wrong in its selective interest in a few pieces of this period. 'Anakreon's Leyer' or 'An die Leyer' (XX, 414), as the translator Bruchmann called it, with its double transition from a heroic to a lyrical mood, could well serve as a motto for the whole of Schubert's music by virtue of its complete and utter charm. Platen's love-lyric 'Du liebst mich nicht' (XX, 409) which Schubert had to transpose from G sharp minor to A minor for his publishers, Sauer and Leidesdorf (an unusual state of affairs, since in the majority of other cases he had to transpose his songs *down* a semitone or tone), symbolizes the refrain by a persistent rhythm and at the same time by the boldest of modulations: the fateful word has to be uttered in every key. Of the five Goethe songs, two – 'Am Flusse' and 'Willkommen und Abschied' (XX, 418, 419) – are less well-known, and probably rightly so, in spite of their fullness and freshness; 'An die Entfernte' (XX, 417), on the other hand, has been undeservedly neglected. It is like a musical letter, half spoken, half sung and extraordinarily simple and spontaneous in its treatment. 'Wanderers Nacht-lied' ('Über allen Gipfeln ist Ruh'; XX, 420) has note quite the same simplicity by reason of a few excessively arioso phrases, and yet it remains the loveliest setting of this hackneyed song. 'Der Musensohn' (XX, 416) is a splendid example of how the simplest and apparently most neutral accompaniment in Schubert's 'strophic song with variations' can change its character:

> *Der stumpfe Bursche bläht sich,*
> *Das steife Mädchen dreht sich*
> *Nach meiner Melodie. . . .**

– a passage in which it becomes sheer scenic painting. How innocent, happy, unassuming and yet ingenious it all is! And Schubert does not need to rely solely on the help of the poet to produce a masterpiece. Collin's 'Wehmut' (XX, 426) contains the whole greatness and unaffected simplicity of Schubert in a nutshell, in its declamatory freedom, its

---

*The dull lad struts
   The prim girl pirouettes
   To my melody. . . .

modulations and its harmonic symbolism ('So wohl – so weh'). And Stolberg's 'Auf dem Wasser zu singen' (XX, 428) contains a nature-scene ('tanzet das Abendrot rund um den Kahn'), the magic of which never palls even though it is thrice repeated – particularly if the singer knows how to treat it with a new and heightened shade of expression each time.

Finally, Schubert reached a pinnacle of achievement in the two Schiller songs of 1823, 'Das Geheimnis' and 'Der Pilgrim' (XX, 431, 432). How far we have travelled from the year 1815, when he had set 'Das Geheimnis' as a strophic song (XX, 105). Emotional intensity and imaginative power here produce a flower of a melodic exuberance in which even suggestions of an Italian style are not out of place.

Ex. 39

Of an equal stature is 'Der Pilgrim', which has the outward appearance of a cantata since, after the measured tread of the first eight verses, it ends with an Adagio in different tempo for the last. Schubert now no longer needed the expedient of recitative; he encompassed a long poem such as this in one single mighty span.

Among all these songs there is one true ballad, 'Der Zwerg', the poem by Matthaeus v. Collin (XX, 425), and dedicated to the poet when it was published as op. 22, No. 1, at the end of May 1823. It is no longer a classical ballad like Schiller's 'Bürgschaft', nor a traditional Nordic one like Goethe's 'Erlkönig', but a more oriental, sombre story which tells of a queen and her dwarf and of how she must suffer death in the depths of the sea because 'she has for-saken him for the king' – a strange tale of sexual mystery. And in the musical form with which Schubert invested it – with its echo of the 'Unfinished' in spite of the dissimilarity of key (A minor instead of B minor), and with its gloomy octaves between the voice-part and the bass of the ac-companiment – the ballad acquires a strange, pale impress-iveness which grips the heart and the imagination. Heart and imagination alike are stirred without our rightly under-standing why; Schubert's contemporaries and posterity de-scribed this effect by the word 'romantic'.

All these songs were written in the depths of gloom and despair over his incurable disease, and it was in this mental state that *Die schöne Müllerin* was composed. The exact chronology is as follows: the first songs in May 1823, fol-lowed by the first two acts of *Fierabras,* then more songs written in hospital, the third act of the opera, and finally the conclusion of the cycle. The title of the first edition runs as follows: '*The Fair Maid of the Mill (Die schöne Müllerin)* – a cycle of songs with text by Wilhelm Müller and set to music for solo voice with pianoforte accompaniment. Dedi-cated to Karl Freyherr von Schönstein. Op. 25.' It was an-nounced on 25th March, 1824 in the official *Wiener Zeitung* and appeared in five issues, I and II 24th March, III–V 12th August. Karl Freyherr von Schönstein was, next to Vogl, the most sensitive interpreter of Schubert's songs and 'ren-dered a great service in introducing Schubert's works into the leading aristocratic circles of Vienna. . . . Furthermore he had a baritone voice; when, as often happened, he sang the songs to Schubert's accompaniment, they had to be trans-posed accordingly.' (Max Friedlaender, in his fine critical edition of 1922, Leipzig, C. F. Peters, p. 24). Kreissle v. Hell-born's version of how Schubert came across the poems has often been told:

One day Schubert called on the private secretary of Count Seczenyi, Herr Benedikt Randhartinger, with whom he was on friendly terms. He had scarcely entered the room, when the secretary was summoned to the Count. He went out at once, indicating to the composer that he would be back shortly. Franz walked over to the desk, where he found a volume of poems lying. He put the book in his pocket and left, without waiting for Randhartinger's return. The latter noticed that the volume of poems was missing as soon as he came back, and called on Schubert the following day in order to recover the book. Franz put down his high-handed behaviour to the interest which the poems had aroused in him, and to prove that his removal of the book had not been entirely unproductive of results, he presented the astonished secretary with the manuscript of the first 'Miller' songs, which he had partially completed during the previous night.

Whether all this is strictly accurate is a matter of opinion.

Anyone who sought to discover a particular 'Viennese' or 'Austrian' atmosphere in *Die schöne Müllerin* would once more find himself on the wrong track, at least so far as the text is concerned. These poems were written in extremely prosaic surroundings – namely, in Berlin. Wilhelm Müller, the son of a shoemaker from Dessau, belonged in 1816 or 1817 to a literary circle of young people, which held its meetings at the house of Councillor Fr. Aug. v. Stägemann and which was not unlike Schubert's circle except that women also took an active part in it. The Berlin equivalent of Schubert among these young men and women was Ludwig Berger, who had already set a number of these same poems to music before Schubert. Here, then, was written, as a kind of semi-dramatic vaudeville, this tale of the true-hearted young miller, who on his travels falls in love with a beautiful and faithless girl and who, after a brief hour of happiness, has to give way to his more dashing rival, the huntsman. The miller and the miller's lovely daughter were favourite figures of Romantic poetry. They already feature in Goethe's lyrics. But the chief inspiration behind Wilhelm Müller's conception was the folk-song, on the model of *Des Knaben Wunderhorn*. There are many obvious indications of this. All the members of Stägemann's cultured circle co-operated in writing *Die schöne Müllerin*; but Müller was the most gifted of them and eventually collected his contributions together in a cycle, which he published in 1821 at the beginning of a volume of poems with the genuinely 'Romantic' title: 'Seventy-seven poems from the posthumous papers of a travelling horn-player.'* There were twenty-

* It says much for Wilhelm Müller that Heinrich Heine thought highly

three pieces with prologue and epilogue, three of which, however, Schubert disregarded. His song-cycle comprises only twenty pieces.

Here again is evidence of Schubert's complete – and completely *deliberate* – independence from Beethoven. Seven years earlier Beethoven's song-cycle *An die ferne Geliebte*, op. 98, had been published, a landmark in the history of song. In this Beethoven took six poems by A. J. Jeitteles and linked them without a break into a single superbly poetical and musical entity by means of longer or shorter interludes and by the device of reverting again to the beginning. This op. 98 is Beethoven's greatest achievement as a song-writer. And it became the starting-point for the song-cycle of Robert Schumann, Carl Loewe, Peter Cornelius and many others. It would be childish to suggest that Schubert was unacquainted with this work of Beethoven's. But he ignored it. He created a scenic drama, through which runs a persistent, though not immediately obvious, connecting thread. Individual songs admittedly belong together, as for example 'Des Müller's Blumen' (IX) and 'Tränenregen' (X), both in the same key and the same time, or 'Pause' (XII) and 'Mit einem grünen Lautenbande' (XIII), both in B flat major and the former ending with a chord which one would not need to repeat at the beginning of the latter, if the cycle were being performed as a whole. But the unity of the work lies deeper. One need only follow the part played by the semi-quaver figure, which is the symbol of the 'brook', and observe how it passes from the busy *piano* of 'Wohin?' (II) to the happiness of the major section in 'Der Neugierige' (VI) and to the troubled anxiety of 'Eifersucht und Stolz' (XV); how, in the second half of the cycle, it is combined with the symbol of the 'green colour' of the huntsman. The last piece, 'Des Baches Wiegenlied' is the finest example of Schubert's delicately balanced psychological sense; the semi-quaver figure moderates to quavers, but the intervals of a fifth persist to the last, like a bitter-sweet after-taste of a sad yet blissful experience. The unity rests further on Schubert's capacity for 'emotional painting' which nowhere produces a more profound effect than here. The rippling, rushing, chat-

---

of him and dedicated to the 'horn-player' a copy of his *Lyrisches Intermezzo*, with the request that he 'should honour it with his attention'.

tering of the brook, the busy clatter of the mill, the gentle plucking of lute-strings are at once realism and reflected imagery; the girl is real – once, at the end of 'Tränenregen' she shows her true, not very sympathetic face – and at the same time seen through her lover's eyes. And to anyone who wishes to trace Schubert's development as a song-writer chronologically, the return to the strophic song is surprising and revealing. For at least half the pieces are pure or varied strophic songs. This is an indication that Schubert was fully conscious of the 'Romantic' literary origin of these songs, the affinity with the folk-song, with *Des Knaben Wunderhorn*, that collection made by two sworn Romantics, which for some strange reason he did not know – or disregarded. He turned accordingly to the simplest of song-forms, the strophic song. But he imbued it with his overflowing musical sense and reserved to himself the full right to vary it or to depart from it completely. He must have felt that the 'popular' character of this simple miller's tale was a poetical masquerade of the kind so beloved by the early writers of the Romantic school. But he contrived to overcome this bogus 'popularity' by means of his own artistic sincerity and his musical maturity.

'THE GOOD EMPEROR FRANZ'

It has been said that Franz Schubert was a completely 'unpolitical animal', a kind of composing machine, who lived in that blissful Vienna which knows only two seasons – the spring, when the trees are decked in green, and the autumn, when people go to the *Heuriger* in Grinzing – and who rose in the morning, sat himself down at his desk and filled sheets of music paper with notes until noon; who spent the afternoon walking in the Wienerwald, his head full of Ländlers, and drank the evening away with his friends in a café or inn. Naturally enough Schubert was not politically-minded like the Heidelberg student Karl Ludwig Sand, who murdered the poet August v. Kotzebue in the belief that he was a reactionary and an enemy of freedom in the pay of the Russians. But like the more closely associated of his friends, he suffered deeply under the oppressive Austrian régime. We know the fate of his school-friend at the Convict, Johann Senn, who in 1820 made so bold as to rebel against the

Imperial Chief of Police and Chief Censor, Count Josef
Sedlnitsky, and who was arrested early one morning during a
search of his lodgings on suspicion of holding 'libertarian
meetings' at an inn with some of his like-minded associates.
Among others, Schubert also happened to be present on this
occasion and was arrested with him. Schubert 'escaped with
a black eye' (O. E. Deutsch, op. cit., p. 130), but Senn fared
worse. He was remanded in custody for fourteen months
and then deported to his native Tyrol, where he eked out a
living in various minor posts and finally ended his days as an
embittered eccentric. It testifies to Schubert's courage that
he continued to set his suspect friend's poems to music in
later years. We know the fate of the Imperial Registrar,
Franz Grillparzer, who, in spite of the literary fame which
he had won in Austria with his dramas *Die Ahnfrau* (1817)
and *Sappho* (1818), managed to 'cause offence' in the highest
quarters with his poems of homage and his dramas of loyalty
towards the House of Habsburg, and had to give vent to his
profound indignation in the privacy of his poetry and entries
in his diary, and who changed from the passionately tor-
mented lover of Kathi Fröhlich into a peevish old bachelor.
What, one might well ask, did Schubert have in common
with Senn, Grillparzer and particularly with his saturnine
friend Mayrhofer?

Political oppression in Austria did not only date from the
time of Napoleon's downfall and the so-called Carlsbad
Decrees, which imposed a strict surveillance over student-
life in Germany and more especially in Austria. The state of
Vienna under the Emperor Franz is described clearly
enough by the blunt and honest Johann Gottfried Seume,
who spent a short time in the Imperial capital during his
celebrated *Journey on foot to Syracuse in the year* 1802. He
first mentions the rumour that the Emperor 'had made Herr
Kasperle of the Leopoldstadt a Baron', which tickled his
sense of humour and which was, in point of fact, supremely
'Viennese'. He then goes on:

There is scarcely a mention of public matters in Vienna, and
you can visit public places for months on end, perhaps, before
you hear one word which has any bearing on politics; such is the
strictness with which they practise orthodoxy in politics no less
than in religion. Everywhere in the cafés there is a reverent hush,
as if High Mass was being celebrated at which everyone scarcely

dared to breathe. Since it is my habit not to fly into a boisterous rage, but instead to talk to myself quite calmly and quietly, my acquaintances several times gave me a friendly warning that walls have ears. On one occasion my carelessness nearly landed me in trouble. As you know, I am no sort of revolutionary, since that usually results in making matters go from bad to worse; but it is a habit of mine to make a little more noise than is perhaps good for me about something I like. For example, the *Marseillaise* has always struck me as an excellent piece of music, and it so happens that, without thinking, I often hum a few bars of it, as indeed I might do with any other piece of music. This actually happened once in Vienna – admittedly in quite the wrong place – and very naturally it acted like a damper on those present. . . .

We are told that Beethoven cheerfully inveighed against political conditions in Austria and against the mental inertia and love of pleasure of the 'Phaeacians' – as he called the Viennese; but he was simply ignored by the authorities, who looked upon him as a harmless lunatic.

'The good Emperor Franz', who succeeded his father Leopold in 1792, owed the aura of sanctity which surrounded his name to Josef Haydn, who had set the Jesuit Father Haschka's loyal words to his immortal melody in January 1797. Schubert had also contributed a little to this loyal transfiguration, with trumpets and drums, when in January 1822, he set to music a four-verse hymn 'Am Geburtstage des Kaisers' (XVII, 3), by Joh. Ludwig Ferdinand Deinhardstein, lecturer in aesthetics and classical literature at the Theresianum; it was performed on the evening before that Imperial occasion by a selected choir of pupils. In it, the full chorus answers a quartet of soloists, accompanied by an orchestra of dignified proportions (although without trombones). But the melody, although after the pattern of Haydn's, lacks the inspiration of its great model. It was the result of a commission which Leopold Sonnleithner had been instrumental in arranging for Schubert, and Schubert for his part carried it out simply and straightforwardly, but without any particular enthusiasm.

Nor would His Apostolic Majesty have been worthy of any such enthusiasm. The Emperor's popularity rested on externals, transparent to the majority of his immediate circle, but equally so to the more sharp-sighted members of the *bourgeoisie*.

Franz, according to *Bilder aus Oestreich aus den Jahren* 1848–

1849 by a German traveller, gave a masterly stage performance in public. By birth and disposition a foreigner, in the disagreeable sense of the word, he played 'the bogus Viennese' throughout his life. The ordinary people of Vienna, of Austria and Styria, possess an indestructible fund of harmless sincerity, cheerfulness and good humour; the man in the street *is* charming. Franz, by nature a suspicious, crafty, coldhearted and narrow-minded prince, without magnanimity, yet with a sharp eye for the weaknesses of the broad masses of the people; so cultured that he could express himself with diplomatic care and precision in both French and Italian – disguised his most carefully calculated thoughts in the simple Viennese dialect, and aped the homely simplicity of the people in gesture, expression and movement, so regularly and for so long that the mask eventually became his natural face. The Emperor's example set the fashion. All the scum of the so-called cultured class wanted to claim association with the lesser orders; Viennese became the diplomatic language of government departments and of the army; even the stateless immigrants who stream into Vienna in their thousands each year in order to seek their fortune in the reflected glory of the Imperial sun, murdered and caricatured the harmless dialect with their own Slav or semi-Slav tongue. The corrupt, blood-sucking, extortionate official, the parrot-like money-aristocrat, the dishonest parasite and the cold-blooded glutton, the upper and lower-class informer—all alike knew how to apply a veneer of Viennese *bonhomie* both at home and abroad, and only the affection and self-complacency with which they bragged so genially, smacking their chests and stomachs, betrayed the fact that they had acquired it by imitation. In the field of literature this play-acting was practised in its most loathsome form by Castelli and Hans Jörgel (Financial Councillor Weis), who for twenty years had habitually aped and debased the language of the country-people with ventriloquists' skill in the ante-chambers and at the tables of aristocratic and royal gentry.*

This judgment is certainly too harsh, particularly in so far as it concerns Castelli, who had himself suffered too much under the censorship of Count Sedlnitsky not to have a sincere hatred for the 'System Franz'. Castelli himself tells an anecdote which illustrates supremely well the character of the man who in his will bequeathed to his people 'his love' and nothing else. Castelli had written a war-poem – it must have been during the campaign of 1809 – which, with the approval of the censors, was given an enormous circulation throughout the Austrian army, and forthwith resulted in his being proscribed by Napoleon. In the event of capture, he would certainly have been shot, like the bookseller Palm.

* E. Vehse, *Geschichte der deutschen Höfe seit der Reformation*, Pt. X, Hamburg, 1852, pp. 123 ff.

After the Austrian defeat, he had no means of reaching safety, and so he hit on the plan of making a personal request to his Emperor to let him travel in one of the many carriages which at that time were leaving almost daily for Hungary, loaded with art-treasures and important State documents. Let him tell the story himself:*

The Emperor had already left the Residenz and had gone to Totis. I made my way there on foot and through the medium of the kindly Imperial Lord Chamberlain, Count von Wrbna, I obtained an audience with the Emperor.

His face showed clearly his grief at the tragic fate of his country, and this gave me hope.

'Who are you?' he asked, 'and what do you want?'

'A poor, provincial clerk who has not even once drawn his full annual salary of 300 florins, because various taxes are still being deducted from him.'

'That is quite in order. I cannot help you there.'

'I am asking for a very different kind of assistance, your Majesty. I have unfortunately been proscribed by the French dictator, with the added injunction that, wherever I am found, I am to be handed over to a military court. I must therefore make good my escape.'

'Of course.'

'But this is impossible, as I have not the means to do so. I am therefore making so bold as to ask your Majesty most graciously to deign to use me as an escort for one of your convoys.'

'You say you have been proscribed. And why is that?'

Humbly and sadly I handed him a copy of the *Moniteur* and said, 'It is all there. Please read it.'

The Emperor did so, shook his head, frowned and then, handing me back the paper, said brusquely: 'So you have written a war-poem? And who, pray, ordered you to do so?'

Schubert's whole life fell within the reign of this man, for the Emperor did not die until 1835. To be fair, he also enjoyed the blessings of this reign after the fall of Napoleon – the peace which the statesmanship of Prime Metternich and his shrewd adviser Friedrich Gentz succeeded in preserving. And whatever foreign critics might say about the simple pleasure-loving Viennese, they were in Schubert's eyes, as in Grillparzer's, a people with a genuine sincerity of feeling, which he found lacking in the North Germans and which endeared his country to him, in spite of all 'depressing experiences'. For this 'uncultured people' a patriarchal government was probably the only right one. For the younger

* *Memoiren meines Lebens*, I, pp. 153 ff. Vienna and Prague, 1861.

members of the rising middle-class, to which Schubert and his friends belonged, it must have been exasperating enough. That Schubert, too, was deeply sensitive about the deathly political hush, the surveillance by vigilant authorities, the decline into philistinism, is shown by one of the entries in the lost diary of 1824 which speaks of his profound hatred for that one-sidedness which 'makes so many wretches think that only what *they* are doing is best, while everything else is of no account. *One* beauty should inspire a man throughout his whole life, it is true; but the splendour of that inspiration should illuminate everything else.' He wanted to be a *complete* human being. And how else is one to explain the poem, which he included in a letter to Schober on 21st September of the same year, except as an expression of resignation over the 'inaction of the times'? As an escape into the world of art, which alone could still mirror at least the reflection of greatness? It is a typically 'Romantic' attitude: art considered not as the expression and transfiguration of life, but as an escape into a dreamland of perfection.

Chapter Eleven

The Period of the Three string Quartets
The Second Visit to Hungary
1824–1826

In the letter to Schober, mentioned in the previous chapter, Schubert continued thus: 'To date things have gone badly with Leidesdorf [his friend and new publisher who had acquired *Die schöne Müllerin*]. He cannot pay nor does anybody buy anything either of mine or of anyone else, except miserable fancy stuff.' And earlier, in August 1824, he had written to Schwind: 'How is Leidesdorf? Is he making any progress or is he already in low water? ... The "Miller" songs make such slow headway too. Every three months a volume manages to struggle off the presses.'

Both letters were written from Zseliz, where Schubert had again gone in May 1824 in the service of the Esterhazy family, with the intention of writing an opera and a symphony in addition to fulfilling his duties as the Count's domestic music-teacher. (In fact he wrote neither the opera nor the symphony.) The visit did his health good, even though he could no longer enjoy the peace of country life as unreservedly as he had done six years earlier: '... Admittedly it is no longer that happy time during which every object seems to us to be surrounded by the bright splendour of youth, but rather a time of fateful recognition of a miserable reality which I try as best I can to beautify by my imagination (thank God!)' (to Ferdinand, in July). If ever he had cherished a youthful passion for one of the two young Countesses, Marie or Caroline – the former was shortly to become engaged – it was now a thing of the past, although he later speaks of a 'certain attractive star' in the castle: 'We imagine that happiness is to be found in places where once we were happy, whereas it lies in ourselves and although I had an unpleasant disappointment and saw repeated here an experience I had already had in Steyr, I am nevertheless better able now to find happiness and peace in myself than I was then.' Someone had obviously found occasion to impress upon him clearly the difference in his status, although during this second visit he was no longer required to live in the staff quarters, but was given a room of his own in the castle itself. He was bored and, in spite of the 'certain star' – probably the Countess Caroline – he sometimes had a 'damnable longing for Vienna'. 'Here I sit alone in the heart of Hungary, where I unfortunately allowed myself to be lured a second time, without even a *single* person with whom I could make intelligent conversation.' No doubt a ray of light in the darkness of this visit was provided by the arrival in August of Karl v. Schönstein, who was a close friend of Count Johann Karl Esterhazy; Schubert eventually accompanied Schönstein back to Vienna in the middle of October – Schönstein sent the Count a humorous description of the journey. Schönstein may also have been responsible for reviving Schubert's interest in vocal music, for, according to a letter to Schober, he had 'written practically no songs since the time you left, but have tried my hand at a number of instrumental pieces'. One of the vocal works, a setting of Friedrich de la Motte-Fouqué's 'Gebet' (XVII, 10) was a direct result of the visit to Zseliz. At breakfast one morning the pious Countess (piety had again become the height of fashion in aristocratic circles since the Emperor's marriage to the bigoted Princess Caroline Auguste of Bavaria in 1816) had requested Schubert to write it, and the same evening it was ready to be sung in the music-room. It is a solo quartet with piano accompaniment, an euphonious piece in the devout key of A flat major with an 'Ascension' at the end. Each voice is given its affectionate solo, interspersed with Italianisms, which are particularly conspicuous in the tenor part, for Schönstein was incidentally a passionate lover of Italian opera.

Schubert received for his services as domestic music-teacher at Zseliz a total of 500 gulden – 100 a month – which compared with what he had earned hitherto from other sources could almost be called a princely salary. (In 1818 he had received only 300 gulden for four months – i.e., seventy-five a month – so we can take it that he had risen in his employer's estimation.) The sale of his songs which comprised op. 1–7 and 10–12 had brought him 480 gulden, supplemented by occasional presents from various individuals to whom he had dedicated them. Up to 7th September, 1824, the date when his A minor Quartet appeared, his published works amounted to thirty; most of these were songs (op. 1–8, 12–14, 19–25) but there were also male-voice quartets (11, 17, 28), the vocal numbers from *Rosamunde* as a kind of hors d'oeuvre, and a few instrumental pieces – Dances (op. 9, 18), the Marches for piano duet (op. 27) and the Sonata for four hands (op. 30), the Variations dedicated to Beethoven (op. 10), and the 'Wanderer' Fantasia (op. 15). It is a tiny fraction of his output, whereas in the case of the 'successful' Beethoven there is scarcely a work for which he was unable to find a publisher, even down to the early works which were included by him in his unbroken catalogue of opus-numbers. If Schubert could only have found a benevolent and whole-hearted publisher and not simply one like Leidesdorf who was himself a luckless individual, subject to fits of melancholy and depression, we would have had from him not only more completed works but more works which, in the event, were never written. And on this subject we will permit ourselves a short digression.

SCHUBERT AND THE PUBLISHERS

There is cause here not for anger but rather for sorrow. Genius is difficult to recognize; and Schubert's genius was, if anything, an embarrassment to him in his search for a publisher. What the publishers wanted from him were saleable articles with which they could do business. On the contrary it is nothing short of astonishing that 'An Schwager Kronos' or 'Der zürnenden Diana' were ever published at all; and that not only Waltzes, Polonaises, and Marches, but also the Piano Sonata in A minor and the String Quartet, op. 29, were accepted. But the fact that not one of Schubert's large-scale and serious instrumental works was printed, until the Piano Trio in E flat in the year of his death, naturally reacted upon the 'market-assessment' of all his works, and gave the publishers an excuse to treat him throughout as a promising beginner and to cut his payments to the bone. One can scarcely exaggerate the bitter resentment which this aroused in

Schubert who, for all his profound modesty, knew who he was and what he had written. The letter from the other Franz Schubert (of Dresden) with which Schubert's dealings with the oldest of all the music-publishing houses then in existence began or, to be more precise, failed to begin, has become universally famous as a musical curiosity. Schubert's friends had sent the manuscript of 'Erlkönig' to the firm of Breitkopf and Härtel and the then proprietor, Gottfried Christoph Härtel, sent it to Schubert's elderly namesake for his professional opinion. The old man's indignation knew no bounds. He was convinced that someone had taken his name in vain: 'I have further to inform you that about ten days ago I received a much-esteemed letter from you in which you enclosed a manuscript of Goethe's "Erl King" which purported to have been set by me. It is with the greatest astonishment that I have to inform you that this cantata was never written by me. I shall keep the same in my possession in the hope of finding out who it was that had the discourtesy to send you such trash and also to discover the fellow who has thus misused my name . . .' That was not a particularly good beginning; and although on 23rd May Härtel asked for the manuscript back and perhaps even studied it carefully, the episode produced no further results. It must have been in the summer of 1822 that Johann Friedrich Rochlitz, the doyen of musical life in Leipzig, met Schubert in Vienna (letter to his wife from Baden, 9th July, 1822). Though he was no longer editor of the *Allgemeine Musikalische Seitung,* he still had considerable influence with Härtel. His reference to that meeting was perhaps, however, a later invention, and on no account did it ever occur to him to recommend the 'young composer', despite the fact that it was due solely to Schubert that a few of his poems acquired some degree of immortality. Later, on 30th April, 1826, he mentioned patronizingly in a letter to Ignaz v. Mosel that he had found some of Schubert's recent works 'very interesting and estimable. Perhaps this talented artist requires only a scientifically trained friend to enlighten him in a kindly manner about himself – as to what he is, what he has, and what he wants to achieve. Then, one hopes, he would discover for himself what he *ought* to do.' Ever since then there have been, and today there still are, people like Rochlitz, with all his same condescension towards the wretched Schubert who did not rightly know what to do with his great talent. They prove how fortunate Schubert was, in spite of everything, to live in Vienna, where warm, spontaneous feeling and understanding still flourished instead of 'intelligence' filtered through 'intellect' or through the Leipzig and Berlin press.

On 12th August, 1826, Schubert at last addressed himself personally to Breitkopf and Härtel.

Dear Sirs,
In the hope that my name is not wholly unknown to you, I am writing most humbly to ask whether you would not be averse to accepting some of my compositions at reasonable terms, since I am particularly anxious to become as well-known as possible in Germany. You may take your choice from the following: songs with pianoforte accompaniment, string quartets, piano sonatas, 4-handed pieces, etc., etc. I have also written an Octet. In any case I should consider it a special honour to be associated with so old and famous an art firm. . . .

The reply, which reached him about a month later, was crushing. Since they (Breitkopf and Härtel) knew nothing whatever about the 'commercial success' of his compositions, they could not see their way to offering him any 'fixed pecuniary remuneration' and must ask him, so far as the first work was concerned, to content himself with a number of free copies. Nor was it even a large-scale work, but one or two pieces for solo piano or piano-duet.

In the first instance Schubert was referred to the Viennese publishers. We are told that, as a young man, he began by approaching Haydn's main publishers, Artaria & Co., with three string quartets (which three?) only to be told by the proprietor, Domenico Artaria: 'I do not take exercise pieces.' The whole story is most improbable, since we are well aware of Schubert's own estimate of his early quartets. Schubert's first published works – according to O. E. Deutsch's admirable article 'Schubert's Publishers' in the 1928 edition of the year-book *Der Bär* – were three songs; 'Am Erlafsee', 'Widerschein' and 'Die Forelle' as supplements to the pocket-books* of 1818 and 1820, for which he naturally received no payment. There followed, thanks to the efforts of his friends and patrons and of Leopold v.

* *Mahlerisches Taschenbuch für Freunde interessanter Gegenden, Natur- und Kunst-Merkwürdigkeiten der Oesterreichischen Monarchie.* Edited by Dr. Franz Sartori.

Sonnleithner in particular, his association with the firm of Cappi & Diabelli, after Haslinger and Diabelli himself had originally refused to publish 'Erlkönig'. Diabelli, or rather Pietro Cappi, who was the only active partner in the firm, undertook the publication of the volumes of songs, op. 1–7 and 12–14, at the composer's risk, and printing costs being met by Schubert's friends. It was only when their commercial success became apparent to him that he offered Schubert 800 gulden for the plates and copyrights of the first twelve opus numbers, which the latter accepted behind his friends' backs. It was a monumental piece of folly. All Schubert's works up to op. 18 were published by Cappi & Diabelli; and it was not until 1823 that Schubert realized that he was being badly treated and grossly underpaid. He proceeded to break off relations with the firm in a letter which was, for him, extremely outspoken, and demanded the return of all his manuscripts. But he fared no better in his new business relationship with Sauer and Leidesdorf, although for different reasons. Ignaz Sauer was a minor musician who had also carried on a hand-to-mouth publishing business since 1800. He happened, at the same time, to be an extremely eccentric individual; Josef Leidesdorf was an insignificant composer and apparently an idealist of the impractical kind. And neither of them – as we already know – had any money. After a few years Schubert was driven to resume his association with Cappi & Diabelli, or with their subsidiaries – for these two gentlemen spent their time entering into new partnerships. During his last years, he tried his luck, so to speak, everywhere; he gave nine works, including the A minor Piano Sonata, op. 42, to a new publisher, Anton Pennauer; made over another three, including the Walter Scott songs and the D major Sonata, to a young relative of the Artaria family, Matthias; published six works with Thaddaeus Weigl, the brother of Josef Weigl and himself an opera composer, a dozen with Tobias Haslinger and finally two with the old, original firm of Artaria & Co.

The fact that he published the volumes of songs, op. 96 and 106, privately in the last year of his life only emphasizes his dissatisfaction; and there is further evidence in the fact that either he himself or one of his friends was constantly engaged in trying to establish a connection 'abroad'. Josef Hüttenbrenner wrote twice to C. F. Peters in Leipzig, who replied with a long, unctuous letter in which he pointed out that he was obliged to take the entire output of his great friends Spohr, Romberg, Hummel, etc., and that this left very little time to spare for an unknown composer. He ended by saying that the agreement would, however, raise few difficulties since 'the young artist's terms are unlikely to be so extreme as not to be readily acceptable'. The only thing missing in this letter was a reference to the high costs of production. Schubert was so disgusted that he apparently did not trouble to reply.

On 12th August, 1826, he wrote a letter to the Leipzig publisher Heinrich Albert Probst which was almost identical to that which he wrote to Breitkopf and Härtel on the same date. Probst was a little diffident about 'the individual, often inspired and at the same time somewhat unusual character of the creatures of [Schubert's] brain' and asked for simpler items: 'a selection of songs, not too difficult pieces for solo piano and piano-duet, written in a pleasant and easily intelligible style'. But when Schubert subsequently sent him three works – we do not know which – he received a rude shock. Probst, by that time, was engaged on the publication of Kalkbrenner's complete works and was overwhelmed with work. In addition, Schubert's figure of eighty gulden for each piece was too high. (15th January, 1827.) It says much for Probst that when he visited Vienna early in 1827, he saw the true worth of Schubert and resumed his association with him (9th February, 1828), though not without repeating his request for works 'which, without sacrificing any of your individuality, are not too difficult to grasp', and mentioning *en passant* that so far as Schubert's idea of payment was concerned 'the terms offered by the Viennese publishers could best serve as a yardstick'. Schubert was reasonable and asked only sixty gulden for a volume containing songs or piano pieces. Probst, however, coaxed from him for sixty gulden the Piano Trio, op. 100, with which Schubert regretfully parted 'in order at last to make a start', although it contained 'six times as much work'. On 2nd October, though he had not yet received a printed copy of the work, he offered Probst his three last piano sonatas, the String Quintet and the Heine songs. But six weeks later he was dead and was therefore probably spared the disappointment of having them turned down.

On the same day that Probst approached Schubert again, the firm of B. Schott's Sons, the publishers of Beethoven's last quartets, *Missa Solemnis* and Choral Symphony, also asked him to send them some of his compositions, without specifying any sum as payment for them: 'We are always ready to welcome piano works or songs for one or more voices with or without piano accompaniment'. On 21st February Schubert offered them a hundred or so works, if one counts each individual song, including the Piano Trio in E flat major, the Fantasia in F minor for four hands, the String Quartets in D minor and G major, three of his operas and the Mass in A flat. He made only a passing reference to the 'Gastein-Gmunden' Symphony 'in order to acquaint you with my striving after the highest in art'. (To think that he might have sent this symphony! Then perhaps it would have survived.) Schott actually asked for the majority of these works, while ignoring the two string quartets, the choruses for female voices and all the songs. Schubert, who had already learnt his lesson, sent only copies of the Trio, the Impromptus and the male-voice chorus 'Mondenschein'. The Trio, which had been sold to Probst in the meantime, was turned down, on the grounds that it was 'probably (too) long'. On 2nd October Schubert was obliged to inquire what had become of the music which he had sent. The male-voice chorus was eventually published in 1830, and the series of Impromptus as op. 142, in 1838, by Diabelli and not by B. Schott's Sons. Schubert had intended to give the Impromptus the opus number 101.

We will not concern ourselves with Schubert's other associations with publishing houses, except for the one with Hans Georg Nägeli of Zürich who approached Schubert through Karl Czerny in 1826 with a request that he should send him a piano sonata for inclusion in a new volume of collected pieces. But when, on 4th July, Schubert demanded the payment of 120 gulden in advance, the celebrated 'improver' of Beethoven's G major Sonata (op. 31, 1) either refused the request in horror or declined to have any further correspondence on the subject. Schubert at any rate summed up his opinion on publishers clearly and concisely in a letter to his parents (25th July, 1827): 'If only one could do honest business with these – [here one must add the word 'dogs' or some other zoological epithet] of art-dealers, but the State, in its wisdom and benevolence, has seen to it that the artist shall remain for all time the slave of every miserable pedlar.'

Nowhere is it easier to differentiate between the 'occasional works' – which in Schubert's case, however, are never quite occasional works in the full sense – and those in which he manifests his 'striving after the highest in art', than in these years between 1824 and 1826, between the A minor and the two last quartets. To the first belongs the series of works for piano-duet which were again – and for obvious reasons – the direct result of his visit to Zseliz. Schubert mentions two of them in his first letter, written in the middle of July to his brother Ferdinand: 'a grand Sonata and Variations on an original theme. ... The Variations have been particularly well received.' And in similar terms to Schwind: '. . . a Grand Sonata and Variations which latter have been particularly well received *here*, but since I do not wholly trust the Hungarians' taste, I leave it to you and the Viennese to pass judgment on them'.

The 'Sonata' was the Duo in C major, which was published posthumously as op. 140 (IX, 12). It is the same Duo which Schumann so long suspected of being the piano arrangement of a symphony, 'until such time as the discovery of the manuscript of the original should convince me to the contrary'. In his heart of hearts he could not decide what to make of the work. 'Familiar as I am with his style and with his particular treatment of the piano, and comparing this work with his other sonatas, in which the true characteristics of the piano are expressed in their purest form, I can only explain this work as an orchestral piece. We can hear string and wind instruments, tuttis, solo passages, drum-rolls; the broad symphonic form, even the echoes of Beethoven's symphonies – as, for example, the Andante of Beethoven's Second in the second movement, and the A major Symphony in the Finale – these, together with some rather more colourless passages which seem to me to have lost something in their transcription for piano, all support my view'. Schumann might also have drawn particular attention to the fanfares of trumpets in the coda of the first movement. But he immediately adds: 'That apart, however, I should like to defend the Duo against the criticism that it is not strictly conceived as a piano-piece throughout, and that it makes impossible demands upon the instrument. . . .' But Schumann, whose knowledge of Schubert as a symphonist rested solely on the C major Symphony, overlooked something. This Duo *is* a piano work and anything *but* a piano transcription or a work originally conceived as a symphony. And not only from the technical point of view – how pianistic, how anti-orchestral the triplet runs in the first movement are, for example! – but because Schubert, as a symphonist, would have limited himself to a quite different range of modulations. What reason would he have had to place before his two young Countesses a disguised symphony? What he had to give them and what he did, in fact, give them was a piece of serious music for their enjoyment in 'large' form, in which the time factor was of no particular importance. On the contrary, the longer this four-handed sonata lasted the better. The two young ladies must also have noted with amusement that the slow movement is largely derived from the Andante of Beethoven's Second and to a lesser degree from the slow movement of his Fifth; on the other hand, however, Schubert's Finale has no connection whatever with the Finale of the Seventh. It is the most important movement, with all the signs of the *genius loci*, Hungarian in rhythm and melody, with a development which is more serious and ingenious than almost any that Schubert had yet written, yet at the same time cast in the form and spirit of a large-scale overture. How little suited the work is to orchestration is proved by Josef Joachim's exercise in that direction. Even if this attempt were better and less flat and less suggestive of Schumann's orchestral style, it would still demonstrate conclusively that the work was conceived in terms of the piano. In contrast to this, it is a simple and perfectly natural matter to orchestrate the sketch of the E major Symphony.

In their way, the Variations, which Schubert wanted to leave to the judgment of the Viennese and which he published in February 1825, as op. 35, with a dedication in French to Count Anton Berchtold, are the more finished of the two works (IX, 16). The 'original theme' in A flat is another march-theme like that of the Variations which he had dedicated to Beethoven; but this time Schubert keeps strictly to the main key throughout all the eight variations (only the fifth is in the minor). The wealth of harmonic invention is utterly enchanting, and the balance between melody and virtuosity complete. The loveliest variations are the third with its duet in strict imitation for the *primo* player, the Nocturne in the minor, and the soft-pedalled 'più lento'. The Finale is a broad Siciliano.

But the most characteristic product of this second visit to the Esterhazys is the 'Divertissement à la hongroise' (IX, 19), even though it was not intended for the young Countesses and was not even written on the spot. But the germ of this work of three movements can be traced back to Zseliz. On 2nd September, Schubert jotted down a 'Hungarian melody', i.e., a short piano piece in B minor, which has a certain affinity with the 'Air russe' of the Moments musicals and which Schubert uses again as the focal point in the Finale of the Divertissement, this time in G minor. It has only recently come to light again and has been published by O. E. Deutsch (Verlag E. Strache, No. 20, 1928). Between the two 'diverting' movements with their alternating sections or episodes there is a short March in C minor (with a Trio in A flat major), and the whole work is no less 'Hungarian' than the 'national' germ from which it grew. For all the characteristic features are present: the melancholy key, the heavily stressed and syncopated rhythms, the passionate tremoli, the *appoggiature* and other 'improvised' *fioriture*, the *appearance* of 'improvisation', the spontaneous invention. But Schubert is not indulging in caricature, as so many genuine or semi-genuine Hungarians and so many of his completely artificial imitators do. He disliked, above all, the restless change of tempo and the oriental, extravagant use of the interval of an augmented second so beloved of gypsy-music. In a D minor section in the first movement there suddenly appears one of the main themes from the Finale of the A minor String Quartet – an invaluable clue to the character of the latter work. When the work was eventually published in April, 1826, Schubert dedicated it to the singer Cathinka Laszny von Folkusfálva, *née* Buchwieser, a somewhat flighty lady who was married to a Hungarian. Liszt later (1838) arranged the work for piano solo, and also made a separate transcription of the March for full orchestra.

For the middle movement of his Divertissement Schubert might equally well have used the first of the three Military

Marches in D major op. 51 (IX, 3) which combines a Hungarian atmosphere in the main section with a Viennese spirit in the Trio and which has achieved world-wide popularity. The two others, in G major and E flat major, are a little less distinctive in character, but are still 'Austrian' enough, particularly the Trio of the latter with its Tyrolean Jodler. On the other hand, the two 'Characteristic Marches' both in C major (IX, 6) and probably written during the same period, are more like French quick marches in 6/8 time. They are written in an unusually broad, painstaking, symphonic style and are useless for 'practical purposes', since one could hardly march to them. There also figures among the four-handed pieces an arrangement of the Overture to *Fierabras* (XXI, 7) which some biographers of Schubert have wrongly attributed to this period. But it was written by Karl Czerny and not by Schubert and was not published until 1827 as op. 76.*

The two Marches (IX, 4 and 5) op. 55 and 66 which Schubert composed 'on the occasion of the death of Czar Alexander I of Russia' and to celebrate the coronation of the Czar Nicholas I of Russia, were written somewhat later, towards the end of the year 1825 and the beginning of 1826. There is an earlier parallel in the Funeral Cantata which Beethoven composed on the death of the Emperor Joseph, and the Festival Cantata which he wrote to celebrate the accession of the Emperor Leopold. Alexander died on 1st December, and Nicholas was crowned Czar on the 24th. We do not know Schubert's view about Czars, but in this instance he probably had their legendary generosity in mind. Nor do we know whether this generosity ever materialized. The two Marches were published early in February, and in the middle of September 1826. They are very dissimilar: the first in the traditional, emotional key of C minor, the Trio in A flat major with a modulation to B minor(!), and very short; the second more of a March-divertissement, not as might be expected in C major but A minor, probably by mental association with the Sarmatian lands of all the Russias. The one thing that is common to both is the fact that they cry aloud for orchestration, particularly in the main section of the first after the passage where two groups of 'wind-instru-

* Schubert wrote his own arrangement which was never published. The MS. is in Paris.

ments' alternate with one another. The A minor March was later – and probably brilliantly – orchestrated by Rimsky-Korsakov.

In contrast to these Marches the two series of four-handed Polonaises, op. 61 and 75 (1825; IX, 25 and 26), the first consisting of six and the second of four, are once more completely pianistic.* The *Frankfurter Allgemeine Musikalische Anzeiger* of 4th April 1827 included a review of the first series which is worth quoting:

> One must not expect true Polonaises here, but short, highly original and for the most part very melodious pieces for the pianoforte in Polonaise rhythm. We would rather, however, that the composer had not persisted in retaining this rhythm throughout the whole of the two volumes, since the result is a monotonous uniformity which the other beauties and original features are scarcely sufficient to outweigh. The pieces are difficult to play because of the modulations which are sometimes surprising and sometimes even a little far-fetched. Highly recommended.

In so far as it expresses surprise at Schubert's harmony, this is a typical contemporary review. But the anonymous writer of it at least appreciated that he was here dealing with short and exquisitely poetic pieces, and he might well have added that the contrapuntal writing in the Trios is also delicately contrived, as for example:

Ex.40

Both main section and Trio are deliberately treated in song form, and no one is obliged to play all six or ten pieces consecutively.

* Op. 75 is earlier than Op. 61 which probably dates from 1825. Op. 75 was written in July 1818.

We are not departing from 'sociable' music when we turn our attention to the two works which Schubert wrote during this period for piano and a solo instrument. The first of these is a Sonata for Piano and Arpeggione in A minor written in November 1824, and first published in 1871 (VIII, 8) with the addition of a 'cello part *ad libitum*. The Arpeggione, also known very appropriately as the Guitare d'Amour, was descended from the Viola da Gamba, with fretted keyboard and six strings. It was the invention of the Viennese instrument-maker J. G. Stauffer and was popularized by the 'cellist, Vincenz Schuster, one or both of whom commissioned Schubert to write this work. He would have been a fool to have wasted any undue energy on this opportunity and on this obsolete instrument. He wrote instead something agreeable and melodious, a first movement which is pleasingly melancholy, a short connecting Adagio in E major and a Finale which is something between a Rondo and a Divertissement. He made full use of the great range of the instrument, but not of its potentialities for double-stopping and (until the final chord) chordal playing. There is an element of tragi-comedy in the fact that this same work has suffered every conceivable form of arrangement, for Schubert is more popular in his 'sociable' and easy-going guise than when he is uncompromising and great.

Of much greater value are the Variations on 'Trockene Blumen' from *Die schöne Müllerin* for piano and flute (VIII, 7), published in 1850 as op. 160 and written in January 1824 for the flautist Ferdinand Bogner who a year later married one of the Fröhlich sisters, Barbara, to his and her misfortune. There is no record of any public performance. In the concert organized by the Fröhlich sisters on 30th January, 1829, half the proceeds of which were set aside for a Schubert memorial, Bogner did not perform these Variations, but a set of Variations by Gabrielsky. He was probably quite right in his choice. It is depressing for any lover of Schubert to see a song of such unique intensity and restraint subjected to a virtuoso treatment and transformed eventually into a triumphal march – a sacrilege which no one but Schubert himself could have been allowed to commit. It was even referred to as 'a popular song'! And from the purely musical point of view each of the seven variations in itself is richer in its modulations and invention than the next, even though Schubert never once departs from the main key. The Introduction, however, is quite incomparable. Schubert cast it in his favourite rhythm and combined all manner of mystery and seriousness with unmistakable echoes of 'Der Tod und das Mädchen'. One would like to suggest that this Andante should be followed simply by the theme – and nothing else.

This work spans the gap leading to the Schubert who is no longer 'sociable' and no longer 'homely' – to the real and great Schubert of the Piano Sonatas in C major, A minor and D major, the String Quartets in A minor and D minor, the Octet and the last Symphony.

During the years 1824 and 1825 Schubert rejoiced in his regained health, or apparent health, and in the companionship of a few friends, and especially of Schwind, whose letters to Schober provide us with the liveliest picture of his existence during this period. He was still very shy and reluctant to take part in any social activity. He avoided the cafés with the exception of one 'where he always goes with Senn', and ten times accepted and then declined an invitation to visit the family of the lawyer Franz Hönig, although there was a charming girl there who might well have taken his fancy. Nor was the creative urge consistently strong, for on 14th February, Schwind reported: 'He is well, and busy again after a certain period of idleness.' There was even a certain amount of friction betwen him and the restive, impetuous Schwind who was at that time in love with Netti Hönig. He had spent the winter of 1824–5 in the Rossau with his family, but he then moved to a charming apartment in the Fruhwirth house next to the church of St. Charles where he lodged with a cooper. From his room he looked out across green fields to the city and he continued to live there until the summer of 1826. At the end of May, however, he set out on another tour and followed Michael Vogl, who had already left on 31st March, to Steyr, where they once more spent a few days with Paumgartner. From there they went on to Linz, where Schubert made an excursion to the church and monastery at St. Florian, and so back to Steyr by way of Kremsmünster. The second half of June and the first half of July were spent in Gmunden – 'very pleasant' – where he began the lost symphony. In the middle of July he went alone to his old friends the Ottenwalts in Linz, made an excursion to Steyregg, and returned again on 19th July. 'He looks so fit and strong, is so full of good spirits and so friendly and communicative that one is really overjoyed to see it,' wrote his host. From Linz he wrote a half-humorous, half-ghoulish letter to Josef v. Spaun., who had himself been exiled for so long in Linz and was now vegetating in Lemberg; and four days later he wrote to his parents from Steyr telling them of his plans: 'We (i.e., himself and Vogl) shall stay here another ten or fourteen days and then set out for Gastein, one of the most famous watering-places, about three days' journey from Steyr. I am greatly looking forward to this trip, since I shall thus get to know the loveliest country and on the way back we shall be visiting Salzburg, which is so famous for its magnificent situation and surroundings. Since we shall not get back from this journey until the middle of September, and have then promised to pay one more visit to Gmunden, Linz, Steyreck and Florian, it is very unlikely that I shall arrive back in Vienna before the end of October.' They did not keep strictly to this programme, however, since they visited Salzburg on the way to Gastein and not on the return journey. They stayed at Gmunden and Steyr again, and Schubert alone returned to Vienna early in October. On 12th and 21st September Schubert sent his brother Ferdinand a detailed, Baedekerlike description of the journey, probably in response to the latter's request.

It was a musical tour. In the first of these letters, Schubert writes. '... The manner and way in which Vogl sings and I accompany, in which at such a moment we seem to be *one*, is something quite new and extraordinary to these people.' He did not, therefore, take great offence at the various eccentricities in which his partner and interpreter indulged; he either overlooked them or pretended he did not hear them. And he himself played his Sonata, op. 42 – we have already mentioned the manner of his performance – and, together with his musical friends, piano duets, the Variations, op. 35 and some of his Marches. He himself published the sonata in the following year, 1826 (with Pennauer), with a dedication to the Cardinal Archduke Rudolf – the same Rudolf to whom Beethoven's *Missa Solemnis* was dedicated (1827) – and with the title of 'Grande Sonate'.

If one excepts the 'Wanderer' Fantasia, it is not only

the first sonata that he published but in the truest sense
a 'Grand Sonata'; yet it was preceded in April 1825 by a
preliminary experiment which is as distinct from his other
sonata sketches, as the sonata itself is from the earlier
sonatas of the period from 1815 to 1823. Is it simply an
experiment? This C major Sonata (XXI, 14), which has been
christened by the publisher of the first edition (1861) 'Whis-
tling – a relic', in the frightful jargon of the popular books
on Schubert, is complete except for the conclusion of the
main section in the Minuet and the end of the Rondo Finale.
Its completion presents no difficult problem and has been
admirably carried out by Ernst Křenek, among others. Its
relationship to the somewhat later A minor Sonata is that of
brother to sister. Indeed the two are twins and it requires
only a glance at the beginning of each to confirm the family
resemblance.

The macrocosm of the two sonatas, if I may so express it, is
identical: four movements, with the Andante following the
first, except that in op. 42 this slow movement consists of a
few variations, and the Finale in rondo-form instead of in
the previous sonata-form. Only the 'microcosm' of the two
works is different: Schubert did not lavish the same meticu-
lous care on the C major Sonata as he did on the A minor
Sonata, which he naturally prepared for press. In both cases,
however, there is a new approach to the problem of unity in
a work of four movements. The second subject in the first
movement of the C major Sonata is closely related to the
first; the two are linked by a unison theme. The development section makes no use of the second subject, as in the
case of the 'Unfinished'; and the movement includes a coda

which sums up what has gone before. In the Andante the
unison theme of the first movement reappears; the dark lyricism of C minor is brightened by an 'alternativo' in A flat
major and ranges into more impassioned regions by means
of recitative-like interjections. The Minuet in A flat has a
Trio in the minor (the notation is G sharp minor) and is
alternately gentle and menacing; the Rondo is sustained by
the contrast between a scale figure in triplets and quaver
figures; but the 'menacing' element in the Minuet and a
quasi-Hungarian chord-figure contradict or darken the playful character of the movement.

The unity becomes still more noticeable in op. 42 (X, 9). A
strange feature is the fact that there is no second subject at
all in the first movement, but only the splitting of a single
theme which is a mixture of mystery and march-like bravado. At the point where the second subject should enter,
this 'split' theme appears in C major and in a charming form.
The development persists, as it were, in trying to achieve an
air of mystery, harmonically and even polyphonically, and
the movement avoids a clearly-defined fatalistic coda. The
'rather agitated' Andante consists simply of two free variations in C minor and A flat major on an intimate song-
theme, which would not be out of place in *Die schöne
Müllerin*; indeed, the horn fifths in the latter variation
underline its affinity with the song-cycle. What is one to say
of so spontaneous an effusion? Is it mere display? Whether it
is or not, it is none the less also art. The third movement, in
the tonic key, is not a Minuet but a Scherzo, restless and
forward-looking, in spite of the ending in A flat major; as a
result the Trio is all the more comforting, a friendly episode.
The Rondo returns again to the fatalism of the first movement, and is once more derived – in its treatment though not
its musical content – from the Rondo of Mozart's A minor
'Paris' Sonata. It is very intimate in character and, in spite of
occasional moments of bravado, provides no spiritual solution. A review in the *Leipziger Allgemeine Musikalische
Zeitung* of 1st March, 1826, which was probably written by
the editor, G. M. Fink, and is, in general, cordial and even
enthusiastic, emphasized that this work only carried the
nominal title of 'Sonata' and could really 'be called, not
without justification, a Fantasia', and that in this respect it
could be compared with the greatest and freest of Beet-

hoven's sonatas – which is certainly an error of judgment of the first order. For it is precisely its independence from Beethoven which distinguishes this sonata; Schubert left the 'macrocosm' of the form untouched and filled it with a new content.

A few months or weeks later there appeared Schubert's Second Grand Sonata, op. 53 (X, 11), dedicated to Carl Maria Bocklet, a competent musician and good friend, four years younger than the composer. He was a violinist at the Theater an der Wien and subsequently won a considerable reputation as a pianist, in which capacity he frequently acted as an interpreter of Schubert's works. The sonata was written in August 1825 at Gastein, immediately after the completion of the lost symphony. It is much more virtuoso in style than the A minor Sonata, and one cannot help thinking that Schubert's consideration for Bocklet had an adverse effect upon the conception of the first movement. It is conventional in form, broad, but also a little empty, and only one theme – the 'un poco più lento' after the second subject, consisting purely of chords and in shifting rhythm – is typical of the 'Romantic', as opposed to the homely, Hummel-like Schubert. And is it not significant that it is precisely this mysterious 'poco più lento' that becomes the chief material for the second movement, headed simply 'con moto' and one of the richest and most intimate which have ever been written? As evidence that Schubert was consciously striving after a sense of unity in this sonata, there is an Andante in A major (XI, 10) which Schubert without any shadow of doubt had originally written for this op. 53. It is a movement of the greatest delicacy and sensitivity and is only spoiled by the ultra-Mozartian character and extreme shortness of its conclusion. One can here recognize the precise moment when Schubert realized that he would have to write another slow movement, linked thematically with the first movement.

The influence of this same theme also persists into the Scherzo, which in its main section makes play with the combination of 3/4 and 3/2 time and is one of Schubert's rare movements with a marked emphasis on the up-beat. For elsewhere – and this, too, is a proof or a characteristic of his natural disposition and of his independence from Beethoven – he is what one might call a 'down-beat' composer, and

even his up-beats are generally quiet. The crown of the
sonata, however, is the final Rondo. It has the same affinity
to Schubert's Dances as his songs have to folk-songs, and in
this case there is no doubt as to the actual prototype or germ
of the movement. It is one of eight short Ecossaises (XII,
26), unfortunately undated, but certainly of an earlier
origin:

The child-like, angelic theme recurs again and again, each
time more richly figured, and an 'alternativo' in G ensures
that we greet each reappearance with renewed delight. We
find it difficult to understand what Schumann meant when
he said that the movement 'hardly fits into its context and is
droll enough in all conscience. One would make a laughing-
stock of oneself, if one were to take it seriously. Florestan
calls it a satire on the Pleyel-Wanhal "night-cap" style;
Eusebius finds in the contrasting outbursts of impetuosity the
kind of faces one makes to frighten children. Both amount to
the same thing – humour.' But why *not* take such a movement seriously? Why not take it seriously precisely because it
is innocent and gay? Should not the softness and the gradual
slowing-down of the conclusion have made the sensitive
Schumann, of all people, realize that Schubert had 'taken it
seriously'?

We are looking a little ahead, when we consider here the
third and last of this group of piano sonatas – the G major,
written in October 1826 and dedicated to Josef v. Spaun
when it was published a year later as op. 78 (X, 12). But this
is where it belongs, since it is the fulfilment and realization
of everything to which the Sonatas in C major, A minor and

D major had aspired. It is perhaps the most perfect of all Schubert's sonatas. In accepting the dedication, Spaun incidentally spoke of Schubert's 'fourth sonata' which shows that the two friends either took for granted the A major Sonata op. 120, or the A minor Sonata op. 143, neither of which had at that time been published, or considered the C major Sonata as a completed work.

In Haslinger's first edition of 1827 the work is called 'Fantasia, Andante, Menuetto und Allegretto' as if it consisted simply of four loosely-connected pieces and as if the first movement was a piece in free form. But this title was only a whim of the publisher, who at least allowed the work to be designated 'Fantasie oder Sonate' on the half-title page. This time Schumann was quite right when he called this last sonata 'Schubert's most perfect in form and spirit' in his comprehensive review of the three sonatas, op. 42, 53 and 78. 'If anyone has not the imagination to solve the riddle of the last movement, let him leave it alone.' And it must have been this movement in particular to which Schumann's eulogistic comment about 'perfect form' referred. It is at once a Rondo and a 'Divertissement'. It includes a dance-like 'alternativo' in E flat major which is self-contained by virtue of its song-form, but at the same time mindful of its true function which is to pave the way back to the first subject or to the recapitulation. It is the purest, gayest complement to the lyricism of the first movement, which this time transfers the heroic or dramatic element, the use of counterpoint as a contrast to lyricism, to the development. What is one to say of the Andante, half lyrical, half defiant, with its moving coda – the whole movement an intensified echo of the Andante of the A major Sonata of 1819? The Minuet, on the other hand, is an intensified echo of the 'Valses nobles' of 1825, which Schubert had published under the preceding opus number (op. 77, XII, 6). Several of these twelve Dances (5, 7, 9, 11) are exactly similar in character; but in none of them is there to be found the B major happiness of the Trio. The only really comparable piece is to be found in the 'Valses Sentimentales', op. 50 (XII, 4) – the thirteenth waltz in A major with its 'tender' love-duet in the right hand.

'I have done little new in the way of songs, but I have tried my hand at several instrumental works, for I have written

two quartets ... and an octet, and intend to write another
quartet. In this manner I want to pave the way to a grand
symphony. ...' (to Leopold Kupelwieser, 31st March, 1824).
The first of these string quartets was the one in A minor,
completed in February and March and played for the first
time on 14th March by Beethoven's 'personal' quartet consisting of Schuppanzigh, Holz, Weiss and Linke, though not
entirely to Schubert's satisfaction – 'rather slowly, but with
great purity and tenderness' (thus Schwind, on the day of the
performance). And wonder of wonders! it was *published*, as
op. 29, 1, in the autumn of the same year. What should have
been op. 29, 2 – namely the D minor Quartet – was not
published until 1831 and then without an opus number; and
op. 29, 3 became op. 161 and had to wait until 1850 before
being published. Schuppanzigh 'was quite filled with enthusiasm', which does him credit, for the A minor Quartet was as
far removed in style and character from Beethoven as it
could be – as far removed as the 'Unfinished' in the symphonic field, and the chamber-music counterpart to the
latter. There is only one characteristic feature which is at all
typical of Beethoven. In the same way that Beethoven used
the heroic theme from the *Prometheus* Ballet three times, for
his Variations, op. 35 and for the Finale of the 'Eroica',
Schubert took for his slow movement the Andantino from
the *Rosamunde* music, which in its grace and buoyant lyricism might well serve as his motto. Here it is expanded, and
intensified at each repetition by the contrast between a pastoral calm and a virile agitation. It is purest Schubert in the
same way that the Andante of the C major Quartet (op. X,
6), is purest Mozart, or the Adagio of op. 59, 1, purest Beethoven. From these three movements one could recognize the
'intelligible', essential character of the three composers down
to the last detail.

Reference has often been made, and rightly made, to the
connection between this Minuet and the setting of a fragment of Schiller's 'Die Götter Griechenlands' of November 1819 (XX, 371):

> *Schöne Welt, wo bist Du?*
> *Kehre wieder, holdes Blütenalter der Natur!**

* Lovely world, where art thou?
  Return once more, thou fair and flower'd age of Nature!

The main subject is an unmistakable quotation, and the change from minor to major a no less unmistakable symbol here than in the song. The resignation of the main section, and the ideal picture of innocent happiness, in the form of a Ländler, is as clear as if it had been expressed in words; in fact it is clearer, for Schubert achieves through the medium of chamber-music something at which he could only hint in a song which was both inspired and restricted by its text. I have already referred elsewhere to the two bars before the entry of the melody which consist of nothing more than harmony, resolved into quiet figuration, and rhythm, isolating the movement, setting it apart and lifting it into a dream-world. Mozart does the same thing in his G minor Symphony with a short 'preliminary statement' of key and rhythm. Beethoven does it in the 'Eroica' with two rhythmic chords, and in the slow movement of the Sonata op. 106 with two ascending 'temple steps'. It is as if the three composers wanted to emphasize what music meant to them; a moment of ordained time, wrested from eternity and projected into eternity again.* Here, in the first movement, the 'lovely world' appears in the C major of the second subject; but in the D minor of the development, Schubert is also thinking of death which is to become the main theme of the following quartet. Behind the lyrical veil everything is eloquent. Can a work with three such movements end on a gay or triumphant note in the fourth? It admittedly ends in the major – A major, but in the same Hungarian disguise which Schubert was to use again in *Die Winterreise* in an exactly similar sense: outwardly exuberant and chevaleresque, but – as a number of mysterious phrases suggest – without any real consolation, in spite of the two loud final chords. We have already attempted to show why this music was so new and, from a harmonic point of view, so extraordinary.

If the germ or kernel of the A minor Quartet was probably the Minuet, in the case of the D minor Quartet it was quite certainly the set of variations on 'Der Tod und das Mädchen'. What Schubert could only suggest in the song here finds exhaustive expression in a fuller, freer, wordless sphere. He does not write 'programme' music, nor do we

* In the autograph of the Octet in the Adagio, there are two very similar 'isolating' introductory bars which Schubert subsequently crossed out.

need to know the song, but we feel unmistakably in this music the symbols of inevitability and consolation. The moving major-ending of the theme assumes the proportions of a true 'ascension' in the coda, after one of the variations in the major, the fourth, has already revealed a momentary glimpse of Heaven. The theme appears each time only lightly disguised or simplified, and in no variation is there any deviation from the main key. One can recognize the difference between the 'sociable' and the deeply serious Schubert when one recalls the variations on 'Die Forelle', or when one remembers that the variations on 'Trockene Blumen' were written a few weeks previously.

The D minor Quartet is of quite different dimensions from the A minor. And yet it is no less concentrated, and its unity is this time clearly illustrated. The march of 'inevitability' (a) becomes a savage threat in the first movement (b), a dance in

the Scherzo and Trio (c) and a new variant of the Dance of Death in the Finale (d), and there is no question that Schubert *intended* this unity. His conscious effort reveals itself in every feature. There is no trace of the easy-going Schubert here; the exposition tends not towards F major or A major, but towards A minor; the development combines both themes, the second of which has already been given its own 'development' within the framework of the exposition. Mendelssohn called the D minor Quartet 'bad music'. But it is this very first movement that one should hold up to anyone who professed to doubt Schubert's capacity for developing his material logically and discursively. The Scherzo has its moment of happiness in the Trio, but even in the Trio the ominous rhythm continues to pulsate. The Finale is a Tarantella of Death, in a combination of rondo and sonata form; a second subject brings a powerful surge of that wave which always recedes again. One is again astonished at the complete indifference to Beethoven. In the first place the A minor and D minor Quartets were written at the same time that Beethoven was beginning to put the finishing touches to his last quartets; but there is equally no indication that Schubert was in the slightest degree influenced by any of the great quartets of op. 59, or by op. 74, or 95. It would be tempting to compare the 'seriousness' of Beethoven's 'Quartetto serioso', op. 95 with the seriousness of the D minor Quartet. Schubert's seriousness is free from pathos; he is more spontaneous; he goes deeper and deliberately avoids the optimistic or triumphant note on which Beethoven ends.

I do not know whether the observation that Schubert's quartets are conceived in terms of the orchestra applies to the A minor and D minor Quartets; but it is certainly true of Schubert's last quartet, the G major, written between 20th and 30th June, 1826 (V, 15). The outward indications of the 'orchestral' character of the work are apparent in the unison passages, in the agitated tremoli in melody or accompaniment, in the groupings of questions and answer. These groupings are admittedly connected with the fact that the first movement, in particular, is entirely dependent upon the interplay of harmonic light and shade, upon the interchange of major and minor within the narrowest compass. If one were to orchestrate it, the result would be something like a pre-Bruckner symphonic movement, except that Bruckner never wrote a movement of such lively construction and such unity of design. And strangely enough, the slow movement – a 'slightly agitated' Andante in E minor – became the model for many of Brahms's movements, romances or orchestral ballads in which an elegiac melody predominates in the bass, with decorative embroidery by the other instruments and with a change of colour provided by an agitated 'alternativo'. There is another strange thing; here is an instance where Schubert compressed and concentrated an instrumental movement into a song, for in Wilhelm Müller's *Winterreise* he found a text to match the melancholy, the bewilderment and the despair of this movement, and in 'Einsamkeit' he recalled it again.* The commentary on the text was, so to speak, in existence before the text itself. Still stranger, the Scherzo in B minor, with a happy Ländler (G major) as its Trio, has something of Schumann's capriciousness, although Schumann, who knew the D minor Quartet

* Cf. Maurice J. E. Brown: 'Instrumental Derivatives in the Songs', *Music and Letters*, XXVIII, 3, 1947.

and estimated it at its true worth, could scarcely have known this G major Quartet. The Finale is the counterpart of the Finale of the D minor Quartet, except that the Tarantella of the latter has here become a kind of 'Reiterstück,' as iridescent as the first movement in harmony and modulation, with a more leisurely second subject which recalls the mood of the Finale of Mozart's D major Quintet. It was the first movement of this Quartet in G which Herren Böhm, Holz, Weiss and Linke ventured to perform at Schubert's celebrated Invitation Concert on 26th March, 1828. We do not know how the audience reacted to it, but the critic of the *Leipziger Allgemeine Musikzeitung* hit the right mark on this occasion when he spoke of 'spirit and originality'.

'Originality' in the cruder sense of the word is lacking in the Octet, on which Schubert worked during February 1824 and which he finished on 1st March (III, 1). It was commissioned by Count Ferdinand Troyer, chief steward to the Archduke Rudolf and himself a composer and a clarinet-player. He himself took the clarinet part when the work was performed privately for the first time in the spring, in the company of some worthy professional musicians – a good testimonial to the democratic spirit of the Viennese aristocracy, at least in the musical sphere. (It was given again by Schuppanzigh at his last Subscription Concert on 16th April, 1827.) It was probably Troyer, too, who, when commissioning the work, stipulated that it should be 'exactly like Beethoven's Septet'. Its similarity to its famous and popular model is carried so far that every member of contemporary audiences must have noticed and enjoyed it. The three wind instruments are the same – clarinet, horn and bassoon; by adding a second violin to the strings Schubert converts the Septet into an Octet. There are six movements as in Beethoven's case, and they are in the same order as in the old-style Divertimento. Where Beethoven writes an Adagio, Schubert, contrary to his usual preference, writes one too; when Beethoven writes an Andante with variations, Schubert does likewise. When Beethoven prepares the way for his Finale with an introduction in the minor, Schubert imitates him. In both works the relationship of keys is absolutely identical. The similarity goes further: Beethoven's Septet had been a *happy* work, even from the point of view of style. It was still pure eighteenth-century music, without emotion and without dualism; and since there is no trace of dualism in Schubert's work either, it was easy and natural for him to take that happy Beethoven as his starting-point.

For all that, this is purest Schubert. It is a resurrection of the old Divertimento in a new spirit which, for want of a better word, we call 'Romantic'. On the surface it is still the old mixture of martial (in the first movement and again in the Finale, in a different form) and pastoral (in the Adagio and the Andante with variations, the theme of which Schubert took from the idyllic love-duet from *Die Freunde von Salamanka*, though not without certain mental reservations). But it is no longer the old 'category' of martial and pastoral. One should perhaps draw a distinction between the martial mood and the act of marching, walking, sauntering; between the pastoral and the bucolic atmosphere in which the shepherd of the eighteenth century no longer blows on his flute, but Pan himself plays his seductive and melancholy music (the clarinet melodies in the Adagio, for example). The first movement, the introduction of which becomes an integral part of the recapitulation (in the same way that the introduction in Mozart's *Zauberflöte* Overture becomes an integral part of the development) could well serve as an overture to Shakespeare's *As You Like It*, if it were not so unmistakably a piece of chamber-music. For in spite of the double-bass, the Octet is, in fact, the purest and most delicate chamber-music, which never oversteps its limits, not even in the somewhat bluffer Scherzo, and least of all in the courtly and suave Minuet. Clarinet and first violin alternate with each other in the leading roles, but each instrument, in its own way, is well provided for, and one would much rather take an active part in the work than simply listen to it.

The Schubert of this period – the Schubert of the piano sonatas, of the three string quartets, of the lost symphony, of the Octet – has become an instrumental composer. Everything that he wrote in the way of vocal music is more of an incidental and occasional nature – with the exception once more of his songs which, in his case, are scarcely ever 'occasional'. This period produced hardly any church music. A *Salve Regina* in C major for a male-voice quartet consisting of two tenors and two basses (XIV, 19), dating from April 1824, was not written as the result of any religious impulse,

but seems rather to have been composed for his 'propa-
gandists' in this field, Herren Suchy or Eichberger and
company. It is a vocal Rondo containing a few expressive
phrases.

Of a very different quality is a setting for male-voice quintet of Schober's poem 'Mondenschein', written in January
1826 (XVI, 27). The combination of the five voices is unusual; solo tenor and a quartet consisting of one tenor and
three basses. It must undoubtedly have been written for a
particular group of singers, even though its first public performance did not take place until two years later with Tietze
as soloist, and then under the title of 'a new Quintet'. It
features a great deal in Schubert's correspondence with his
publishers and the opus number, 102, was his own choice,
although he did not live to see the work published. It is, in
fact, a major work and a masterpiece, full of magical harmony and sensitive modulation, and in the visionary middle-
section Schubert completely forgot Tietze and his vocal ambitions. The three songs for male-voice quartet which Pennauer published as late as October 1828 were written
somewhat earlier, probably in 1825: they are 'Wehmut', a
setting of a poem by Heinrich Hüttenbrenner, 'Ewige
Liebe' (Ernst Schulze) and 'Flucht' (C. Lappe). Hüttenbrenner was a friend of Schubert's youth, but his association with Schulze and Lappe did not begin until
1825, so that it is possible to date these songs fairly accurately. One wonders how the last two songs at any rate could
ever have been published and how they managed to escape
the notice of the censors. For Schulze was bold enough to
write lines like these:

> Gewagt und gewonnen! schrieb mancher aufs Schwert;
> Gewagt und zerronnen ist mir nur (nun?) bescheert . . .*

and Lappe wrote A Hymn to Freedom, which he was at least
prudent enough to call 'Die Freie', so that it could also be
mistaken as a reference to 'Nature and the open air'. In
'Wehmut' Schubert reproduces the sound of the 'evening
bell' in the main section by means of a persistent 'ding-dong'
effect in the first bass part: Peter Cornelius's device of 'one
tone' was not therefore so very original. Later, in a setting of

---

* 'Dared and won!' many a man used to engrave upon his sword;
'Dared and failed!' is all (now?) my portion. . . .

J. G. Seidl's 'Das Zügenglöcklein' (XX, 507), Schubert
reproduced the sound of the bell that tolls when a man is on
the point of death, in the upper register *above* the voice part.
'Ewige Liebe' maintains from beginning to end an an-
apaestic rhythm which one might describe as 'revolutionary'.
'Die Flucht' alternates between homophonic and freely imi-
tative sections and in any discussion of Schubert's political
faith one should not forget these songs. It says much for his
courage or for his simple-mindedness that 'Flucht' was performed in public under the title of 'a new vocal quartet' in
one of Georg Hellmesberger's concerts on 20th March, 1825.
On the other hand there is no mention of any public performance of 'Ewige Liebe', nor strangely enough of the
completely unpolitical 'Wehmut'.

A very different kind of song is the Latin 'XVIth century
Drinking-song' – 'Edit Nonna, edit Clerus' – (in the Collected Edition, XVI, 29, it is wrongly given as fourteenth
century), which Schubert wrote at Gmunden in July 1825
apparently for his host Ferdinand Traweger. The four male
voices rattle it off merrily like a millwheel; the *pianissimo*
passages are particularly impish. If this is a 'convivial' song
which could equally well be sung out-of-doors, then the setting of Mayrhofer's 'Gondelfahrer' for male-voice quartet
and piano (XVI, 9), written in March 1824 and published in
August, is as much a concert-piece as any song, and we shall
see later that about the same time Schubert also set this text
as a song, in the same key, but otherwise differing from the
choral version in every respect.

This 'Gondelfahrer' is something new among Schubert's
songs for accompanied male-voice quartet. We have a letter
from him – undated but probably written early in 1823 – to
Leopold Sonnleithner, who had apparently asked him to
compose some new quartets for the Society of Friends of
Music. Schubert declined the invitation: 'You yourself know
how the later quartets were received; people have had
enough of them. I might of course be successful in inventing
some new form, but I cannot be certain of doing so. But as
my future fate is something very near to my heart, you yourself will, I know, admit that I must go forward cautiously.
. . .' Here Schubert has indeed taken a step 'forward'. There
is no longer any need or opportunity for a guitar accompaniment, no final 'round', no special consideration for the first

tenor. It is an impressionist picture of the purest artistic design, a gondolier's song in which the piano creates the 'atmosphere', the rhythm of the waves and the sound of bells borne on the night air above San Marco. He has here found the 'new form', the new spirit. This same spirit permeates the short setting for male-voice chorus of J. G. Seidl's 'Grab und Mond' (XVI, 41) written in September 1826, with its bold hollow fourths which lead from the tonic to the recapitulation in A flat minor.

Two choral songs from Sir Walter Scott's *Lady of the Lake,* one for male-voice quartet, the other for a terzet of women's voices, are of a quite different character and belong in another category. On the other hand a setting of a poem from Goethe's *West-östlicher Divan* ('Im Gegenwärtigen Vergangenes', XVI, 15) is quite certainly an experimental sketch or a preliminary study for 'Gondelfahrer' and can only have been written in the year 1824. It is like a cantata in style, with solos and duets, and ends with the usual 'round'; yet in spite of the extremely primitive accompaniment it is no longer a 'convivial' song, although it is possible to imagine it being sung in a gathering of serious and thoughtful people, young or old. In the first duet, for the two tenors, Schubert uses the same imitation in which the charm of the later 'Gondelfahrer' lies. It is the fact that he set this 'ultra-symbolical' and esoteric song to music which distinguishes him from hundreds of other choral composers:

> . . .*denn es ziemt, des Tags Vollendung*
> *Mit Geniessern zu geniessen.**

On New Year's Day, 1824, he wrote the 'Lied eines Kriegers' for bass-solo and unison male-voice chorus with piano accompaniment (XX, 464), in which he avoids the somewhat banal 'heroism' of the text by turning to a minor key – banal, since it is concerned with a chorus of spirits. Did Schubert see himself and his friends in this picture? Another short 'occasional' piece, 'Der Tanz' (XVII, 14) was written in the middle or towards the end of 1825 to celebrate the recovery of little Irene Kiesewetter, daughter of an aulic councillor, who, at the age of fourteen, had conceived an inordinate passion for dancing. It was apparently commissioned by her anxious father and the cheerful piece, writ-

*'. . . for it is fitting to enjoy the close of day with like spirits.'

ten almost in the style of a gallop, was performed by two pairs of friends, male and female. Two years later, Schubert had to write something more ambitious for a similar occasion.

We last left Schubert as a song-composer after *Die schöne Müllerin*, and the intervening period confirms what he had written in that much-quoted letter to Schober from Zseliz in September 1824: '... since you left, I have written practically no songs'. He had become an instrumental composer. Between *Die schöne Müllerin* and *Die Winterreise* – that is to say, up to February 1827 – he wrote only some four dozen songs, and of these four dozen posterity has neglected at least half, unlike Schubert's contemporaries, who thought highly of some of the songs, such as Lappe's 'Der Einsame' or Seidl's 'Im Freien', which present-day taste finds insipid. The names of poets such as these provide half the explanation for this change in Schubert's creative outlook. The great names of this period are those of Friedrich Rückert, who stands on the threshold of it (1823); Schiller, to whom Schubert returned for the last time with his setting of 'Dithyrambe' (XX, 457), which is a 'round' rather than a song for bass-voice; and Goethe, to whose *Wilhelm Meister* Schubert turned for the last and final time in January 1826 in a group of four songs (XX, 488–91). The brothers August Wilhelm and Friedrich Schlegel appear very occasionally. In his choice of texts it was as if he had become, so to speak, short-sighted and unable to see beyond his immediate Viennese circle. Luckily, however, this circle led him abroad again, to translations from the English, to Sir Walter Scott and Shakespeare. He again set a number of Johann Mayrhofer's poems, in spite of the strained relations which now existed between him and his friend. The effect of this was to bring into greater prominence Franz Xaver v. Schlechta, a fellow-pupil of Schubert's at the Seminary and his life-long admirer; Carl Lappe, who had already achieved some degree of immortality through Beethoven's setting of one of his poems, and with whose 'Flucht' we have already made our acquaintance; Christoph Kuffner, an official in the Imperial War Ministry; Johann Gabriel Seidl, like Schlechta a friend of his youth, who in 1824 also tried to persuade Schubert to set his opera libretto *Der kurze Mantel* to music – a suggestion which Schubert wisely declined. A personal meeting in Gastein with Johann Ladislaus Pyrker, the Patriarch of Venice, resulted in Schubert setting two more of his poems to music, which he published two years later as op.79 with a dedication to the poet. Pyrker had proved very generous when Schubert dedicated the three songs of op. 4 (including 'Der Wanderer') to him in 1821; but on this occasion it does not seem to have occurred to him to put his hand in his pocket. This Austrian circle fortunately still included Matthaeus v. Collin, for Collin's 'Nacht und Träume' became one of Schubert's 'immortal' songs. But some distance outside this circle stand Wilhelm v. Schütz and Ernst Schulze, whose fashionable epic in clever *ottave rime, Die bezauberte Rose* attracted the attention of Schubert and his friend and medical adviser Bernhardt as suitable material for an opera in 1824 and 1825. But after March 1825, Schubert was solely interested in Schulze as a lyric poet and in his 'poetical diary'.

Of particular importance for him was his association with Jakob Nikolaus Craigher, a man of his own age, who was born in Veneto and had moved from Pest to Vienna in 1820. He was on friendly terms with Friedrich v. Schlegel and the painter, L. F. v. Schorr, and shared their interest in foreign literature and in mastering it through the medium of skilful translation. On 23rd October, 1825, he wrote in his diary: 'Schubert has made an agreement with me, by which I am to provide him with faithful translations of a number of songs by English, Spanish, French and Italian classics, which he will then set to music and have published with the original text. . . . He has also taken a few new songs of mine with him, which he will probably set to music'. Schubert not only set two of these 'new songs', 'Totengräber's Heimweh' and 'Die junge Nonne', but also Craigher's translation of Colley Cibber's 'The Blind Boy' ('Der blinde Knabe'), a different version of which had already been set to music by Franz Lachner and Simon Sechter. Schubert had already taken a practical interest in English literature in the spring and summer of 1825. In April (while he was still in Vienna and before starting on his tour) he had set The Lay of the Imprisoned Huntsman' ('Das Lied des gefangenen Jägers') from Scott's *Lady of the Lake*, and in Linz he completed the beginning of this cycle – the only one between *Die schöne*

Müllerin and the *Wilhelm Meister* songs – with four songs and two choruses, for which he used the Bremen Professor Ph, Adam Storck's translation of the Scottish bard's romantic narrative poem. Sir Walter Scott's tales in poetry and prose had been the height of fashion in both Germany and Austria for some ten years, and *The Lady of the Lake*, in particular, was one of J. M. Vogl's favourite books. These songs were sung in Gmunden and Linz 'with the greatest success'; and in 1826 Schubert published them as op. 52, in two books containing seven numbers, with a dedication to Countess Sophie v. Weissenwolff of Steyregg near Linz, where he had enjoyed the most generous hospitality. He set great store by this publication: 'But I intend to follow a different procedure with the publication of these songs from the usual one, which produces so very few results, since they bear the celebrated name of Scott at their head, and so might arouse more curiosity and, with the addition of the English text, might also make me better known in England. ...' (Letter to his parents, 25th July, 1825.) The English text does not always lend itself to German translation and to a declamatory style, and Schubert would have had to make many adjustments to get the two to correspond.

Another chance occurrence led him to Shakespeare. In 1824, an amateur publisher, Josef Trentsensky, had undertaken a 'Viennese' collected edition of Shakespeare's works, based on August Wilhelm Schlegel's translations, for the plays which Schlegel had omitted, and for the sonnets and the epic poems, new versions had to be provided by young Viennese writers. One of these – and the most diligent and prolific – was Eduard v. Bauernfeld whom Schubert had met in January 1822 together with another of these 'English scholars', Josef Fick, at the house of the Professor of Theology, Vincentius Weintritt, who was incidentally one of the leading victims of Viennese reaction and imperial bigotry. (The fact that Schubert frequented this house is further proof that, so far as politics were concerned, he was either not entirely disinterested or he was disarmingly ingenuous.) Bauernfeld translated, among other things, *Antony and Cleopatra* (in collaboration with Ferdinand v. Mayerhofer) and *The Two Gentlemen of Verona*, and it is his versions which Schubert used for his corresponding songs. For the third and subsequently most famous song – the Serenade

('Ständchen') from *Cymbeline* – Schubert relied on Schlegel's translation.

There is no doubt that he himself considered his settings of Scott's poems as his most important achievement among the songs of this year. The Collected Edition scatters them ruthlessly throughout three different volumes, but they constitute one single entity. It is as if Schubert had deliberately sought to provide an echo of the poem in seven musical pictures: first, Ellen's slumber-songs for the warrior and for the huntsman; the 'Boating Song' for male-voice chorus as a triumphal reception for Sir Roderick the Victorious (XVI, 10); and as a counterpart, the dirge of women and maidens ('Coronach'; XVIII, 1); finally 'Norman's Song', Ellen's 'Ave Maria' and 'The Lay of the Imprisoned Huntsman'. If one so wished, one could detect a deliberate intention in the sequence of keys – from D flat major by way of E flat major, C minor, F minor, C minor to D minor. Schubert uses the 'brighter' keys only for occasional contrast.

It is inevitable that these settings of the younger Scottish bard recall those of the older, Ossian. There is no longer anything rhapsodic or adventurous in these later songs. Schubert has become a 'Classicist'. Ellen's slumber-song for the warrior ('Soldier, rest! thy warfare o'er') is a vocal Rondo, with episodes treated in a more martial style. The two choruses ('Hail to the Chief'; 'He is gone on the mountain') are strophic songs, and both are conceived in a more theatrical manner than many choruses in Schubert's operas; and 'Ave Maria' ('Ave Maria! Maiden mild') is a strophic song. Schubert had the whole picture clearly before his eyes; thus the 'harp accompaniment' in 'Soldier, rest!' can only be explained by reference to the two previous lines of Scott's poem:

> *She sung, and still a harp unseen*
> *Filled up the symphony between.*

In the huntsman's slumber-song ('Huntsman, rest! thy chase is done') the horn-call in the accompaniment sounds as in a dream or half-dream; 'Norman's Song' ('The heath this night must be my bed') – a premonition of death and victory, the last verse of which turns quite naturally to the major – with its persistent iambic, martial rhythm in the accompaniment, is the realization of what Monteverdi may

have had in mind two centuries earlier with his *stile con-
citato*. 'The Lay of the Imprisoned Huntsman' ('My hawk is
tired of perch and hood') is strangely enough – and yet, on
second thoughts, not so very strangely – an emphatic Polonaise in the minor. The prisoner sees visions of freedom, of
dancing and hunting; the accuracy of the strophic setting is
remarkable. One need scarcely waste words describing the
simplicity of the accompaniment and the (Italian) sensitivity
of the vocal line in 'Ave Maria'. Schubert used this song to
demonstrate to his father the difference between bigotry and
his own piety. 'People wonder greatly at my piety,' he wrote
in a letter to his father from Steyr on 25th July, 'which I
have expressed in a hymn to the Holy Virgin, and (which), it
seems, grips every spirit and turns it to devotion. I believe
this is because I never force myself to devotion and never
compose hymns and prayers of that kind, except when I am
involuntarily overcome by it. Then, however, it is usually
the right and true devotion'.

Of somewhat later origin, i.e., March 1826, is the 'Romance of Richard Coeur-de-Lion' ('Romanze des Richard
Löwenherz'; XX, 501) taken this time from Scott's *Ivan-
hoe*. It has the same simplicity of form, the same unity
in the accompaniment with its knightly dignity and its flourishes of trumpets, and it is of the same high quality. Schubert, at any rate, thought it worth publishing entirely on its
own two years later as op. 86, without any dedication.

The three settings of Shakespeare songs are much more
'accidental' in their origin, rather in the same way that
Haydn's settings of Shakespeare were. The paean to Bacchus
(XX, 502) is a compact 'round', in which the phrase
'Füll'uns, bis die Welt sich *dreht*' cast a spell over Schubert.
The two others, the 'Serenade' from *Cymbeline* (XX, 503)
and 'To Sylvia' ('An Sylvia') from *The Two Gentlemen of
Verona* are deservedly famous – the former by virtue of the
unaffected reticence of its melody and the fragrance of its
accompaniment, the latter by reason of the persistent bass-
figure which symbolizes so charmingly the ever-present
Sylvia.

We will return now to the songs of 1824 and to the settings
of poems by the 'Viennese circle', and with these it does not
always follow that weak words beget weak music. This is
admittedly true of Kuffner's 'Glaube, Hoffnung und Liebe'

(XX, 462) in which Schubert set three chorale-like verses between two treated in freer style; the text itself was not exactly inspiring. But he transformed Lappe's* 'Im Abendrot' (XX, 463) into a hymn of profound and impressive solemnity; and in 'Der Einsame', the real title of which should be 'Der Zufriedene' (XX, 465), he both illustrated and idealized the philistinism of the *Biedermeier* period. This song was a success and was published separately and without dedication as op. 41. Of the four Mayrhofer songs, with which Schubert finally took leave of his friend, 'Der Sieg' (XX, 458, a bass-song cast in a rhapsodic and cantata-like mould, is like a reminiscence of the untroubled past. A completely personal note is also struck in 'Abendstern' (XX, 459), with its melancholy quotation from the Allegretto of Beethoven's A major Symphony. Schubert published neither of these songs – and why should he not sometimes have sung to himself and for himself alone? The most characteristic of these last Mayrofer songs is the 'Tristan-like' 'Auflösung' (XX, 360):

> *Verbirg dich, Sonne,*
> *Denn die Gluten der Wonne*
> *Versengen mein Gebein. . . .*
> *Geh unter, Welt, und störe*
> *nimmer die süssen*
> *Aetherischen Chöre. . . .†*

Schubert sets this like a man intoxicated, with an ecstatic figure and tremolo in the bass, and repeated the words 'Geh unter, Welt, geh unter', at the end, as if in the last stages of exhaustion. It is a forerunner of the great orchestral 'Liebestod' of the summer of 1859. Not one of the songs which separate the settings of Mayrhofer from those of Scott is without distinction; Schlechta's 'Des Sänger's Habe,' with its jingling interludes – reminiscent of Hugo Wolf – is quite outstanding, as are the settings of Craigher's 'Totengräber's Heimweh' (XX, 467) in spite of the somewhat affected nature of the poem, and the same poet's 'Der blinde Knabe' (XX, 468), for all the excessive sentimentality of the text. The striding chorale-like rhythm of Schlechta's 'To-

---

* Lappe, it is true, did not belong to the Viennese Circle.
† Hide thyself, Sun, for the flames of ecstasy consume my body. . . . Perish, O World! and disturb no more the sweet, ethereal choirs. . . .

tengräberweise' (XX, 496), a rather more elegant variant of
a conventional poetic theme, transforms it into one of Schubert's most impressive songs, and it becomes a compendium
of his favourite modulations. The counterpart is Schlechta's
'Fischerweise' (XX, 495) in which voice-part and the bass of
the accompaniment indulge in a kind of thematic teasing of
each other – in exactly the same way as in Ernst Schulze's
'Auf der Bruck' (XX, 477); from a musical point of view
both these songs fall into a category of their own together
with the setting of Shakespeare's 'To Sylvia'.

The two songs of this period which have become most
famous are the ballad-like 'Die junge Nonne' (XX, 469) with
its pious modulation to the major and the pious sound of a
little bell at the end, and the setting of Collin's 'Nacht und
Träume'. Both were published together as op. 43, the
author of the latter poem being given on that occasion as
Schiller instead of Collin. The song has only one single dynamic marking: 'pianissimo', and in its noble simplicity it
provides a test of delivery to which few singers are equal.
Indeed, for the delivery of Schubert's songs in general,
neither the Italian or quasi-Italian lyrical style nor the melodious enunciation of the words is in itself sufficient; the
ideal delivery for his songs lies somewhere between the two,
with alternate emphasis on each.

Schubert's principal method of 'integrating' a song consists at this stage of a persistent figure in the right or left
hand of the accompaniment, within which he reserves to
himself only the full freedom and flexibility of modulation.
Rhapsodic treatment and recitative have disappeared; he can
now say all that he has to say within the framework of the
strophic song with variations. For 'Refrain-Lieder' like the
four settings of poems by J. G. Seidl (XX, 508–11), published as op. 95 and 'dedicated to the poet', or like Castelli's
'Echo' (XX, 513, and probably the first of 'Six Cheerful
Songs' written for Weigl's publishing-house), all of which
might be described as Italian canzonettas with German text,
he employs nothing more elaborate than a simple, charming
melody and the simplest accompaniment. But when Seidl
provides him with something more deeply emotional, like
'Wiegenlied' (XX, 512) something equally profound and personal blossoms in Schubert, too, in his favourite and most
characteristic rhythm. As in the settings of Seidl, so also in

those of Schulze, one has the same feeling that Schubert set
them as if they had been written by Goethe, that his music
weighs too heavily on the words, that he has far outgrown
such poetry. Schulze, indeed, tried occasionally to imitate
Goethe, as in the case of 'Im Freien' (X,X 494), the form and
spirit of which have their origin in Goethe's 'An den Mond',
and on which Schubert lavished all the abundant fullness of
his heart. The setting of the second of two scenes from Wilhelm v. Schütz's 'oriental-scented' play *Lacrimas* (XX, 483,
484), with its animated freedom of delivery over a 'symphonic' accompaniment, ranks among Schubert's boldest
and finest songs. It could well be included as a girl's confession of her love in some opera as yet unwritten.* The
second of the Pyrker songs, 'Die Allmacht' (XX, 479) – the
first, 'Heimweh' (XX, 478), i.e., the nostalgia of a moun-
taineer, suffers too much under the handicap of the text – is a
magnificently hymn-like and completely personal rebirth of
the pathos that was Gluck's or Beethoven's.

The harmony between poetry and music becomes complete when we turn to the settings of the greater poets. Of
those with words by the brothers Schlegel, to whom Schubert had probably been attracted again through his association with Craigher, the most arresting is Friedrich
Schlegel's 'Fülle der Liebe' (XX, 480) which is not only a
counterpart to Platen's 'Du liebst mich nicht', but also an
interpretation or an explanation of the Andante from the D
major 'Gastein' Sonata. The song and the sonata were both
written in August 1825. What the song expresses within its
narrower limits

> *Ein sehnend Streben*   *teilt mir das Herz*
> *Bis alles Leben*   *sich löst in Schmerz . . .*
> *Ein Zauber waltet*   *jetzt öber mich*
> *Und der gestaltet*   *dies all nach sich . . .†*

---

*This W. v. Schütz owes such immortality as he has achieved
solely to Schubert; he was a protégé of W. v. Schlegel and a prolific
writer. Schubert probably met him through their mutual acquaintance
Matthaeus v. Collin; yet he is not without interest in a biography of
Schubert, since he was the author of a drama entitled *Graf und Gräfin von
Gleichen.*

> †A yearning desire   rives my heart
> Until all life itself   dissolves in pain. . . .
> A magic power   now casts its spell over me
> And bends   all this to its will . . .

the sonata-movement can release in full and unchecked flood:

The four Rückert songs are all of the first order: 'Greisengesang' (XX, 456), conceived for a noble baritone voice, with its alternation between major and minor; the charming and popular 'Lachen und Weinen' (XX, 455); the intimate and devotional 'Du bist die Ruh' (XX, 454); and above all 'Dass sie hier gewesen' (XX, 453), which one might call 'impressionistic', were it not also a piece of the most delicate, spiritual sensitivity. Finally Schubert achieved the ultimate perfection in the four *Wilhelm Meister* songs, op. 62, of January 1826 with which he took leave of Goethe (XX, 488–91). He here set the Harper's song, 'Nur wer die Sehnsucht kennt', to music for the fifth and sixth time – once, in keeping with its context in the novel, as a duet or antiphon between Mignon and the Harper:

He [Wilhelm Meister] fell into a reverie, his heart full of ardent longing, and how in harmony with his feelings was the song which at that very moment Mignon and the Harper were singing with profound expression as an irregular duet:
'Who alone has felt the pangs of longing....'

Schubert follows Goethe exactly: the lyricism of the begining changes to a dramatic tension at the words

*Es schwindelt mir, es brennt mein Eingeweide ...**

* My head reels, my heart burns within me ...

and this tension is echoed again in the repetition of the lyrical beginning. We have already seen that this 'process' is the
counterpart and explanation of many of Schubert's slow
movements. The other setting of the text is a very simple,
concentrated song. Between 'Heiss mich nicht reden' and 'So
lasst mich scheinen' there is a melodic, harmonic and rhythmic affinity: the former is in E minor, the latter in B major;
the one is an expression of earthly pain, the other a heavenly
vision.

Chapter Twelve

The Last Years
End and Beginning
1826–1828

During no period of his life is the dualism in Schubert's music – that of the most gifted Viennese composer of his time and of the great 'Romantic' classicist – more clearly defined than during his last years. He had become a well-known composer and now had to make every effort to become still better known. In order to find a public and publishers for the 'serious' works which he had already written or was about to write, he had no alternative but to compromise, so far as he was able. But in spite of this, he kept his paramount objective steadily in view. Nothing demonstrates this more clearly than the programme of his celebrated 'Private Concert' of March 1828 which consisted 'entirely of works composed by himself', after the model of Beethoven. In none of these works did he fall below his own high standard, and he even treated his audience to the first movement of his G major String Quartet; and thanks to the co-operation of a sensitive interpreter like J. M. Vogl, the choice of songs was equally effective and sober. He chose some of his best works, but only those with which he was on certain ground. It is a fact, however, that during his last two or three years, he also wrote several 'lighter', more approachable, virtuoso pieces, for which he could count on an appreciative public.

Before we turn to these works, we will touch briefly on his last and, in a literal sense, unfinished opera. Since we do not know it, we cannot really discuss it in any detail. But is it not symbolical that the one work of Schubert's which death cut short should be an opera – a work in that field which it was never given to him to master? It would probably have been his best and most mature stage-work, and perhaps he would

this time have had the courage to put into practice the pro-
gressive achievements of *Lazarus*. But it is still doubtful
whether it would have influenced the history of opera, which
was moving towards Marschner and Wagner along the path
which Weber had shown.

Fierabras had marked the end of Schubert's 'careless' or
naïve operatic phase. Perhaps he realized that he had
reached a dead end; perhaps he had learnt that the writing of
an opera demands something more than hurriedly providing
libretto with music – however good that music may be. It
says much for his more critical frame of mind that, as we
have already seen, he resisted Johann Gabriel Seidl's repeated requests (1st July, 1824) that he should write the incidental music for the production at the Theater an der Wien
of his dramatic fairy-tale *Der kurze Mantel*, although he
originally condescended to do so*. On the other hand it
appears to have been Schober who was responsible (rightly
or wrongly) for the fact that nothing came of a suggestion of
Schwind's (in a letter dated 14th February, 1825) that he
should prepare a libretto for Schubert based on the biblical
story of David and Abigail.

But he never gave up his plans for an opera. One of his
younger friends and his most recent bosom-companion,
Eduard v. Bauernfeld, made the following entry in his diary
in March 1825: 'He wants an opera libretto from me, and
suggested *The Enchanted Rose* (*Die bezauberte Rose*). It
told him that a *Count of Gleichen* (*Graf von Gleichen*) was
running through my head.' Although Bauernfeld was no less
prolific and even more dexterous in his own sphere than
Schubert was in the musical field, he nevertheless showed a
certain sense of discrimination in not embarking upon a
dramatization of Ernst Schulze's mawkish and over-
polished poem. At best the result would have been nothing
more than another tale of knights, singers and fairies with
marches, processions and melodramatic music off-stage; despite Schulze's immaturity (like Schubert, he died young) his
verses are none the less very charming and would have been
infinitely coarsened and banalized in the process. The plot
would not even have offered an opportunity for a love-duet,
since the hero does not 'rescue' the heroine until the final

* Cf. O. E. Deutsch: 'Concerning two operas which Schubert never
wrote' in *Moderne Welt*, special Schubert-number, 1928.

scene, up to which point he has not been permitted to have any conversation with her. As we know from O. E. Deutsch, Schulze had, in a different way, already 'stood proxy' to one of Schubert's most famous songs, for the text of Schober's 'An die Musik' derives from a stanza (II, 41) of *Die bezauberte Rose,* which it simply paraphrases:

> *Du holde Kunst melodisch süsser Klagen,*
> *Du tönend Lied aus sprachlos finsterm Leid,*
> *Du spielend Kind, das oft aus schönern Tagen*
> *In unser Nacht so duft'ge Blumen streut,*
> *Ach, ohne dich vermöcht'ich nie zu tragen,*
> *Was feindlich längst mein böser Stern mir beut!*
> *Wenn Wort und Sinn im Liede freudlich klingen*
> *Dann flattert leicht der schwere Gram auf Schwingen.* *

With *Der Graf von Gleichen,* however, Bauernfeld really 'got down to business', to use his own expression. (2nd May, 1826.) 'Dramatic and musical contrast: orient and occident, janissaries and chivalry, romantic and domestic love, etc. – in short, a Turkish-Christian sketch. The verses flow fairly easily for me.' No doubt. A few days later he wrote in jocular vein to Schubert: 'I have composed *and* sung most of the numbers in the *Count of Gleichen*'. To which Schubert replied: 'It is very clever of you to have done the opera. I only wish I could see it in front of me already. They have asked for my libretti here to see what can be done with them. If only your libretto were ready now, I could submit *that* to them and if they recognized its worth (which I do not doubt) I might make a start on it, God willing, or send it to Mme Milder in Berlin.' It is highly significant that he himself no longer had any confidence in his previous operas; but it was another monumental piece of ingenuousness on the part of the author and the composer not to have foreseen that the Imperial Censor would never pass an opera, the plot of which not only accepted the possibility of bigamy but even glorified it.

* Thou lovely Art of sweet melodious sadness, thou Song echoing out of mute and sombre grief, thou dancing child who oft doth scatter such fragrant flowers from happier days into the darkness of our night, ah! without thee I could never bear the slings and arrows of outrageous fortune. When word and thought echo their kindly message in song, then grievous sorrow lightly takes wing.

Not even Goethe could find a social and dramatic solution, for in his *Stella* of 1775 he treated the problem of bigamy and wavered between a reconciliatory and a tragic ending; as far as we are concerned the one point of interest is the fact that during the twenties this problem was still being treated in operatic form in Weimar as well as Vienna, for on 5th December, 1822, Eckermann wrote: 'This evening at Goethe's house I heard the rehearsal of the first act of a partly completed opera, *The Count of Gleichen,* by Eberwein . . .' and again on 6th April, 1825, he spoke of the 'popular quartet' from this opera.

If we can believe his diary, Bauernfeld finished the libretto on 9th May, after one week's work. 29th May, however, is the more probable date (cf. O. E. Deutsch, op. cit., p. 530). 'Informed Schubert about it (the libretto), and he replied without delay. He is burning to receive it. . . .' And at the end of July 1826 when Bauernfeld returned from a holiday tour of Carinthia and the Salzkammergut, the great moment arrived. 'When we alighted that evening at Nussdorf, Schwind and Schubert rushed out of the café to meet me. Great rejoicing! "Where is the opera?" asked Schubert. "Here!" – I solemnly handed him the *Count of Gleichen*.' This time, however, Schubert seems to have been a little more circumspect and did not set to work immediately. Obviously a light had dawned. 'Schubert is delighted with the opera, but we are afraid of the censor' (August 1826) – and not without justification, either. Then, on 26th October: 'The opera libretto is forbidden by the censor. Schubert wants to compose it nonetheless.' The next mention of the opera does not occur until 31st August, 1827: 'Schubert is composing the *Count of Gleichen*.' And we are told that during the last year of his life he was still sketching 'completely new harmonies and rhythms' for the work. This is something unusual; for sketching had certainly not been Schubert's method for his earlier operas, except, perhaps, *Sakuntala*. But listen to Bauernfeld himself:

In August 1826 I brought the finished opera with me, and Schubert at once [?—the first page of the sketch bears the date, June 17th, 1827!] set to work on it. He had previously sent the text to the manager of the Kärntnertor Theatre, who was somewhat anxious about the reactions of the censor. Grillparzer expressed his readiness to arrange for the opera to be produced

at Königsstadt Theatre (in Berlin) in the event of it being forbidden in Vienna. During the following winter, Schubert had
roughly sketched out the whole of the music and played and even
sung some of it to me at the piano. It sounded very charming
and poetic! However it still lacked the orchestration, which was
merely indicated here and there and the detailed filling-in of
which alone could supply the proper colouring. But while he
was still engaged on this task, death overtook him suddenly.
It was not until nearly forty years later that Schubert's own
manuscript of the score was brought to light again through the
untiring efforts of Herbeck, who set to work eagerly to complete
the orchestration of the opera according to the Maestro's [!]
indications. The individual numbers which were performed at
one of the Society's concerts aroused a universal interest in the
whole musical work, for which I was fortunate enough to have
been allowed to provide the poetic foundation. . . .

And now we have to rely upon Ludwig Herbeck's description in his biography of his father (*Johann Herbeck*, Vienna,
1885, p. 206 ff):

Schubert's manuscript came into Herbeck's possession. It can
really be described as nothing more than a sketch, for only the
voice-parts are completed in detail, while of the accompaniment
merely the bass is indicated here and there. From this Herbeck
revised and completed the first number, a male-voice chorus
('Morning-song in the Forest' – 'Morgengesang im Walde') which
came into his hands with a number of loose sheets of music,
without his realizing that this charming piece was the introductory chorus to an opera. Apart from this chorus, Herbeck completed the scene which follows it up to the line 'Thou dost darken
my every moment with pain and dread'; then from the words
'Hearken to what I tell thee' (19 bars before the commencement
of the *Allegro assai*; the immediately preceding passage must
have been lost, since Herbeck would scarcely have started his
orchestration in the middle of a phrase) as far as 'my face is
too hideous in her sight'; then from the final 'A ship, a ship!'
to 'Warm blood and a merry spirit.' Herbeck included his
completed version of Suleika's charming aria 'Ye flowers, ye
trees' and also the quartet in the Jubilee Concert of the Male-
voice Choral Society in 1868. Of the music to the first acts
Herbeck also orchestrated the chorus 'We praise thee, flower of
the world', which occurs between the two above-mentioned
numbers, and the song 'A thousand women'. From the second
act, however, he seems to have completed only the 'Chorus of
Reapers'. Herbeck's filling-in is for the most part complete.
Only in a few places are there gaps in the orchestration, which
one can claim, without laying oneself open to the charge of
exaggeration, to have been carried out in a manner fully worthy
of the spirit of Schubert.

Herbeck's versions of 'Morgengesang im Walde' and
'Rüdiger's Heimkehr' for tenor solo, male-voice chorus and

orchestra were later published by C. A. Spina in Vienna; both Schubert's autograph and Herbeck's orchestrated version of the quintet (the quartet mentioned above?) and Suleika's arietta passed into the possession of Nikolaus Dumba and thence into the Vienna City Library.

We cannot make any comment on 'Morgengesang im Walde' in this last opera of Schubert's. But as regards his setting of J. G. Seidl's 'Nachtgesang im Walde' (XVI, 1; April 1827) we know that it was written for a 'private concert given by Herr Jos. Rudolf Lewy, horn-player at the Kärntnertor Theatre'. Four male voices alternate loudly and softly, and in homophony throughout, with four horns in E. The piece would be too long for stage purposes and is a little too primitive for the concert-room. It might almost have been composed by Conradin Kreutzer.

This brings us to the Schubert of the last years – the Schubert who more than ever was intent upon winning, and indeed *had* to win, his public, and we will begin with the two works for violin and piano which he did *not* include in the programme of his public concert. Both were written for the same players, his friend C. M. v. Bocklet and the very young violinist Josef Slawjk. The first, the Rondo, op. 70 (VIII, 1), was played for the first time in private at Domenico Artaria's house early in 1827 and a little later published by him; the second, the Fantasia, op. 159 (VIII, 5), was written in December of this year and performed at a matinée concert of Slawjk's on 20th January, 1828. Both works are, so to speak, makeshifts for the violin concerto which Schubert never wrote. The title of the Rondo reads: 'Rondeau brilliant'. And from the technical point of view, both works bear the same relation to the imaginary violin sonatas which, with the possible exception of the A major, op. 162, Schubert also failed to write, as the 'Wanderer' Fantasia bears to the intimate piano sonatas. The most dazzling technical skill is demanded of both players. The Rondo, in C minor, is constructed exactly on the pattern of the Finale of the Piano Sonata, op. 78, except that it has a dignified introduction which later reappears as a kind of development section, after the model of the first movement of the Octet. It is followed by a lyrical middle-section in G major, which corresponds approximately to the long middle-section in E flat in the

Finale of op. 78. The Rondo theme is Hungarian, one might almost say Polish, in character, and as if to make assurance doubly sure, Schubert combines it with flowery touches of lyricism and a triumphant flourish at the end. Schubert allows himself no half-measures, but he makes it easy for the listener. The work was subsequently reviewed in glowing terms in the *Wiener Zeitschrift für Kunst* of 7th June, 1828:

... Although the whole piece is brilliant, it does not owe its existence to mere figurations such as grin at us in a thousand different contortions from so many compositions and are a weariness of the spirit. The spirit of invention has here often beaten its wings mightily indeed and has borne us aloft with it. Both the pianoforte and the violin require an accomplished performer who must be equal to passages which have not achieved as it were, their right of citizenship by countless repetition, but which reveal a new and inspired succession of ideas. The player [sic!] will feel attracted in an interesting way by the beautiful interchange of harmonies. ...

In spite of the flowery language of this appreciation which could well serve as an example for many others, the writer recognizes and expresses admirably the difference between a 'fashionable' composer and Schubert.

In the Duo in C major, op. 159, Schubert sets the listener a much more difficult task. As in the 'Wanderer' Fantasia, the movements or sections are interlinked, though no longer in the sequence and spirit of a sonata of four movements, but in a more complicated manner. An 'Andante molto' – again, how unwilling Schubert is to write the word 'Adagio', for this 'andante molto' is a decidedly slow Andante! – of a soft and dreamy tension throughout, is followed by an Allegretto in A minor, *all' ongarese* as in the other Duo, but this time of a more noble character in spite of the stronger colouring, and with a charming tendency towards 'canon'; and as a Finale, a set of variations (in A flat major) on his song 'Sei mir gegrüsst'. But after the third variation the 'Andante molto' returns in an altered and abbreviated form as an introduction to a march-like 'Allegro vivace' which is still recognizable as a variation under its jaunty disguise, and which assumes a 'winding-up' role after the return of the theme. The 'brilliant weakness' of the work naturally lies in the superficial treatment of the passionate song-theme, which,

as in the earlier example of 'Trockene Blumen', is much too
good for such treatment. This time Schubert fared badly at
the hands of the critics. Thus *Der Sammler* on 7th February,
1828: 'Herr Franz Schubert's Fantasia for Pianoforte and
Violin . . . lasts rather longer than the time that the Viennese
are prepared to devote to their aesthetic pleasures. The hall
gradually emptied and your correspondent admits that he,
too, is unable to say how this piece of music ended.' And the
Leipziger Allgemeine musikalische Zeitung of 2nd April was
short and to the point: 'A new Fantasia . . . made no appeal
of any sort. It would be a fair judgment to say that the
popular composer has frankly gone off the rails here.'

But the 'popular composer' certainly satisfied his contemporaries when he wrote a Nocturne in E flat major for
piano trio (VII, 5) which was published as op. 148 in 1844. It
must have been written about the time of the Duo op. 159,
since it uses and further develops the theme of the 'Andante
molto'. It is a singularly empty Adagio, with a few contrasts
and modulations. Yet though no one but Schubert could
have composed it, it is written, as it were, with his left hand
and foreshadows hardly at all the two great Piano Trios of
his last years.

These two Piano Trios, op. 99 and op. 100, the one in B flat
major (VII, 3) written during the summer of 1827 and the
other in E flat major completed in November of the same
year, are, after the 'Trout' Quintet, the two works in which
Schubert achieved the purest blend of the 'sociable' spirit
with that of true chamber-music. He never heard a public
performance of the B flat major nor, strangely enough, did
he even offer it to a publisher, not even to Schott; he only
heard it performed privately at Josef v. Spaun's house on
28th January, 1828, with Bocklet at the piano and Schuppanzigh and Linke on the violin and 'cello respectively. The
E flat major, on the other hand, was frequently played and
was even published by Probst in Leipzig during the composer's lifetime, in October or November 1828. Bocklet
played it with Schuppanzigh and Linke on 26th December,
1827, and it was repeated on the occasion of the great Schubert concert in March 1828 when the violinist J. Mich-
Böhm took the place of Schuppanzigh.

Schumann compared the two Trios and as usual expressed
himself with admirable clarity on the subject of them.

Once glance at Schubert's Trio (op. 99) – and the troubles of our human existence disappear and all the world is fresh and bright again. Yet some ten years ago a Trio by Schubert passed across the face of the musical world like some angry portent in the sky. It was his hundredth opus and shortly afterwards, in November 1828, he died. This recently published Trio seems to be the older of the two works. There is absolutely no evidence of any earlier period in its style and it may well have been written just before the familiar E flat Trio. Yet the two works are essentially and fundamentally different. The first movement, which, in the E flat Trio, is eloquent of extreme anger and passionate longing, is here a thing of grace, intimate and virginal; the Adagio, in the E flat Trio a sigh, rising to spiritual anguish, is here a blissful dream-state, a pulsating flow of exquisitely human emotion. The Scherzos are very similar to each other; yet to my mind, that of the B flat Trio is superior. I will not attempt to choose between the two last movements. To sum up, the Trio in E flat is active, masculine, dramatic, while the B flat is passive, feminine, lyrical. . . .

That is as truly and beautifully expressed as almost everything that Schumann, with his feelings for pure musicianship and humanity, wrote about Schubert. The later Trio is certainly superior to the earlier. But if anyone should tend to underrate the first movement of op. 99, he will perhaps appreciate it more fully when he realizes that it is yet another paraphrase of a song – this time of 'Des Sängers Habe' (XX, 466) of February 1825:

> *Schlagt mein ganzes Glück in Splitter*
> *Nehmt mir alle Habe gleich,*
> *Lasset mir nur meine Zither,*
> *Und ich bleibe froh und reich!**

The musical and spiritual connection is unmistakable. Schumann's 'grace' and 'virginal purity' acquires a new aspect – that of gallantry, sweetness and light. The same is true of the Rondo which is no less clearly derived from the song 'Skolie' written on 15th October, 1815:

> *Lasst im Morgenstrahl des Maï'n*
> *Uns der Blume Leben freun*
> *Eh' ihr Duft entweichet!†*

* Shatter all my happiness in pieces, take from me all my wordly wealth, yet leave me only my zither and I shall still be happy and rich.
† Let us, in the bright May morning, take delight in the life of the flower, before its fragrance disappears.

If anyone is of the opinion that Schubert was incapable of
remembering his own song after an interval of twelve years
– occasionally he did in fact forget what he had written – let
him draw his own comparison:

These symbols, with their remarkable similarity, grew at
least from the same spiritual subsoil. But do not let these
parallels give rise to the mistaken idea that Schubert was
attempting to write 'programme-music'. What he was trying
to achieve was to expand and develop in a less constricted
form what he had expressed in musical terms in the song,
and to intensify this expression by means of musical, as opposed to poetical, contrasts. The two elements in one of these
contrasts – the second subject of the first movement and the
middle section of the Rondo – have a direct connection with
each other. Schubert is here striving after a higher unity
within a sonata-framework, though in a different sense from
what he had set out to achieve in the 'Wanderer' Fantasia.
The Scherzo employs a waltz-like subject in its main section,
which is transformed into a true waltz in the Trio. The key-
relationship of the four movements could not be more
normal or more 'classical'; even the 'andante un poco mosso'
(Schumann calls it 'Adagio') is in the immediate key of E flat
major. But in its melody and harmony it becomes, as it were,
a compendium of all that is most sensitive in Schubert – a
'dream-state' which is not completely blissful but disturbed
occasionally by a sense of pain. Bocklet is said to have embraced Schubert and kissed him after the performance at
Spaun's. That is a better reaction than the assertion that

Beethoven wrote more concentrated piano-trios or that the effectiveness of Schubert's trios is unfortunately prejudiced by the fact that nowadays piano, violin and 'cello have become the customary combination for better-class café ensembles. When I read some critics of Schubert I am reminded of Heine's comment on the celebrated victor of Waterloo – that he was as stupid as all men who have no heart. For in Heine's view ideas do not come from the head, but from the heart. As a matter of interest, it is actually in a *piano-trio* of Beethoven's that we find the clearest foreshadowing of Schubert – the 'Allegretto ma non troppo' of op. 70, No. 2.

In the Piano Trio, op 100, Schubert's intention to give a definite sense of unity to the four movements is crystal-clear. The first movement develops, most unusually, a Scherzo idea, but contrasts and combines it with a hesitant second subject and an exquisitely lyrical third, which recalls, the 'Unfinished' and which one could quote as a further illustration of Schubert's harmonic sensitivity. Consequently the Scherzo itself belongs rather to an older type, in spite of its direction 'scherzando', and the 'canon' treatment at the beginning between strings and piano in octaves reminds one instinctively of Haydn. There is a story attached to the Andante in C minor (once again the key relationship is extremely simple). Schubert is credited with having used in it a Swedish folk-song which he had heard the tenor Isaac Albert Berg sing at the Fröhlich sisters' house. The story is not improbable, for the melody hovers in typical folk-song fashion between minor and major mediant and minor and major dominant. Schubert added a march-like accompaniment which give it an ominous colouring, and developed it into a grandiose ballad, with emotional outbursts and with one of his most moving inspirations. And these various ideas return in a disguised form in the Finale. It begins with all the outward appearance of innocence in a Mozartian 6/8 time and 6/8 spirit; but the 'Swedish theme' returns twice; it is a broadly-designed movement which hovers between sonata and rondo-form.

'The 'sociable' mood is more evident again in the works for four hands which Schubert wrote during the last years of his life. In February 1827 he wrote a set of variations on a theme from Hérold's opera *Maria* ('Was einst vor Jahrèn',

'Sur la rivière') which were published in the autumn as op.
82, and dedicated to 'His Reverence Herr Cajetan Neuhaus,
Professor of Theoretical and Practical Philosophy at Linz',
of whose relations with Schubert little or nothing is known.
Hérold's opera had been performed in December 1826 at the
Kärntnertor Theatre, in Castelli's translation. Here is
further confirmation that, apart from his own themes, Schubert chose only French and never Italian ones as subjects for
variation; and once again this song of the miller Lubin is
emphatically march-like in character. It is not until the
eighth, last and most developed variation that Schubert
refers again to the imitation of the 'mill' in the first part of
the song; for the rest, he treats the theme with the utmost
freedom, varies the time and the key (from C major to C
minor, and from A flat major to A major), links the sixth
variation with the seventh by means of a modulating half-
close, and provides, if not a feast of romantic enchantment,
at least a festival of sound. The *Leipziger Allgemeine Musikalische Zeitung* of 6th February, 1828, probably again in
the person of its editor G. W. Fink himself, duly declared,
not without certain reservations and admonitory advice, that
the work was 'the most successful that Schubert has yet
given us', one, in fact, 'that must be numbered among the
best of recent times'.

Fink could have said this with much greater justification
of the F minor Fantasia, which was published as op. 103 by
Diabelli after Schubert's death, but which Schubert himself
had intended for Countess Caroline Esterhazy (letter to
Schott dated 21st February, 1828). He made a fair copy of it
in April, and with Lachner played it to the delighted Bauernfeld on 9th May. Like the 'Wanderer' Fantasia or the Duo
op. 159, it is a cycle of four movements in free sonata-form –
Allegro – Largo – Scherzo with Trio – Finale, the latter,
however, introduced by a return on a higher level to the first
movement. But in a musical and spiritual sense it is a return
to Zseliz in transfigured retrospect. The 'Allegro molto moderato' begins in a typically Hungarian minor, but soon
modulates to a happy major; the Largo in F sharp minor
contains the much-criticized 'declaration of love' *all' italiana*, but the critics may perhaps understand it and accept it
more kindly, when they realize that Schubert had just heard
Paganini play and – somewhat later, it is true – had said of

the Adagio of Paganini's Second Concerto, op. 7, that he had
heard an angel singing in it. The Scherzo and Finale introduce an unexpected tendency towards a contrapuntal spirit.
It was for Schubert a 'discovery' and for that reason is all the
more enchanting. Schubert must have realized this. It was
perhaps in order to bring discoveries of this kind under
greater control that he considered taking instruction from
Simon Sechter during the last months of his life.

Shortly after this, in May 1828, Schubert wrote the sonata-
movement for four hands, which Diabelli published as a
'characteristic Allegro' under the trivial title of 'Le
bensstürme' (IX, 23; op. 144). The 'storms' are hardly con-
sistent with the direction 'Allegro ma non troppo' – 'not too
fast'. In spite of its sonata-form and extended development,
the movement has more of the majestic character of an overture and is a very formal and rather empty piece, with the
exquisite second subject in the recapitulation in the major as
a bright episode. The return to A minor suggests a con-
tinuation which Schubert never wrote. Instead, on 3rd June
at Baden, he wrote, as a kind of competition with Franz
Lachner, another four-part Fugue in E minor (IX, 28)
which, as already remarked, recalls Mozart's Fugue in G
minor (K. 401) to a quite extraordinary degree. This Fugue
of Mozart's, completed by Stadler, had been widely familiar
since 1800. It had been frequently printed and it is as if
Schubert had just discovered it or had been reminded of it
while contemplating his alleged ' contrapuntal deficiency'.
Like its Mozartian model, it scarcely rises above the level of
an exercise-piece. The story goes that Schubert and Lachner
(to whom we owe the correct dating of the work) played
their mutual efforts on the organ of the monastery church at
Heiligenkreuz. Schubert's Fugue was published by Diabelli
in 1844 as op. 152 in its organ-arrangement as a four-handed
piece. In the case of Mozart, then in his twenty-sixth year,
the G minor Fugue marked the beginning of a crisis which
he was granted another ten years to surmount. In the case of
Schubert, there remained only a few months, and death
spared him or deprived him, at the age of thirty-one, of any
further approach to the problem. For us, however, this unimportant 'occasional' work has a profounder significance.
It shows us how exclusively Schubert's music was founded
on the 'classical' period, and how little it occurred to him to

delve deeper into the past. He wrote good and not-so-good works, but never one which was ambiguous or hybrid in style. For him, the history of music began with Mozart and Haydn; and in his eyes, the contrapuntal style which he occasionally used for his church-music was Mozartian or, to be more precise, Viennese. We know that he had some of Bach's fugues in his possession in 1824 (probably those from the *Well-tempered Clavier*), but we do not know what impression they made on him. In 1817 there had appeared Muzio Clementi's *Gradus ad Parnassum*, with its strict, pedagogic distinction between old-and new-style brilliance, and it is almost inconceivable that Schubert was not familiar with the work. But as far as he was concerned, all this savoured of the schoolroom and of the past. His own development was uniform and unbroken.

There remains, as the final apotheosis of all Schubert's compositions for four hands, the Rondo in A major which was published a year after his death by Artaria as 'Grand Rondeau', op. 107 (IX, 13). It is like a symbol of friendship, of sympathetic co-operation to a common end; the idyllic atmosphere is scarcely, and then only briefly, disturbed by a middle-section in the manner of Weber. This Rondo says in unpretentious, Viennese language what the slow movement of the C major Symphony expresses with intense gravity and slightly *all' ongarese*. It is one of the few works of Schubert's in which one can detect the local colour which permeates his 'Deutschen' and waltzes.

An amusing offshoot of these four-handed works is the Children's March in G major, with a trio in C major (IX, 7). It was written on 12th October, 1827, for little Faust Pachler of Graz, who could naturally only manage something very elementary, while the adult player on the left-hand half of the keyboard – in this case his mother – undertook the lion's share. Faust Pachler was the small son of Schubert's hosts at Graz, the lawyer Dr. Karl Pachler and his wife Marie Leopoldine, herself an accomplished pianist, who had also met Beethoven at Vöslau in 1817. An autumn trip to the capital of Styria in company with his friend Johann Baptist Jenger had already been planned in 1826, but had to be postponed because Schubert was short of money. But the journey was eventually made in the autumn of 1827. The two friends took the mail-coach on 2nd September, and three days later heard a performance of Myerbeer's *opera seria, Il crociato in Egitto* at the Graz Theatre which, according to Anselm Hüttenbrenner, Schubert (not unsurprisingly) disliked. On the 8th, Schubert took part in a charity concert organized by the Styrian Music Society; he contributed his choruses 'Gott in der Natur' and 'Geist der Liebe', and accompanied 'Norman's Gesang' from his Scott songs. They made coach excursions into the surrounding countryside and generally speaking enjoyed themselves on their host's beer and on the light Schilcher wine which is produced on the hillsides around Graz. This lasted less than three weeks, for on the 20th the two friends took leave of their hosts and reached Vienna after a journey of four days (which Jenger has described in detail). On the 27th Schubert wrote to the Pachlers to thank them for their hospitality: 'I am already beginning to realize that I was only too happy at Graz and I cannot yet acclimatize myself to Vienna again. It is admittedly a little large, but on that account it is devoid of friendliness, sincerity, genuine thoughts, reasonable words and above all, intelligent deeds . . .' 'In Graz I soon discovered the natural and sincere way of keeping company . . .' But although at the end of his letter he expressed the hope that he would be able 'to show my gratitude in a suitable manner', Frau Pachler had to remind him to write the promised Children's March. Schubert dispatched it on 12th October with the – to us – amusing comment that it would not meet with the approval of the small recipient 'since I do not feel myself cut out for this kind of composition'. On 4th November, Dr. Karl Pachler's birthday, the little piece was given its first performance.

Another 'occasional' piece of these last years is the Allegretto in C minor – with a middle-section in A flat major – which Schubert wrote on 26th April, 1827 'as a memento for my dear friend Walcher' (XI, 12). Ferdinand Walcher, somewhat younger than Schubert and an official in the Imperial War Ministry, left on 5th May for Venice, which was then the main base of the Imperial Fleet. It is a touching little piece, of the most straightforward symbolism: after a kind of 'It must be', the melody returns, as if in consolation, in the major, implying as it were: 'It is only au-revoir'; and the middle-section speaks in even tenderer tones. If the piece were included among the Moments musicals or Impromptus, it would be universally popular.

The four piano sonatas, on the other hand, which Schu-

bert composed during the last ten months before his death
are anything but occasional works; the first, which is known
as op. 142 under the title of 'Four Impromptus', was written
in December 1827 (XI, 3), and the other three (X, 13, 14, 15)
in September 1828. It is true that the title of the first was his
own invention (in the MS. and in the letter to Schott dated
21st February, 1828) and he even agreed to separate editions
of the individual movements, probably, however, for the
simple reason that he thought that they would stand an
easier chance of being sold as 'impromptus' than as a sonata.
Schumann was not deceived when the work was subsequently published, with a dedication to Liszt:

I find it difficult to believe that Schubert really gave these
movements the title of 'Impromptus'. The first is so obviously
the first movement of a sonata, so completely developed and
finished that there can be absolutely no doubt about it. The
second Impromptu is, in my opinion, the second movement of
the same sonata; in key and character it goes hand in hand with
the first. Schubert's friends alone must know what became of the
two final movements, and whether Schubert completed the
sonata or not; one might perhaps treat the fourth movements as
the Finale, yet although the key supports this view, the carelessness of the general construction tends to contradict it. These
are therefore speculations which only a study of the original
manuscripts could resolve. ... As for the third Impromptu, I
would almost be inclined to believe that it was never written by
Schubert, or if it was, that it is a product of his boyhood. It
consists of a set of moderately or completely undistinguished
variations on an undistinguished theme. It lacks all trace of that
inventiveness and imagination which Schubert elsewhere displays
so vividly, and above all in the *genre* of the variation. So play the
first two Impromptus together, follow them with the fourth so
as to end on a lively note, and you will have, if not a complete
sonata, at least one more lovely reminder of Schubert. ... In the
first movement it is the light, fantastic ornamentation between
the lyrical moments which lulls us to sleep; the whole movement
must have been written in a passionate moment, as if in recollec-
tion of the past. The second movement is of a more contem-
plative nature, such as we find frequently in Schubert's music;
the third movement (the fourth Impromptu) is different, with
a certain sulkiness and yet a quiet charm of its own; it reminded
me constantly of Beethoven's 'Rage over a lost penny', a quite
ridiculous and little-known work.

There are some more precise details which Schumann
might have mentioned. As a sonata movement, the first

movement is unusual, since the development is *replaced* by
that 'light, fantastic ornamentation which lulls us to sleep',
and returns in the form of a quasi-coda. It is as if sonata-
form, in this the year of Beethoven's death, was tending to
return to its original binary design and to eliminate all trace
of the dramatic element. The clearest evidence, however,
that this is no separately conceived and independent piece is
the return of the first subject in the last ten bars. It cries
aloud to be carried further to a logical conclusion, a function which is met by the Allegretto in A flat major which
here takes the place of the Minuet. It is a Sarabande – an
echo of the Allegretto from Beethoven's Piano Trio, op. 70,
2, and a presage of all the romantic magic of which the
piano was later to be capable. The Finale is a Rondo in that
'late-period' form of Schubert's with which we are now familiar, with an extended middle-section, 'Allegro scherzando',
that is full of whimsical fancy not only in its melody and
harmony but also in its rhythm which makes play with the
interchange between 3/8 and 6/8. We are disappointed at
Schumann's condemnation of the slow movement – five
variations on Schubert's favourite theme with which we are
so familiar from the A minor Quartet and the *Rosamunde*
music. One could vindicate them by a comparison with
Weber's variations which the Polonaise rhythm of the second
one invites ('Polonaise', in spite of the fact that it is in
common time). But they need no vindication. They are so
sonorous, their 'virtuosity' is so artless, and they fit so
exactly into their context.

Shumann's essay on 'Schubert's last compositions' does
not tell us much about the three Piano Sonatos in C minor, A
major and B flat major of September 1828 (X, 13, 14, 15)
although they were dedicated to Schumann himself by the
publisher Diabelli. The last of these he finds

remarkable enough, impressive in a different way from his others,
by virtue of a much greater simplicity of invention, a voluntary
resignation to brilliant novelty, where elsewhere he makes such
high demands, and by the spinning out of certain general musical
ideas, instead of linking episode to episode with new threads,
as he does elsewhere. Thus it ripples along from side to side,
always lyrical, never at a loss for what is to follow next, as if it
could never come to an end. Here and there the even flow is
broken by occasional spasms of a more violent kind, which,
however, pass quickly. If my imagination seems, in this assess-

ment, to be coloured by the idea of his illness, I must leave the matter to calmer judgment.

Now in September 1828, Schubert was no more ill than usual. It was not the thought of death that disturbed him but the thought of Beethoven. He wanted to dedicate this sonata to Hummel, but he would probably not have done so, had he still been able to dedicate it to Beethoven. Who could possibly write piano sonatas in 1828 without thinking of the consummate achievements of the great master of the sonata? It is as if Schubert had felt it his historic duty to carry on this work. The scrupulous care with which he approached these three sonatas tends to bear this out, for there exist extremely interesting manuscript sketches for each of them. He begins in the manner of Beethoven in the C minor Sonata and ends in the same manner in the B flat major. But at the same time (and Schumann's delicate sense of discrimination has detected this) he returns to his own individual style, to his pre-1825 type of piano sonata, to its directness and intimacy, and to its relationship with his songs. This is most clearly noticeable in the Adagio (sic! – but is it not once again an Andante?) of the C minor Sonata, which is as closely related to the 'Andante molto' of the E flat major Sonata of 1817 (X, 7) as brother to sister: in both movements the character of the middle-section is almost completely identical. The Andantino of the A major Sonata has a direct connection song – 'Pilgerwise' (XX, 429).

*Ich bin ein Waller auf der Erde
und gehe still von Haus zu Haus . . .*

*I am a pilgrim on the earth, and pass
silently from house to house . . .

I hope no one will accuse me of suggesting that Schubert had the *text* of the song in mind, when he was writing this movement. But the key is the same, the emotion is the same, expressed in purely musical terms and contrasted and intensified by a middle-section which, in its declamatory freedom, originality and imaginative fancy, is one of the most remarkable things that Schubert ever wrote. Finally, the 'Andante sostenuto' of the B flat major Sonata, in C sharp minor or *D flat* minor, is suggestive not of illness but of farewell and transfiguration. It is the climax and apotheosis of Schubert's instrumental lyricism and of his simplicity of form. The repetition is enriched and sublimated by the material, the 'experience' of the middle-section, and in a particularly lovely manner here by virtue of the consoling sincerity of this middle-section.

The criticism which it is fashionable to level against the first movements of these three sonatas ceases to be valid when one realizes that Schubert did not want to write a development and attached no importance to such a section. In the C minor Sonata, he begins in the heroic manner of Beethoven, introduces the second subject in the normal relative key, and even begins the development as if it were meant to provide a dramatic solution. But it trickles away into an agitated, chromatic *pianissimo* section which leads back by way of a short crescendo to the heightened energy of the recapitulation. In the A major Sonata everything that could be called 'development' finds its way into the exposition, and in place of the development proper Schubert spins a dreamy, ballad-like web of sound, the very existence of which is its own best justification. The first movement of the last sonata is again cast in a completely different mould. It has a song-like theme, and this theme originates from the depths of the Mignon songs. If the reader compares it with the first version of 'So lasst mich scheinen, bis ich werde' (XX, 395), he will appreciate this, in spite of the difference of key. Schubert first treats it in exactly the same way as the first movement of the four Impromptus, op. 90. That is to say, he carries the melody into the realm of emotional, eloquent modulations, particularly in the 'development', but provides it with contrasts from the same emotional range of heartfelt, 'virginal' hesitation. Of the three dance-movements, all of which are in the main key of their respective sonatas, the first is a Minuet, the other two Scherzos. The most delicate is that of the B flat major Sonata, 'vivace con delicatezza', which moves in a completely unreal world, the unreality of which is only emphasized by the comparative harshness of the Trio.

Of the three Finales, that of the C minor Sonata is a Tarantella in extended rondo-form, with lyrical and emotional episodes in dance-style; and the last in B flat major is an echo of Beethoven – of the movement with which the latter replaced the original Finale of the B flat major Quartet, op. 130. Schubert, therefore, was familiar with this. It is easy to prove that his movement lacks Beethoven's degree of logic and concentration. Nor is it cast in that rondo-form for which Schubert showed such a strong predilection from the G major Sonata, op. 78, onwards, but combines it with what is this time a genuine sonata-form development. The finest of these Finales is that of the A major Sonata. Its relation to the song 'Im Frühling' (XX, 497)

> *Still sitz'ich an des Hügels Hang,*
> *Der Himmel ist so klar....**

is so obvious that one need not quote the two examples. On the other hand it is the fulfilment of that genial music-making for which Haydn or Beethoven (in the Finale of the G major Sonata, op, 31, 1) created the prototype. In Schubert's hands this geniality is transformed into utter happiness and we would willingly forgo the final *coup,* the return to the first movement in the last bars.

These three or four piano sonatas, however, are not Schubert's last word as a piano composer. He had his final say in the short pieces of his last years which he wrote and which were published in part by the publishers Haslinger, Diabelli and Leidesdorf, under the title of Impromptus or Moments musicals. It is easy to understand why they are his 'last word'. For he was an inventive spirit, a composer of the spontaneous, striking inspiration, and not one, like Haydn or Beethoven, who could fashion something great out of a trivial idea. It is, *mutatis mutandis*, the same relationship as that of the volatile Verdi to Richard Wagner, the strategist in the field of developing and combining musical motives. And perhaps Schubert himself recognized that the three

* Silent I sit upon the hillside, the sky is so clear ...

piano pieces of May 1828 (XI, 13) in E flat minor, E flat major and C major fell short of these exacting requirements, since he did not publish them, although they were written with an eye to their being more readily acceptable than sonatas to a publisher such as Probst. The three pieces certainly belong together. The middle one, in E flat major, possibly provides the key. It is typically *all' italiana*, a somewhat love-sick Venetian cavatina, with two episodes or Trios which both lack what I call the 'microcosm' of a work, in that they are too monotonous. The first, in E flat minor, is *alla francese*, as evidenced by the middle-section which is a typical Romance in the style of Kreutzer or Rode. Originally it had a second middle-section in A flat – an Andantino, also *molto alla francese*.

The last piece is *all' ongarese*, similarly with a middle-section which this time is too broad and empty, and with a rather noisy coda.

The Schubert of the perfect lyrical piano-piece appears in the ten numbers which were published, partly during his lifetime and partly after his death, as 'Impromptus', op. 90 (XI, 2; only Nos, 1 and 2 during his lifetime) and 'Moments musicals', op. 94 (XI, 4). They have no connection whatever with Beethoven's 'Bagatelles'. The Bagatelles were genuine by-products, musical ideas, often consisting of only a few bars. They are comparable with the sketches of a great painter, fully executed and unmistakable in their individuality, like a drawing of Michelangelo's or Rembrandt's, yet capable of development. In Schubert's Impromptu or Moment musical there is nothing sketchy. Each must be simple in form, yet with every detail filled in – the 'microcosm' is all-important. As Willi Kahl has pointed out in *Archiv für Musikwissenshaft*, III (1921), Schubert was not the creator of this form; it was not, so to speak, an 'original' of his. His predecessors were Wenzel Joh. Tomaschek (born 1774), whose name had already appeared with Schubert's in 1821 in the announcement of an almanac; and Tomaschek's countryman Joh. Hugo Worzischek (born 1791) who was similarly represented along with Schubert in a collection of German Dances which was published in the New Year of 1823. Previous to 1827 Tomaschek had written eight volumes of 'Eclogues', 'Rhapsodies', and 'Dithyrambs', and the title of 'Impromptus' had already appeared in 1822 in the op. 7 of Worzischek, who lived in Vienna from 1813 onwards and died there in 1825. This title was current not only in Prague or Vienna (for example in Capek's 'Impromptu brilliant', op. 6 of 1826) but also, since the end of 1822, in the Germany of the post-Weber school (in Heinrich Marschner's op. 22 and 23, for example). Even Weber himself wrote a 'Momento capriccioso'.

It can be clearly proved that Schubert was familiar at least with the Viennese publications in this *genre*. But he or his publishers adopted only the names. Is not the E flat major Andante from the Sonata in A flat major of 1817 (X, 3) already the most perfect Impromptu? And if anyone chose to explain or characterize the Moment musical in C sharp minor, No. 4, by quoting certain Preludes from the *Well-tempered Clavier* as a model, is it not equally true that the middle-section of this same E flat major Andante was already completely in the manner of Bach? Was not the 'Air russe', which Schubert included in his Moments musicals, written in the year 1823? It is their deeper, Schubertian originality which distinguishes these pieces. The first C major revolves around the note G as its focal-point which, as it were, flings open the door *fortissimo* to the development of a single, barely contrasted musical idea, and closes it again *pianissimo* – a development full of the most moving modulations and of spontaneous, even faintly contrapuntal surprises. The second would be somewhat in the nature of an *étude*, if it were not also full of poetry and if it did not contain a pounding middle-section *all' ongarese*. The third in G flat major (transposed into G major by the publisher) gives voice to that inner lyricism for which Schubert found similar expression in so many of his mystical or 'cosmic' songs. It is a pre-Mendelssohn 'Song without Words'. The last, in A flat major, is a variant of the second, but the last remnant of its *étude* character has vanished in the 'cello melody of the main-section and in the elegiac character of the Trio (C sharp minor).

We have already spoken of the 'Air russe', No. 3, of the 'Moments', op. 94 – a musical epigram or 'Divertissement en miniature'. No. 6, an Allegretto in A flat major, is also of an earlier origin (1825) and was published by Sauer and Leidesdorf in one of their collected volumes. It is a variant of the 'Sarabande' from op. 142, only more poignant and more deeply overshadowed by suffering; it could well be a Minuet from an unwritten sonata. The violent outburst of No. 5 in F minor contrasts with the gentleness of the A flat major Andantino, No. 2. The minuet-like C major of No. 1, which could be a counterpart to the Minuet of the A minor String Quartet, is contrasted with the dark and savage C sharp minor of No. 4, perhaps the most original of all, in spite of the alleged, and indeed possible, influence of Bach.

We will confine ourselves to a brief mention of the Dances of these last years – the twelve 'Graz Waltzes', op. 91, which were written, as their title suggests, at Graz, and which have a distinct uniformity even down to the key-plan (XII, 7), and the twenty 'Last Waltzes' published as op. 127 (XII, 8), which also include a number of waltzes dating from the year 1815. In the same category as the Graz Waltzes is the spirited 'Graz Gallop' in C major (XII, 24), published without an opus-number in a collection of seventeen 'Favourite or Popular Gallops', in which Johann Strauss, senior, and Josef Lanner were represented. Lanner and Strauss carried on Schubert's 'Viennese tradition' – a tiny, though the most popular, element in his character.

The jump from these smaller and occasional works to the two great intrumental works of the year 1828 – the last Symphony and the String Quintet – could not be greater. We do not know whether the symphony continued the train of ideas which Schubert had set in motion in the lost 'Gastein' symphony, or whether it marks the beginning of a new development. The Quintet, however, is linked not with the 'lighter' chamber-music works with piano which the year 1827 produced – the Trio op. 100 and the virtuoso Duos – but with the two string quartets of 1826. Here, too, as in the three piano sonatas of September, it is as if Schubert had been encouraged by Beethoven's death to embark upon a rivalry from which he had shrunk during the lifetime of the man whom he had held in such awe and reverence. And it was not a quartet that he wrote, but a quintet – a class of chamber-music to which Beethoven contributed only a few, early examples, op. 4 of 1795 and op. 29 of 1801. The former was an arrangement of an octet, and even if Schubert happened to have known it, it could not have made any impression on him. As for op. 29, he adopted the key, but not the instrumental combination, for he used two 'cellos instead of two violas. Whether he had a model for it, and if so, what that model was is a matter for conjecture. It cannot have been Boccherini, for the 'alto violoncello' in the latter's quintets is nothing more than a viola; it was much more probably one of George Onslow's quintets.

We are breaking the chronological sequence by considering the Quintet (IV, 1) first, for it was written during August and September and therefore *after* the Symphony which was begun in March. On 2nd October he offered it to Probst and mentioned that it had not yet been tried out; it is doubtful whether, in fact, he lived to hear it. Probst naturally did not accept the offer; the work was not published until 1853 or 1854, and then by Spina as op. 163.

It is a work *sui generis*. It may well be that Schubert did in fact embark upon it, because he no longer had cause to fear the critical presence of Beethoven; but the first movement, at least, contains much more than 'C major elements' of Beethoven and Mozart – from the Quintet (K. 515), for example, the 'Jupiter' Symphony, and the Quartet from op. 10, from which the development section as a whole and the virile, pugnacious figure after the first *fortissimo* are derived. When, during the recapitulation, the first violin 'quickens' the main theme with its 'figure', we are at once reminded of the beginning of Mozart's Quintet. But that is the sum total of Schubert's dependence on or connection with the past in this work. Even if the three following movements were not so incomparably Schubertian, this Quintet is so orchestral in conception and feeling that it scarcely comes within the scope of chamber-music. The second 'cello is treated quite differently from the first. It has essentially a 'supporting' function, and this again suggests the influence of Onslow, who replaces the 'cello by a double-bass in some of his quintets. I have always felt that with a 'single' instrumental combination the weight of tone is unbalanced, and have longed to hear the work played by a 'double' string quartet with a double-bass in place of the present second 'cello. The clearest indication of the orchestral character is to be found in the tempestuous Scherzo with its 'horn' fifths and sheer exuberance of sound. The Trio certainly provides an extreme contrast: D flat major as against C major, Andante sostenuto as

against Presto, common time as against 3/4, and all five
instruments pitched in so low a register that one might well
imagine that the two violins had been replaced by violas. A
new meaning is given to the conception of a 'Trio' with the
contrast between unison passages in recitative style and harmony full of suspensions like a moment of thoughtful con-
templation. And this time Schubert does not write an
Andante but a sonorous, lyrical Adagio, in E major, once
again with a strong contrast of key (F minor) and dynamics,
a contrast of that spontaneous passion rooted in mystery,
which elsewhere he avoids. A tremor of this passion lingers
on into the repetition of the lyrical section and stirs once
again in the moving coda. The Finale reverts to a mood of
rollicking informality and recalls the Finale of the youthful
C major String Quartet, which was so natural and so carefree. It is as if two congenial spirits were strolling together,
and as they walk they interrupt each other to point out new
and enchanting beauties around them, or to draw each
other's attention to strange, mysterious things. Schubert
could surpass his C major Symphony only by this unique,
unsurpassable work.

The history of the C major Symphony (I, 7) is well-known.
When Robert Schumann moved to Vienna in the autumn of
1838 in the naïve hope of finding there a more fruitful
milieu for himself and his art than his own native Germany,
he not only visited Schubert's grave, but also Schubert's
brother Ferdinand. And it was in the latter's house, at the
beginning of 1839 – or to be more precise, on 1st January –
that he discovered this symphony among 'a fabulous pile' of
manuscripts.

Who knows how long it would have lain neglected there in
dust and darkness, had I not immediately arranged with Ferdinand Schubert to send it to the management of the Gewandhaus
concerts in Leipzig, or to the artist himself who conducts them
[Mendelssohn]. . . . The symphony reached Leipzig, where it
was performed, its greatness recognized, performed again and
received with delighted and almost universal admiration. The
enterprising publishing firm of Breitkopf and Härtel bought the
work and the copyright, and thus the orchestral parts are now
available to us, soon perhaps to be followed by the full score,
for the benefit and enjoyment of the whole world.

The publication of the score hung fire, however, and it did

not appear until 1849 or 1850. And the 'almost' universal admiration was true only of Leipzig. Schubert himself had submitted the symphony to the Vienna Philharmonic Society shortly after completing it, but when it was declined on the grounds that it was 'too long and difficult' Schubert offered in its place his early C major Symphony which, as a matter of interest, was not performed until after his death either. At first Paris and London also found the work 'too long and difficult'; on the first of these occasions (1842) the orchestra of the illustrious London Philharmonic Society covered itself with as little glory as Habeneck's Paris orchestra which, during the rehearsal of the work in 1844, refused to go any further than the first movement. Mendelssohn had a great affection for the work and conducted it on two further occasions after 21st March, 1839; and on 15th December, 1839, the Vienna Philharmonic condescended to play the first two movements, although not without inserting an aria from Donizetti's *Lucia di Lammermoor* between them. After this performance the critic of Castelli's *Allgemeine Musikalische Anzeiger* wrote: 'The two movements of the Symphony certainly left no one in no doubt as to the composer's thorough grounding in the art of composition, but Schubert seemed to be unable fully to succeed with tonal masses. The result was a kind of skirmish of instruments, out of which no effectual pattern emerged. True, a red thread ran through the whole, but it was too pink for one to detect it correctly. In my opinion it would have been better to have left the work strictly alone.' Posterity will never discover how the author of this review could discover even a pink thread running through the whole of a work of which he only knew half.

As regards Schumann's celebrated review, posterity has concentrated on one quotation in particular – the reference to the 'heavenly lengths' – and has quite misunderstood it, for Schumann used the phrase in a completely non-critical sense. But Schumann had something much profounder to say on the subject of the great C major Symphony. 'Deep down in this symphony there lies more than mere song, more than mere joy and sorrow, as already expressed in music in a hundred other instances; it transports us into a world where we cannot recall ever having been before.' We today can recall that world, however; it exists in Schubert's own music, at the beginning of his D major Symphony, and the similarity between it and the beginning of this symphony is still more marked when we remember that its first subject was originally constructed purely on the notes of a common chord.

What Schumann meant was that the work is not eloquent. It is not an expression of Schubert's personality in the way that Beethoven's Fifth Symphony, for example, was an expression of Beethoven's personality. It is neither rhetorical nor heroic. Schumann rightly emphasized the 'masculine origin' of this symphony and its complete independence from those of Beethoven. It is as if Schubert had not known of the existence of Beethoven's Ninth with its final eruption into vocal utterance nor of the humorous and archaistic Eighth. Schubert is here still living or living again in that paradise of pure music-making from which Beethoven had been driven forth. He is as unaffected by the emotionalism of the works of Beethoven's 'middle' period as by the latter's moving attempt to conquer this emotionalism and to speak a sublimer, more spiritual language.

For us who do not know the 'Gmunden-Gastein' Symphony, the C major Symphony represents a return to the Symphony in E major, by-passing on the way the 'Unfinished', which is a work *sui generis*. The orchestral combination which it uses is similar, including the trio of trombones; indeed, it is somewhat simpler, since Schubert here dispenses with one of the two pairs of horns. The same insistent urge towards physical unity prevails, and the degree of concentration is greater (the phrase 'heavenly lengths' can really be applied only in the most superficial sense). There is evidence of this not only in the linking of the 'mysteriously veiled' introduction to the first movement by means of the theme which first expresses itself in such mystical language on the trombone – how important a part is played in this work by the interval of a third, either in its pure form or linked by the intermediate note! – but also in the simple key-relationship of the individual movements (A minor for the Andante, C major for the Scherzo). How simple and direct it all is – the transition to the second subject in E minor (in the Quintet it becomes A flat major), the quiet passage leading to the recapitulation, the contrast between thematic and 'lyrical' treatment in the Scherzo and Trio, the daemonic energy of the Finale! Scherzo and Finale are clearly linked

by the four-note figure which later achieves its apotheosis in
the Finale, where it transforms the daemonic energy into a
grandiose climax, into the terrible and menacing utterance
of the Commendatore in *Don Giovanni*. As for the Andante
all' ongarese, one cannot improve on Schumann's lovely description – the elementary interchange between minor and
major, between rhythmic undercurrent and lyricism, the
'poignant voices', the passage 'where a horn calls as if from
the distance, and all is hushed, as if a heavenly visitant were
moving gently among the orchestra'. Even this 'Andante con
moto' does not sound entirely new to us; it goes back to an
early type of movement which is most clearly illustrated
perhaps in a fragmentary Allegretto in C minor for piano
(XXI, 13), in much the same way that the anonymous
character of the first movement is illustrated in the early D
major Symphony and in many of his overtures. How far this
symphony points into the future beyond the whole Romantic period; how 'modern' it is!

During his last years Schubert took a renewed interest in
church music, stimulated perhaps by the publication (as op.
48) and performance of his C major Mass of 1816 in the
autumn of 1825, but quite certainly by a spiritual urge, too.
It was an artistic rather than a religious urge, for in the Mass
it was possible to say things and introduce artistic devices
which were denied to other fields, including opera. At the
same time, other influences were at work. Besides the masterpiece of this period, the Mass in E flat major, there are a
number of secondary works which were the outcome of
purely external circumstances. Among them are the
'Gesänge zur Feier des Heiligen Opfers der Messe nebst
einem Anhange: Das Gebet des Herren' (XIII, 7; 1826), for
which Schubert received a hundred gulden from the author
of the text, Joh. Phil. Neumann. Neumann, Professor of
Physics at the Polytechnic Institute, had already been associated with Schubert in 1820 in a joint plan for an opera based
on Kalidasa's Indian drama *Sakuntala* which, however, got
no further than the sketching of two acts of the libretto.
Neumann was a disciple of the eighteenth-century Rational-
ist school, and of the movement to popularize church music –
the same movement to which Mozart had earlier contributed
his two Church Songs, K. 343, at the request of his employer,

Archbishop Colloredo, or Michael Haydn his *Deutsche Messe* of 1782. Schubert's 'Gesänge' consist of eight numbers and an 'epilogue', which correspond to the *Kyrie, Gloria, Evangelium and Credo, Offertorium, Sanctus, Benedictus, Agnus Dei* and *Amen*; the 'epilogue' corresponds to the *Paternoster*. The whole poem is treated in the manner of a song, each section varying from two to four stanzas, and Schubert duly set it in homophonic song-form for mixed chorus and wind orchestra, with short postludes after the majority of the numbers. Once again there are occasional phrases which recall *Die Zauberflöte*. We do not know Schubert's opinion of attempts like these to popularize or 'humanize' the church ritual. The Viennese consistory at any rate showed both a degree of humanism and good taste in permitting the publication and distribution of the work, although not, of course, for liturgical use.

A very similar work is the setting of the Hebrew text of the 92nd Psalm, for baritone-solo and mixed chorus, which Schubert wrote in July 1828 for the chief Cantor, Salomon Sulzer. Sulzer was also a reformer of Jewish religious singing – intent (to quote the entry under his name in Schilling's *Universal-Lexicon der Tonkunst* of 1838) 'upon organizing a ritual of divine worship re-animated by the conceptions of true religiousness and the spirit of the times, or rather, upon creating such a ritual for the first time. It is to the particular and lasting credit of the esteemed Cantor that, in his pursuit of this object, he contrived to enlist the aid of the foremost composers in the Imperial city, and their valuable contributions redound to the enviable honour of the literature of choral music'. Without a doubt the most enviable is Schubert's contribution. It is a simple setting, consisting of an antiphonal exchange between individual voices and the combined chorus, with, as a matter of course, a solo for the distinguished Cantor's own baritone in the middle-section, and a few 'quasi-oriental' flourishes. Schubert must have been familiar with Jewish singing, although the work could not have been written without Sulzer's help and advice in the matter of correct declamation. It certainly cannot have been this pure and beautiful piece that Liszt had in mind when he, or rather Princess Sayn-Wittgenstein, described in a hideous spate of words a service conducted by Sulzer (in *Die Zigeuner und ihre Musik*). If the reader is further interested in the

matter, he will find information in Sulzer's foreword to the
first volume of his *Schir Zion* and Birnbaum's (a pupil of
Sulzer's) account of the incident in the library of the
Hebrew Union College in Cincinnati and also in the records
of the Vienna Kultusgemeinde.*

The setting of A. Schmidl's 'Hymne an den Heiligen
Geist', for two four-part male-voice choruses, is not church
music, but religious music in exactly the same sense as the
Neumann 'Mass' hymns. Schubert wrote it in May 1828
(XVI, 42) and added a wind-orchestra accompaniment in the
following October, together with minor alterations to the
score and even to the text. It is a powerful work in its interchange between soloists and chorus and in the close interplay
of the two alternating choruses. And even if a certain amount
of 'choral society' influence manages to creep in, as for
example the 'conspirator-bass' in the second part ('Verlass
auf unserm Pfad uns nicht'), at least the ecstatic close, dying
away to nothing, is not designed for effect.

The greatest and most important of the church works of
these last years is, of course, the Mass in E flat major (XIII,
6) started in June and finished in July, between the C major
Symphony and the String Quintet. It is a dualistic work, and
we know nothing of the circumstances which led Schubert to
write it. Could it have been that he wanted, some three years
after the application for a post which he had made in April
1825, to pave the way for a new one by adding to his tally of
church music? Joseph Eybler, who had succeeded Salieri as
Chief Court Director of Music, was then sixty-three years
old (actually he survived Schubert by nearly twenty years)
and his assistant, Joseph Weigl, was not much younger. Such
'practical considerations' would explain some of the conventionalities of the E flat Mass. Unlike the Mass in A flat
major, the key sequence of the various movements of this
work (in the conventional E flat) is quite normal: *Kyrie,
Credo* and *Sanctus* are in the main key; the *Agnus Dei*
begins, according to tradition, in the relative minor (C
minor); the *Gloria* is in B flat major, and the key relation-
ships within the individual movements are perfectly simple
and straightforward. The use of counterpoint always occurs
in the traditional and proper place. In this respect Schubert

* For this information I am indebted to Dr. Eric Werner, Professor of
Jewish Music in Cincinnati.

obviously wanted to avoid giving any offence.

On the other hand he was incapable of keeping his passionate feelings and his imagination completely in check. In the case of this Mass, too, he would have had to wait a long time for it to be performed and generally accepted. It was only a sense of piety and the high regard in which his late brother was held that made it possible for Ferdinand Schubert to arrange a performance of the work at the Parish Church of Mary the Comforter on 15th November, 1829. On 20th March, 1830, the Vienna critic of the *Berliner Allgemeine Musikzeitung* wrote as follows:

> The most recent work in the field of church-music was a posthumous Mass by Franz Schubert, two public performances of which have already been given by the composer's brother. Even though the actual performance cannot be described as having been successful, it is none the less just possible that an absolutely perfect rendering of the work might produce a lasting impression. It almost seems as if the prospect of death lay heavy on the late master's heart and mind, while he was engaged upon this Mass.

It was no Berliner, but a Viennese who had the temerity to write such impudent nonsense.

It is perfectly true that, when he departed from the 'traditional' approach, Schubert did not make the contemporary critics' task particularly easy. From the point of view of style, the Mass is very new. It is a choral Mass. There is admittedly a constant interchange between soloists and chorus, but at no point does a soloist predominate, not even in the 'Christe' section of the tender yet earnest *Kyrie*. In the most important and, from the composer's point of view, difficult movements of the *Gloria* and the *Credo*, everything is expressed with a pregnant and concentrated terseness. The old distinction between the *Missa Solemnis* (or *Missa Lunga*) and the *Missa Brevis* has completely vanished. In the *Gloria*, Schubert repeats the opening section after the 'Gratias', and also uses the same music for the 'Quoniam' so that these three pillars support only the two musical arches of the 'Gratias' and the 'Domine Deus'. The 'Gratias' is divided between the upper and lower voices of the chorus and forms no more than a delicate contrast to the more substantial paean ('Allegro moderato e maestoso') of the 'Gloria', with its soaring figure on the violins. In the 'Domine Deus' there

is admittedly a change of time and key, and it is one of the
boldest and at the same time one of the most genuinely
'spiritual' movements which has ever been written for a
Mass. A 'liturgical', though undoubtedly spontaneous,
melody on the trombones gives it its spiritual, one might
almost say Gregorian, colouring. But simultaneously there
rises in the chorus and on the strings an agitated episode, full
of the most expressive harmony – 'Agnus Dei, qui tollis pec-
cata mundi, miserere nobis!' For the fugue, Schubert uses
the same 'Magnificat' subject which Bach developed in the E
major Fugue of the *Well-tempered Clavier, Book II*. He
treats it chromatically and introduces three *stretti*, each separated from the next by a progressively shorter interval.
Both here and in the 'Et vitam' fugue of the *Credo* and in the
joyful neutrality of the 'Hosanna' in the *Sanctus*, his mind
was unfortunately a little too intent upon the Emperor
Franz and his musical advisers. It is in these sections that the
dualism of the work lies. In every other respect the *Credo* is
a masterly movement with its rapid change of expression
and its stability of form, underlined by the return of a drum-
roll which ushers in the quiet solemnity of the central idea.
Even in this, the longest movement of the Mass, there is only
a *single* episode, the 'Et incarnatus' (A flat major, 12/8), a
Rondo in canon-form for the solo soprano and two solo
tenors, into which is woven the deeply emotional, even explosive, 'Crucifixus'. In the *Sanctus* there is the traditional
thrice-repeated cry, rising each time to a self-contained
climax. The *Benedictus* is a melodious Andante in A flat
major, with wonderful responses from the wind instruments.
(Here, incidentally, is another difference from the Mass in A
flat, for the flute is omitted throughout). The most remarkable movement is the *Agnus Dei*. Schubert uses, as his chief
material, a double theme, one part of which is identical with
the subject of Bach's C sharp minor Fugue from the *Well-
tempered Clavier, Book I*, and with the main theme of his
own 'Doppelgänger'. 'Der Doppelgänger' was written in
August, and consequently here is the one single instance
where Schubert took an idea originally developed on broad
symphonic lines and subsequently concentrated it into the
narrower compass of a song.

In addition to these spiritual and religious works there is a
number of 'secular' choral works of every type, for male or

female-voice chorus, with or without accompaniment. They
are of considerable significance, despite the fact that they are
scarcely known today. The most effective of them is the
setting of Klopstock's 'Schlachtlied' – Schubert himself
called it 'Schlachtgesang' – as a double-chorus for eight
men's voices (XVI, 28). It is the martial counterpart to the
above-mentioned setting of A. Schmidl's 'Hymne an den
Heiligen Geist' of May (or October) 1828, except that Schubert dispenses completely with the interplay between soloists
and chorus. I do not know what led him to set the old bard's
piously heroic triplets to music, on 28th February, 1827,
some sixty years after they were originally written. There
was certainly – and happily – no martial occasion for him to
do so in the Austria of Metternich's day. At any rate he
thought highly enough of the chorus to end his public concert of March 1828 with it; it was probably performed by
members of the Philharmonic Society. This time the choral
forces cannot be too strong, and the rousing and stirring
effect is assured. It is at its most marked when the two choruses join forces after every second verse or sing in unison;
the martial rhythm, and the triumphant cadences are maintained from beginning to end. After the concert, the critic of
the *Leipziger Allgemeine Musikalische Zeitung* expressed
himself in the following complimentary terms: '... conceived with genuinely Germanic power and a faithful
reflection of the august bard's sublime words'.

A work which appeals to us more today, because it is not
martial but 'Romantics', is the choral setting of J. G. Seidl's
'Nachthelle' (XVI, 13), which Schubert wrote in September
1826 for a 'damnably high tenor' (Walcher's letter of 25th
January, 1827), four-part male-voice chorus and piano. It
was performed on 25th January, 1828, by Herr Tietze and
chorus at a social evening of the Society of the Friends of
Music. It is a charming antiphonal Nocturne, with a passionate emotional outburst, and the piano paints the setting, the
twinkling of the stars, with chords in the upper octaves. A
little later, in July 1827, Schubert wrote a similar and still
lovelier piece – the 'Ständchen', which was sung by
Fräulein Josephine Fröhlich and the lady-pupils of the
Conservatoire at his concert of March 1828. There is a story
attached to it. Louise Gosmar, one of Anna Fröhlich's
pupils, had asked Franz Grillparzer to write a poem for a

serenade in honour of her birthday, and Anna invited Schubert to set it to music. Schubert accepted the invitation and immediately wrote a setting for contralto solo, men's voices and piano (XVI, 14), which prompted Anna to remind him that she only had young ladies' voices at her disposal and not tenors and basses; whereupon Schubert rewrote the chorus for sopranos and contraltos (XVIII, 4). On 11th August, 1827, Louise Gosmar's birthday, the serenade was sung for the first time in the garden of the Langs' house at Döbling; it was performed in public on 24th January, 1828, at an evening concert of the Philharmonic Society. Schubert had to be fetched from an ale-house to listen to it, and the story goes that after the performance he said to Anna Fröhlich: 'Really, you know, I never realized it was so beautiful.'

And beautiful indeed it is. The original version is the lovelier of the two, for the deep voice of the contralto – much more delicately suited to the lover's role than a tenor – hovers above the men's voices like a star above gently ruffled water. The chorus of women's voices must sing with great restraint in order not to mask it. But the magic of the piece cannot be destroyed, except if it is sung by boys' voices. This magic lies in the exquisite, eloquent modulation, in the calm and delicacy of the vocal line of the solo-part which the supporting chorus echoes now gently, now with a sense of urgency. And the farewell, uttered in the softest of pianissimos, reveals a certain quiet sense of humour. We are at once enchanted and amused.

The more robust counterpart to this heavenly work is 'Mirjams Siegesgesang' (XVII, 9) – likewise a setting of Grillparzer's words, for soprano solo (actually a mezzo-soprano), mixed chorus and piano, and written in March 1828. It describes in ecstatic retrospect the destruction of Pharaoh and his cavalry, and could equally well be called a large-scale cantata or a short oratorio. It consists of several episodes which are contained within a musical framework, with the soprano leading, the chorus following and written throughout in *alfresco* style. The piano accompaniment cries aloud for orchestration – trumpets and side-drums, for example, in the very first bar; and this orchestration, which Schubert undoubtedly planned for a later and more suitable occasion, was in fact subsequently carried out by his friend Franz Lachner. The work is unmistakably modelled on

Handel, and yet everything is so spontaneous and fresh that one is utterly charmed by the imitation, even in the somewhat too 'elementary' final fugue.

It is another great step (and a step downwards at that) from these pieces to the comic terzet – 'Der Hochzeitsbraten' (XIX, 2) – with words by Schober, which Schubert wrote in November 1827 to amuse his friends, and which was probably performed as a 'grand Finale' on the occasion of the last Schubertiad at Spaun's house on 28th January, 1828 – which ended hilariously 'with practically everyone present drunk'. This terzet has a curious history. An obscure musician named Anton Fischer (1778–1808), who had moved to Vienna from Bavarian Swabia in 1798, had published in 1805 a comic terzet entitled 'Die Advocaten', for two tenors and a bass with piano accompaniment. The young Schubert copied it out at the end of 1812, and it was probably performed early in 1813 at his father's house. A second, slightly altered copy found its way into the hands of a friend, 'perhaps Joseph Hüttenbrenner' (O. E. Deutsch, op. cit., p. 644), and was published under Schubert's name in May 1827 – in other words, while he was still alive. Apparently this was done with his tacit agreement, even though it is a completely worthless and absurd piece (XIX, 1). Yet six months later he himself tried his hand at this *genre* with 'Der Hochzeitsbraten' and even offered the piece to Schott for publication along with his great quartets and one of the piano trios, emphasizing at the same time that 'it had been successfully performed'. It was published posthumously as op. 104. The 'plot' is simple. The betrothed couple, Therese and Theobald, need a cheap joint of meat for their wedding celebrations the following day, and although the bride is at first nervous of the idea, she nevertheless acts as beater when her fiancé goes out poaching. But the huntsman Caspar watches the pair, and hears – like us – the fateful shot. Emerging from his hiding place, he threatens them with prison and the penitentiary. But eventually he relents and accepts an invitation to the wedding-feast, with the idea of filling the bill of bridegroom rather than guest. The model for this kind of banality à la Dittersdorf and Weigl was Mozart's 'Ständchen' (K. 441c) which was published, also by Schott, in 1810, and was frequently printed under Haydn's name; Mozart kept trivialities like this strictly to himself. The prettiest thing in this 'Hochzeitsbraten' is the minuet-like song of rejoicing at the end, in which the betrothed couple sing a yodelling-song and the huntsman joins in derisively, while adding his private observations in recitative.

During these last years there are 'detours' and one purely 'occasional' work even in the field of song, in which Schubert was so completely himself and made so few compromises. This work is the 'Drei Gesänge von Metastasio' which he composed for the singer Luigi Lablache and dedicated to him when it was published as op. 83 in 1827 (XX, 579–81). Lablache, who was born in Naples three years before Schubert, was certainly the most celebrated bass of his day. He was at that time singing at the Kärntnertor Theatre, and we are told that Schubert made his acquaintance at Kiesewetter's house. Lablache also frequented the company of Frau v. Laszny (where he is said to have taken the second bass part in Schubert's 'Gondelfahrer' on one occasion), and of Giannatasio del Rio, where *Der häusliche Krieg* was performed with piano accompaniment (O. E. Deutsch, op. cit., p. 667). Of these three songs only two, incidentally, were actually written by Metastasio – 'L'incanto degli occhi' and 'Il traditor deluso'. The latter is from *Gioas re di Guida* where, however, it is put into the mouth of a woman and not a gallant, as in Schubert's setting. The text of the third, 'Il modo di prender moglie' is the work of an unknown poet, and can only have been written after 1817, since it is designed exactly after the model of Figaro's first aria in Rossini's *Barbiere*. It was purely Schubert's admiration for Lablache's qualities, for the sweetness and range of his voice, the ease with which he could alter his register, and his universality, that led him to compose these three songs. For the first aria is lyrical, the second – in the form of a recitative and aria – runs the whole gamut of the emotions, and the third, an imitation of 'Largo al factotum' from a musical point of view, too, even down to the 6/8 time, is a *buffo* scene in the grand manner. The style throughout is distinctly Italian, but without a single trace of exaggeration or parody. This group of songs is the last and most significant proof of Schubert's lack of 'national' prejudice – Weber could never have written anything similar –and of his genuine affection for *bel canto*.

The 'detours' are two songs in *concertante* style. The first is a setting of L. Rellstab's poem 'Auf dem Strom' for tenor and French horn in E (XX, 568; March 1828) which without a doubt was written expressly for Schubert's celebrated concert, at which it was performed by Herren Tietze and Lewy. The other is 'Der Hirt auf dem Felsen', based on Wilhelm Müller's poem 'Der Berghirt', for soprano and clarinet (XX, 569), which was composed in October 1828 and published posthumously as op. 129. It was written as a concert-piece for Anna Milder, who sang it for the first time in Riga in March 1830. 'Auf dem Strom' is what the Italians would call a 'Partenza', a song of farewell, and an attempt to see how far a simple three-stanza song was capable of treatment in an Italian style, with its echoes and interludes for horn and piano. If any of Schubert's songs was influenced by the spirit and 'sentiment' of Beethoven's *An die ferne Geliebte*, it was this one. It is significant of the closely-woven combination of voice-part, piano and horn that the horn provides the basis for the final chord. 'Der Hirt auf dem Felsen' resembles more closely a *scena* in *concertante* style. Schubert supports the fiction, at least at the beginning, that the wistful and rather melancholy singer, in his solitude, plays the interludes upon a shawm. The rejoicing at the coming of spring, with which the monologue ends, assumes the character of a duet. The charm of the song lies in its naturalness. In both pieces the piano is relegated to a purely primitive accompanying role which is quite alien to Schubert's genuine songs.

Schubert's 'genuine songs' found their culminating point during these last years in a new cycle with poems by Wilhelm Müller. This was *Die Winterreise*, consisting of twenty-four songs in two parts, the first written in February and the second in October 1827; the former published in January 1828, and the latter, posthumously, at the end of the following December. In the interval the poet had also died at an early age. Spaun has told us that during his illness, Schubert spent his last conscious moments correcting the proofs of the second part. And Mayrhofer took the writing of this cycle as proof that Schubert's mood became much more melancholy during his latter years. Schubert, he said, had been seriously ill for a long time, he had experienced much disillusionment and life had lost its brightness. For him, winter had come. The irony of the poet, rooted in despair, appealed to him, and he gave poignant expression to it. During the conception and writing of the cycle he seems to have been depressed and reserved, and Spaun begged Schubert to tell him the reason. 'You will soon hear and understand why,' Schubert is said to have replied. Later he invited Spaun to come to Schober's house where he was going to sing 'a cycle of terrifying songs'. 'I am curious to hear your reaction to them. They have affected me more deeply than has been the case with any other songs.' And when, during the performance, his friends found them difficult to understand and Schober confessed that only 'Der Lindenbaum' really appealed to him, Schubert replied that these songs gave him more pleasure than all his others, 'and they will one day give you pleasure too'.

It betrays a certain lack of familiarity with the process of creative activity to imagine that it was simply the poetic content of these songs which 'affected' Schubert. They naturally moved him profoundly, otherwise he would never have set them to music; they exactly matched his condition and his mood. But what affected him much more closely was the problem of their exhaustive interpretation. His remark referred only to their artistic or aesthetic merit, for with this cycle there can scarcely be any question of 'pleasure' in the ordinary sense of the word. The central character is a youth, disappointed in love and disillusioned with life, who sees only death as the ultimate end of his wintry journey. In setting these poems, the main problem lay in the verbal exuberance of the text and in the danger of unnaturalness and sentimentality. Schubert therefore adopted an approach that is, if possible, still simpler, but at the same time still more intense and concentrated, than in *Die schöne Müllerin*. The key-system appears to be and is quite haphazard, due no doubt to the fact that the emotional curve is not so simple as it is in the earlier cycle, where it rises to a climax and then dies down again. The individual scenes or episodes are less closely connected; Schubert does not therefore mind occasionally using the same key for consecutive songs, and it is purely by chance that the first of the two parts begins in D minor and also ends in D minor, after one of those favourite transpositions down a tone or a third, which Schubert here resorts to for practical reasons on four

separate occasions. But it is by no means accidental that the
second part begins in E flat major, a key which is never once
used in the first part and which here symbolizes a new
upward surge of the spirit –

> *Was hat es, dass es so hoch aufspringt, mein Herz?**

Nor is it accidental that the bright major keys are used so
sparingly. The strongest contrast is the E major of 'Der Lindenbaum' which follows the D minor, A minor and C minor
of the first four songs. The major mode has the principal
function of symbolizing the happiness of the past, while the
minor represents the darkness of the present. This contrast is
at its most striking in the first song, in which the wanderer
leaves behind the town where his former happiness had
turned to disillusionment; and in 'Rückblick', with its elementary alternation between G minor and G major and its
passionate phrase in the region of B flat major ('und ach,
zwei Mädchenaugen glühten'), one of Schubert's loveliest
inspirations. He does not avoid strophic form, but uses it less
frequently than in *Die schöne Müllerin*. For the hero and
vehicle of these lyrical out-pourings is not the simple miller's
lad, but a sensitive young man much like Schubert's own
idealistic and 'cultured' friends. He had an excellent model
in Mayrhofer. For this very reason 'Der Lindenbaum',
which has been reduced to a folk-song and sung to death, is
in fact anything *but* a folk-song. This fact is emphasized by
its prelude and postlude, with the distant horncall and echo
in the highly sensitive accompaniment, and by the use of a
minor key for one verse.

It seems to me that the thirty-one year old Schubert's *Winterreise* is another of the products of that second 'childhood',
that blending of extreme simplicity and impressive power
which only a great genius achieves at the end of his journey.
For Schubert was young and yet old when he came to write
Die Winterreise, in the same way that Mozart was young
and yet vastly old when he was writing *Die Zauberflöte.*
Schubert lavished all his resources upon this cycle – his
genius for line and colour, for sensitive feeling and painting,
for 'emotional description', and simplified them all without
destroying their intensity. The melodic line in 'Der greise
Kopf' has always ranked as an example of 'draughtsmanship'

* What ails thee, my heart, that thou leapest so?

– a silhouette in music. The lazy flapping of the crow ('Die Krähe') is both a piece of descriptive writing and a symbol of inevitability. The barking of dogs at night in the village is at once a noise and something dimly comprehended between sleeping and waking. The signpost ('Der Wegweiser') bears upon its outstretched finger the letters: DEATH. Sometimes the symbolism retires into the background. The bravery of 'Der Mut'

> *Fliegt der Schnee mir ins Gesicht,*
> *Schüttl'ich ihn herunter;*
> *Wenn mein Herz im Busen spricht,*
> *Sing ich hell und munter. . . .**

has a ring of bravado; but the bravado is spasmodic and wears a 'Hungarian' mask. And the end, 'Der Leiermann', with its monotonous melody over hollow fifths, is quite calm, quite unemotional. There is no outburst, but simply a pause on the brink of insanity.

The songs which were written between *Die Winterreise* and *Schwanengesang* recall an episode by Anselm Hüttenbrenner in his reminiscences, during the years when Schubert shared lodgings with Mayrhofer and sat at his desk every morning from six till one.

When I visited him in the afternoon, he would immediately play me what he had just written and would ask for my opinion. If I was particularly enthusiastic about a song, he would say: 'Yes, that is certainly an excellent poem. It puts a good idea into one's mind at once and the melodies follow so thick and fast that composing it is a real pleasure. One can get nowhere with a bad poem. One racks one's brains and nothing but dry dust comes out. I have discarded before now many poems that people have urged me to set to music.'

He does not seem to have remained faithful to this praiseworthy principle of discrimination either before or after the Graz period. Before starting out on his journey he set two more of Sir Walter Scott's songs, 'Anne Lyle's Song' ('Lied der Anne Lyle') from *The Legend of Montrose* (XX, 541) and 'Norna's Song' ('Gesang der Norna') from *The Pirate* (XX, 542), which he published as op. 85 in March 1828, probably as the first of a new series of songs by the Scottish bard. 'Gesang der Norna' is a strophic ballad which

---

* When the snow flies in my face, I shake it off; When my heart speaks within me, I sing right loud and blithely . . .

would fit perfectly into the first act of some Nordic opera. In 'Lied der Anne Lyle' there occurs, at the entry of the voice-part, exactly the same abrupt modulation from C minor to E flat major, which determines the 'Nordic' character of the melody in the slow movement of the E flat major Trio. There is a direct connection here, not only in the harmony and melody, but also in the rhythm. But Scott towers above the other poets of this period like a demi-god, and one wonders regretfully what Schubert would have been able to give to posterity, if during these years a few volumes of Eichendorff's, or Mörike's poems had come into his possession, instead of his having to content himself with what was immediately to hand. A typical example is 'Das Lied im Grünen', a poem by the Court actor Friedrich Reil which Schubert set in June 1827 (XX, 543) and the pedantry of which culminates in the allusion to Wieland and Kant. Yet in the matter of key and treatment, it achieves its 'apotheosis' in the Rondo of the A major Piano Sonata, and thus at any rate it served its purpose.

In a letter to a friend of his in the autumn of 1827, Ernst v. Feuchtersleben tells us that 'Schubert returned from Graz recently, full of enthusiasm but richer by only two songs'. The first of these is 'Heimliches Lieben' (XX, 544), a setting of a poem by Caroline Louise v. Klenke, the mother of the disagreeable Frau v. Chézy. It is not strictly speaking a song, but rather an arioso with conventional piano accompaniment and Karl Czerny was not entirely unjustified in later (1838-9) arranging it as a piano solo. The other is the ballad 'Edward' (XX, 545), the text of which Schubert had probably found at the Pachlers' house in a copy of Herder's *Stimmen der Völker*, printed first as a song and then in dialogue form. If it were not for its somewhat richer and fuller harmonization, it could well take its place in a 'Berlin' song collection of forty years earlier, and would have satisfied Goethe completely. It was one of the pieces which, together with 'Heimliches Lieben', were intended to be dedicated to Frau v. Pachler; in its place there appeared in op. 106, published privately, 'Das Weinen' (XX, 546), 'Vor meiner Wiege' (XX, 547), and the earlier 'An Sylvia (XX, 505) which seemed more suitable than the gloomy old Scottish ballad. The texts of 'Das Weinen' and 'Vor meiner Wiege' were the work of Karl Gottfried v. Leitner, a native

of Graz, where he was a professor at the Lyceum, and a
friend of the Pachlers; since he had moved to Cilli in Styria
as a teacher in 1827, Schubert could not have known him
personally. He had already set his 'Drang in die Ferne' (XX,
424) to music some years earlier, and it was obviously the
Pachlers who had renewed Schubert's interest in his poetry.
He accordingly also set 'Der Wallensteiner Lanzknecht beim
Trunk' (XX, 548), 'Der Kreuzzug' (XX, 549), 'Des Fischers
Liebesglück' (XX, 550), 'Der Winterabend' (XX, 551), and
'Die Sterne (XX, 552) – the last written in January 1828, at
which point his interest in Leitner fortunately ceased. For
Leitner is pedantic and sentimental, and 'Das Weinen' and
'Vor meiner Wiege' are only redeemed by Schubert's genu-
ine sincerity and sensitive feeling. In 'Vor meiner Wiege'
there is a section in the major which symbolizes the past as in
Die Winterreise. 'Der Kreuzzug' recalls the early 'Ritter
Toggenburg' and the only refinement is the discreet treatment of the voice-part in the midst of the march; the monk
retires into the darkness of his cell while the column of crus-
aders passes on its way into the brightness of day. The
richest of these songs, from the musical point of view, is 'Der
Winterabend', and the most original, 'Die Sterne', which
recalls in its rhythm the Moment musical, op. 94, 5, yet
vividly illustrates, with its quick tempo and lightness of
touch, the twinkling of the stars. 'Der Lanzknecht' is nothing
like powerful enough, and like 'Der Kreuzzug' it is a tribute
to the 'Nazarene' cult of early Romanticism.

There followed, after January 1828, a break in Schubert's
output of songs. In March he began the C major Symphony,
and in May he said what amounted to a final farewell to
Viennese poetry, which had found its highest expression in
Mayrhofer's lyrics, with a setting of Franz v. Schlechta's
'Widerschein' (XX, 553). It belongs in the same category as
his Italian or pseudo-Italian songs in the jocular manner of
Castelli, and is in fact only the final version of a song written
during his 'Italian' period in 1820, in which year the original
version had appeared in a Leipzig pocket-book.

It is as if Schubert was conscious of the vacuum into which
he had been forced by his dependence upon the poetry of his
countrymen, and which not even the greatest or rather the
only great one among them, Franz Grillparzer, was capable

of filling. For although Grillparzer was not only a dramatist but also a lyric poet of the first order, he lacked the gift for light, polished, musical verse. After the above-mentioned break in his song-output, Schubert turned his attention northwards. With one single exception, his last songs are settings of poems by Ludwig Rellstab and Heinrich Heine. Rellstab had visited Vienna in the year 1825, and had expressed himself in highly critical terms about the state of music there. Schubert's attention had probably been called to him as a result of this. Schindler tells a different story, according to which he himself had first been responsible for introducing Schubert to a number of Rellstab's poems which had apparently been discovered among Beethoven's posthumous papers without any indication as to their authorship. This tale is probably nothing more than a piece of trumpet-blowing on the part of the 'Ami de Beethoven', arising from his *penchant* for playing the Boswell to Beethoven's Johnson. Be that as it may, in March Schubert took some verses of Rellstab's as the basis for his concert-piece 'Auf dem Strom' which we have already mentioned, and at the end of April he copied a setting of Tellstab's melancholy poem 'Herbst' into the album of the young violinist Heinrich Panofka, a pupil of Mayseder. It is an elegy of three stanzas in E minor and could well have been written by Mendelssohn if it were smoother and its emotion less passionately felt.

Without Schubert, Rellstab would scarcely be known today as a lyric poet. Son of a literary-minded composer and publisher, and two years younger than Schubert, he has become primarily famous as a critic; his satirical novel about 'Henriette [Sontag], the beautiful singer', his campaign against Spontini, and his support for C. M. Weber (with whom he struck up a friendship in 1824) – these are all part of Berlin stage-history. His poems were published in 1827, and one would scarcely suspect the acute critic behind this sensitive, lyrical wanderer through the world of nature.

Schubert had originally planned to publish the seven Rellstab lyrics and the six Heine songs – to which we shall return directly – as a cycle, with a dedication to his friends. At the head of this cycle he had placed an eighth song, 'Lebensmut' (XX, 602), which has only survived in fragmentary form, and which he subsequently rejected. We do not know the reason for this, for it is a bright and resonant song in attractive Polonaise rhythm, and would have made an excellent introduction. In October, however, he offered his settings of poems by 'Heine of Hamburg' separately to the publisher Probst, evidently because he was hard up for money. Eventually, after his death, the publisher Haslinger, assisted by Ferdinand Schubert, restored them to their proper place alongside the Rellstab songs, added Schubert's last song, a setting of J. G. Seidl's 'Die Taubenpost', and published the whole collection in two volumes under the conventionally sentimental title of *Schwanengesang*. Thus, instead of ending with the grandiose setting of Heine's 'Der Doppelgänger', Schubert's song-output finishes on a somewhat commonplace note. For 'Die Taubenpost' (XX, 567) is not much more than a charming song, in which the one poignant feature for us today is the quotation from 'Trockene Blumen' ('Dort schaut sie zum Fenster heimlich hinein') which ushers in the closing phrase; the dove, which so faithfully bears the lover's greetings, is the longing of a passionate heart.

The Rellstab songs recapitulate much of what we have already said about Schubert in conclusive and mature terms, and they also underline something new: the *conversational* role of the piano accompaniment. 'Liebesbotschaft' ('Rauschendes Bächlein', XX, 554) could well take its place in *Die schöne Müllerin* were it not for this new emphasis which transforms the song into a recital-piece, for all its intimacy and spiritual depth. 'Krieger's Ahnung' is the final echo of the cantata-like type of song which found its first expression in the Ossian songs. 'Frühlingssehnsucht' (XX, 556) belongs in the same category – is it, in fact, a category? – as 'Der Musensohn'; 'Ständchen' is a successor to the Shakespeare Serenade except that with its extravagant touches it is sentimental in a mildly humorous way. 'Aufenthalt' ('Not too fast, but vigorously' – so runs the musical direction) recalls 'Die junge Nonne', though without its dark emotionalism. A particularly effective touch is the unison of the voice-part with the bass of the accompaniment. 'In der Ferne' (XX, 559), if it recalls anything, reminds one strangely of Purcell or of a 'ground' by some other seventeenth-century master, except that no composer of the old classical school would have dared to write the powerful ending in the major. 'Abschied' (XX, 560) is the ultimate expression of that blend of sentimentality and commonplace which 'Der Einsame' or 'Im Grünen' could only partially convey.

Schubert probably made his acquaintance with Heine's poetry at Schober's house. On 12th January, 1823, Franz v. Hartmann noted in his diary that they had there started to read, *inter alia*, Heine's *Reisebilder*, which were published in May 1826: 'Much that is charming. A great deal of wit. False tendencies', was his impression. In 'Die Heimkehr', with which the *Reisebilder* open, Schubert found the six songs which he set to music and provided with titles, which Heine had omitted to do.

Here, after a long interval, Schubert once more encountered a true and genuine lyric poet, whose allegedly 'false tendencies' could not affect him. By 'false tendencies' Hartmann probably meant something of a political nature and with nice instinct detected Heine's contempt for everything Teutonic; whereas it is much more the false over-emphasis of sentiment in, for example, 'Atlas' (XX, 561) which we find disturbing today:

*. . . die ganze Welt der Schmerzen muss ich tragen.**

Schubert takes this seriously and at the same time gives it a somewhat operatic colouring (the form of expression is quite different from that in the incomparable setting of Goethe's 'Prometheus'). 'Ihr Bild' (XX, 562) reminds one perhaps of the Mignon songs, yet throughout it there is a final, concentrated, eloquent – one might almost say, *wounding* – simplicity, down to the hollow chord which divides the second verse from the last. 'Das Fischermädchen' (XX, 563) and 'Am Meer' (XX, 565) belong together: the one, a rather courtly and yet in some respects sinister barcarolle, the other, a vision and an emotional outburst – an outburst, so to speak, which has threatened from the very start in the violent dissonance of the first chord. There are no models of any kind for 'Die Stadt' (XX, 564) and 'Der Doppelgänger' (XX, 566). 'Die Stadt', with the town dimly visible through the mist across the grey canal, is the prototype of the impressionist song; 'Der Doppelgänger' the blending of impressionist and dramatic power – a piece of lyrical 'theatre' or theatrical lyricism. We are standing on the threshold of a new development.

*. . . I must bear the whole world of sorrows.

Chapter Thirteen

Schubert and his Attitude to Death

"Nullique ea tristis imago"

This short digression is not intended as a sentimental excursus after the style of the popular (one might almost say over-popular) biographies of Schubert, but as a brief exercise in speculation which should be applied to each of our great composers, but which in Schubert's case assumes a doubly great importance in view of his early death. It is essential, too, because it proves in the most conclusive way that Schubert is not simply to be compared to Goethe's 'singer who sings like the bird that dwells among the branches', but that he is one of those great composers whom one can no more pat benevolently on the back than one can Bach, Beethoven or Wagner, and whose early consummation only makes him that much greater.

Great composers must also be great men, and all of them have to grapple with the problem of death, both as men and as musicians. It is one of their fundamental problems, by which we recognize them. It is a matter of complete indifference to us what George Philipp Telemann thought about death. But it *is* important that life, death and the hereafter lie at the heart of the philosophy and creative achievement of his less prolific and less successful contemporary, Johann Sebastian Bach. It can fairly be said that no composer thought more about death or stood in greater awe of it than Bach; that none was more deeply absorbed in the physical agony of dying as symbolized in the passion and death of Christ. The only counterpart is to be found in a painter, Matthias Grünewald. For him the pain was only bearable because this bitter act of dying was the assurance of the life to come, of rest eternal; because death opened the door to that Heaven for which he longed so fervently. Bach welcomed death, although he feared it; and between his fear and his longing stood only an indomitable and rocklike faith.

Schubert knew nothing of Bach's Cantatas and Passions, not would he have understood them. He was no Lutheran Christian nor – as we have already attempted to show – was he unhesitating in his acceptance of Catholic dogma; and he was not so fortunate as Mozart, the fatalist, whose Masonic associations made possible his cheerful resignation to the inevitable. 'Since death is the true and ultimate goal of our earthly life, I have accordingly so acquainted myself with this, the truest and best friend of man, during these past few years that not only does his image no longer strike terror to my heart, but calms and comforts me greatly! . . . I never lie down to sleep without thinking that (young though I am) I may never wake tomorrow – and yet there is not one among my acquaintances who can say that I am moody or dismal company – and for this happiness I thank my Maker every day and from the bottom of my heart I wish no less for all my fellow-men.' Beethoven, the optimist, had none of this fatalistic cheerfulness. His Funeral Marches are the mirror of his certainty in the immortality of greatness. It is not a Christian conception of immortality. The 'Et vitam venturi saeculi' of his great Mass is triumphant in a comparatively unreligious sense; the symphony which he dedicated 'to the memory of a great man' contains a heroic elegy and raises a triumphal arch.

Yet does not this letter of Mozart's recall Schubert's letter of July 1825 to his father which we quoted in an earlier chapter, in which he poked gentle fun at his hypochondriac brother for having doubtless thought nine times that he was going to die, 'as if death were the worst that could happen to us mortals'. For Schubert, as for Mozart, it was not the worst thing. When we speak of his attitude to death, we are not thinking of such youthful and picturesque affairs as Schiller's 'Leichenphantasie', of Pope's biblical and ecstatic defiance of death, 'The Vital Spark', of the many dirges and grave-diggers' songs, of the melancholy of Matthisson and the sentimentalities of Schubart, or of Ossian's threnodies. These only prove the persistence with which Schubert's imagination revolved round the subject. And they do not move us particularly. But when, in 1817 or 1818, we come to Mayrhofer's 'Fahrt zum Hades' and to Schiller's 'Gruppe aus

dem Tartarus', we find ourselves face to face with Schubert's
hopelessness and despair. He is credited with having said: 'It
sometimes seems to me as if I did not belong to this world at
all.' The remark sounds authentic. He belongs to that
'gloomy shore' where

'... neither sun nor stars shine, where no song is heard,
where no friend is to be found ... Oblivion breathes an air of
peace that is heavy with death ...'

It seems as if a poem of this kind was the direct result of a
conversation between Schubert and his friends, and had
been immediately set to music by him. The unity of poet and
composer is no less complete here than in an exponent of the
'Gesamtkunstwerk'.

Beside this classical, Homeric conception of death stands
another which is no less classical and unchristian. In the year
1769, one of the greatest of German literary figures,
Gotthold Ephraim Lessing, wrote a 'study' on: 'How the
ancients pictured death.' The quotation from Statius at the
head of the present chapter is taken from this essay. It is not
only *un*christian, but *anti*christian. Death is not a pun-
ishment for the original sin of Adam and Eve, who ate of the
tree of knowledge. The ancients did not picture death as the
grim skeleton which haunts the *danses macabres* of the
Middle Ages and of Hans Holbein, but as the brother of
gentle sleep, with torch reversed. Death is a friend.

> *Gieb deine Hand du schon und zart Gebild,*
> *Bin Freund, und komme nicht zu strafen.*
> *Sei guten Muths ich bin nicht wild,*
> *Sollst sanft in meinen Armen schlafen.**

Schubert varied and transfigured this picture of death as the
gentle friend of youth in his D minor String Quartet. And it
is echoed again in so many of his movements (and not only
the slow movements), where this transfiguration and exquisite melancholy are no less distinct, even though they remain
unuttered and seem like some carefully guarded secret. It is
Schubert's profoundest acknowledgment of this world and
of the next. Lessing's remark – '... it is a proof of true, of
rightly comprehended true religion, if it brings us back at

---

* Give me thy hand, thou fair and gentle creature. I am a friend and
come not to punish thee. Be of good cheer! I am not fierce. Thou shalt
sleep peacefully in my arms.

every point to the idea of beauty' – is equally applicable to Schubert. Time and eternity dissolve in beauty. One of the simplest and loveliest of his songs, 'An die Nachtigall', written on 22nd May, 1815, and instinct with music and with an inescapable sense of melancholy, has always struck me as a confession of love for the inevitability of death and farewell. And what else does the second and final movement of the 'Unfinished' express? Does not this sense of fulfilment also show why this work could not possibly be finished? It summons up another symbol of classical antiquity, the image of the butterfly, of transformation, of Goethe's 'Die and be born!' The butterfly is Schubert's music, born of earthly sorrow, shot through with the radiance of an eternally melancholy beauty.

It is a matter for the mystics to decide whether or not the writer of such music welcomed death with it. At the grave's edge, Goethe's aged Faust thus warns the spirit-messenger who is standing so silently within his room:

'Beware that thou utterest no magic word!'

She utters none and yet the darkness of eternal night falls on Faust. And in his short life Schubert had heard so many magic words of this kind and had given them magical life in his music.

Chapter Fourteen

Illness and Death

A few weeks after the beginning of his new phase of development, Schubert was dead. Early in October he had gone on another walking-tour to Eisenstadt with Ferdinand and two other friends, during which he seemed to have regained his former cheerfulness. But on his return the old headaches began again. Yet these pains, which had become habitual, had no direct connection with his last illness. This was enteric fever. On 12th November he wrote to Schober: 'I am ill. For eleven days I have eaten and drunk nothing and wander back and forth between my chair and my bed, weak and exhausted. Whenever I take any food, I cannot manage to keep it down . . .' And 'in this desperate plight' he begged for something to read. Franz Lachner, who visited him with Bauernfeld on 17th November, found him still in full possession of his faculties, and spent several hours 'with the most modest and sympathetic of friends', discussing plans for an opera. Bauernfeld and Lachner mention *Der Graf von Gleichen*, but Schubert probably wanted a new libretto. On 18th November he became delirious and could only be confined to his bed with difficulty. And on the 19th, at three o'clock on a Wednesday afternoon, he died.

He was buried on 21st November. The details of the funeral – the grief of his family and his friends' dismay – have been frequently described. For his grave Grillparzer wrote the famous inscription about 'the rich treasure, but yet much fairer hopes' which death had cut short. This is both true and untrue. To the present day opinions have varied widely on the degree to which Schubert's work was completed or left incomplete. Schwind, who heard the news of his friend's death in Munich, summed it up better: 'Schubert is dead, and with him has gone our happiest and loveliest possession.'

He was right in a deeper sense than he could have realized. For with Schubert's death an epoch in the history of music ends. Both as a man and as a composer he stands on the threshold of what we now call the Romantic Period. He is one of those composers who, like Mozart and Beethoven and yet more positively than either of them, 'take no thought for the morrow', who follow unreservedly and without heed a single impulse – to create; who, in their music, find – partly of their own free will and partly out of sheer necessity – the only means of meeting the challenge of human existence and of the universe. But he is not a typical Romanticist like all the other composers who came into the world during the twenty years which followed his birth; he is even less typical than his older contemporary, Weber. He is without spiritual discord; he still has the honesty and courage to express the full sensuousness and richness of life. He is a romantic Classicist and belongs in the great company of Haydn, Mozart and Beethoven. He does not suffer from that 'ineffectual exaggeration' with which Grillparzer reproached German Romanticists and which applies equally to their poetry and to a substantial part of their music. He left no successors. The feeling that he inspires in later ages is an infinite longing for a lost paradise of purity, spontaneity and innocence.

Index to Proper Names

Index of Works, excluding Songs

List of Songs